AIR DISASTER

VOLUME 2

by Macarthur Job

Illustrated by Matthew Tesch

By the same author

AIR CRASH
the story of how Australia's airways were made safe
Volumes 1 and 2
(Aerospace Publications)

THE OLD AND THE BOLD
(Iona Books)

AIR DISASTER
Volume 1
(Aerospace Publications)

ACKNOWLEDGEMENTS

Usually when an author comes to the point of acknowledging all those people who have helped him in his task of compiling a book so full of technical and other detail as this one, it is difficult to know where to begin. As I observed in Volume 1, no book encompassing the disciplines and experiences represented in a detailed survey of a number of diverse airline accidents, each one of them highly significant in its own way to the future safety of airline operations as a whole, could be written without the ready assistance and advice of a number of people.

In this case however, I do not have that difficulty, and at the outset I unreservedly acknowledge the outstanding contribution that artist Matthew Tesch, himself a commercially qualified pilot, has made to this volume. His effort and commitment to excellence throughout the 12 months it has taken to produce this book has far exceeded the artist's usual role of creating the many graphic illustrations that bring the text to life.

His encyclopaedic knowledge of the world airline industry supplied a store of minute detail, particularly for some of the captions and tables, on manufacturers' various versions of basic aircraft types, serial numbers, airline delivery dates, fleet numbers and airline liveries. He also assumed the role of technical editor, constantly checking on expressions of technical detail and consistency of style – at times difficult for the author to see for himself, immersed as he is in the task of first absorbing, then explaining, the web of technical detail and circumstances that conspired to bring about the accidents.

Without Matthew Tesch's outstanding collaboration, *Air Disaster*, Volumes 1 and 2, would not have been what they are. On his behalf I would like to thank those who assisted his own research – Mick Hodges, Mike Clayton of Aironautica, Bob Warn, Peter Marosszeky and the staff of United Airlines.

Two published works by other aviation authors have also made a particular contribution to the finished product.

Impact Erebus (Hodder and Stoughton, 1983), by former senior Air New Zealand pilot, Captain Gordon Vette, was especially useful in understanding the basis for Royal Commissioner Justice Mahon's findings at the conclusion of his Inquiry into the Erebus accident, and an extract from this book is included in Chapter 5, which reviews the whole circumstances of this tragic episode. Captain Vette subsequently consented to write the foreword to this second volume of *Air Disaster*, for which I sincerely thank him.

And without Betty Tootell's *All Four Engines Have Failed* (Andre Deutch Ltd in association with Hutchinson [Australia] Pty Ltd, 1985) one important airline safety object lesson would certainly have been entirely missing from the pages of this second volume. In the absence of any available official report on the so-called "Jakarta Incident", during which a British Airways Boeing 747 flew into a cloud of volcanic dust, sustaining a total loss of engine power, the dramatically detailed and well researched narrative by Betty Tootell provided an excellent basis for the account in Chapter 7.

As before, I am indebted to Dr Rob Lee, Director of Australia's Bureau of Air Safety Investigation, for continuing to allow me access to the Bureau's library of overseas accident investigation reports, as well as to the Bureau's Russell Sibbison, Data Manager, Safety Analysis Branch, and to Stuart Spinks and Andrew Watson, respectively Manager and Administration Officer of the Bureau's Melbourne Field Office, for their unfailing helpfulness.

As with my earlier books, my aviation mentors of long standing, Stanley Brogden OAM, and John Watkins OBE, have continued to provide advice and encouragement. Stanley Brogden's own erudite summing up of the Royal Commissioner's report on the Erebus Inquiry, published in *Aircraft* magazine in July 1981, was a most helpful addition to the volume of material available on this accident, and I acknowledge my indebtedness to him.

Other aviation colleagues upon whose expertise I have again drawn include Captain John Laming, Norman King and Peter Bacon, respectively Flight Engineer Manager and Senior Check Flight Engineer with Qantas, Bob Fripp, Ron Smith, Brian L Hill, and aviation antiquarian John Hopton. My thanks and appreciation go to them all.

Once again my thanks to Jim Thorn and Maria Davey at Aerospace Publications for their patience, enthusiasm and support in seeing an extremely demanding project through to its worthwhile conclusion.

And finally thanks to my wife, Esma, for her own untiring literary editorship of the text, ensuring that an essentially technical subject remained readable to those who are not themselves aviators or technocrats!

Macarthur Job
Melbourne, Victoria
March 1996

Published by Aerospace Publications Pty Ltd (ACN: 001 570 458), PO Box 3105, Weston Creek,
ACT 2611, publishers of monthly Australian Aviation magazine.
Production Manager: Maria Davey

ISBN 1 875671 19 6

Proudly printed in Australia by Pirie Printers Pty Ltd, 140 Gladstone Street, Fyshwick 2609
Distributed in Australia by Network Distribution, 54 Park Street, Sydney 2000. Fax (02) 264 3278
Distribution in North America by Motorbooks International, 729 Prospect Ave, Osceola, Wisconsin 54020, USA.
Fax: (715) 294 4448. Distribution throughout Europe and the UK by Airlife Publishing Ltd, 101 Longden Rd,
Shrewsbury SY3 9EB, Shropshire, UK, Fax (743) 23 2944.

FOREWORD

by Captain Gordon Vette

Former Air New Zealand Senior Check and Training Captain,
author *Impact Erebus* (Hodder and Stoughton, 1983)

I greatly admire the superb work done by Macarthur Job and Matthew Tesch in *Air Disaster*, Volumes 1 and 2, and I am honoured to write this Foreword to the second volume,

Airline flying today is the safest form of transport yet devised. Yet for most of us who have devoted our working lives to crewing these aircraft, past accidents provide us with cues to enhance safety even further.

The extraordinary depth of understanding demonstrated by Messrs Job and Tesch in the pages of this book – the distillation of the facts behind each of the accidents covered, often from a mountain of conflicting evidence – and their crafting and illustrating of the stories of these human tragedies, serve the aviation industry well. The work provides excellent reference material that will inform new pilot intakes, as well as spur the efforts of those of us who are dedicated to looking beyond so-called "pilot error" to search for systemic and latent problems within organisations as a whole.

In writing this Foreword, I am of course especially mindful of the Air New Zealand Mt Erebus disaster, covered in Chapter 5, and some of the behind-the-scenes aspects of that particularly unhappy event. It is my hope that others may gain a deeper understanding of the complexities of this and other accidents. Blame achieves little – indeed it can be counterproductive. Only by minimising errors, recognising that they can never be entirely eliminated, and making systems and organisations as error-tolerant as possible, can air safety continue to be enhanced.

My own research and investigations into the Mt Erebus accident culminated in this hypothesis:

The crew of Flight 901 were authorised by the Civil Aviation Division of the Ministry of Transport, and by Air New Zealand, cleared by McMurdo Centre, and descended VFR in excess of VMC conditions at McMurdo. The shifting of the waypoint to behind Mt Erebus; the aircraft's three independent navigation systems showing the DC-10 to be on track in accordance with the crew's map preparation; and the visual counterfeit of Lewis Bay for McMurdo Sound (a powerful illusion created by sector whiteout), all confirmed the mental set of the crew, who saw exactly what they expected – right up to the moment of impact.

On hearing my submissions to the Royal Commission, Counsel for First Officer Cassin, Roger MacLaren QC, compared the tragedy of Flight 901 to the deliberate deceptions of the old Cornish wreckers, who would lead unsuspecting ships to their doom on the rocks by moving light beacons on the coast. Although far from the intent, the result in this case was the same. My evidence was accepted by the Royal Commissioner, Mr Justice Mahon, and formed the basis for his Erebus Report.

Yet sadly, several forces conspired to mask the true cause, and the unshakeable reluctance of both the then New Zealand Prime Minister and the Chief Executive of Air New Zealand to accept that there was any systemic error on the part of the airline, precipitated my early retirement and the shelving of the Erebus report.

Subsequently, the Privy Council went on to declare: "It is an understandable weakness of human nature on the part of airline management responsible for flight operations that they should shrink from acknowledging, even to themselves, that something they had done or may not have done could be the cause of such a horrendous accident".

An airline aircraft despatched, authorised and finally cleared under VFR, is permitted to fly below Minimum Safe Altitudes prescribed for IFR – in fact at 500 feet above the sea, or 2000 feet above mountainous terrain. Without this rule, most airline operations could not take place. Photographic evidence clearly showed that the crew of Flight 901 did not infringe even the enhanced VMC visibility requirements specified for Antarctica by Air New Zealand and the Civil Aviation Division of the Ministry of Transport.

Only one computer-generated master flight plan for Antarctica was held in Air New Zealand's company computer and this had been used by all previous flights to McMurdo. The crew of Flight 901 could not have expected this to change only hours before their departure. Their not being notified of the change could be likened to someone loading an NDB on to a truck, moving it to the other side of a mountain, and setting its beacon transmitting again – without telling anyone!

My own aviation career spans more than 47 years and 21,000 hours of flying and instructing – on aircraft types as diverse as the old Tiger Moth to the Boeing 747. Study of human factors in aviation over these years has taught me never to jump to obvious conclusions, but to look further – and to remember the calibre of the crew, asking the question: "If that crew were trapped into their demise, could any other normal crew be similarly trapped in the same circumstances?" In aircraft accidents, the crew are the "active failure" – but are seldom around to defend themselves. So we need always to search diligently for the true cause – in the face of all the politics and the opposition from those with positions to defend.

I look forward to the good safety educational results that *Air Disaster*, Volumes 1 and 2, will bring to the aviation industry. Works of this calibre make us aware of the pathogens within a system than can combine to expose even the proudest safety record holders to failure.

Gordon Vette
Auckland, March 1996

CONTENTS

INTRODUCTION

Sixty years ago, pioneer Imperial Airways pilot, Captain Gordon Olly, declared in his book, *A Million Miles in the Air*, "It is an essential mental attribute of the flying man that he should concentrate when he is up in the air; that he should keep himself ceaselessly on the alert."

And so say all of us! Indeed, not just of 'the flying man' only, but of all who are in any way involved in the operation, maintenance and management of aircraft operations. Captain Olly's quaintly worded declaration could in fact be said to be the theme of this book.

For if humankind has learnt any clear principle in the 93 years that have now passed since the first heavier-than-air machine lifted itself off the ground under its own power, it is that aviation appears to have an inexhaustible supply of unpleasant surprises for those who in any way presume to take it for granted. Or, as the Flight Safety Foundation is wont to put it: *aviation in itself is not inherently dangerous, but like the sea, is terribly unforgiving of any carelessness, incapacity or neglect.*

That is not in any way to point the finger at the hapless crews and their passengers who were the victims of the salutary aviation events described in the pages that follow. The author, himself a commercial pilot of over 40 years experience, was only too conscious as he wrote the stories of these tragedies that, "there but for the grace of God go I".

Indeed, as Captain Gordon Vette has so aptly pointed out in the foreword to this volume, apportioning blame can in fact be counterproductive – and that only by minimising errors and seeking to make aviation systems as error-tolerant as possible, can air safety continue to be enhanced.

That ongoing process is exactly what this book is about and, as in Volume 1, in identifying crew members unfortunate enough to be caught up in these tragic learning experiences, it seeks only to be authentic in "telling it as it was".

Volume 2 thus continues the theme established in Volume 1, examining the way hitherto unsuspected hazards of jet age aviation have come to light through costly real-world experience. Yet for all their individual trauma, those experiences have progressively helped to evolve a superb global transport system whose safety standards surpass even the normal hazards of everyday life – statistically, the risk of dying in bed is greater than that of doing so in an airline accident! Considering the frequency of airline flights taking place the world over, 24 hours a day, every day of the year, in all types weather, the safety standard achieved is astonishing.

As this volume was in preparation, the world's justifiable confidence in air travel was underlined by two major anniversaries: 20 years of accident-free revenue flying by the world's only supersonic airliner, the Concorde; and a quarter of a century of operations by the epoch-making Boeing 747, whose advent in 1970 changed the lives of literally millions of the world's people, bringing international travel within their reach for the first time in history.

But even with all this technical success, and the overall standards of safety that have been achieved, the art and science of advanced aeronautics in all types of flying conditions are not yet fully perfected. Nor has the complex relationship between technological progress on the one hand, and human frailty on the other, been fully resolved. In aviation, perhaps more so than in other fields of human endeavour, mankind remains as much a victim of himself as of the elements around him.

The instances chosen for inclusion in this book are either notable examples in their own right, or are representative of failures resulting from these causal factors. As in Volume 1, their other qualification for inclusion was that comprehensive reports on the accidents themselves, their circumstances, and their subsequent investigations, were available.

The fact that all the aircraft types featured in this volume happen to be products of either Boeing and McDonnell Douglas is simply a reflection of the make up of today's global airline industry – the days of the Comets, the Caravelles and the Tridents, types which ranked in Volume 1 as mainline equipment, are now gone. Airbus Industrie types are also missing – but for the opposite reason. It is only comparatively recently that Airbus Industrie's expanding numbers of aircraft in the world airline fleet began to be manifested in accident statistics. A number of Airbus investigations were in progress when this volume was planned, but because of the lack of definitive information on these accidents, it was obvious that justice could not be done to them at that stage.

The same applies to the airlines whose names appear in the pages of this book – the coverage is simply a reflection of numerical predominance – and of course of the expert, frank and open reporting of the investigating authorities whose comprehensive reports enabled the reviews to be written. The inclusion of particular case histories in the book certainly does not imply that the accident record for any aircraft type, airline, or nation leaves something to be desired!

Readers may notice, that as the case histories covered in both Volume 1 and Volume 2 become more recent, so their investigations have become more complex and wide-ranging. As a result, reviewing the investigations included in Volume 2 has demanded considerably greater and more detailed analysis.

In airline operations today, a single isolated event rarely results in an accident. Rather, a chain of events develops that changes what might have been an uneventful flight into a disaster. If events had been different at any one link in the chain, the accident would not have happened.

After examining 10 years of accident data from around the world, researchers at Boeing have found that as the severity of accidents increase, so do the number of links in the causal chain. In other words, the worst accidents provide the most opportunities to break the accident chain and are therefore, at least theoretically, the most preventable. According to the Boeing team, more than four prevention opportunities present themselves during events leading to a typical fatal accident – more than four points at which different actions or procedures could sever the causal chain and thus prevent the accident happening.

The Boeing air safety research team has therefore proposed the development of a "prevention strategies" philosophy, rather than the traditional one of simply seeking to correct problems that an investigation has revealed – as Australians might put it, "shutting the stable door after the horse has bolted".

The Boeing team has identified no less than 37 prevention strategies – changes to training, procedures, and operations – that have the potential to break the causal chain in the majority of accident cases. A number of air safety investigation authorities throughout the world are already responding to this challenge.

It will be interesting, as time goes by, to see how this new approach, involving a moving away from traditional cause-analysis attitudes to a prevention-analysis mode, will affect the already high safety standards of the world airline industry.

Much emphasis has been placed, both in the foreword to this book, and in Chapter 5, on the effects of computerised operational technology on crew responsibility and flight safety. But the accident in Antarctica is not the only one that raises questions on this subject.

Reviewing the circumstances of the final tragedy in this book is to be appalled by the fact that, had that Boeing 767 been an earlier version of the type, fitted with engines that were mechanically rather than electronically controlled, that accident *could not* have happened.

The horror that overwhelmed the Lauda Air Boeing 767 is by no means the only jet transport crash to have evoked reservations on the efficacy of computerised electronic control systems over the 10 years or so that have passed since this technology was introduced. Others, together with a number of alarming inflight incidents, have also raised doubts, not only as to whether the systems had been subject to sufficient proving, but whether in fact they could actually be counter productive to crew reactions in an emergency.

There is an impression in the industry that zealous software designers and programmers, few of whom have first hand flying experience of any sort, let alone of airline operations at 'the sharp end', are committed, as far as is presently acceptable, to designing pilots out of the loop.

Why? Because, as one manufacturer's software designer put it, '80% of accidents are caused by pilots'!

But those who determine the philosophy of this new technology need to be mindful that there is a reverse side to this coin that rarely rates a mention today: *It is quite impossible to assess the number of accidents that don't happen – because pilots are there to prevent them!*

Considering the harsh operational lessons that so often have had to be learned with each step forward in aviation, the wisdom of 'hastening slowly' with new control technology, as in all ventures into the realm of the new and the untried, should need no emphasis.

Macarthur Job
Melbourne, March, 1996

FROM THE ARTIST...

The pleasure and privilege of continuing to collaborate with Mac Job and Maria Davey in the creation of *Air Disaster*, Volume 2, is axiomatic, and the sentiments that I expressed in my Artist's Note which prefaced Volume 1 apply in equal measure to the work entailed in Volume 2.

Indeed, as readers will see, preparing the contents of Volume 2 has proved even more demanding, if that is possible. Although it contains four less chapters than *Air Disaster*, Volume 1, the highly complex nature of many of the accidents reviewed in Volume 2 have demanded greater and more detailed examination and analysis. The overall result is that Volume 2 contains considerably more material than Volume 1, all of it prepared with the same commitment to accuracy and authenticity as the content of Volume 1.

Here, in respect of Volume 1, a small corrigendum must be acknowledged. After the publication of this first volume, Gertjan Bart was kind enough to write from The Netherlands, with photographic proof, to point out that KLM's 747 PH-BUF *was* wearing the-then new 'blue-top' livery at the time of the Tenerife disaster. Your artist had been sufficiently vexed by his inability to reconcile aircraft deliveries with repainting dates that he raised the question with the airline itself before producing the art for Vol 1, Ch 18. KLM's Head Office reply advised that the aircraft was still in the old 'white-top' scheme at the time of the accident, and the drawings were done accordingly.

During the course of preparing this second volume, I had the good fortune to meet former United Airlines Captain Al Haynes (and his delightful wife, Darlene), and to renew my acquaintance with former Air New Zealand Captain Gordon Vette – two of the more luminary names of the many within the pages of this book. Circumstances conspired to end, in ways identical in degree if different in application, the flying careers of both these men. But neither faltered, and both have gone on to communicate the fruits of their rich experience in the wider cause of safety in the skies. Both these contacts contributed to my understanding of the events in which they were involved and the latter kindly consented to write a Foreword to Volume 2.

It is to another, however – to the man whom many have described as the 258th victim of the Mt Erebus crash – that I dedicate my work in this book: the late Peter Thomas Mahon. To the former Royal Commissioner, the enduring legacy of whose illuminating exposition *Verdict on Erebus* (Collins, Auckland, 1984) continues to inspire – truth-seeker *par excellence* – thank you for the courage of your example.

Matthew Tesch
Sydney, March 1996

GLOSSARY OF AERONAUTICAL TERMS AND ABBREVIATIONS

ADF: Automatic Direction Finder. Previously known as radio compass.

Aileron: Control surfaces on (usually) outer sections of wing trailing edges, controlling bank and roll of aircraft.

AINS (Area Inertial Navigation System): An extremely sophisticated navigation system available to airline operations. Comprising three independent inertial systems to ensure accuracy, the system also responds to radio navigation aid inputs. Capable of accurately navigating aircraft on area navigation routes or great circle tracks from takeoff to final approach anywhere in the world. (see also INS)

Airspeed Indicator (ASI): Instrument measuring speed of aircraft through air, expressed in knots.

Air Traffic Clearance: Approval by Air Traffic Control for aircraft to taxi, takeoff, climb, enter controlled airspace, descend or to land.

Air Traffic Control (ATC): System of directing all aircraft operating within designated airspace by radio. Divided into sectors such as Tower (aerodrome control for takeoffs and landings), Departures, Control (en route aircraft), and Approach.

Altitude: Height of aircraft as shown on altimeter adjusted to local barometric pressure.

Angle of attack: Angle at which wings meet airflow.

Artificial horizon (AH): Instrument displaying aircraft attitude in relation to real horizon.

Asymmetric flight: Multi engined aircraft flying with one engine inoperative.

ATIS: Automated terminal information service. Continuous, recorded radio transmission of meteorological conditions at airport.

Attitude: Lateral and longitudinal relationship of aircraft to horizon.

Attitude indicator: See artificial horizon and flight director.

Bunt: Sudden nose down manoeuvre of aircraft, usually producing uncomfortable negative G.

"Clean" (aircraft): Aircraft in normal cruising configuration, with high lift devices and undercarriage retracted.

Control Area: Designated area of airspace in which all aircraft movements are under radio direction of Air Traffic Control.

Control Zone: Designated airspace encompassing terminal area of an airport in which all aircraft movements are under radio direction of Tower Controller.

Co-ordinates: Latitude and longitude of a position anywhere on the earth's surface, estimated to one minute of an arc.

CVR (Cockpit Voice Recorder): Sophisticated, "crash proof" tape recording equipment fitted to airline aircraft to record flight crew conversations and radio transmissions. The tape is a 30 minute closed loop which is continuously recycled, providing a complete audio record of the last 30 minutes of any flight.

Directional gyro (DG): Instrument accurately registering direction aircraft is heading. When aligned with compass, provides immediate indication of changes in magnetic heading.

DME: Distance Measuring Equipment. Radio navigation aid providing pilot with constant readout of distance from selected radio beacon.

Elevation: Height of terrain above mean sea level. Abbreviated AMSL.

Elevators: Control surfaces at rear of horizontal tail (tailplane), controlling nose attitude of aircraft.

Endurance: Time (expressed in minutes) aircraft can theoretically remain in air before fuel is exhausted.

ETA: Estimated time of arrival

ETD: Estimated time of departure.

Fin: The vertical aerofoil member of an aeroplane's tail assembly or empennage. Provides directional stability in flight. Known as the vertical stabiliser in US aviation parlance. (See also rudder).

FDR (Flight Data Recorder): Complex "crash proof" instrument fitted to airline aircraft to continuously record operating parameters during flight. Early FDRs using stylus scribing on metallic tape recorded only four parameters – airspeed, altitude, heading and vertical acceleration. Today's digital FDRs (DFDRs) simultaneously record some 70 aircraft performance parameters, including instrument readings, flight control movements, engine performance and secondary control settings.

Flaps: Adjustable surfaces on aircraft's wing trailing edge. When lowered, flaps increase lift of wing, thereby reducing stalling speed, and increase drag, steepening aircraft's glide angle.

Flight Director: Complex, computer controlled flying instrument combining inputs of other flying and radio navigation instruments in single large dial located directly in front of each pilot.

Flightplan: Document prepared by pilot on official form before departure, providing details of proposed flight – track to be followed, waypoints, computations of wind effects, headings and speeds for each leg, all-up weight at departure, and progressive fuel burn.

Flight Level (FL): Expression of height in hundreds of feet, based on standard barometric altimeter setting of 1013.2 millibars. Eg, 12,000 feet on standard altimeter setting would be FL120. Differs from altitude in that the latter is based on actual barometric altimeter setting for a particular area or airport.

"G" (gravities): Expression of force acting on aircraft and its occupants in flight, measured in multiples of earth's gravitational force.

GMT (Greenwich Mean Time): Standard world time used for navigation regardless of location of ship or aircraft. Now generally referred to as UTC (Co-ordinated Universal Time).

Ground speed: Actual speed of aircraft over ground. May be greater or less than airspeed, according to wind.

HF (High (radio) Frequency): Radio propagation in the frequency band from 3 to 30 MHz. Permits communication over long distances, but reception can be subject to atmospheric and electrical interference. Used by aircraft operating beyond range of VHF and UHF radio propagation.

HSI (Horizontal Situation Indicator): Instrument on the pilot's flight instrument panel capable, of displaying position information in ILS, VOR or NAV modes. When selected in NAV mode, displays distance to the next waypoint in top left-hand corner, ground speed top right-hand corner, and plan view of aircraft's position left or right of track, thus providing instant information on aircraft's position and speed.

INS (Inertial Navigation System): Long range navigation system used by modern transport aircraft. Using highly sensitive gyros and inertial weights, it has the ability to sense and measure every movement of the aircraft, and with its associated computer, continuously plot the aircraft's position. Linked to an autopilot, the system will fly the aircraft along a designated track. Most systems contain three inertial platforms which monitor each other, and will isolate one if it malfunctions. (See also AINS.)

ILS (Instrument Landing System): Electronic approach aid which enables a pilot to carry out an approach for landing when weather conditions preclude visual contact with the ground.

IFR (Instrument Flight Rules): Stipulated procedures for navigating aircraft by reference to cockpit instruments and radio navigation aids alone. Enables flight regardless of visibility. Normal operating procedure for airline flights.

IMC (Instrument Meteorological Conditions): Weather conditions in which visibility is less than specified for visual flying, and in which flight is legally possible only under IFR.

Knot: One nautical mile per hour. Equivalent to 1.853km/h

Lowest Safe Altitude (LSA): Designated minimum altitude for particular air route, providing minimum of 1,000 feet clearance above underlying terrain.

MAC: Mean Aerodynamic Chord.

MSA (Minimum Safe Altitude): Altitude below which IFR aircraft may not descend unless specifically to do so by ATC. Takes into account high terrain underlying an air route.

Mach number: Figure expressing relationship between true airspeed of aircraft and speed of sound.

Mach buffet: Turbulence like condition, felt initially in flying controls at high Mach numbers (ie as aircraft approaches speed of sound). As Mach number increases, manifestations can include large changes of trim and heavy buffeting of the aircraft itself.

Mayday (repeated three times): Radio telephony version of former morse code "SOS" distress call. Derived from the French "m'aidez" – "help me".

N1: RPM of Stage 1 fan of turbofan jet engine, expressed as a percentage of normal maximum fan speed.

N2: RPM of gas turbines of turbofan jet engine, expressed as a percentage of normal maximum turbine speed.

Nautical mile (nm): Measure of distance used for navigation in the air and at sea. Equal to one minute of an arc of latitude on the earth's surface. Is 800 feet longer than a statute mile and equivalent to 1.853km.

Navaid: Radio navigation aid.

NBD: Non directional beacon. Ground based medium frequency radio transmitter sending continuous signals in all directions for use by aircraft fitted with ADF (radio compass).

NOTAM (Notice to Airmen): Message concerning changes to serviceability of aerodromes, radio and navigation facilities.

Octas ("eighths"): Expression of cloud amount. Eight octas (or eighths represents a completely overcast sky; four octas a half clouded sky.

Pitot-static system: System of instruments, connecting tubes and air sensors for measuring altitude, airspeed, and rate of climb or descent.

Precipitation: (Meteorological) Rain, hail, sleet or snow in or falling from cloud.

Preflight (inspection): "Walk around" inspection of aircraft by pilot, usually immediately prior to flight.

QFE: Code expression designating altimeter setting in millibars for particular airport. When set on subscale of altimeter, instrument reads aircraft's height above that airport.

QNH: Code expression designating altimeter setting in millibars – when set on subscale of aircraft's altimeter, instrument reads aircraft's height above mean sea level.

Radial: Bearing to or from VOR radio range.

Radio Compass: See ADF above.

Radio Range: Type of radio beacon providing defined aircraft tracks to or from that navigation aid.

Rate One turn: Shallow standard rate turn used in instrument flight conditions.

RPM (rpm): Measure of engine speed expressed in revolutions per minute.

Rudder(s): Control surface(s) at rear of vertical tail (fin) controlling yawing movement of aircraft.

Sigmet: Warning signal issued by Aviation Meteorological Service when weather conditions suddenly deteriorate.

Slats: Aerodynamic device fitted to leading edge of wings to delay onset of stall.

TACAN (UHF Tactical Air Navigation Aid): Military navigation and communications unit. Civil aircraft can usually interrogate the DME element of a TACAN.

Trim: Adjusting control of aircraft in climb, level flight and descent, so pilot is not required to maintain continuous pressure on elevators, ailerons or rudder.

Turn and bank indicator: Instrument displaying rate of turn and if turn is "balanced" with correct amount of bank – ie neither skidding outwards nor slipping inwards.

SAR: Search and Rescue.

Spot height: Height noted on chart showing elevation of prominent mountain peak.

Stalling speed: Low airspeed at which aircraft wings suddenly lose lift. No connection with engine "stall". Is absolute minimum airspeed at which aircraft can maintain flight.

Tailplane: Horizontal aerofoil member of an aeroplane's tail assembly or empennage. Provides longitudinal stability in flight. Known as the stabiliser in US aviation parlance. (See also elevators.)

Transponder: Radio device fitted to aircraft which, when triggered off by certain radar wavelengths, emits a signal visible on ground radar screens. Signal usually includes additional information such as altitude of the aircraft.

UHF (Ultra High (radio) Frequency): Frequency band of 300 to 3000 MHZ. Aviation use confined mainly to military aircraft.

V (code): Schedule of indicated airspeeds stipulated for different phases of flight (see following).

V_1: Decision speed during takeoff. Aircraft is committed to fly when this speed is passed.

V_r: Rotation speed. Speed at which aircraft is "rotated" into liftoff attitude by raising the nosewheel off the runway.

V_2: Takeoff safety speed. Minimum control speed plus safety margin to allow for engine failure and other contingencies.

V_{ne}: Never exceed speed.

V_{ref}: Flap reference speed. Landing speed for stipulated number of degrees of flap extension.

Vasis: Visual approach slope indicator. System of lights located on ground on either side of runway to indicate correct angle of descent to approaching aircraft.

VSI (Vertical Speed Indicator): Instrument displaying rate of climb or descent in feet per minute.

VHF (Very High (radio) Frequency): In general use for in-flight radio communications on air routes. Its frequency band from 30 to 300 MHZ is largely free from interference and static, but range is limited to "line of sight".

VFR (Visual Flight Rules): Stipulated flight procedure for navigating aircraft visually, clear of cloud, in Visual Meteorological Conditions.

VMC (Visual Meteorological Conditions): Weather providing specified range of visibility, making it possible for pilots to use visual means to avoid obstructing terrain and other aircraft.

VOR: Very High Frequency Omni directional Radio Range.

CHAPTER 1

"We've lost *both* engines!"

– DC-9 Captain to Atlanta Air Traffic Control Centre

Southern Airways McDonnell Douglas DC-9-31 N1335U [47393]
(F/n 934) – April 4, 1977

Severe thunderstorms with hail were forecast for the DC-9's 25 minute flight at 17,000 feet. But who could have suspected conditions would be extreme enough to flameout both engines?

Shuttle service to Atlanta

Southern Airways' Flight 242 from Muscle Shoals, in northwestern Alabama, to Atlanta, Georgia, with an en route call at Huntsville, was but one of a number of scheduled DC-9 services being operated by the company throughout the southeastern states of the USA on April 4, 1977.

Founded immediately after the war with headquarters at Huntsville, Alabama, Southern Airways Inc had progressively established itself as a successful regional airline, initially operating DC-3s. As its network grew, linking more and more major centres in the Deep South, the company base was transferred to Atlanta, by now the "hub" of its operations. And in the early 1970s it upgraded its airline services to jet operations, acquiring a fleet of DC-9s.

Today's Flight 242, under the command of Captain Bill McKenzie, and scheduled to depart Muscle Shoals at 3.15pm, was expected to be little different to the service from Atlanta which the same aircraft and crew had flown only two hours earlier. Indeed, as one of the company's frequently flown routes, it was extremely familiar to them. Early that morning in fact, after overnighting at a motel in Muscle Shoals, they had flown their first service for the day

to Atlanta via Huntsville. Both legs of the flight were comparatively short, the first only 57 nautical miles (104km) on an easterly heading to Huntsville, and the second another 133nm (244km) on to Atlanta on a southeasterly heading.

Complex weather pattern

The weather over the eastern half of the United States was far from ideal. The National Weather Service chart showed a deep low centred over the southern tip of Lake Michigan, producing an occluded front, extending from the low pressure centre to southwestern Indiana, with a cold front continuing south to Louisiana and out into the Gulf of Mexico.

In addition, a warm front, aligned northwest-southeast, lay between southwestern Indiana and western North Carolina and continued eastwards to the Atlantic coast. A squall line extending northeast from near Meridian, Mississippi, was passing through northern Alabama, northwestern Georgia and southeastern Tennessee as far as the vicinity of Knoxville.

Ceilings between 1000 to 2000 feet were expected, broken to overcast, with layered clouds to 15,000 feet, and visibility five to eight km in haze

and moderate rainshowers. There were scattered thunderstorms with tops to 35,000 feet, a few of them severe near the cold front, reaching to 55,000 feet. Moderate to severe icing conditions existed in the thunderstorms above freezing level at 12,000-14,000 feet. Wind gusts in excess of 50 knots and hail of 18mm or more in diameter could be expected with the passage of the cold front.

In addition to the area forecast, SIGMETs issued by weather offices in the southern states were in force, as well as two Tornado Watches issued by the National Severe Storms Forecast Centre. These generally predicted tornadoes east of Huntsville, with a few severe thunderstorms reaching to 58,000ft, extreme turbulence, wind gusts to 70 knots, and hail up to 75mm in diameter.

Capt McKenzie was provided with these Tornado Watches and SIGMETs before boarding the aircraft at Muscle Shoals for the afternoon flight to Atlanta, together with reports for a number of terminals along the aircraft's route. But there was little to suggest that actual inflight conditions would be significantly different from those of only two hours before when, on their outbound flight from Atlanta, they encountered heavy rain and hail, and

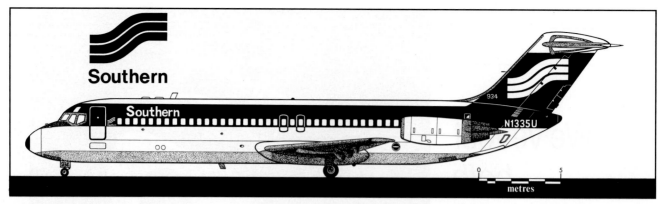

Profile drawing of the ill-fated DC-9, N1335U. Southern Airways took delivery of this aircraft in June 1971, the last of five new DC-9-31s ordered from McDonnell-Douglas. Sistership N97S [47245] was written off in November 1970, but other Series 30 DC-9s were acquired second-hand from Hawaiian, Allegheny and other operators. (Matthew Tesch)

their descent from 19,000ft into Huntsville had been made on instruments.

For the experienced Captain McKenzie, 54, the adverse forecast held few terrors. He had been with Southern Airways since 1960, flying the company's routes for 17 years and, with nearly 20,000 hours in his logbook, was familiar enough with the vagaries of the local weather. His First Officer, Lyman Keele, 34, was also a seasoned pilot. Trained in the US Navy, he had spent a year flying in Southeast Asia as a carrier pilot aboard the *USS Hancock*. Still a member of the Navy Reserve, he flew military aircraft regularly from Dobbins Air Force Base on the outskirts of Atlanta.

Taking off from Muscle Shoals at 3.21pm, the DC-9 landed at Huntsville 20 minutes later after an uneventful flight. The stop at Huntsville was short, neither of the pilots leaving the flightdeck. With no further communications from the company's despatch office in Atlanta, the pilots passed the time in small talk with the cabin crew, Flight Attendants Cathy Lemoine and Sandy Ward.

As the 81 passengers for Atlanta came aboard, Cathy Lemoine, on duty in the forward cabin, spoke to the captain again. "What's it going to be like from here to Atlanta?" she asked. The outbound flight had been rough. "Just like it was coming up here," he replied.

"Going to have to keep ourselves in our seats, eh?"

"Depends on how many people you've got – in any case we only have about 10 minutes level ..."

The ground crew passed the aircraft's manifests, together with the latest terminal forecast for Atlanta, up to the flightdeck and, as the pilots began their prestart checks, First Officer Keele read the forecast to the captain. It indicated that Atlanta was overcast by layers of cloud at 2700, 5000, and 25,000 feet, and that the surface wind was blowing at 27 knots, gusting to 40 knots.

At 3.50pm, as the engines were started and the aircraft began to taxi, it began to rain at Huntsville and the crew turned on the windscreen wipers. Four minutes later the DC-9 took off, setting course for

Atlanta with an estimated time interval of 25 minutes. The flight planned route was direct from Huntsville to the Rome VOR, a distance of 88nm, climbing to 17,000 feet, then a descent into Atlanta, a further 45nm.

At 3.58pm the DC-9 crew called Memphis [Air Route Traffic Control] Centre and the controller told them a SIGMET, warning of hazardous weather, was current for the Tennessee, southeastern Louisiana, Mississippi, and northern and western Alabama areas. Advising them to monitor VOR broadcasts within a 150nm radius of the SIGMET area, the crew were then instructed to contact Atlanta Centre.

Between 3.59 and 4.02pm, the Atlanta controller was talking to a TWA flight about deviations to the east of its track around thunderstorms between Chattanooga, Tennessee, and Rome, Georgia, and at 4.03 he contacted an Eastern Air Lines flight which had just crossed the storm area northwest of Rome. "How would you classify your ride through that line up there?" the controller enquired. "Do you recommend

Another of Southern's DC-9s – short-bodied Series 14 N3303L [45698] – makes a textbook touchdown at Miami. This aircraft was originally one of a Delta Air Lines batch of 14 DC-9-14s, another of which, N3305L, was lost in an encounter with the wake turbulence of a DC-10 while crew-training at Greater Southwest International Airport, Texas, on May 30, 1972 (refer Air Disaster, Vol 1, Chapter 10). The remaining 13 DC-9-14s were sold to Southern Airways during 1972-73. (Airline Publications)

anyone else coming through it?" The Eastern Air Lines flight answered that "it wasn't too comfortable, but we didn't get into anything we would consider the least bit hazardous."

Loss of communication – and a broken windscreen

At 4.03pm the Southern Airways DC-9 reported to Atlanta that it was "level at 17,000 [feet]," and at 4.06 Atlanta cleared the DC-9 to descend to and maintain 14,000 feet. The aircraft acknowledged the instruction. But over the following two minutes, four further transmissions to the aircraft went unanswered. Finally, in response to yet another call, the DC-9 told Atlanta to "standby".

Atlanta now transmitted: "Roger, maintain 15,000 if you understand me" and the aircraft's reply contained the first indication that all was not well: "We're trying to get it up there," the crew transmitted. A few seconds later the DC-9 reported: "OK – we just got our windshield busted and – we'll try to get it back up to 15 – we're 14." This was followed 15 seconds later by: "Our left engine just cut out." Atlanta replied: "Roger, and lost your transponder, squawk 5623."

Half a minute later came the further dramatic announcement: "The other engine's going [out] too!"

Loss of power on both engines

The full implications of this transmission were not immediately apparent to the controller: "Say again," he requested.

DC-9: "Standby – we've lost both engines! Get us a vector to a clear area, Atlanta!"

Atlanta: "Continue present southeastbound heading – TWA's off to your left about 14 miles at 14,000 feet and says he's in the clear."

DC-9: "OK ... want us to turn left?"

Atlanta: "Contact approach control 126.9 and they'll try to get you straight into Dobbins [Air Force Base]."

DC-9 (urgently): "Give me a vector to Dobbins if they're clear."

Atlanta: "Call on 126.9 – they'll give you a vector to Dobbins."

During the next three minutes, Atlanta Centre made three more transmissions to the DC-9, all of which went unanswered. Then both Atlanta Approach Control and the TWA flight directed calls to it, but again there was no response. However, at 4.13pm the DC-9 transmitted to Atlanta Approach: "Atlanta, do you read Southern 242?"

Approach Control: "Southern 242, Atlanta ... go ahead."

DC-9: "We've lost both engines –

N89S [47042], the first of Southern's DC-9-31s, is seen here in the company's earlier livery. The cleaned-up triple-banded "S" scheme retained the basic navy blue-and-white look, but deleted the yellow cheatline trims and radome cap, and was occasioned by Southern's effort to reposition itself as a medium haul carrier, not just a short-sector regional operator. By the time of the New Hope disaster, Southern was carrying 3,000,000 passengers a year, 90% of them on its fleet of two dozen DC-9s of assorted marques. In June 1979, the airline merged with North Central to become Republic Airlines, the latter name disappearing also when it was absorbed into Northwest. ("Airliners" magazine)

how about giving us a vector to the nearest place – we're at 7000 feet."

Approach Control: "Roger, turn right, heading 100 degrees – will be vectors to Dobbins for a straight-in approach Runway 11 – your position is 15, correction 20, miles west of Dobbins at this time."

DC-9: "OK – 140 degrees heading and 20 miles."

Approach Control: "Make it a heading of 120, Southern 242 – right turn to 120 degrees."

DC-9: "OK – right turn to 120 and ... you've got our squawk, haven't you, on emergency?"

Approach Control: "I'm not receiving it, but radar contact, your position is 20 miles west of Dobbins."

DC-9: "OK."

DC-9 (half a minute later): "All right, listen – we've lost both engines, and ... I can't ... tell you the implications of this ... we've ... only got two engines. How far is Dobbins now?"

Approach Control: "19 miles."

DC-9: "OK – we're out of ... 5800 feet – at 200 knots."

Approach Control: "Southern 242 – do you have one engine running now?"

DC-9: "Negative – no engines."

DC-9 (half a minute later): "Approach Control, what's your Dobbins weather?"

Approach Control: "Standby."

Approach Control: "Southern 242, Dobbins weather is 2000 scattered, estimated 7000 overcast, visibility seven miles."

DC-9: "OK, we're down to 4600 now."

Approach Control: "Roger and you're approximately ... 17 miles west of Dobbins at this time."

DC-9: "I don't know whether we can make that or not."

DC-9 (20 seconds later): "Is there any airport between our position and Dobbins?"

Approach Control: "No sir, the closest airport is Dobbins."

DC-9: "I doubt we're going to make it – but we're trying everything to get something started."

Approach Control: "Roger, well there is Cartersville – you're approximately 10 miles south of Cartersville – 15 miles west of Dobbins."

DC-9: "Can you give us a vector to Cartersville?"

Approach Control: "All right, turn left, heading 360 degrees ... direct vector to Cartersville."

DC-9: "360 degrees, roger."

DC-9: "What's the runway heading? ... and how long is it?"

Approach Control: "Standby."

Approach Control: "The runway configuration ... at Cartersville is ... 360, running north-south, and the elevation is 756 feet, and ... trying to get the length now ... it's 3200 feet long."

DC-9 (15 seconds later – in desperation): "We're putting it on the highway ... we're down now to nothing!"

Forced landing

At 4.18pm the DC-9, approaching on a northeasterly heading, attempted a landing on Georgia's State Spur Highway 92, just southwest of the little community of New Hope, the site of a major battle during the Civil War more than a century before. But the two lane highway, only seven metres wide and flanked on either side by pine forests and electricity poles, offered scant prospect for avoiding disaster.

As the aircraft continued its approach, its port wing clipped the tops of two trees beside the road. Two hundred metres further on and now within the township itself, the wing again hit a tree alongside the highway, after which both wings began striking trees and poles on either side of the road as the DC-9, its undercarriage and flaps fully extended, descended towards the ground.

Disastrous consequences

Nearly 400 metres after striking the first tree, the aircraft's main undercarriage touched down on the highway. But almost simultaneously the port wing struck an embankment, veering the DC-9 off the road to the left – with tragic consequences. Knocking down road signs, poles, fences, and trees, breaking up and exploding into flames as it went, the hurtling, out-of-control airliner finally struck a service station-grocery store. Demolishing its petrol pumps, together with five cars and a motor truck standing in front of it, and setting these ablaze, the burning wreckage of the DC-9 eventually skidded to a stop amongst trees 385 metres further on.

Volunteer firemen from the nearby New Hope fire station responded immediately, frantically directing their efforts to contain fierce fires in the service station building and among the vehicles, as well as the blazing aircraft wreckage itself. The service station fire, ignited by short-circuited powerlines, was fed by fuel from the broken petrol pumps. One fire engine fought this fire, while the other tackled the remains of the DC-9.

Both pilots were killed instantly in the impact, as were 31 of the passengers. Another 20 died in the fire. Eight people on the ground also lost their lives, among them the daughter and two grandchildren of the service station proprietor, who were about to drive away from the forecourt when their car was struck by the aircraft. Both flight attendants, who suffered only sprained necks and abrasions of the legs, were able to free themselves from the wreckage.

Cathy Lemoine, in the forward cabin, found herself hanging upside down, restrained by her seatbelt. After releasing herself she fell onto debris in the galley area. Unable to open the main cabin door, she climbed through an opening in the fuselage, jumped to the ground, and ran to a nearby house to get help.

Sandy Ward, in the aft attendant's seat, felt the aircraft strike the ground about six times before coming to rest. Fire erupted after the first or second impact, moving rapidly rearward through the upper part of the cabin. Protecting her hand with her apron, she undid her seatbelt and stood up. A wall of fire confronted her, and smoke caused her to cough repeatedly. After struggling unsuccessfully to open the rear bulkhead door, she moved forward because the flames had diminished, and walked out onto the ground. She began pulling passengers from the wreckage until an explosion forced her away.

A local doctor and a nurse arrived on the scene shortly afterwards and immediately began rendering what aid they could to the many injured and burnt. They also took responsibility for notifying the nearest available hospitals, together with arrangements for evacuating the survivors by helicopter and ambulance.

Survivors

Twenty-one of the 81 passengers survived the crash and fire, but sustained a variety of serious injuries. Many were burned about the head, face, hands, and lower legs, and three had fractured spines. Arm, hand, and leg fractures were common and most passengers had numerous abrasions. Nine sustained injuries combined with burning or smoke inhalation. The feet of a number of the survivors were cut and some were also burned because they had no shoes for protection. The flight attendants had briefed the passengers to remove their shoes to prevent damage to evacuation slides. Lacking any advice from the flightcrew, they had no way of knowing the circumstances of the landing – and no reason to deviate from standard procedures.

One passenger had covered his head with his leather jacket and wedged a pillow between his face and the seatback in front of him just before impact. After the aircraft stopped, he removed the jacket and moved forward, leaving the aircraft through a hole in the fuselage. His head was burned by melted plastic dripping from the ceiling.

Investigation

Investigators from the National Transportation Safety Board, who arrived at the site from Washington DC early next morning, found that the DC-9 had crashed at an elevation of 1020 feet, 26nm west-northwest of its destination airport at Atlanta.

The total wreckage area was about 580 metres long and 90 metres wide. The fuselage forward from the leading edge of the wing, though untouched by the fire, was destroyed by impact forces. The forward flight attendant survived only because the structure had shielded her. Most of the survivors from this section were ejected during its fragmentation and were seriously injured. The passenger seats had separated from their tracks and were scattered, all showing evidence of compression buckling.

The nose section itself came to rest inverted. Although the centre windscreens were intact, the outer panes were shattered and the inner panes cracked.

The midships portion of the fuselage, containing the wing centre section, was severely damaged by fire, together with all the passenger seats and cabin floor. Both wings had been torn off. The rear fuselage was also damaged by fire, with most of the seats separated from their tracks and fire damaged.

The undercarriage was extended and the spoilers retracted. The trailing edge flaps were lowered 50 degrees and the leading edge slats fully extended. All control surfaces were accounted for, and all damage was found to be caused by impact. The leading edges of the wing slats, the fin and the tailplane contained numerous indentations from 1.5mm to 3mm deep – damage inflicted by hailstones.

Both engine nacelles also had dents in their leading edges. The fan blades on both engines were generally in good condition but the fronts of their spinner fairings were dented. The low-pressure compressors on both engines were severely damaged aft of the third stage rotor, and the high-pressure compressors had extreme damage in all stages – bent and broken trailing edges of stator vanes, and bent and broken rotor blades. Many of the rotor blades in the lower stages were bent forward, and most of the blades in the higher stages were either broken or missing. Blade roots were lodged among the stator vanes in the last three stages of the high-pressure compressors, with all the fragments severely battered.

The combustion case drain valves contained metal chips, and all turbines had overheated. All blades in the four turbines of the starboard engine were burned and broken, and the last three stages of the nozzle guide vanes had melted.

According to one of the survivors, a commercial pilot who had been seated on the left at the rear of the cabin, just forward of the engine air intake, the flight was normal until the aircraft encountered severe turbulence, followed by very heavy rain, a lightning strike on the port wingtip, and hail. Almost simultaneously with the onset of the turbulence, the power was reduced on the engines.

The hail increased in intensity and size, then the starboard engine failed, followed by the port engine shortly afterwards. He thought the cabin lights went out after the light-

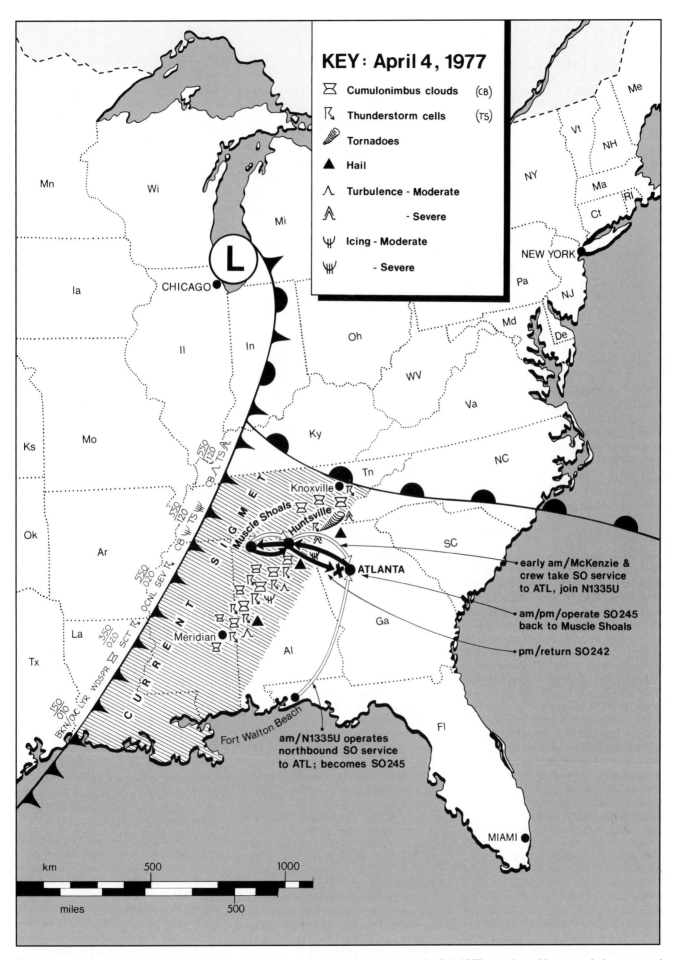

⋈ Cumulonimbus clouds (CB)

↳ Thunderstorm cells (TS)

🌀 Tornadoes

▲ Hail

⋀ Turbulence - Moderate

⋀ - Severe

Ѱ Icing - Moderate

Ѱ - Severe

Mn

Wi

Mi

Ia

L

CHICAGO

Il

In

Oh

NY

Me

Vt

NH

Ma

RI

Ct

NEW YORK

Pa

NJ

Md

De

WV

Va

Ks

Mo

Ky

NC

550
120
CB ⋀ TS ⋀

550
120
CB Ѱ TS Ѱ

Knoxville

Tn

Muscle Shoals

Huntsville

550
020
OCNL SEV ⋉

Ok

Ar

SC

ATLANTA

early am/McKenzie & crew take SO service to ATL, join N1335U

am/pm/operate SO245 back to Muscle Shoals

pm/return SO242

La

350
020
SCT ⋉

Meridian

Al

Ga

150
010
BKN/OVC LYR WDSPR ⋈

Tx

Fl

Fort Walton Beach

am/N1335U operates northbound SO service to ATL; becomes SO245

MIAMI

C U R R E N T   S I G M E T

km	500	1000

miles   500

Map of central and eastern United States, showing main weather systems present on April 4, 1977, together with sectors being operated that day by Southern DC-9 N1335U. (Matthew Tesch)

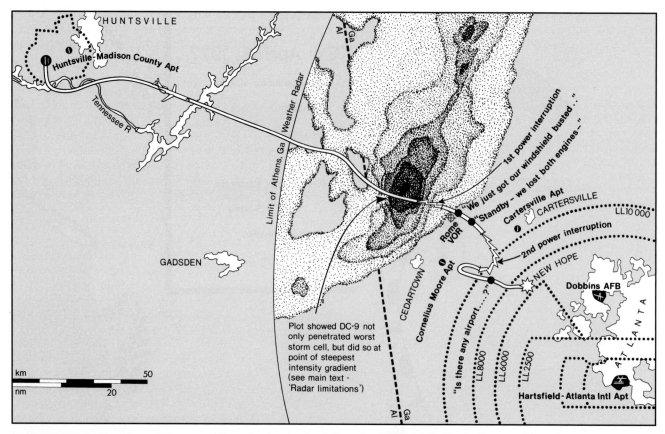

Larger scale map of northern Alabama and Georgia, showing track flown by N1335U from Huntsville to accident site, as determined by investigators from radar plots and eyewitness sightings. Some published accounts of this accident have speculated that the seemingly inexplicable turn back towards the west might have been the result of the crew's sighting of Cornelius Moore Airport through breaks in the rain and cloud as they descended. Loss of visual contact, or a sudden realisation of the airport's unsuitability have similarly been held as the reason for the further course reversal back towards the southeast. The second interruption to the DC-9's electrical power at this time, however, obliterated any evidence there might have been on the CVR to support this theory. The stippling shows areas of storm activity recorded by National Weather Service radar at the time of the aircraft's total loss of engine power, its density indicating the estimated intensity of precipitation. (Matthew Tesch, with acknowledgement to NTSB)

ning strike, but before the hail began. He estimated the turbulence lasted between one and two minutes, the heavy rain from 45 to 60 seconds, and the hail a similar time. The engines failed shortly after the hail ceased.

Just before the starboard engine failed, he heard loud popping noises from an area ahead of the engine. Similarly, just before the port engine failed, he heard it surging, accompanied by loud popping. He also noticed the spinner fairing of the port engine was dented. He then heard the Auxiliary Power Unit (APU) being started, followed by the sound of it running.

Both flight attendants recalled similar details. They received no indication from the pilots about what had happened in the heavy hail encounter, or how they intended to land.

A post-accident weather analysis established that the storm system which moved across northeast Alabama and northwestern Georgia on the afternoon of April 4 was one of the severest in the United States for three years. It was also one of the fastest moving systems on record, and included some 20 tornadoes and 30 severe thunderstorms.

Flight Recorders

The DC-9 was equipped with a Sundstrand Flight Data Recorder (FDR). Though its case was damaged, all traces on the foil recording medium were clear. The FDR traces indicated two instances of electrical power interruption. From the time the aircraft began to taxi at Huntsville until the first power loss, 15 minutes 7.7 seconds elapsed. After electrical power was restored, the FDR operated for two minutes 24 seconds before power was lost again. After the second resumption of power, the FDR operated for five minutes 40.2 seconds until the crash.

The aircraft also had a Collins Cockpit Voice Recorder (CVR). The CVR case was damaged by fire, but the recording tape was intact and, except for the power interruption, yielded a complete record of the crew's comments and radio exchanges from the time the aircraft was on the ground at Huntsville.

Playing and transcribing the CVR tape added to the record of events derived from the crew's radio transmissions, and provided a dramatic word picture of the development of the accident and the crew's des-

perate attempts to avoid a disaster.

This extract from the CVR transcript begins just after 3.58pm, six minutes after takeoff from Huntsville and just after Huntsville Departure Control transferred the DC-9 to Memphis Centre. With the first officer flying the aircraft, and the captain handling the radio communications, the flight deck exchanges continued as follows (local pm time is shown in hours, minutes and seconds):

3.58.10: CAPT: Memphis Centre, Southern 242 is with you – climbing to 17,000.

3.58.16: MEMPH: Southern 242, Memphis Centre, roger.

3.58.22: CAPT: As long as it doesn't get any heavier, we'll be all right.

3.58.25: F/O: Yeah, this is good.

3.58.26: MEMPH: Memphis Centre – attention all aircraft: SIGMET – hazardous weather – vicinity Tennessee, southeastern Louisiana, Mississippi, northern and western Alabama and adjacent coastal waters – monitor VOR broadcast within a 150 mile radius of the SIGMET area.

3.58.27: CAPT: Oh ###! [expletive].

3.58.45: MEMPH: Southern 242, contact Atlanta Centre on 134.05.

3.58.50: CAPT: 134.05 – Southern 242, good day.

3.59.00: CAPT [evidently as aircraft runs into heavy turbulence]: Here we go – hold 'em cowboy!

4.00.21: F/O: I can handle this all the way over ...

4.02.57: CAPT: I think we'd better slow it up right here in this stuff.

4.03.14: (Sound of light rain)

4.03.20: CAPT: Atlanta, Southern 242 – with you – level 17.

4.03.24: ATLAN: Southern 242, Atlanta, roger – altimeter 29.56.

4.03.48: CAPT: Looks heavy – nothing's going through that!

4.03.54: CAPT: See that?

4.03.56: F/O: That's a hole, isn't it?

4.03.57: CAPT: It's not showing a hole, see it?

4.04.05: (Sound of rain)

4.04.06: F/O: ###! [Expletive – evidently as aircraft is severely jolted]

4.04.08: F/O: Do you want to go around that right now?

4.04.19: CAPT: Hand fly at about 285 knots.

4.04.30: (Sound of hail and rain)

4.05.53: F/O: Which way do we go across here? I don't know how we get through there, Bill.

4.05.59: CAPT: I know you're just going to have to go out!

4.06.00: F/O: Yeah – right across that band!

4.06.01: CAPT: All clear left approximately right now – I think we can cut across there now.

4.06.12: F/O: All right – here we go.

4.06.25: F/O: We're picking up some ice, Bill.

4.06.29: CAPT: We're above 10 degrees.

4.06.30: F/O: Right on 10!

4.06.55: (Noise of heavy hail and rain)

At this stage, Flight Attendant Sandy Ward, speaking from her station at the rear of cabin, announced that passengers should keep their seatbelts securely fastened:

4.07.22: FLIGHT ATTENDANT [on cabin PA system]: Keep your seatbelts on and securely fastened – there's nothing to be alarmed about. Relax – we should be out of it shortly.

4.08.34: ATLAN: Southern 242, do you read Atlanta?

A little more than a minute after Sandy Ward's announcement, prompted by the fact that the heavy hail and turbulence, far from easing, had become even more severe, and there had been an interruption to the aircraft's electrical supply, the same flight attendant addressed the passengers again:

4.08.38: FLIGHT ATTENDANT [on PA system]: Please check to see that all carry-on baggage is stowed completely underneath the seat in front of you – put all carry-on baggage underneath the seat in front of you. In the unlikely event that there is a need for an emergency landing, we do ask that you please grab your ankles, I will yell from the rear of the aircraft – there is nothing to be alarmed about, but we have lost temporary APU power at times. So in the event there is any unlikely need for an emergency, and you do hear us call, please grab your ankles. Thank you for your co-operation and just relax – these are precautionary measures only.

4.08.46: CAPT: Atlanta, Southern 242, standby ...

4.08.49: ATLAN: Roger, maintain 15,000 if you understand me – maintain 15,000, Southern 242.

4.08.55: CAPT: We're trying to get it up there!

4.08.57: ATLAN: Roger.

4.09.15: CAPT: OK – Southern 242 – we just got our windshield busted and – we'll try to get it back up to 15,000, we're at 14,000.

4.09.25: ATLAN: Southern 242 – you say you're at 14,000 now?

4.09.27: CAPT: Yeah – couldn't help it.

4.09.30: ATLAN: That's OK – are you squawking 5623?

4.09.36: F/O [evidently attempting to increase power]: Left engine won't spool!

4.09.37: CAPT: Atlanta – our left engine just cut out!

4.09.42: ATLAN: Southern 242, roger – and lost your transponder – squawk 5623.

4.09.43: F/O: I am squawking 5623 – tell him I'm level at 14,000.

4.09.49: CAPT: Atlanta, 5623 – we're squawking!

4.09.53: ATLAN: You've lost an engine – and busted a windshield?

4.09.56: CAPT: Yes sir, Atlanta!

4.10.00: ATLAN: Southern 242 – you can descend and maintain 13,000 now – that'll get you down a little lower.

4.10.02: CAPT: Autopilot's off.

4.10.03: F/O: I've got it – I'll hand fly it.

4.10.04: F/O: My God! That other engine's going too!

Aerial view of the crash site, with the fragmented wreckage of the DC-9 visible in the centre and right of the picture. The highway on which the crew attempted their forced landing runs from left to right through the centre of the picture. The pine forest on either side of the narrow road rendered their task impossible.

Miraculous escape for the residents of this New Hope home, with a substantial section of the DC-9's fuselage 'netted' by a stand of trees only metres from their front door. (World Wide Photos/Patrick Stephens Ltd)

4.10.05: CAPT: Got the other engine going out too!

4.10.08: ATLAN: Southern 242 – say again?

4.10.10: CAPT: Standby – we've lost both engines!

4.10.14: F/O: All right, Bill – get us a vector to a clear area.

4.10.16: CAPT: [urgently]: Get us a vector to a clear area, Atlanta!

4.10.20: ATLAN: Continue present southeastern heading – TWA's off to your left about 14 miles at 14,000 and says he's in the clear.

4.10.27: CAPT: Want us to turn left?

4.10.30: ATLAN: Southern 242, contact Approach Control – 126.9 – and they'll try to get you straight into Dobbins.

4.10.36: F/O: Give it to me – I'm familiar with Dobbins – tell them to give me a vector to Dobbins if they're clear.

4.10.38: CAPT: Give me a vector to Dobbins if they're clear.

4.10.41: ATLAN: Southern 242 – 126.9. They'll give you a vector to Dobbins.

4.10.50: F/O [anxiously]: Ignition override – it's got to work!

4.10.56: (Power interruption for 2 minutes, 4 seconds.)

4.13.11: CAPT: Atlanta Approach, Southern 242, we've lost both engines – how about giving us a vector to the nearest place – we're at 7000 feet?

4.13.16: FLIGHT ATTENDANT [on PA system]: Ladies and gentlemen, please check that your seatbelts are securely across your pelvis area on your hips.

4.13.18: APP: Southern 242 roger, turn right heading 110 – will be vectors to Dobbins for a straight-in approach Runway 11, altimeter 29.52, your position is 15, correction 20, miles west of Dobbins at this time.

4.13.31: CAPT: OK – 140 heading and 20 miles.

When the flight attendants were convinced both engines had failed, they began briefing the passengers on emergency landing procedures. They demonstrated how to open the exits, how to assume the brace position, and instructed the passengers to remove sharp objects from their clothing, to check luggage was stowed securely, and to remove their shoes to prevent damage to the evacuation slides. After their briefings, Flight Attendant Lemoine opened the flightdeck door to tell the pilots the passengers were prepared for an emergency landing, but First Officer Keele only yelled at her to sit down. She saw the windscreen was shattered.

4.13.35: APP: Southern 242, make it a heading of 120, right turn to 120.

4.13.40: CAPT: OK, right turn to 120 – you've got our squawk, haven't you, on emergency? F/O [concerned]: Declare an emergency, Bill!

4.13.45: APP: I'm not receiving it, but radar contact on your position is 20 miles west of Dobbins.

4.14.03: F/O: [with increasing anxiety]: Get those engines ...!

4.14.24: CAPT: [with obvious concern but calmly]: All right, listen Approach. We've lost both engines, and

– I can't – tell you the implications of this – we've only got two engines – how far is Dobbins now?

4.14.34: APP: Southern 242 – 19 miles.

4.14.40: CAPT: OK – we're out of 5800 at 200 knots.

4.14.44: F/O [mentally calculating]: What's our speed? Let's see – what's our weight Bill? Get me a bug speed!

4.14.45: APP: Southern 242 – do you have one engine running now?

4.14.48: CAPT: Negative – no engines.

4.14.59: CAPT: Bug speed 126 (Sound of trim noise)

4.15.04: CAPT: Just don't stall this thing out. F/O: No – I won't. CAPT: Get your wing flaps (Sound of lever movement)

4.15.57: CAPT: OK – we're down to 4600 now.

4.15.59: F/O [anxiously]: How far is it? How far is it?

4.16.00: APP: Roger, and you're approximately ... 17 miles west of Dobbins at this time (Sound of windscreen wipers coming on)

4.16.05: CAPT: I don't know whether we can make that or not.

Meanwhile, in the cabin the forward flight attendant, Cathy Lemoine, called Sandy Ward on the intercom to tell her the situation on the flightdeck. They then discussed preparations for an emergency landing.

4.16.25: CAPT: Is there any airport between our position and Dobbins?

4.16.29: APP: No sir – closest airport is Dobbins.

4.16.34: CAPT: I doubt we're going to make it – but we're trying everything to get something started.

4.16.38: APP: Roger, well there is Cartersville – you're approximately 10 miles south of Cartersville, 15 miles west of Dobbins.

4.16.44: F/O: We'll take a vector to that – yes, we'll have to go there.

4.16.45: CAPT: Can you give us a vector to Cartersville?

4.16.47: APP: All right, turn left, heading 360 – direct vector to Cartersville. F/O: What runways? What's the heading of the runway?

4.16.53: CAPT: What's the runway heading?

4.16.58: APP: Standby.

4.16.59: CAPT: And how long is it?

4.17.00: APP: Standby.

4.17.08: CAPT: [with resignation]: Like we are, I'm picking out a clear field.

4.17.12: F/O [forcefully]: Bill, you've got to find me a highway!

4.17.17: CAPT: Let's get the next clear open field ...

4.17.21: F/O: No!

4.17:35: CAPT: See a highway over there – no cars! F/O: Right there – is that straight?

4.17.39: CAPT: No!

4.17.45: F/O: [decisively]: We'll have to take it!

4.17.50: APP: Southern 242, the runway configuration at Cartersville is ... 360, running north-south, and the elevation is 756 feet ... trying to get the length of it now ... it's 3200 feet long.

4.17.58: (beep on undercarriage horn – followed by steady horn for four seconds.)

4.18.02: CAPT: Approach – we're putting it down on the highway – we're down now to nothing!

4.18.07: F/O: Flaps? CAPT: They're at 50. F/O: [with apprehension]: Oh ... Bill ... I hope we can do it!

4.18.14: F/O: I've got it – I got it!

4.18.15: F/O: I'm going to land right over that guy.

4.18.20: CAPT: There's a car ahead!

4.18.25: F/O: I've got it, Bill – I've got it now!

4.18.30: CAPT: OK – don't stall it!

4.18.31: F/O: We're going to do it right here!

In this starboard side view of the main wreckage, the scorched and blackened trunk of the conifer in the middle background stands where the DC-9's empennage has been torn off. Visible in the picture are the base of the leading edge of the fin (top right), the dismembered "U" of the aircraft's registration, and the damaged but largely intact nacelle of the No.2 engine.

The forward fuselage, though untouched by the fire, was destroyed by impact forces. In this closeup of the wreckage of the DC-9's inverted nose section, only the pilots' broken instrument panel remains recognisable.

At about this moment, the rear flight attendant, Sandy Ward, sighted treetops through a cabin window and yelled to the passengers:

4.18.32: FLIGHT ATTENDANT [on PA system]: Bend down and grab your ankles now!

The forward flight attendant, Cathy Lemoine, repeated the command, and the passengers responded. There were no signals from the flightdeck that the landing was imminent.

4.18.34: F/O: I've got it!

4.18.36: (Sound of breakup lasting three seconds.)

4.18.43pm: End of CVR tape

Engine tests

At the request of the National Transportation Safety Board, the engine manufacturer conducted tests to investigate the effects of ingesting large amounts of water on an operating JT8D-7 engine. The program included water ingestion tests, compressor rig tests, and spin pit tests of individual compressor disk and blade assemblies.

At flight idle thrust, with ingestion rates exceeding 18 percent (by weight) water-to-air, the high pressure rotor rpm decelerated to below generator cutout speed. When the water ingestion rate was reduced, the rotor speed recovered and remained stable. The engines did not surge or flameout during the testing. At lower ingestion rates and higher power settings, the engine operation remained stable. The tests also showed that water did not collect in the air bleed cavities or compressor cases, and that the compressor rotors were not damaged.

The compressor rig and spin pit tests were to determine whether liquid water trapped in the bleed cavities could hit the compressor blades and cause damage similar to that sustained by the DC-9's engines. Water jets were directed at the rotating compressor blades and rotors until the blades failed. All failures were high frequency fatigue failures and occurred in the aerofoil near the platform.

By contrast, the blades in the DC-9's engines had failed from overload bending at random points on the aerofoil. In addition, many of the blade roots had been torn from the disk slots, whereas none of the blades were torn from the slots during the rig tests.

A review of the engine compressor's developmental history and an analysis of its test data showed that, during water ingestion, the high-pressure compressor's sensitivity to stalls and surges was substantially increased. When water was ingested in large quantities, surging in the higher stages of the compressor could produce upstream overpressures and aerodynamic forces in excess of any experienced during the developmental and service histories of the JT8D engine. The forces generated could be high enough to deflect the blades in the sixth stage and cause them to clash with the upstream stator vanes.

Analysis

The tests carried out during the investigation, the review of JT8D engine compressor research data, and passenger and flight attendant evidence produced a viable theory of how the DC-9's engines were damaged so severely.

The intensity of the rain and hail in which the aircraft was flying before engine power was lost was clearly sufficient to cause the engine rpm to drop below that required for operation of the generators. This was supported by the 36 second loss of electrical power which began at 4.07:57pm. Significantly, it was evident that engine speed was lost shortly after the power levers were retarded to low settings – very likely flight idle – probably as the first officer sought to slow the aircraft to turbulence penetration speed.

Engine speed obviously increased on at least one engine about 36 sec after the first loss of electrical power because the CVR, FDR and radios returned to operation. Although the recovery to at least generator operating speed could have been related to reduced water ingestion, it was more likely because the power levers were advanced – a normal reaction to a loss of engine rpm. Additionally, the crew were attempting to climb, requiring higher thrust settings.

Survivor evidence verified that both engines surged and stalled in heavy rain just before they failed – the condition shown, at low rpm, to produce overpressures in the low-pressure compressors sufficient to cause blades to deflect and clash against the vanes. Moreover, throttle advancement under these conditions was likely to aggravate the situation.

The investigators concluded therefore that, after engine rpm was first lost, the levers were advanced, and the resulting surging and stalling caused blades in the low-pressure compressors to clash against the vanes, as shown by the damage found in the low-pressure compressors of both engines. The sixth-stage blades had deflected forward to clash with the fifth-stage stator vanes, breaking pieces from both blades and vanes. The fragments were then ingested into the high pressure compressors, causing extreme damage. The lack of typical foreign object damage, including hail damage, to the fan blades and the blades in the forward stages of the low-pressure compressors, showed clearly that hail ingestion was not responsible.

If the power levers then remained at relatively high settings with the compressors damaged, high fuel flow, in conjunction with reduced compressor efficiency, would result in excessive temperatures in the turbine sections of the engines. The damage to both engines clearly indicated that this occurred before the engines finally failed, with the result that they were no longer capable of producing thrust.

After the engines ceased to function, electrical power was again interrupted for about two minutes. Undoubtedly, this time, it was restored by the APU, because once

again the CVR and FDR began functioning. Survivor evidence, CVR comments, and the condition of the APU as found in the wreckage, showed it was operating at the time of the crash.

With the complete failure of both engines, a catastrophic accident was almost inevitable, unless the DC-9 was able to reach a suitable airfield within gliding distance. Certainly the probability of completing a landing on a highway or in a field without major damage or injury was extremely low.

Three airfields were potentially available to the DC-9, with Dobbins Air Force Base by far the best choice. This major airport, elevation 1068ft, located on the northwestern outskirts of Atlanta, lay about 26nm southeast of the aircraft's position when the second engine failed. Its concrete Runway 11-29 was 3050 metres long and 100 metres wide, and the airport was equipped with both approach surveillance and precision approach radars, as well as fire fighting and crash rescue facilities.

The other two aerodromes were even closer, but were general aviation airfields. Cartersville Airport, elevation 756 feet, was only eight nm northwest of the DC-9's position. Its one asphalt runway, aligned 18-36, was 976 metres long and 20 metres

wide. Cornelius Moore Airport, which lay 10nm to the southwest, had one asphalt runway, 1220 metres long and 23 metres wide, aligned 10-28. Its elevation was 973 feet. Neither of these airports had crash rescue equipment.

Reconstructing the aircraft's actual track flown from the evidence contained in the FDR and the radar plots recorded by Atlanta Approach Control, it was clear that, just over a minute after the second engine failed, the crew made a 180 degree turn back towards the west-north-west, instead of continuing toward Dobbins Air Force Base, as the Atlanta controller had suggested almost immediately he was informed both the DC-9's engines had now failed.

Confirmation of this critical change of heading came from several witnesses on the ground who, at about 4.15pm, saw the DC-9 flying clear of cloud on a westerly heading. It then made a left turn and flew back towards the east. The only thing unusual about the aircraft was its complete lack of engine noise.

Because the CVR was inoperative, the investigators were unable to determine why the crew did this. Possibly, shortly after the loss of the engines, the aircraft emerged from cloud and the pilots, busy trying to

Cutaway view of a Pratt & Whitney JT8D engine. Major components referred to in the text are labelled. (Matthew Tesch, with acknowledgement to United Technologies)

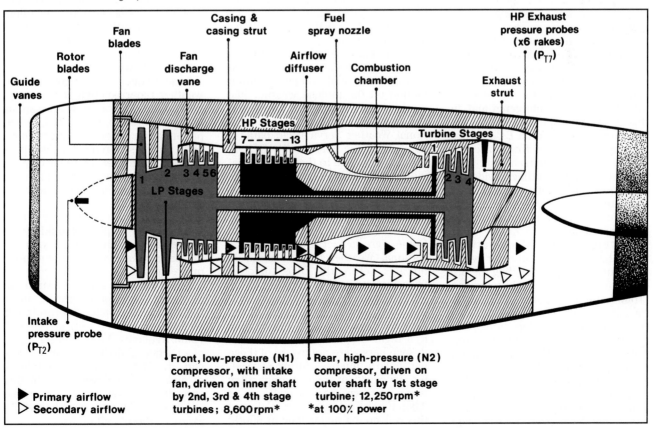

restart the engines and the APU, made the 180 degree turn to remain in visual conditions while they did so. Whatever the reason, the crew's decision was to cost them dearly – had they maintained their heading towards Dobbins, they could probably have reached its generously proportioned runway with height to spare.

The option of attempting a landing at Cornelius Moore Airport, which was only four nm further west at the time the DC-9 turned back towards the east, would have been available had the crew known of the airport's location. But they were evidently not aware of it because when the first officer said, "Get us a vector to Dobbins," the captain responded with a request for "… a vector to the nearest place." Atlanta Approach Control was unfortunately not able to help because Cornelius Moore was outside the airspace for which the controller was responsible, and not shown on his map displays.

In any case, the outcome of an attempt to land at Cornelius Moore could only be guessed at. Its short runway, the difficulties of judging an accurate approach without engine power, and the lack of firefighting and rescue facilities at the airport, made it by no means certain that a landing would have been successful. Much the same could be said of an attempt to land at Cartersville, the airport suggested too late by Atlanta Approach when it became clear the DC-9 had no hope of being able to reach Dobbins.

It could not be determined why the captain did not take over control of the aircraft, at least in the final stages of the emergency landing. It is standard procedure for a captain to take control in an emergency and, in this case, the captain's total flying experience and time on DC-9s were far superior to the first officer's. Moreover, the CVR transcript suggests that the first officer, evidently a forceful personality, twice refused the captain's advice to select an open field, instead of a highway, for their forced landing.

Southern Airways' operations manual set out procedures for avoiding thunderstorms, including the options of delaying flights on the ground or deviating en route. Clearly the company did not intend its crews to fly through thunderstorms, and the investigators sought to determine why this crew chose to enter a thunderstorm cell that was extremely hazardous.

As the crew continued towards Atlanta in instrument conditions, they would not have been able to sight the towering thunderstorm near Rome, but were obviously receiving radar returns from it. At 4.03:48pm, when the aircraft was about 35nm west-northwest of the Rome VOR, the captain commented: "Looks heavy – nothing's going through that!"

Radar limitations

Why the captain changed his mind can never be known for certain, but it seems the crew thought they discerned a "hole" in the weather system. In any event, the aircraft continued on the same heading for just over a minute, then began a right turn. Given the intense precipitation levels of the storm only a short distance away, the aircraft's radar should certainly have been showing a "contour hole" – an area where the very intensity of the precipitation prevents any radar return, producing a misleading blank spot amid the radar echoes being displayed on the aircraft's radar screen.

This "contour hole" deception is a well known phenomenon familiar to experienced airline pilots. In this instance however, because the aircraft was already flying in heavy rain, the radar could have been affected by attenuation, distorting the appearance of the contour hole to the extent that it was interpreted by the captain as an area actually free of precipitation. The captain's comment: "All clear left approximately right now…," at 4.06:01pm seems to confirm this, because the aircraft's heading was then altered to the left – as it proved, into the most intense area of the storm.

Other than the echoes visible on the aircraft's radar, it was evident that the crew had no specific information on the intense weather just west of the Rome VOR. However, the investigators found that the National Weather Service had data, in addition to the general SIGMET information passed to the aircraft, that would probably have altered the crew's decision to fly through it. Detailed reports of intense thunderstorms, with hail and cloud tops above 40,000 feet, to the west of Rome were in fact prepared by the National Weather Service some 20 minutes before the DC-9 took off from Huntsville.

The normal means of communicating such information to Southern Airways crews was via the company's flight despatch system. Yet the despatchers were not aware of these particularly intense storms until after the accident, even though they were first reported near Rome at 3.00pm. The investigators believed this reflected a major flaw in Southern's despatch system – an apparent inability to monitor severe storm systems affecting its route structure.

An alternative means of passing this severe weather information to the aircraft would have been through en route ATC units. These units also had the capability to track severe weather systems by radar. But according to the controllers, Atlanta Centre had little with which to confirm the particularly severe weather located in the Rome area. None of the radar reports from the National Weather Service had been made available to ATC personnel, and they had received few reports from pilots.

Weather information

Given the availability of sophisticated weather detection and tracking systems – automated and digitised radar, Doppler radar, and satellite cameras transmitting pictures of weather systems every 30 minutes – the National Transportation Safety Board concluded that existing methods of passing critical weather information to aircraft were insufficient to assure an adequate level of safety.

A means of relaying severe weather data directly to ATC units for immediate internal distribution would, the investigators believed, significantly improve controllers' knowledge of the location and intensity of severe weather. The controllers could then pass the information directly to pilots. Under the current system, because en route controllers could be of little assistance, crews had to rely too heavily on their aircraft's weather radar for guidance.

Studies however showed that the X-band frequency used by airborne weather radar equipment is susceptible to attenuation by water vapour and precipitation, particularly when precipitation covers the aircraft's radome. In these circumstances, pilots could misinterpret the radar display, which was one reason why airborne radar should not be used as a storm penetration aid.

For maximum effectiveness, X-band radar displays should be interpreted when the aircraft was flying in an area free of water vapour or precipitation.

For regional airlines such as Southern Airways, operating short flights, radar display interpretation could obviously be critical. Aircraft could frequently be in rain for much of a particular flight and, for this reason, crew training on the limitations of airborne radar was vital. In this case, the investigators believed, the DC-9 crew might not have been fully aware of these limitations.

CHAPTER 2

"Are we clear of that Cessna?"

– Boeing 727 First Officer to Captain

Pacific Southwest Airlines Boeing 727-214 N533PS [19688] (F/n 206), and Cessna 172 Skyhawk N7711G – September 25, 1978

Faultless inflight visibility, a primary airport control zone, state-of-the-art ATC radar equipment, a computer controlled conflict alert warning system, and experienced crews in both aircraft, all failed to prevent a horrific midair collision that took the lives of 144 people.

The morning service to San Diego

The bright autumn morning was just the sort of day for which the State of California is legendary – fine and calm, with cloudless blue skies and mild temperatures. And for Pacific Southwest Airlines, the thriving Californian company with headquarters at San Diego, the day showed every promise of being yet another excellent one for business.

Among the airline's many scheduled trips was PSA Flight 182, a daily morning Boeing 727 service from Sacramento, the state capital, to San Diego via Los Angeles. A breakfast flight, it was usually well patronised by business executives on their way to one day meetings or conferences in the relaxed southern city, and today was no exception.

In command of PSA Flight 182 this Monday morning was Captain James McFeron, 42, a 14,000 hour pilot with 12 years' command time on Boeing 727s. His experienced crew comprised First Officer Robert Fox, 38, with 10,000 hours, half of which had been gained on Boeing 727s, and Flight Engineer Martin Wahne, 44, with similar experience to the first officer. Four flight attendants were in the cabin to look after the passen-

gers, some of whom were company aircrew "deadheading" their way back to base at San Diego. One of them, another Boeing 727 captain, occupied the forward jumpseat immediately behind McFeron's position on the flightdeck.

Departing Sacramento on schedule at 7.20am, the Boeing landed 45 minutes later at Los Angeles where more passengers came aboard, bringing the total passenger complement to 128. Among those boarding at Los Angeles was a prominent lawyer, Mrs Valerie Kantor, wife of a Californian Democrat Party executive. The aircraft took off again for San Diego International Airport, known locally as Lindbergh Field, at 8.41am.

Like the first leg of the trip, the en route section of the flight was entirely uneventful in the superb morning visibility. First Officer Fox was flying the aircraft from the right hand seat, with Captain McFeron handling the radio communications. At 8.53am, the Boeing having been transferred from the en route air traffic control frequency, Captain McFeron made his first contact with San Diego Approach Control, reporting they were at 11,000 feet on descent. Approach Control cleared the

Boeing to continue descending and, four minutes later at 8.57am, Captain McFeron reported they had left 9500 feet and had the airport in sight. San Diego Approach Control then cleared the Boeing for a visual approach to Lindbergh Field's Runway 27. The Boeing would be making a right hand circuit, joining on the downwind leg.

A training flight

In the San Diego area that morning at 8.15, a Cessna 172 Skyhawk had taken off from Montgomery Field, a general aviation aerodrome six nautical miles northeast of the international airport, for a period of instrument flying training. The Cessna, N7711G, belonged to the Gibbs Flite Center at Montgomery Field, and was under the command of flying instructor Martin Kazy, 32, a commercial pilot with some 5000 hours' flying experience.

His pupil was 35 year old David Boswell, a sergeant in the Marine Corps who, though relatively inexperienced in terms of flying hours, also held a commercial pilot licence. Boswell was undergoing training with the Gibbs Flite Center for an instrument rating.

Pacific Southwest Airlines' Boeing 727 N551PS [20679], an Advanced model 214 and a later sistership to the ill fated N533PS. After 1977 the company livery – broad cheatline and "rooster's tail" on the fin – consisted of triple bands of orange, vermilion and dark red. The company logo was also modified to show PSA as a thick black outline and offset shadow. (Boeing)

The training session in the Cessna was to include Instrument Landing System (ILS) approaches, but because Montgomery Field was not equipped with this radio navigation aid, the Cessna had been approved by San Diego air traffic control to proceed to Lindbergh Field to carry out practice ILS approaches to Runway 09, the reciprocal of Runway 27 in use.

In radio contact on the Lindbergh Tower control frequency, the Cessna carried out two practice ILS approaches to Runway 09, terminating each with a 'go round' instead of a landing. At 8.57, at about the same time as Approach Control was clearing the Boeing 727 for a visual approach to Runway 27, the Cessna completed its second ILS and, from its position just to the west of the airport, put on power and began climbing out to the northeast in preparation for a further practice approach, this time to Runway 27, using one of Lindbergh Field's two NDB radio navigation aids. The Lindbergh tower controller then instructed the Cessna to change frequency and contact San Diego Approach Control.

Meanwhile the approach controller called another Pacific Southwest Airlines flight that was approaching

to land ahead of the Boeing 727 to advise it that "Traffic will be a Cessna 172, just making a low approach off Runway 09, northbound. Contact Lindbergh Tower now, 133.3."

Apparently not hearing all this transmission, Captain McFeron queried: "Was that for us?" The approach controller replied: "No, that was for the other company flight, sir."

But two minutes later, just after 8.59, Approach Control did call the Boeing with a traffic advisory: "Traffic [at] 12 o'clock, one mile, northbound," the controller informed the aircraft. Captain McFeron responded: "We're looking."

A few seconds later again the approach controller further advised the Boeing: "Additional traffic at 12 o'clock, three miles, just north of the field, northeastbound – a Cessna 172 climbing VFR out of 1400 [feet]". This time First Officer Fox responded: "OK – we've got that other 12."

Immediately afterwards the Cessna itself called Approach Control to report it was now at 1500 feet and "northeastbound". The approach controller told the Cessna it was identified on radar and instructed it to remain VFR at or below 3500 feet and to maintain a heading of 070 degrees pending radar vectoring for

its practice NDB approach to Lindbergh Field's Runway 27. The Cessna crew acknowledged the instruction and read back the clearance.

This then prompted the approach controller to further advise the Boeing: "Traffic at 12 o'clock, three miles, now out of 1700 [feet]", and Captain McFeron immediately responded: "Traffic in sight."

"OK, sir," Approach Control replied, "Maintain visual separation, contact Lindbergh Tower [on] 133.3."

The approach controller then informed the Cessna: "Traffic at six o'clock, two miles, eastbound – a PSA jet inbound to Lindbergh, out of 3200, has you in sight," and the Cessna acknowledged the transmission.

At this stage the Boeing 727, having descended to 3200 feet, was swinging smoothly to the left onto an easterly heading to enter a downwind leg parallelling Runway 27 and about two nautical miles to its north.

Captain McFeron now changed frequency and reported to Lindbergh Tower that they were on the downwind leg of the circuit. In acknowledging his call, the tower controller also told the Boeing there was "Traffic, 12 o'clock, one mile, a Cessna."

After a pause, evidently while the Boeing crew were again scanning their field of view for the light aircraft, Captain McFeron replied: "OK – we had it there a minute ago ... [further pause of six seconds] ... I think he's passed off to our right."

Changing the subject, the tower controller then enquired: "How far are you going to take your downwind [leg]? Company traffic is waiting for departure."

"Probably three to four miles," Captain McFeron replied.

Instructing another Pacific Southwest Airlines aircraft awaiting takeoff to "taxi into position and hold," the controller told the Boeing 727 crew they were "cleared to land" and McFeron acknowledged the clearance. The waiting aircraft was then cleared for takeoff, departing from Runway 27 one minute later.

Though the Boeing 727's crew did not realise it, the Cessna, having unexpectedly turned 20 degrees to the right from its previous heading of 070 degrees, was now also flying an easterly heading ahead of them as it continued its climb. Thus, as the Boeing extended its downwind leg to the northeast of the airport, gradually descending, it was rapidly overtaking the Cessna from behind, with both aircraft on different radio frequencies.

Meanwhile in the ATC approach control facility, the automated "conflict alert" warning began flashing on the approach controllers' radar screen and its aural warning sounded, indicating that the predicted flightpaths of the Boeing and the Cessna would enter the computer's warning parameters. However, as such conflict alerts were a relatively common occurrence in Lindbergh Field's busy control zone, and the Boeing crew had already indicated they had the Cessna in sight before changing to the tower frequency, the controllers took no action other than to again call the Cessna to remind its crew of the Boeing's presence behind them. "Traffic in your vicinity," the approach controller warned the Cessna 50 seconds later, "A PSA jet has you in sight – he's descending for Lindbergh." There was no acknowledgement from the Cessna. The reason why was soon to become tragically plain.

Midair collision

At about this time, a number of people on the ground beneath the flightpaths of the two aircraft, in the quiet residential suburb of North Park, saw the descending Boeing 727 overtaking the climbing Cessna from almost immediately behind. While they watched with horrified fascination as the remaining gap be-

Pacific Southwest Airlines operated more than 30 Boeing 727s of all marques. This head on view shows the black painted "mouth" which gave the company's aircraft their characteristic "smiling face" feature. N533PS was the 11th 727 delivered to the airline and the sixth of an initial order for seven 727-200s. (Flight International)

tween the large and small aircraft rapidly closed, they saw the Boeing bank momentarily to the right. At the same time, the Cessna's suddenly pitched nose up, and the inevitable impact was taken on the underside of the leading edge of the Boeing's starboard wing.

The noise of the collision was like a sonic boom[1], the impact attracting the attention of many other witnesses on the ground. Looking up they saw thick black smoke enveloping the starboard inner wing of the Boeing 727, from which the remains

of the shattered Cessna and other aircraft parts were falling. As the smoke began to clear, clouds of vaporised fuel could be seen streaming from the Boeing's badly damaged wing and the aircraft began banking into a shallow descending turn to the right.

Moments later, a bright orange fire broke out in the leading edge of the Boeing's damaged starboard wing, apparently as the fuel pouring from severed lines and tanks caught fire. The intensity of the fire grew rapidly, until flames were streaming back beyond the trailing edge. At the same time the aircraft's angle of bank and descent progressively increased, until it was diving towards the ground at a steep angle while banked about 50 degrees to starboard, obviously out of control.

Ten seconds after the midair collision, Captain McFeron made his final transmission to Lindbergh Tower, his voice eerily calm: "Tower, we're going down – this is PSA."

Apparently not yet appreciating the enormity of the situation, the tower controller answered: "OK, we'll call the [emergency] equipment for you."

Five seconds later the Boeing, still steeply banked and nosedown, plunged with enormous violence into the closely settled suburb of North Park, erupting "like an atomic explosion" as one traumatised eye witness described it, into an intense fireball and a mushroom cloud of black smoke. The time of impact was a few seconds after 9.02am.

Scene of devastation

Emergency services that converged on the suburban crash site through San Diego's morning peak traffic from all over the city – fire brigades, ambulances and police vehicles, all with sirens wailing ominously – were confronted with a scene of utter devastation.

No less than 22 houses, spread over four suburban blocks, together with numbers of motor vehicles, lay destroyed or badly damaged, many of them burning fiercely. Little remained to show that the cause of the wholesale destruction had been a fully functioning modern airliner carrying a near full load of business passengers. With the exception of the three badly damaged tail-mounted engines and sections of the tail assembly, the entire aircraft structure was fragmented. Much of this scattered wreckage had been further destroyed by the intense fire, much of it still burning.

Fragments of human bodies – all that was left of the 135 occupants of the Boeing 727 – lay scattered in the streets, in trees, on rooftops and in suburban backyards. In addition to those on board the aircraft, seven residents of North Park were dead – killed by the impact in their houses, in their cars, or as they walked in the street.

The crushed, broken but unburnt wreckage of the Cessna lay upside-down in a street just over a kilometre northwest of the devastation. Both its occupants had obviously been killed instantly in the midair collision.

A Cessna 172 Skyhawk II – an aircraft similar to the one involved in the accident.

On site investigation

National Transportation Safety Board investigators who arrived in San Diego from Washington DC later that day established that the Boeing 727 had struck the ground in a southwest heading, almost the reciprocal of the direction in which it was flying at the time of the collision, in a steep nosedown attitude while banked about 50 degrees to the right. The fuselage, from the nose to the airstair compartment in the tail, was completely fragmented, with a major portion of the wreckage consumed by fire.

Simplified map of central and southern California, showing route being operated by the Boeing 727 on the morning of the accident. The stage lengths would be similar to a Brisbane/Sydney/Canberra service. (Matthew Tesch)

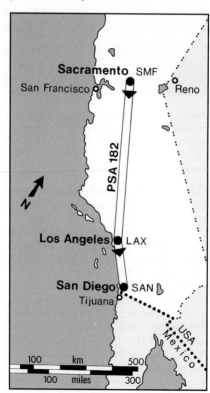

The starboard wing was also destroyed, but lying amongst its wreckage were the crushed remains of the Cessna's port wing fuel tank.

The Boeing 727's port wing, though not demolished to the extent of the starboard wing, was nevertheless severely damaged by ground impact and fire, but a section containing the No 3 and No 4 leading edge slats was identifiable. The slats were in the extended position, while the wing's three spoiler panels (inflight speed brakes) were retracted. Measurement of the wing flap jackscrews showed that the flaps were extended 15 degrees at the time of impact.

All three engines had separated from the aircraft structure and were severely damaged, but there was no evidence of any pre-impact malfunction, and it was obvious that they were under power at the time of the crash.

Examination of the Cessna's wreckage showed that, together with the port fuel tank, a portion of its port wing was missing. Both the fin and rudder had separated from the tail assembly and were bent to the left. From the tail assembly forward to the port side door post, the upper structure of the fuselage was crushed downwards, while the rear fuselage behind the cabin was severely buckled upwards.

Various pieces of the Boeing 727's starboard wing leading edge flap system were found embedded in the crushed Cessna wreckage, including sections of the No 5 and No 6 flaps, and the forward end of the No 5 flap actuator, with the piston rod and attachment bracket assemblies still attached. The actuator rod assembly was in the extended position, but bent about 75° inboard, with a small portion of the Cessna's propeller blade jammed between the piston rod and the end of the actuator. The Cessna's engine and propeller had separated from the fuselage and,

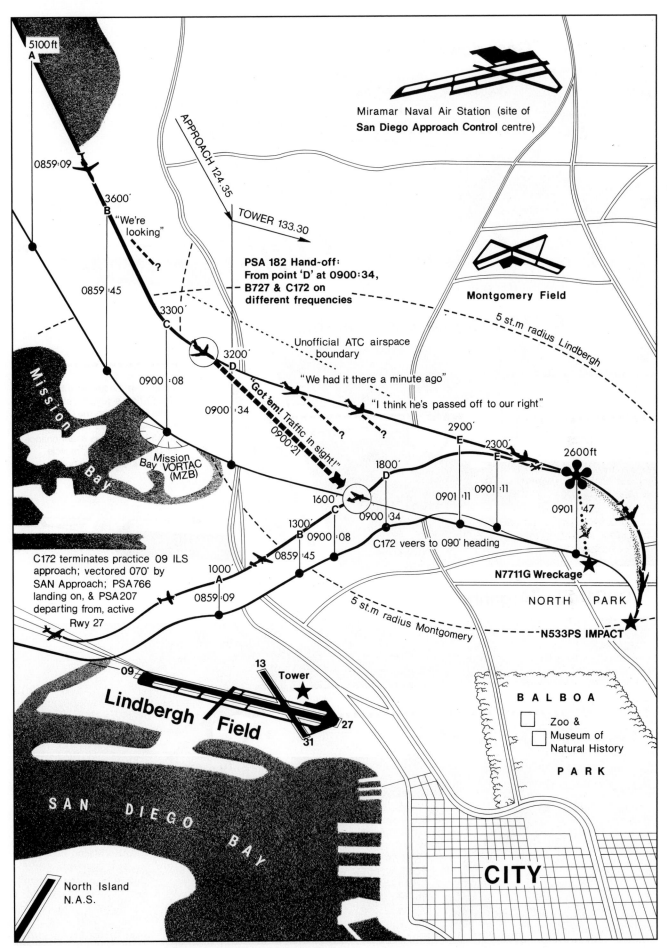

5100ft
A
0859:09
B 3600'
"We're looking"
?
0859:45
C 3300'
0900:08
D 3200'
0900:34
"Got 'em! Traffic in sight!"
0900:21

APPROACH 124.35
TOWER 133.30

PSA 182 Hand-off:
From point 'D' at 0900:34,
B727 & C172 on
different frequencies

Unofficial ATC airspace
boundary

"We had it there a minute ago"
"I think he's passed off to our right"
?   ?

Miramar Naval Air Station (site of
San Diego Approach Control centre)

Montgomery Field

5 st.m radius Lindbergh

2900'
E
2300'
E
2600ft
1800'
D
0901:11   0901:11
0901:47
1600'
C
0900:34
1300'
B 0900:08
C172 veers to 090' heading
N7711G Wreckage

Mission
Bay
Mission
Bay VORTAC
(MZB)

C172 terminates practice 09 ILS
approach; vectored 070' by
SAN Approach; PSA766
landing on, & PSA207
departing from, active
Rwy 27

1000'
A
0859:09

0859:45

5 st.m radius Montgomery

NORTH   PARK

N533PS IMPACT

09
13
Tower
Lindbergh
Field
27
31

BALBOA
☐ Zoo &
☐ Museum of
Natural History

PARK

SAN   DIEGO   BAY

North Island
N.A.S.

CITY

North facing aerial perspective of the San Diego area, showing relationship of Lindbergh and Montgomery Fields, together with flightpaths and ground tracks of the Boeing and Cessna during the minutes leading to the collision. (Matthew Tesch, with acknowledgement to NTSB and Rand McNally)

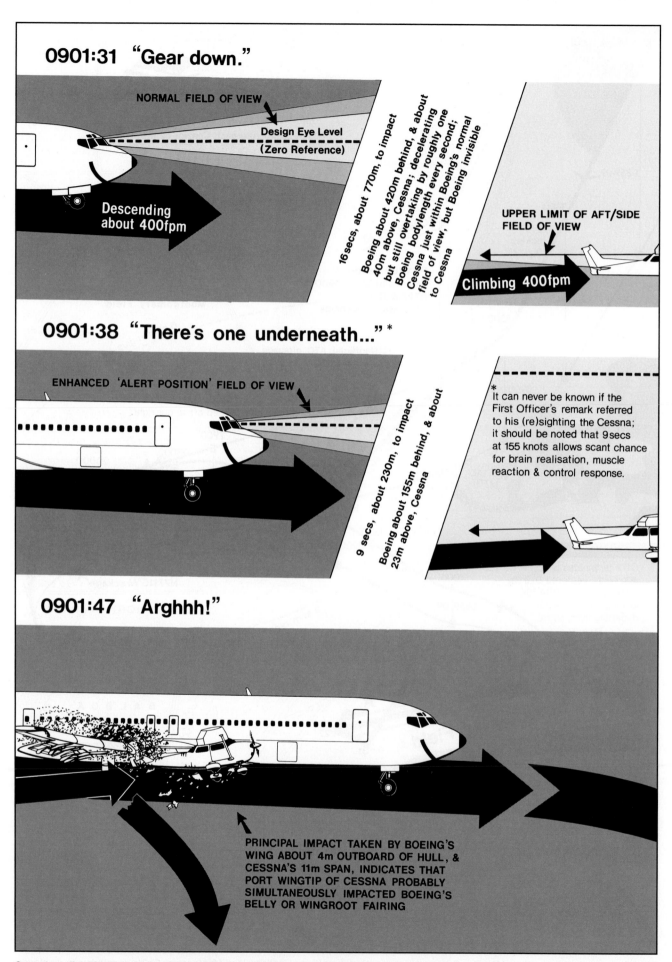

0901:31 "Gear down."

NORMAL FIELD OF VIEW

Design Eye Level (Zero Reference)

Descending about 400fpm

16secs, about 770m, to impact

Boeing about 420m behind, & about 40m above, Cessna; decelerating but still overtaking by roughly one bodylength every second; Cessna just within Boeing's normal field of view, but Boeing invisible to Cessna

UPPER LIMIT OF AFT/SIDE FIELD OF VIEW

Climbing 400fpm

0901:38 "There's one underneath..." *

ENHANCED 'ALERT POSITION' FIELD OF VIEW

9 secs, about 230m, to impact

Boeing about 155m behind, & about 23m above, Cessna

* It can never be known if the First Officer's remark referred to his (re)sighting the Cessna; it should be noted that 9 secs at 155 knots allows scant chance for brain realisation, muscle reaction & control response.

0901:47 "Arghhh!"

PRINCIPAL IMPACT TAKEN BY BOEING'S WING ABOUT 4m OUTBOARD OF HULL, & CESSNA'S 11m SPAN, INDICATES THAT PORT WINGTIP OF CESSNA PROBABLY SIMULTANEOUSLY IMPACTED BOEING'S BELLY OR WINGROOT FAIRING

Sequence showing the two aircraft's final seconds of flight as their flightpaths converged. The field of view available to the captain and first officer of the 727 during the first two stages in the sequence is also illustrated. (Matthew Tesch)

although the propeller remained bolted to the crankshaft, a portion of each of the two blades had broken off.

Flight Recorders

The Boeing 727 was equipped with a four parameter Flight Data Recorder (FDR) providing traces for airspeed, altitude, magnetic heading and vertical acceleration; and a Cockpit Voice Recorder (CVR) fitted with a continuous tape so as to provide a record of radio communications and flightdeck conversation over the last 30 minutes of any flight.

The two units were recovered from the scattered wreckage, but both had been damaged and subjected to intense heat. The metal foil recording tape of the FDR was heavily encrusted with deposits of combustion, and only by repeated chemical and ultrasonic cleanings was it possible to finally read out the altitude, airspeed and heading traces. The vertical acceleration trace remained indecipherable.

Despite severe external damage, the CVR on the other hand yielded a tape in excellent condition, and the final five minutes of the flight were read out without difficulty and transcribed.

The FDR record did not add a great deal to the information available to the investigators from witness and other evidence. It confirmed that the Boeing was maintaining a magnetic heading of just under 090 degrees at the time of the collision, and that, after it entered the descending turn to the right, the heading progressively increased to 200 degrees by the time of ground impact.

The FDR also showed that the aircraft was descending through an altitude of 2650 feet AMSL (2350 feet above ground elevation) and at an indicated airspeed of 155 knots when the collision occurred. The relative impact speed between the two aircraft would thus have been of the order of 65 knots (120kmh). Small blips on the altitude and airspeed traces of a 1.5 second gain of 100 feet, producing a decrease of two knots over the same brief period, at about the time of the collision, suggested an instinctive backward movement of the control column by the first officer as the Cessna became

This horrifyingly spectacular picture of the Boeing 727 plunging to destruction seconds after its collision with the Cessna 172 was captured on film by San Diego professional photographer Hans Wendt, who at the time happened to be taking some views of a service station in the residential suburb of North Park. The midair impact has torn off the Boeing's Nos 5 and 6 leading edge flaps, together with a section of the No 5 leading edge slat, and peeled a portion of the starboard wing leading edge back to the main spar. The raging fire in the starboard wing is being fed by severed fuel lines, the flames streaming back behind the trailing edge almost as far as the Boeing's tail. Despite almost full up elevator and full opposite aileron, the crew are unable to check the steep angle of dive or the increasing angle of bank. Note the undercarriage, lowered before the collision in preparation for landing. (Hans Wendt via NTSB)

visible to him at the last moment. From this point on, the altitude trace abruptly decreased, while the airspeed trace increased, rising to just under 220 knots when the recording was terminated by ground impact.

The transcript of the CVR on the other hand, yielded a great deal of information of value to the investigation.

As the Boeing 727 descended into the San Diego area, the supernumerary captain occupying the forward jump seat was conversing with Captain McFeron on company working conditions of mutual interest, but this discussion ended as the aircraft began its gradual turn on to the downwind leg of the Lindbergh Field circuit. From this point on, except for an occasional word or exclamation, only the three flight crew members spoke, all their exchanges being related to the conduct of the flight. This included radio exchanges between the flight engineer and the company's operations office at Lindbergh Field, relating to the servicing required for the aircraft after landing, which concluded only a minute before the collision.

However, the CVR also contained the occasional remark which the investigators were unable to definitely attribute to any one of the four individuals known to be on the flightdeck. They were finally unable to determine whether this unidentified voice was one of the four known flightdeck occupants, or whether

there was a fifth person on the flightdeck occupying the second jumpseat.

The radio exchanges with San Diego Approach Control and the flightdeck conversation recorded by the CVR during the final two minutes and eight seconds of the flight are as follows. Seconds to the collision (c) and to final impact with the ground (g) are shown in italics in brackets before each exchange:

(c120, g140): APP: Cessna 7711G, radar contact, maintain VFR at or below 3500, fly heading 070, vector [for] final approach course.

(c97, g117): CESSNA [acknowledging]: 7711G on the heading and VFR below 3500.

(c90, g110): APP [to Boeing]: PSA182, traffic at 12 o'clock, three miles, out of 1700.

(c84, g104): F/O: Got him!

(c83, g103): CAPT [to Approach Control]: Traffic in sight.

(c82, g102): APP: OK sir, maintain visual separation, contact Lindbergh Tower 133.3. Have a nice day now!

(c79, g99): F/O [flying the aircraft]: Flaps two.

(c71, g91): CAPT [to Lindbergh Tower]: Lindbergh, PSA182. Downwind.

(c67, g87): TOWER: PSA182, Lindbergh Tower, traffic 12 o'clock, one mile, a Cessna.

(c64, g84): F/O: Flaps five.

(c62, g82): CAPT: Is that the one we're looking at?

(c62, g82): F/O: Yeah – but I don't see him now.

(c61, g81): CAPT [to Tower]: OK – we had it there a minute ago.

(c58, g78): TOWER: PSA182, Roger.

(c58, g78): CAPT: I think he's passed off to our right.

(c57, g77): TOWER: Yeah.

(c53, g73): CAPT [to F/O]: He was right over here a minute ago.

(c52, g72): F/O: Yeah.

(c51, g71): TOWER: How far are you going to take your downwind, PSA182? Company traffic is waiting for departure.

(c48, g68): CAPT: Ah, probably about three to four miles.

(c46, g66): TOWER: OK.

(c38, g58): TOWER: PSA182 – cleared to land.

In this second picture by Hans Wendt, snapped a split second before the aircraft disappeared from view behind the building in the foreground, the angle of bank has steepened considerably, providing a clearer view of the wing damage inflicted by the collision with the Cessna. The aircraft's rudders, centred in the first picture, are now deflected to the left as the pilots make a final desperate attempt to recover control. Note the glare of the wing fire reflecting from the rear fuselage. (Hans Wendt via NTSB)

(g14): F/O [with emphasis]: We're hit man – we *are* hit!

(g12): CAPT [quietly but positively]: Tower – we're going down – this is PSA.

(g10): TOWER: OK – we'll call the equipment for you!

(g7): UNIDENTIFIED: Whoo!

(g7): Sound of stall warning.

(g6): CAPT [to Tower]: This is it, baby!

(g6): UNIDENTIFIED: Bob ... [name of F/O]

(g5): F/O: #### [Words deleted on transcript]

(g4): UNIDENTIFIED: ### [Words deleted on transcript]

(g2): CAPT [probably speaking on cabin public address system]: Brace yourself!

(g1): UNIDENTIFIED: Hey baby ...

(g1): SECOND UNIDENTIFIED: Ma, I love you ...

(g0): End of recording.

Photographs

The Boeing's steep descending turn to destruction was successively captured on film by a Mr Hans Wendt, a professional photographer who was engaged in an assignment at a service station in North Park that morning and fortunately had a loaded camera within reach when the midair collision occurred.

Two of the photographs he was able to take before the aircraft disappeared from view behind a nearby house graphically portrayed the plight of the stricken Boeing as a result of the collision and were quickly seized upon by the press and published in newspapers around the world. Enlargements of these highly spectacular photographs were used by the investigators to try to determine the position of the aircraft's control surfaces and the state of its fuel and hydraulic systems as it dived out of control.

Study of the enlarged prints revealed that the No 5 and No 6 leading edge flaps were missing from the starboard wing, together with a section of the No 5 leading edge slat. In addition, a major portion of the wing's leading edge was peeled back to about the front spar. Because of the extent of the wing fire towards the trailing edge of the wing in the vicinity of the inboard aileron, it was not possible to determine whether any of the control surfaces in that area were missing.

In Boeing 727 aircraft, hydraulic lines to the leading edge devices are routed forward of the front spar, but from the photographs it was not possible to determine whether these

(c37, g57): CAPT [acknowledging]: PSA182's cleared to land.

(c34, g54): CAPT [to flightdeck crew generally]: Are we clear of that Cessna?

(c32, g52): F/E: Supposed to be!

(c31, g51): CAPT: I guess.

(c30, g50): F/O: Flaps 15.

(c25, g45): SUPERNUMERARY CAPT [laughing]: I hope!

(c24, g44): CAPT [positively]: Yeah – before we turned downwind, I saw him about one o'clock – probably behind us now.

(c14, g34): F/O: Gear down.

(c11, g31): Sound of undercarriage extending and locking down.

(c6, g26): F/O: There's one underneath ... I was looking at that inbound there.

(c1, g21): CAPT: Whoops! [probably as first officer instinctively pulls back on control wheel on sighting Cessna immediately in front on his side].

(c1, g21): F/O [involuntarily]: Arghhh!

(c0, g20): Metallic crunching noise of collision.

(g19): SUPERNUMERARY CAPT: Oh ####! (expletive deleted on transcript).

(g18): CAPT [reassuringly]: Easy baby, easy baby.

(g16): CAPT [to F/O]: What have we got here?

(g15): F/O [grimly]: It's bad.

(g15): CAPT: Eh?

lines were broken or merely flattened. However, fuel lines from the fuel pumps to the fuel pressure sensors are located immediately behind the leading edge flaps. If severed, these lines would spray out fuel for as long as the fuel pumps remained in operation.

Except for the aircraft's upper and lower rudders which were centred in the first photograph and positioned about 10 degrees to the left in the second, the deflections of the other control surfaces were the same in both pictures: the port wing spoilers were fully up, the port wing aileron was fully up, the starboard wing aileron was down, the elevators were almost fully up, the trailing edge flaps were set at 15 degrees, and the leading edge devices were fully extended.

Cockpit visibility

The investigators carried out a study of crew visibility pertinent to the midair collision using a binocular camera successively mounted in the two pilot positions and the forward jumpseat position in a Boeing 727-200, and in both pilots' seats of a Cessna 172. Because the position of the Boeing flight engineer's seat at the time of the collision was not known, photographs were not taken from this crew seat. The photographs were designed to show a panoramic view of the flightdeck and cockpit window layouts as would be seen by each crewmember rotating his head fully from one side to the other.

The photographs taken from the captain's and first officer's seats on the Boeing's flightdeck showed that the Cessna would have been almost centred on their windscreens between 170 and 90 seconds before the collision. After that time it would have been visible on the lower portion of the windscreen, just above the windscreen wipers. Movement of either pilot to an "alert" position – that is, leaning forward to scan for an airborne target – would have elevated the Cessna slightly during the last 80 seconds. Any view of the Cessna would have been hidden from the occupant of the forward jumpseat by the captain's head and shoulders.

Similar photographs taken from the control seats of the Cessna showed that only for a very brief period, some 90 seconds before the collision, would the Boeing have been visible to either pilot – and then only on the upper portion of the port side door window. For the remaining time to the collision, the Boeing would have been hidden by the port wing and cabin structure.

Some idea of the enormous destruction caused by the crash of the Boeing into the residential suburb is evident from these two general views of the wreckage trail. Note the crushed motor vehicle at left in the second picture. (Ron Smith)

Air Traffic Control (ATC) procedures

Under the ATC arrangements in place in the San Diego area at the time of the accident, a 15 nautical mile radius Terminal Radar Service Area (TRSA), with a base altitude of 4000 feet, overlaid the San Diego terminal area airspace. Within this TRSA, ATC provided radar vectoring, sequencing and separation for all IFR and participating VFR aircraft. At altitudes below the TRSA, ATC provided radar vectoring, sequencing of all arrivals, and traffic advisories.

The San Diego Approach Control facility was equipped with search radar providing azimuth and range information at lower levels of flight within a 50nm radius of the airport, and an Automated Radar Terminal System (ARTS) computer. Its radar screens displayed primary and secondary returns from aircraft, with alphanumeric data tags for those that were transponder equipped. Both the Boeing 727 and the Cessna were equipped with altitude encoding transponders, and their data tags on the radar screens displayed their identifications, computed ground-speeds and altitude readouts.

The radar and transponder data were also transmitted by microwave link to Lindbergh Tower where they were displayed on a bright radar indicator suspended from the tower ceiling above the tower controller's position. This display did not include alphanumeric data or altitude readouts, however.

San Diego Approach Control's conflict alert system had been commissioned only six weeks before the accident. Its aircraft separation parameters were 375 feet vertically, 1.2nm horizontally, and 40 seconds "look ahead". Any aircraft track computer projections which intruded into these areas would initiate an alert.

Analysis

Why did this disastrous midair collision occur? Why was it that highly experienced pilots in both aircraft, near perfect visibility, qualified and seasoned air traffic control staff, powerful search radar, an automated radar terminal computer, and the latest development in ATC radar technology, an automated conflict alert system, all failed to prevent this appalling accident?

Local standing orders for approaches to Lindbergh Field from the north required approach controllers to instruct southbound jet and turboprop aircraft "to maintain at or above 4000 feet until clear of the Montgomery Airport traffic area." During the investigation it was found that not all controllers were adhering to this procedure. Some controllers were clearing aircraft for a visual approach, but monitoring

their altitude readouts. If it appeared than an aircraft would descend below 4000 feet before clearing the Montgomery Field area, the controller would restrict the descent or co-ordinate it with the Montgomery Field tower controller.

On this occasion, the approach controller who handled the Boeing 727's descent prior to the collision said that because the aircraft was not going to enter the Montgomery Field traffic area, he did not issue it with the 4000 foot restriction. The approach controller explained that the Boeing was outside the Montgomery Field traffic area when he cleared it for a visual approach, and that he monitored the aircraft's progress on radar. For this reason, he believed there was no need either to place the restriction on the Boeing, or to co-ordinate its passage with the Montgomery Control Tower. However, the evidence showed that the Boeing 727 did pass through the southern edge of Montgomery Field's airspace.

In any event, all southbound airline aircraft in the San Diego area were required to be restricted to the 4000 feet descent limit, and if the restriction had been imposed, even though there was no actual traffic conflict in the Montgomery Field traffic area, it is possible that the accident would not have occurred.

Although an IFR flight, the Boeing's crew had accepted a visual approach clearance to Lindbergh Field.

In the existing visual flight conditions, its crew were thus required to "see and avoid" other aircraft. The radar traffic advisory services available in the San Diego area below 4000 feet were designed to assist pilots in this vital responsibility.

Beginning two minutes 20 seconds before the collision, the Boeing was given three advisories of conflicting traffic by Approach Control, and one by Lindbergh Tower. Thirty seconds after 8.59am, the approach controller informed the Boeing there was another aircraft a mile directly ahead, heading north. Captain Mc Feron's reply indicated they had not sighted it, but were "looking". The aircraft concerned was a Grumman T-Cat on a northerly heading en route from Imperial Beach, 11nm southeast of Lindbergh Field, to Gillespie Field, an aerodrome to the north of San Diego, at an altitude of 3500 feet.

Nine seconds later, the approach controller called the Boeing again to report there was "additional traffic", three miles directly ahead, this time a Cessna 172 "just north of the field" heading northeast and climbing through 1400 feet.

Immediately after clearing the Cessna to proceed VFR below 3500 feet and to maintain a heading of 070 degrees, the approach controller again called the Boeing to report that the "traffic" was "at 12 o'clock, three miles [ahead], out of 1700 [feet]." This traffic advisory did not include the direction of movement or the aircraft type as required by ATC procedures, but the controller's inference was that it also referred to the Cessna. In any event, Captain McFeron reported back a few seconds later, "Traffic in sight." The approach controller then cleared the Boeing to "maintain visual separation" and to contact Lindbergh Tower on its own frequency.

The Boeing's acceptance of this clearance from Approach Control meant that its crew were responsible for separating their aircraft from the traffic that had been pointed out to them. While there was no doubt that it was the Cessna the approach controller was pointing out in his third traffic advisory to the Boeing, the investigators could not be certain whether or not Captain McFeron was referring to the Cessna when he called "traffic in sight".

About the time of the midair collision, Lindbergh Tower controllers were in contact with only two other airborne aircraft – another company aircraft, Flight PSA207 which had just been cleared for takeoff, and a Cessna 401 which was nine nm east of the field. Exhaustive enquiries by

In this view of the devastation created by the Boeing as it plunged into the suburban area at high speed, one of the aircraft's battered JT8D engines is the only recognisable item of wreckage.

Emergency crews pick their way among the havoc as they search for remains of those killed in the accident. The dorsal fin air intake for the Boeing's No 2 engine – one of the few airframe components still identifiable – lies on its side at the left of the picture.

the investigators to determine whether there could have been another light aircraft in the vicinity of the Boeing during the three minutes leading up to the accident indicated that this was unlikely, though not impossible.

The tower controllers had no knowledge of any such traffic, nor was any such aircraft tracked by San Diego Approach Control. For there to have been another light aircraft ahead of the Boeing in a position to be mistaken for the Cessna, it would have had to be operating in violation of ATC regulations and without detection by the controllers.

The flightdeck visibility study showed that, at the time Approach Control issued their second and third traffic advisories to the Boeing, the Cessna would have been centred on both pilots' windscreens. The CVR transcript showed that both pilots sighted an aircraft in the same area in which the approach controller said the Cessna was flying, and that they identified it as a Cessna. It was likely therefore that the Boeing crew did have the Cessna 172, N7711G, in sight shortly after it was pointed out to them.

It was also evident that the Boeing's transmissions to the approach controller convinced him that the crew had the Cessna in sight and were capable of maintaining visual separation from it. Approach Control's two subsequent advisories to the Cessna that "a PSA jet ... has you in sight" confirmed this.

The last traffic advisory to the Boeing came only 15 seconds later, after it had been transferred to the Lindbergh Tower frequency, the tower controller pointing out that there was a Cessna one mile directly ahead. Again however, the advisory did not include the direction in which the Cessna was flying. Even so, the CVR transcript left no doubt

that the crew associated this fourth advisory with the Cessna they had already reported sighting. But it also showed that after this earlier sighting, and before receiving the Tower's advisory, the crew had either dismissed it as not posing a hazard, or had simply lost sight of it. The fact that the two aircraft were now operating on different ATC frequencies – the Boeing on the Tower's and the Cessna on Approach Control's – did nothing to help resolve the confusion.

Although the Boeing's reply to the Tower initially indicated the crew had lost sight of the Cessna, subsequent transmissions gave the controller the impression it had passed off to the Boeing's right and was no longer a hazard. It was most unfortunate that, when the Boeing crew were not able to re-sight the Cessna, they did not convey this fact unambiguously to the tower controller.

A further difficulty was the fact that, about this same time, the Cessna, without notifying the Tower, turned from its assigned heading of 070 degrees on to an easterly heading similar to that of the Boeing. A ground track plot of the two aircraft's positions carried out during the investigation showed that, if the Cessna had maintained its 070 degree heading as instructed, it would have cleared the Boeing's descent path with an altitude separation of about 1000 feet.

Why the Cessna deviated from this heading could not be determined. In the Lindbergh Field traffic area it was

The wreckage of the Cessna 172 after recovery from the crash site, as seen from the port side. Beginning from the rear with the aircraft noseup at the instant of the collision, the Cessna has been "filleted" through the midline of the fuselage, the nose and engine having been torn off altogether. (Ron Smith)

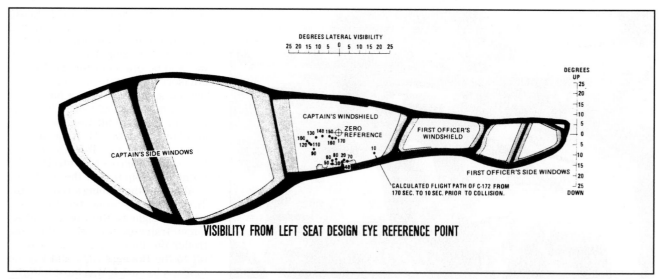

DEGREES LATERAL VISIBILITY

VISIBILITY FROM LEFT SEAT DESIGN EYE REFERENCE POINT

Diagrams produced during the investigation as a result of a detailed cockpit visibility study, showing the Boeing pilots' field of view from both the left and right control seats. The relative positions of the Cessna as seen from the Boeing flightdeck during last 170 seconds prior to the collision are indicated by the dots. The numbers indicate seconds to the collision. During the last 80 seconds the crew's difficult-to-see tail-on view of the Cessna was almost obscured by the base of the Boeing's windscreen frame and the windscreen wipers. (NTSB)

subject to the direction of ATC and the pilot-in-command should either have complied with the ATC instruction he had been given, or informed the controller otherwise. Some of the Cessna's transmissions were in any case garbled and not altogether clear – no doubt the result of the instructor allowing his student to try to "sort it out for himself" – fly the aircraft, hold to an IFR standard, and handle the communication and frequency changes, all at the same time.

The investigators' flightdeck visibility study further showed that, at the time the Boeing crew received the Tower's traffic advisory, the Cessna would have been positioned at the bottom of both pilots' windscreens, just above the windscreen wiper blades. However, if their seat adjustments were such that the pilots' eyes were lower and slightly aft of the flightdeck's design eye reference points, the Cessna could have

been masked altogether by the aircraft structure immediately below the windscreen. In this case, they would not have been able to see it without leaning forward – or raising their seats.

But, even if the pilot seat positions were not a factor in obscuring the crew's view of the Cessna, their ability to sight it at this stage would have been more difficult than at first. With the Cessna now on almost the same heading as the Boeing, its apparent movement across the pilots' field of vision would have ceased. Furthermore, looking at it tail on, the apparent size of the target would have been a good deal smaller than previously. Even though the white surface of the Cessna's wing should have presented a relatively bright target and the sun was well above the horizon, so that the pilots would not have had excessive glare to contend with, the most difficult aspect of try-

ing to sight the Cessna would have been the fact that its altitude was less than that of the Boeing – in other words the Boeing crew would have been looking for it, not against the clear sky, but below the horizon, against the background of the suburban residential area beneath it. Even a white painted light aircraft can be extremely difficult to discern at a distance when it is superimposed on the variegated visual pattern created by closely settled suburban housing. The problem is compounded if, as in this case, the light aircraft has no apparent motion, making it especially difficult to pick out.

Half a minute after 9am, when Approach Control warned the Cessna there was "traffic at 6 o'clock, two miles, eastbound, a PSA jet inbound to Lindbergh ... has you in sight," it was still maintaining its 070 degree heading. But it made its turn onto the easterly heading very shortly af-

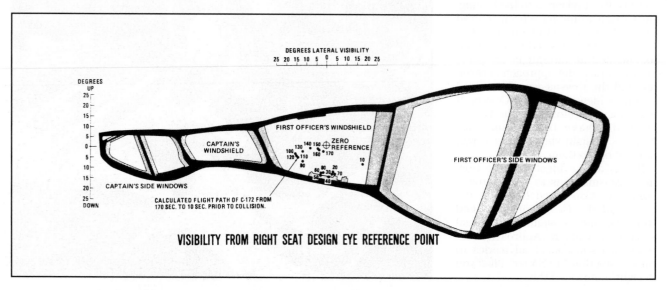

DEGREES LATERAL VISIBILITY

VISIBILITY FROM RIGHT SEAT DESIGN EYE REFERENCE POINT

terwards, and from that time, as established by the cockpit visibility study, it was impossible for the Cessna pilots to see the Boeing. However, as the Cessna crew were told they were being overtaken by a jet aircraft whose crew had them in sight, it would be unrealistic to expect the Cessna pilots to set about manoeuvring their aircraft in order to sight the Boeing.

Regardless of the Cessna's change in heading, the Boeing was the overtaking aircraft and therefore had the responsibility to pass "well clear" of the Cessna. Air traffic regulations did not define the meaning of "well clear" in terms of actual distance or height, and its interpretation was a matter of pilot judgement. However, Pacific Southwest Airlines' Chief Pilot told investigators that he considered half a mile would have been an adequate margin for such a manoeuvre, even though it placed the aircraft within the parameters of the ATC conflict alert warning system.

The conflict alert warning in fact began sounding 19 seconds before the collision. Neither the approach controller nor the approach co-ordinator handling the Boeing 727 were startled by the alert, they told the investigators, because they were so accustomed to them during shifts when there was no actual conflict, or no aircraft close enough together to require the controllers to initiate avoiding action. Since being commissioned, the system had averaged no less than 13 conflict alerts a day, some of them "nuisance alerts".

ATC procedures nevertheless required the controller to take appropriate action to resolve conflict, and to decide if and when the conflict was resolved. But this action did not necessarily require the controller to notify the pilots that their aircraft were in a conflict situation.

In this case, based on all the information available, and exercising his experience and judgement, the approach controller decided that the Boeing crew were complying with their visual separation clearance and overtaking the Cessna within the separation parameters of the conflict alert computer. He had pointed out the Cessna traffic to the Boeing and, in acknowledging this advice, the Boeing crew said they had the traffic in sight, and would maintain visual separation. As far as the approach controller was concerned therefore, there was no real conflict. No action was thus required, other than to remind the Cessna crew of the presence of the Boeing. The approach co-ordinator concurred with this decision at the time.

There is no doubt that both the approach controller and the approach co-ordinator were misled by their belief that the Boeing crew had the Cessna in sight, as well as by their extensive experience of similar conflict alerts when no action on their part was necessary. Nevertheless, the failure of ATC procedures to require pilots to be notified of conflict alert warnings resulted in a situation that failed to make full use of the system. Had this requirement existed, it is possible that the crews of the two aircraft would have been able to take evasive action in time to avoid the collision.

From the evidence of eye witnesses to the collision, as well as that of the FDR, it seems that the Boeing's first officer and at least one of the pilots in the Cessna did sight each other an instant before the collision, for both attempted to take avoiding action. In all probability in instinctive reactions, both aircraft were pulled noseup. But these actions came much too late and in any event probably cancelled each other out. Given the distance of the Boeing 727's flightdeck ahead of the wing where the impact occurred, it is very likely that the pilots did sight the other's aircraft something less than a second before the collision. One can only speculate as to the inner feelings of each pilot as they suddenly sighted the other aircraft looming alongside their cockpit side windows.

The practice of issuing "maintain visual separation" clearances in busy primary airport traffic areas was a matter of concern. The practice achieved little, other than to place crews in "see and avoid" situations, even though flying in areas where the ATC system has the radar capability to provide safe vertical and lateral separation. Had this positive separation been provided at San Diego on September 25, 1978, the Boeing 727 and the Cessna 172 would not have collided.

The investigation also indicated that flight crews operating in "see and avoid" situations exercise less vigilance when they are receiving radar assistance than when radar is not available. Instead of endeavouring to sight and maintain visual contact with other traffic, they tend to rely on controllers to point out the traffic, particularly any aircraft which may be in conflict with their own.

The same tendency to relax vigilance appeared to apply to controllers, particularly when an aircraft had reported "traffic in sight" and the controllers believed its crew had a better grasp of the conflict situation than they did. But even when

the crew of an aircraft accepts the burden of maintaining separation, controllers should not assume their ability to do so will remain unimpaired. Controllers should always be ready to update pilots' traffic information and to immediately alert them to changes in a traffic situation.

The principle of "redundancy" remains a cornerstone of all aspects of aviation safety. Such redundancy between pilots and controllers is only achieved when both exercise their individual responsibilities to the full, regardless of who has assumed or been assigned the primary burden for the safety of the operation.

Findings of the investigation

• The primary cause of the midair collision was that the crew of the Boeing lost sight of the Cessna, but did not make this fact clear to ATC.

• ATC failed to appreciate that the Boeing crew had lost sight of the Cessna, or even that there was some doubt as to its position. This should have been evident from the Boeing's transmissions.

• It was possible that another light aircraft, unidentified and operating without a clearance, could have confused the Boeing crew's attempts to sight the Cessna.

• ATC procedures were not well co-ordinated, resulting in the use of visual separation clearances when radar services were available. Radar separation procedures would have provided positive lateral and vertical separation between the two aircraft.

• The pilot in command of the Cessna neither maintained the heading assigned by ATC, nor informed the controller that the aircraft was diverting from this heading. Had it remained on its assigned heading, the collision would not have occurred.

• Approach Control failed to warn either aircraft of the conflict alert.

• Approach Control did not restrict the Boeing to a minimum height of 4000 feet when over the Montgomery Field traffic area. Had it done so, the collision would not have occurred.

All in all, this appalling but entirely avoidable accident was a vindication of the case for positive ATC control and aircraft separation in primary control zones, regardless of the quality of the prevailing visibility – proof positive, if any more were needed, that the concept of "see and avoid" separation with modern high speed jet aircraft is simply asking too much of human capability.

Footnote:
(1) Both the midair and ground impacts were in fact recorded on seismological instruments at the San Diego Museum of Natural History.

CHAPTER 3

"Mayday! We're not going to make the airport!"

– DC-8 First Officer to Portland Tower

United Airlines McDonnell Douglas DC-8-61 N8082U [45972] (F/n 2482) – December 28, 1978

With an hour's fuel in reserve, an undercarriage malfunction in the circuit area did not pose any great crisis. But in the course of preparations for an emergency landing, the crew appeared to 'lose the plot'. On final approach, fuel became exhausted and the DC-8 crashed short of the runway.

Service to Portland

United Airlines' Flight 173, a domestic east-west transcontinental service from New York to Portland, Oregon, via Denver, Colorado, was being operated on Tuesday, December 28, 1978, by one of the company's stretched DC-8-61s. A long range aircraft capable of seating up to 257 passengers, the type had rendered excellent service since being introduced to the airline's longer routes 10 years before.

The crew rostered for this mid-winter daylight flight reflected the experience and background to be expected aboard a large aircraft of the old established airline. In command was Captain Malburn McBroom, 52, a pilot with United Airlines for 27 years, and a captain since 1959. With a total of nearly 28,000 hours, he had logged 5500 hours as captain on DC-8s. First Officer Rodrick Beebe, 45, who had been with the company for 13 years, had over 8000 hours' experience, while the flight engineer, Second Officer Forrest ("Frostie") Mendenhall, 41, had 11 years' service with the company. In addition to his 3900 hours as a flight engineer, well over 2000 of which were in DC-8s, he was

a qualified Commercial Pilot with multi-engine ratings.

The long 1500nm morning flight from John F Kennedy International Airport, New York, across two thirds of the United States to Denver, Colorado, was entirely without incident. At this strategic inland airport, a major hub for so many internal air services in the USA, the DC-8's tanks were replenished with 21,200kg of turbine fuel and the cabin refurbished for the remaining two and a half hour flight to Portland, Oregon.

Shortly after 2.30pm, Pacific Standard Time, 181 passengers, including six small children, were ushered aboard under the care of the five cabin attendants, the four engines were started, and the aircraft taxied out. On the flightdeck, in addition to the three crew members, was another company captain travelling as a passenger. He occupied one of the two jumpseats.

At 2.47pm, with First Officer Beebe flying the aircraft and Captain McBroom handling the communications, the DC-8 took off from Denver and was cleared to Portland on its IFR flightplan. The weather forecast was favourable and the planned time interval to Portland was two hours

26 minutes, for an ETA of 5.13pm in clear weather conditions. As the fuel required for the flight was 14,480kg, the aircraft was carrying a reserve of 6720kg, adequate to cover the mandatory FAA requirement for a 45 minute reserve, plus the company's usual 20 minute contingency reserve.

As with the morning flight from New York, the flight to Portland was smooth and routine and at 5:06pm, just after darkness had fallen and right on schedule, with the carpet of lights that was the city of Portland now spread out before them, Captain McBroom called Portland Approach Control to report they were at 10,000 feet on descent. Portland Approach told the aircraft to maintain its heading for a visual approach to Runway 28. Acknowledging the instruction, Captain McBroom added that they had the field in sight.

Undercarriage problem

Some three minutes later, after the DC-8 had been cleared to continue its descent to 6000 feet, First Officer Beebe called for the flaps to be extended 15 degrees, then asked for the undercarriage to be lowered. But, as the captain moved the undercarriage selector to the down posi-

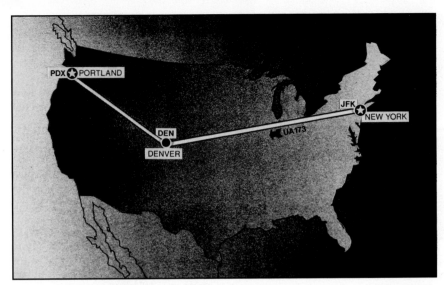

Map showing transcontinental New York/Denver/Portland route of Flight UA173 on December 28, 1978. (Matthew Tesch)

tion, something went wrong. Instead of the usual sound of the retraction mechanism in transit, followed by the normal moderate thump of the wheels locking down, there was an immediate shudder and loud thump which shook the whole aircraft, quickly followed by a second, lesser thump. At the same time the aircraft yawed momentarily to the right.

No "in transit" light illuminated on the instrument panel during this time, and only the green nose leg lamp was now showing, with nothing to indicate that the main undercarriage had extended at all. At this stage, the Portland Approach Controller, oblivious of the malfunction, called the descending DC-8 again: "United 173 heavy [the "heavy" denotes that the DC-8's wake turbulence could pose a hazard for other aircraft], contact Portland Tower now, 118.7".

Captain McBroom responded: "Negative, we'll stay with you – we'll stay at 5000 [feet]. We'll maintain about 170 knots – we've got a gear problem. We'll let you know."

This was the first indication to anyone on the ground that the DC-8 was in difficulties, and Portland Approach immediately replied: "Roger, maintain 5000 – turn left, heading 200." Two minutes later the Portland Approach controller added: "United 173 heavy, turn left now, heading 100, and I'll just orbit you out there until you get your problem right."

McBroom acknowledged the controller's instruction then, on the cabin PA system, made an announcement that he was concerned about the condition of the undercarriage and that they would "circle around while the crew did some checking."

To the passengers and cabin crew, the captain's words came as no surprise. They too had heard and felt the severe shudder and loud thump and feared something was wrong.

Emergency landing preparation

For the next 23 minutes, while Portland Approach continued to vector the DC-8 in a holding pattern above rolling hills on the outskirts of the city to the south and east of the airport, the crew considered and tried all possible emergency and precautionary measures to assure themselves that all three undercarriage legs were locked in the full down position. Second Officer Mendenhall went back to the passenger cabin where, shining a torch from the nearest cabin windows, he did his best to visually check the mechanical indicators on the upper surfaces of both wings, which extend through the wing when the main undercarriage is down and locked. They appeared to indicate the undercarriage had extended, though he could not be entirely sure.

At Captain McBroom's request also, the senior flight attendant came forward to the flightdeck while he outlined the situation to her, explaining that, after they had "run a few more checks," he would let her know what he intended to do.

At 5.38pm, the captain contacted the company's Line Maintenance Control Centre in San Francisco by radio to explain the undercarriage malfunction and what the crew were doing to ensure that it was fully extended. He reported they had some 3200kg of fuel on board and would hold for another 15 or 20 minutes while the cabin crew prepared the passengers for an emergency evacuation. Second Officer Mendenhall also spoke to engineers at the maintenance centre, detailing the symptoms of the undercarriage problem.

"OK – you estimate you'll make a landing about five minutes past the hour?" the San Francisco Centre asked finally, seeking confirmation of the time.

"Yes – that's good ball park," the captain responded, "I'm not going to hurry the girls. We've got about 165 people on board and we want to take our time and get everybody ready – and then we'll go. It's [the weather] as clear as a bell here and no problem."

Still flying at 5000 feet, the DC-8 continued to orbit under the direction of Portland Approach, maintaining a triangular pattern to the south, which kept it within about 20nm of the airport.

At 5.45pm the senior flight attendant reported back to the flightdeck to appraise the captain of progress in preparing the passengers and cabin for the emergency landing. The aircraft had now been holding for more than half an hour and, with some of the passengers becoming restive, she was anxious that they were authoritatively informed of what was happening. Her exchange with the captain was cordial and calm, if not entirely without anxiety.

CAPT: How are you doing, Dory?

FLT ATT: We're ready for your announcement – you have the signal for protective position? That's the only thing I need from you right now.

CAPT: OK – what would you do? Have you any suggestions about when to brace? Want to do it on the PA system?

FLT ATT [hesitating]: I'll be honest with you ... I've never had one of these before ... my first, you know.

CAPT: All right, what we'll do is we'll have Frostie [the flight engineer] ... a couple of minutes before touchdown, signal for a brace position.

FLT ATT: OK – he'll come on the PA? And if you don't want us to evacuate, what are you going to say?

CAPT: We'll either use the PA, or we'll stand in the door and call.

FLT ATT: OK – one or the other. We're reseating passengers right now and all the cabin lights are full up.

CAPT: All right.

FLT ATT [with emphasis]: We're ready for your announcement anytime.

While the senior flight attendant returned to continue supervising preparations in the passenger cabin, Second Officer Mendenhall was still trying to determine if the main undercarriage had extended properly. But, with the time just on 5.47pm, First Officer Beebe's mind was on the DC-8's remaining fuel.

FLT ENG [looking out at wing]: I can see the red indicators from here, but

Sistership to the DC-8 lost at Portland, United's 5th Super 61 – N8073U [45813] – is shown in its delivery colours during 1967. The ill fated N8082U (United's 17th aircraft of the type) was one of a trio accepted in May 1968 in similar livery. The giant airline's 34th and last DC-8-61, N8099U [46066], was delivered in June 1969.

I can't tell if there's anything lined up.

F/O: How much fuel have we got left, Frostie?

FLT ENG: 5000 [pounds/2270kg].

OFF DUTY CAPT [in jumpseat]: Less than three weeks – three weeks to retirement – you better get me out of here!

CAPT: Don't worry!

OFF DUTY CAPT: If I might make a suggestion, you should put your coats on ... both for your protection and so you'll be noticed ... so they'll know who you are.

CAPT: Oh – that's OK.

OFF DUTY CAPT: But if it gets hot [in case of fire], it sure is nice not to have bare arms.

CAPT: If anything goes wrong, you just charge back there and get ... off – OK?

OFF DUTY CAPT [vacating his jumpseat in preparation for moving back into the passenger cabin]: I told the girl to put me where she wants me – I think she wants me at a wing exit.

CAPT: OK fine, thank you.

With that, the off-duty captain left the flightdeck to provide support to the cabin crew. The time was now almost 5.49, and Beebe again asked about the remaining fuel showing on the gauges. When Captain McBroom replied, "Five" [5000 pounds], Mendenhall made a comment on the fuel pump lights, to which the captain responded: "That's about right – the feed pumps are starting to blink." On this model DC-8, the total usable fuel remaining when the inboard feed pump lights illuminate is 5000 pounds (2270kg).

McBroom then asked Mendenhall to update the landing data card which, prior to the undercarriage malfunction, the flight engineer had prepared in the usual way.

CAPT: Hey, Frostie!

FLT ENG: Yes, sir?

CAPT: Give us a current card on weight – I figure about another 15 minutes.

FLT ENG: 15 minutes?

CAPT: Yeah – give us 3-4000 on top of zero fuel weight.

FLT ENG [aside]: Not enough! 15 minutes is going to really run us low on fuel here.

Second Officer Mendenhall nevertheless completed the landing data card as he was bidden. As he did so, First Officer Beebe asked him about his radio discussion with the maintenance centre in San Francisco. The time was now 5.51pm and the aircraft was about 18nm south of the airport in a turn towards the northeast.

F/O: Maintenance have anything to say, Frostie?

FLT ENG: They said, 'I think you guys have done everything you can.' I said we were reluctant to recycle the gear for fear something was bent or broken, and we wouldn't be able to get it down again.

F/O [to captain]: Think we ought to warn these people on the ground?

CAPT: Yeah – we'll do that right now. [Turning to flight engineer] Call the United terminal – give them our passenger count including laps [infants] – tell them we'll land with about 4000 pounds [1816kg] of fuel and to give that to the fire department. I want United mechanics to check the airplane after we stop – before we taxi.

Second Officer Mendenhall did so promptly and, when the company terminal at Portland Airport sought confirmation that the aircraft would be landing at 6.05pm, he checked once more with the captain: "They want to know if we'll be landing about five after," the flight engineer asked. The captain replied, "Yes,"

and Mendenhall relayed this to the company. The time now was 5.54pm and the aircraft was about 17nm south of the airport, heading northeast.

CAPT: All done?

FLT ENG: Yes, sir – and ready now for the final approach, final descent check.

When these checks were completed, First Officer Beebe again queried the quantity of fuel remaining, and Mendenhall told him 4000 pounds – 1000 pounds in each of the four tanks. Then Captain McBroom spoke to Mendenhall again:

CAPT: You might just take a walk back through the cabin and see how things are going – OK? I don't want to hurry them, but I'd like to do it in another ... 10 minutes or so.

Mendenhall was gone from the flightdeck for the next four minutes, during which McBroom and Beebe discussed the competence the senior flight attendant was displaying, the procedures to be followed in the event of an evacuation after landing, whether the wheel brakes would have antiskid protection and the technique to be used during the approach and landing. Shortly after 6.01, Mendenhall returned to the flightdeck to report that the cabin crew would be ready for the landing in "another two or three minutes."

CAPT: OK – how are the people?

FLT ENG: Well, they're pretty calm and cool. Some of them are obviously nervous, but for the most part they're taking it in their stride. I stopped and reassured a couple of them – they seemed a little bit more anxious than some of the others.

CAPT: OK – well about two minutes before landing – that will be about four miles out – just pick up the PA mike and announce: 'Assume the brace position!'

FLT ENG: We've got about three [3000 pounds/1362kg] on the fuel – and that's it.

CAPT: OK – on touchdown, if the gear folds or something really jumps the track, get those boost pumps off ... you might even get the valves open.

At this stage, with the aircraft about five nm south of the airport on a southwest heading as it flew yet another wide orbit, the Portland Approach controller asked the crew for a status report, and how much longer it would be before they landed. This time Beebe replied to the call:

F/O: Yeah – we have an indication our gear is abnormal – it'll be our intention in about five minutes to land on Runway 28 Left. We would like the [fire] equipment standing by.

Our indications are the gear is down and locked, but we've got our people prepared for an evacuation in the event that should become necessary.

APP: OK – advise when you'd like to begin your approach.

CAPT: Very well – they've about finished in the cabin – I'd guess about another three, four – five minutes.

APP: If you could give me souls on board and amount of fuel?

CAPT: 172 and about 4000 – well, make it 3000 pounds [1362kg] of fuel. And you can add to that 172, plus six laps – infants.

For the following three minutes, the three flightcrew members were occupied in a further discussion on checking the undercarriage warning horn as additional evidence that the wheels were fully down and locked, and whether the automatic spoilers and antiskid systems would operate with the undercarriage circuit breakers out.

Then, a little after 6.06pm, by which time the aircraft was about 17nm south of the airport on a south-westerly heading, the senior flight attendant came back to the flightdeck to make her final pre-landing report.

CAPT: How are you doing?

FLT ATT: Well, I think we're ready.

CAPT: OK.

FLT ATT: We've reseated – they've assigned helpers, and shown people how to open exits – they've got able bodied men by the windows. The [off-duty] captain in the first row of coach after the galley – he's going to take that middle galley door – its not far from the window ...

CAPT: OK – We're going to go in now – should be landing in about five minutes.

Fuel exhaustion

While McBroom was still speaking, Beebe called out to Mendenhall: "I think you've just lost number four ... better get some crossfeeds open there or something."

FLT ATT: I'll go and make the five minute announcement – I'll be sitting down now.

F/O [to McBroom as senior flight attendant leaves the flightdeck]: We're going to lose an engine!

CAPT: Why?

F/O: Fuel!

F/O [sharply to Mendenhall]: Open the crossfeeds, man!

Conflict and confusion reigned on the flightdeck for 15 seconds, then Beebe exclaimed: "It's flamed out!" McBroom immediately called Portland Approach to request a clearance to Runway 28L. The DC-8 at this stage was 19nm south-southwest of the airport and turning left. Portland Approach provided vectors for a visual approach to runway 28L and instructed the aircraft to report when the airport was in sight.

FLT ENG: We're going to lose number three in a minute, too – it's showing zero!

CAPT [emphatically]: You've got a thousand pounds – you've got to!

FLT ENG: 5000 in there ... but we lost it!

CAPT: All right.

FLT ENG: Are you getting it back?

F/O: No number four – you've got that crossfeed open?

FLT ENG: No, I haven't got it open. Which one?

CAPT: Open 'em both – get some fuel in there! Got some fuel pressure?

FLT ENG: Yes, sir.

CAPT [with relief]: Rotation! Now she's coming! OK – watch one and two. We're showing down to zero or a thousand.

FLT ENG: Yeah.

CAPT: On number one?

FLT ENG: Right!

F/O: Still not getting it!

CAPT: Well, open all four crossfeeds.

FLT ENG: All four?

CAPT: Yeah.

F/O: All right – now it's coming!

CAPT [with concern]: You've got to keep 'em running!

FLT ENG: Yes, sir!

F/O [with frustration]: Get this ### [expletive] on the ground!

FLT ENG: Yeah – it's showing not very much more fuel ...

CAPT [to Approach Control]: United 173 has the field in sight now – we'd like to turn left for 28L.

APP: OK – maintain 5000 [feet].

FLT ENG: We're down to one on the totaliser. Number two is empty!

More than 22 years old when this picture was taken in January 1991, N8091U [45995] (re-engined with CFM56 high bypass turbofans and redesignated a DC-8-71), displays the orange-red-blue cheatlines which United adopted in June 1974. This scheme, the airline's first major postwar livery change, is representative of N8082U's appearance at the time of its loss. The fuselage title remained "United" as before, but the company name condensed "Air Lines" into a single word. The "double U" symbol on the fin was the first entirely new graphic device introduced since the airline's traditional shield motif appeared in 1936. The picture is also noteworthy because it shows Portland Airport's slush covered apron in wintry Oregon twilight – conditions similar to those at the time of the accident. (Keith Myers)

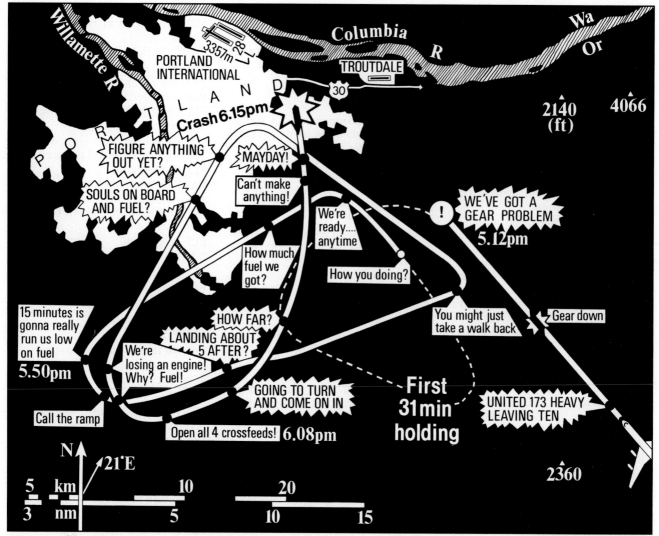

Map of the greater Portland area – from the Columbia River to the ranges and peaks of the Mount Hood National Forest parks to the east. The recorded flightpaths and deduced ground tracks of the DC-8 during the latter part of its holding are superimposed. (Matthew Tesch, with acknowledgement to NTSB)

CAPT [to Approach Control]: United 173 is going to turn towards the airport and come on in.

APP: Turn left, heading 360 – and verify you have the airport in sight.

CAPT: We have the airport in sight.

APP: United 173 is cleared for visual approach – Runway 28L.

CAPT [to Mendenhall]: Reset that circuit breaker momentarily – see if we get gear lights.

The flight engineer complied with the request and the green nose undercarriage lamp illuminated.

CAPT: Yeah – nose gear's down.

With the time now almost 6.11pm, the captain requested the DC-8's distance from the airport.

CAPT [to Approach Control]: How far do you show us from the field?

APP: I'd call it 18 flying miles.

FLT ENG: Boy – that fuel sure went to hell all of a sudden – I told you we had four [4000 pounds].

CAPT: There's an interstate highway type thing along that bank on the river – in case we're short.

CAPT [a minute later]: That's Troutdale [Portland's general aviation airport] over there – about six of one and half a dozen of the other.

F/O [anxiously]: Let's take the shortest route to the airport.

CAPT [to Approach Control]: What's our distance now?

APP: 12 flying miles.

CAPT: About [another] three minutes – four.

FLT ENG [urgently]: We've lost two engines, guys! We just lost two engines – one and two.

F/O: You've got all the pumps on and everything?

FLT ENG: Yep!

APP: United 173, contact Portland Tower, 118.7 – you're about eight or niner flying miles from the airport.

CAPT [with alarm]: They're all going – we can't make Troutdale!

F/O: [also with alarm] We can't make anything!

CAPT: OK – declare a Mayday!

F/O [to Approach Control]: Portland Tower, United 173, Mayday! We're ... the engines are flaming out – we're going down! We're not going to be able to make the airport!

Crash into trees

At 6.15pm, the DC-8, now flying a heading of 345 degrees towards the airport, but with all four engines finally starved of fuel, descended in darkness into a wooded area of suburban Portland only six nm east-southeast of the runway threshold. Initially striking the tops of 35 metre high trees, the aircraft tore an increasingly deep 40 metre wide swathe through the trees as it sank towards the ground.

Narrowly missing a multistorey block of flats, the aircraft demolished an unoccupied house, tearing off the outboard port wing, before colliding with an embankment bordering a street, which wrenched off the undercarriage. Bouncing and slithering across the street, the fuselage tore down telephone poles and high tension wires, struck a second unoccupied house situated amid trees, and finally came to rest amongst the remains of this building.

Although the aircraft was effectively destroyed by the numerous successive impacts, the greater part of the long fuselage remained intact and no fire broke out, thanks no doubt to the fact that no fuel remained. As a result, the emergency cabin lighting illuminated automatically as the aircraft skidded to a stop and 156 of its 189 occupants, including four of the aircraft's five flight attendants, were able to clamber from the wreckage with only minor injuries.

While no less than 39 emergency vehicles, alerted by Portland Airport authorities, were converging on the scene of the accident, local residents in the neighbourhood of the crash were the first to come to the aid of survivors.

One man had felt something shake his house and, not knowing what it was, thought a car had hit an electricity pole. Soon afterwards he saw numbers of dishevelled people walking on the road and he yelled at them to stay away from the fallen power lines. They yelled back that they were "from the plane." At first he didn't know what they were talking about, but then it dawned on him that an aircraft had crashed. "They were cold," his wife said. "We gave away blankets and sleeping bags. A lot had lost their shoes. A stewardess was barefoot and said her feet were freezing. My husband gave her a pair of his socks. They were all thirsty too – I don't know how many glasses of water I handed out."

Another family tended to the needs of about 30 survivors in their home, all of them with minor injuries of varying degrees.

Not surprisingly, rescue teams when they reached the wreckage found the most severe fuselage damage had been sustained by the nose section of the aircraft. Tree impacts had broken the flightdeck away completely and demolished the lower starboard side of the fuselage as far back as the fifth row of passenger seats.

Ten occupants, all seated on the starboard side in the forward section of the fuselage between the flight engineer's station on the flight-deck and row five of the passenger cabin, had been killed in the crash. The victims included the flight engineer himself, Second Officer Mendenhall, and the senior flight attendant. A little girl of three was the only survivor of a family of five travelling in this part of the cabin. Both her parents and her two sisters were killed, while she suffered a broken leg and head injuries.

Captain McBroom sustained a broken ankle and broken ribs, serious head lacerations, and back injuries, while First Officer Beebe was seriously injured and in a critical condition. Twenty other passengers also received serious injuries. The most seriously injured were seated in the forward portion of the cabin close to those killed, an area of the fuselage penetrated by a large tree.

Some passengers were injured during the evacuation of the cabin. Two sustained fractures and others lacerations and abrasions when they fell from exits, or as they climbed down to the ground through wreckage and crash debris. In addition to the captain and first officer, 22 survivors were conveyed to hospital by helicopter or ambulance.

Impact and breakup sequence of the DC-8. This simplified illustration of a "textbook" forced landing in "impossible" terrain shows how the deliberate, progressive demolition of the wings, undercarriage and empennage absorbed the worst of the decelerative forces, thereby retaining maximum structural integrity – and survivability – in the fuselage. (Matthew Tesch)

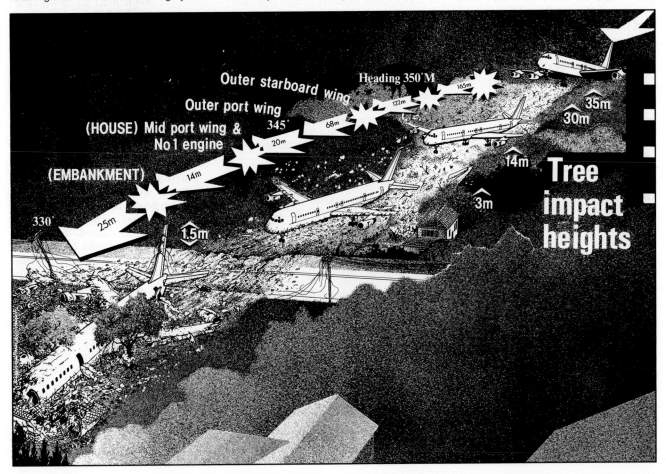

Although the DC-8 had come down in a suburban area with houses and apartment blocks in the immediate vicinity, there were no ground casualties. One of the police taking part in the rescue operation commented: "It's just amazing – if they had to crash, they couldn't have put it down in a better place."

While going through the wreckage, rescuers were startled to hear something moving around inside the fuselage. Investigating, they found a fully-grown German Shepherd dog exploring the remains of the under-floor baggage compartment. The dog's container pack had been demolished, but the animal was quite unhurt!

Wreckage examination

The accident occurred five nm southeast of Portland International Airport at an elevation of 285 feet. The wreckage trail was 1554 feet (474 metres) long and 130 feet (40 metres) wide.

The fuselage, from about the fifth row of passenger seats forward, had sustained severe impact damage. The upper structure of the flight-deck, including the front windows, had separated and lay to the right of the fuselage just forward of the in-board end of the starboard wing. The lower section of the flightdeck, together with crew seats, instrument panel, and the nose structure with the nose leg assembly still attached, had come to rest upside down.

All sections of the fuselage were accounted for, all structural damage having been caused by impact with

numerous large trees and with the ground. The lower starboard side of the cabin, between the fourth and sixth rows of passenger seats below window level, had been torn away. The remainder of the underside of the fuselage sustained heavy damage from impact with trees and tree stumps. The cabin interior, from row six to the aft bulkhead, was relatively intact, but some windows had been smashed and the fuselage dented by trees and separated components of the main undercarriage.

Both wings had been torn from the fuselage immediately outboard of their attachment points. No 2 engine had broken away from its pylon and was lying by the wing trailing edge. No 1 engine remained attached to the port wing. A 1.8 metre section of the outer port wing had been sheared off and was found near the first house. The inner portion of the starboard wing, with No 3 engine and pylon still attached, lay just forward of the starboard tailplane. The outboard section, with No 4 engine, lay beside the fuselage. Apart from impact damage, all four engines were found to be capable of operation, but none were rotating at impact.

The tail assembly sustained only moderate damage, the leading edge of the fin having caught on high tension wires.

Both main undercarriage legs had been wrenched from their mountings, but were fully extended at the time of the crash. Examination of the starboard main retraction mechanism revealed corrosion in the threads of an

attachment eyebolt which had pulled away from the actuator cylinder piston rod. The nose leg had extended normally.

Flight Recorders

The DC-8's Fairchild Flight Data Recorder (FDR) was undamaged. A readout of the final 16 minutes of the recorded traces revealed that electrical power to the recorder had terminated 44 seconds before the crash. The quality of the recording on the aircraft's Sundstrand Cockpit Voice Recorder (CVR) was good and the entire tape was transcribed.

Survivor evidence

The DC-8 was equipped with a monitoring system to check the fuel consumed along the intended route. This consisted of a computer print-out which predicted the amount of fuel used between several points en route. The crew were able to check the actual fuel used against the predicted fuel use at each of these points.

When interviewed in hospital, the captain told investigators that the flight from Denver to Portland was perfectly normal and that they were very close to the predicted fuel consumption over the entire trip. Trouble began only when the undercarriage was selected down for landing.

"As the landing gear extended," he explained, "it was noticeably unusual ... it seemed to go down more rapidly ... it was a thump, thump in sound and feel ... much out of the ordinary for the aircraft. It was noticeably different and we got the nose gear light but no other light."

A passenger told investigators: "We were making a normal approach and I remember the pilot announcing we were at 5000 feet just before the gear went down. The gear made a terrible, terrible jolt – we knew immediately that something was wrong."

During his interview, Captain McBroom said that, in preparing for the emergency landing, he had neither designated a time limit to the senior flight attendant, nor asked her how long it would take to prepare the cabin. Rather, he had assumed 10 or 15 minutes would be reasonable and that some preparations could be made on the final approach to the airport.

When all four engines finally flamed out, with no hope of reaching the runway, the captain was faced with an extremely critical and immediate decision. From the height at which the massive aircraft was flying, he had only 77 seconds in which to select an area for the inevitable crash landing somewhere amongst the darkened suburbs of outer Portland that lay below them.

Rescue teams work under floodlights by the broken off nose section of the DC-8. This picture, looking aft into the aircraft's long fuselage, reveals the largely intact overhead bins and passenger seats on the port side of the First Class cabin. On the starboard side, "Jetescape" hatch 1R has been prised open. The after dark forced landing of the huge aircraft in a timbered, built up residential suburb with so few casualties was a remarkable achievement on the part of captain and crew. (with acknowledgement to AP/Wide World Photos)

But here McBroom had an advantage: he had flown the route to Portland many times and knew the area well. He quickly discarded the idea of landing on the highway that parallelled the nearby Columbia River because of the peak hour traffic it would be carrying at this time of the evening. He also rejected the possibility of ditching in the river itself, because of its current and icy midwinter temperatures.

"There were several possibilities – none of them good," the captain said. "I found this one possible spot – a grove of trees with houses on each side." Because the area was dark and there were no lights in it, he assumed there were no houses among the trees. He took the aircraft in, deliberately nosing it between two trees so as to take the main impact with the wings.

Considering that the DC-8 came down amongst trees in the dark, the casualty rate was extraordinarily low – an undoubted tribute to the captain's good judgement. Contributing to this outcome too was the fact that all the aircraft's fuel had been consumed, thus preventing an explosive fire with its inevitably disastrous consequences. McBroom himself gave much of the credit for the high survival rate to the senior flight attendant killed in the crash. "She was in charge of preparing the cabin and did it in such a good way," he said. "She was a damn good stewardess."

Most of the passengers, though they knew why the aircraft had been holding for so long, thought the aircraft was finally landing on the runway. Because they had received no warning from the flight crew, they were caught completely by surprise when the wings began striking trees. "When I felt the first bump, I thought, 'Oh good – nothing went wrong.'" one survivor said, "Then, all of a sudden ...!" Another told investigators: "We hit hard. We knew then we weren't on the runway. At that point a stewardess yelled: 'Grab your ankles!'"

One woman explained that her husband changed seats with her while the aircraft was holding: "I was sitting next to a middle [overwing] exit. But he thought a man should be there to open the hatch. After the crash, he opened the emergency hatch next to him and started helping people out. He didn't know his leg was broken."

Analysis

The investigation confirmed that the DC-8 burned fuel at a normal rate between Denver and Portland, and that it arrived in the Portland area with its planned reserve of 13,800 pounds (6265kg) of fuel.

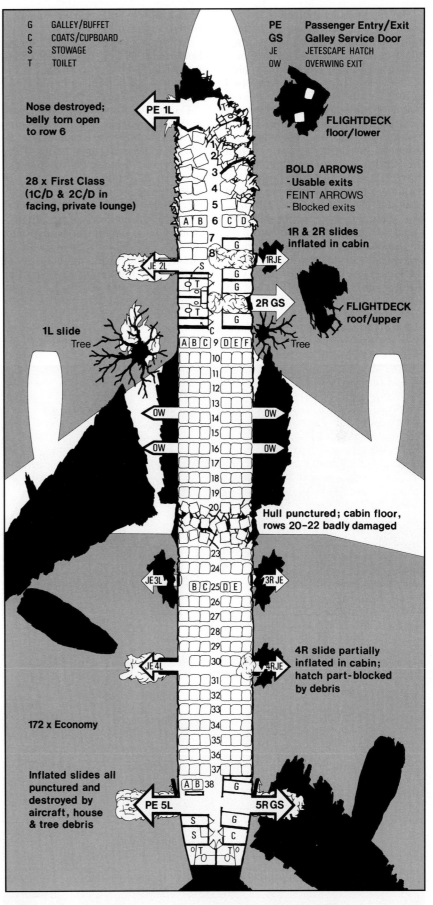

Representative interior configuration of a United Airlines DC-8-61, with damage incurred in the Portland crash indicated. In addition to the twin pairs of passenger entry and galley service doors, and the four overwing exits, the DC-8-61 was also fitted with six "Jetescape" doors which hinged down and out from floor level. (Matthew Tesch, with acknowledgement to United Airlines)

The first problem which faced the crew was the unsafe undercarriage indication, followed by a loud thump, an abnormal vibration, and an abnormal yaw. The investigation revealed that severe corrosion had developed in the mating threads where the actuator of the starboard main retract cylinder assembly connected to the piston rod end. The corrosion resulted in the parts separating when the undercarriage was selected down, allowing the main leg to immediately free fall into the extended position. The shock of this fall disabled the microswitches for the main undercarriage position indicators on the flightdeck. Meanwhile, the nose and port undercarriage legs were extending normally, the time delay creating a momentary difference in aerodynamic drag and producing a transient yaw to the right.

At the time the aircraft began holding at 5000 feet while the crew investigated the problem, some 6054kg (13,334 pounds) of fuel remained in the tanks.

Company procedures for dealing with undercarriage system failures on the DC-8-61 were adequate. The Irregular Procedures section of the DC-8 flight manual instructed the crew to determine the position of both the main and nose visual indicators, and "if the visual indicators indicate the gear is down, then a landing can be made at the captain's discretion." The flight engineer's check of the visual indicators for both main legs showed that they were down and locked, and the flightdeck indicator for the nose leg showed the normal green "geardown" light.

Yet from the time the captain informed Portland Approach of the problem until contact with company line maintenance at San Francisco, some 28 minutes elapsed. Certainly the abnormal undercarriage extension was cause for concern and it was proper for the crew to assess the situation before communicating with company line maintenance. However, the procedures prescribed in the manual were brief, the weather was good, the area was devoid of heavy traffic, and there were no other problems that should have delayed communication with the company.

Company maintenance staff in San Francisco then verified that the crew had done everything possible to ensure the integrity of the undercarriage. The investigators believed that, at the conclusion of this radio discussion about 30 minutes before the accident, the captain could have safely made a landing.

Instead however, the captain called the senior flight attendant to the flightdeck to brief her on preparing the cabin for a possible abnormal landing. But he did not specify a time within which this was to be accomplished, as required by the flight manual. In the absence of any such constraint, the senior flight attendant probably had the impression that time was not as important as thorough preparation.

The investigators believed that, whenever a flight deviates from its flight plan, the crew should evaluate the potential effect on the aircraft's fuel status. In this case, the crew knew that evaluation of the undercarriage problem and preparation for the emergency landing would involve extended holding.

Regardless of whether they were aware of the actual fuel remaining in the tanks at this stage of the flight, the crew certainly knew the initial fuel load was based on normal consumption for the two hour 26 minute flight, plus a reserve that included 45 minutes at normal cruise, and a contingency margin of an additional 20 minutes. They should therefore have been conscious that fuel would become critical after an extended period of holding.

Proper crew management includes constant monitoring of fuel remaining as it relates to time, including allowing for a missed approach, should this become necessary. Such planning should also consider the possibility of inaccuracies in the fuel quantity indicators. This necessitates establishing a deadline for an

Starboard main undercarriage of a Super DC-8, viewed from beneath the wing trailing edge, looking forward. The close-up photos (opposite) label the main components. (via Matthew Tesch)

approach to land, with constant checking of both time and the aircraft's position relative to the runway. In this instance however, the crew clearly did not adhere to such procedures. On the contrary, the CVR transcript indicated insufficient attention to the fuel state, even after prolonged holding.

In analysing the crew's actions, the investigators had to consider if they could have been misled by inac-curacies in the fuel measuring system. However, comments and radio transmissions in which the fuel quantities were mentioned indicate the system was reading accurately.

Had the crew related any of these fuel contents readings to fuel flow, they should have known that fuel exhaustion would occur about 6.15pm. Other evidence of failure to assess the effect of the prolonged holding was the captain's declared intention at 5.51pm to land at about 6.05 with 4000 pounds of fuel on board. Yet, two minutes earlier, he had acknowledged that only 5000 pounds remained. In reality, in the 16 minute interval between 5.49 and 6.05, the DC-8 would have consumed at least 3000 pounds.

Further evidence of the crew's lack of concern was provided by what took place between 17 and 13

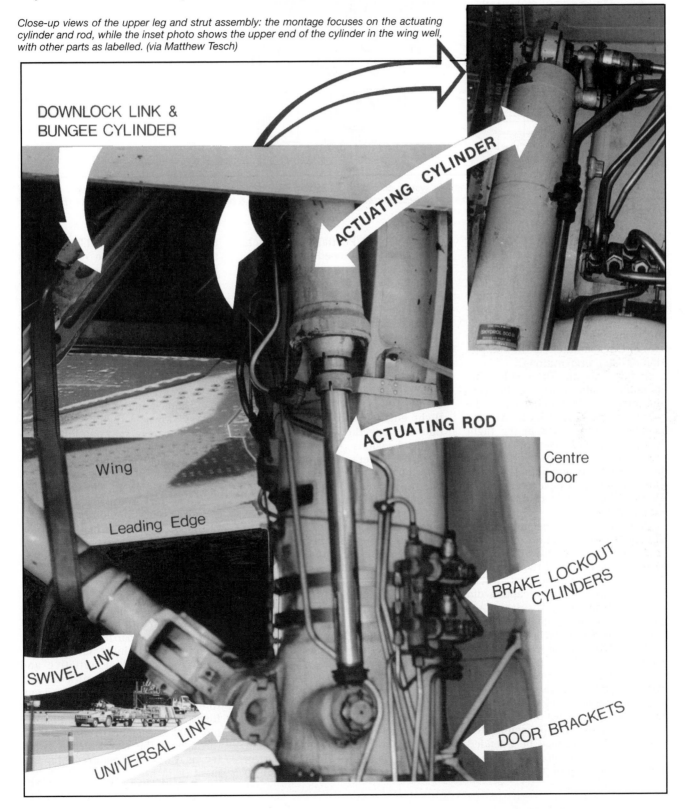

Close-up views of the upper leg and strut assembly: the montage focuses on the actuating cylinder and rod, while the inset photo shows the upper end of the cylinder in the wing well, with other parts as labelled. (via Matthew Tesch)

DOWNLOCK LINK & BUNGEE CYLINDER

ACTUATING CYLINDER

ACTUATING ROD

Wing

Leading Edge

Centre Door

BRAKE LOCKOUT CYLINDERS

SWIVEL LINK

UNIVERSAL LINK

DOOR BRACKETS

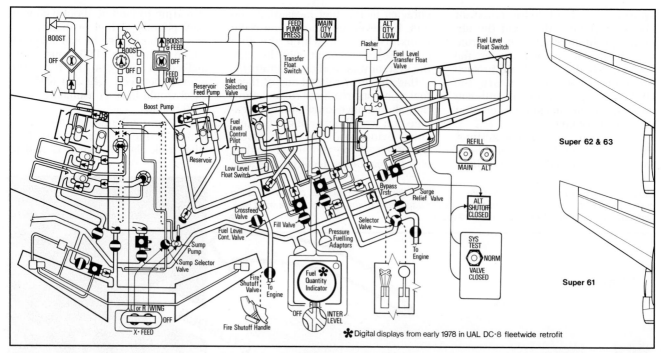

Although this schematic diagram depicts the fuel system of a DC-8-62 (which, like the Super 63, featured extended wing tips, additional tankage and other modifications), it is valuable nonetheless, showing particularly (centre top & bottom) the source and flightdeck indications of a low fuel state. (Matthew Tesch)

minutes before the crash. Just after the flight engineer's observation at 5.58pm that only some 4000 pounds now remained, he left the flightdeck at the captain's request to check preparations in the cabin. On his return four minutes later, he gave McBroom an estimate of another two or three minutes for the completion of cabin preparations.

At this stage the DC-8, still flying its holding pattern, was not far from the airport, with nothing left to be done on the flightdeck. All the checks, as prescribed in the flight manual and recommended by company line maintenance by radio, had been completed, and both Air Traffic Control and the company terminal at Portland had been alerted to the aircraft's plight.

Under these circumstances, there appears to have been no reason not to continue inbound towards the airport in order to meet the estimated landing time. But the first officer then accepted, and the captain did not question, a vector from Approach Control which would take them away from the airport again and further delay the landing appreciably. It was at this point that the crew's continuing preoccupation with the undercarriage problem and cabin preparation became crucial – and an accident inevitable.

Although on two occasions the captain had confirmed he intended to land about 6.05pm, this ETA was not adhered to, nor was a revised

ETA given to Portland Approach. This only strengthened the investigators' belief that the undercarriage problem had a disorganising effect on the crew. Even after No 4 engine had flamed out, and with the fuel totaliser indicating only 1000 pounds, the captain still persisted in resetting circuit breakers to recheck undercarriage light indications.

Although a captain is in command and responsible for the performance of his crew, the first officer's and flight engineer's inputs are important because they provide backup for his decisions.

A first officer's main responsibility is to monitor the captain. In particular, he provides feedback for the captain. If the captain infers from the first officer's actions that his judgement is correct, the captain could be reinforced in an error of judgement. Although the first officer in this case made several subtle comments on the aircraft's fuel state, it was not until after the No 4 engine flamed out that he finally uttered: "Get this ... on the ground!" If he had recognised the critical nature of their situation, he failed to convey it to the captain.

A flight engineer's responsibility, aside from management of the aircraft's systems, is to monitor the captain's and first officer's actions as they relate to the aircraft's performance. Although the flight engineer told the captain at 5.50pm that an additional 15 minutes was "going to

really run us low on fuel," he took no action to ensure the captain was fully conscious of the time to fuel exhaustion. And, on returning to the flightdeck just before 6.02, he conveyed no concern about the fuel state. Although he commented that only 3000 pounds of fuel now remained, he neither mentioned the time remaining to fuel exhaustion, nor the urgency for expediting the landing.

The accident exemplified a recurring problem in the airline industry – a breakdown in flightdeck management during a malfunction of aircraft systems in flight, one that had been dramatically underlined by the loss of Eastern Air Lines' Lockheed TriStar N310EA in the Everglades National Park in Florida, almost exactly six years previously (refer *Air Disaster*, Volume 1, Chapter 12). Responsibilities need to be divided among the crew while a malfunction is being resolved. But in this case no one was delegated to physically monitor the fuel state.

As a result of this accident and its investigation, the National Transportation Safety Board concluded that assertiveness training, including the need for individual initiative and effective expression of concern, should be a part of the standard curricula in the training of all airline flight and cabin crew – the philosophy that has since become known throughout the world airline industry as Cockpit Resource Management (CRM).

CHAPTER 4

"American 191, do you want to come back?"

– Chicago Tower Controller to DC-10

American Airlines McDonnell Douglas DC-10-10 N110AA [46510]
– May 25, 1979

For the 271 people aboard a regular afternoon service to Los Angeles, their departure from Chicago on the eve of a holiday weekend seemed normal and full of promise. Little could they know their gleaming widebodied jet concealed a fatal flaw – and that, only half a minute after liftoff, everyone of them would be dead.

Friday May 25, 1979, a pleasant, sunny afternoon, if a bit windy at Chicago, Illinois, was the eve of the USA's Memorial Day weekend, and passenger traffic out of the city's O'Hare International Airport was even more hectic than usual for one of the world's busiest airline terminals, not least for the giant domestic carrier American Airlines.

Among the company's many services whisking excited holiday makers away to their weekend destinations was a regular DC-10 flight right across the continent to Los Angeles, California, where the late spring weather promised to be even balmier. This service, American Flight 191, had been operated by the company's fleet of DC-10s since the airline, as the launch customer for the type, had first introduced this widebodied, long range design to the route eight years previously.

Powered by three 40,000 pound (18,145kg) thrust General Electric CF6-6D turbofan engines, this Series 10 version of the DC-10 had a maximum brake release weight of 430,000 pounds (195,043kg), and a range of more than 3600nm. Seating 270 passengers in a mixed class configuration, the aircraft was popular with both the airline's customers and its crews.

The DC-10-10 allocated to this day's flight, scheduled to depart at 3pm, was N110AA, an aircraft which had provided excellent service throughout the near 20,000 hours it had flown since being delivered to the company in 1972. It was under the command of Captain Walter Lux, 53, a 22,000 hour company veteran who had been flying DC-10s almost from the time of their introduction to American Airlines. His crew were also mature – First Officer James Dillard, 49, had almost 10,000 hours, and Flight Engineer Alfred Udovich, 56, had 15,000 hours. Ten flight attendants were on duty in the spacious cabin.

Everything was perfectly normal and routine – a scene totally familiar to all experienced air travellers – as the 258 passengers filed aboard from the departure lounge and the cabin crew showed them to their seats. Understandably, many of them were in high spirits as they stored their hand luggage in the overhead lockers, sat down and fastened their seat belts.

Ready right on schedule, the doors were closed and, on the flightdeck, the crew started all three engines. On the control pedestal between the two pilots was the usual takeoff data card, completed to show the gross weight of the aircraft was a heavy 379,000 pounds (172,066kg), the takeoff flap setting 10 degrees, the critical engine failure speed (V_1) 139 knots, rotation speed (V_R) 145 knots, and takeoff safety speed (V_2) 153 knots.

At 2.59pm, Central Standard Time, the DC-10 was cleared to taxi to the holding point for Runway 32 Right. The sky was clear, and the wind from the northeast, blowing strongly at 22 knots, with occasional gusts to 28 knots.

The distance to the runway threshold was short and, despite the volume of traffic using the airport, there was no delay before the aircraft was cleared to taxi into position on the runway and line up. At 3.02:38, (ie 38 seconds after two minutes past three), the DC-10 was cleared for takeoff. A few seconds later, the captain's voice acknowledged positively: "American 191 under way."

To the air traffic controller watching from the control tower, the DC-10's acceleration and roll seemed perfectly normal until some 6000 feet (1830 metres) down the runway, just before it rotated into the takeoff attitude. But at this point, pieces of the port (No 1) engine pylon fell away from the aircraft, and white vapour began to stream from the mounting. A moment later, during the rotation itself, the controller was aghast to see the entire No 1 engine and pylon tear itself loose from the aircraft, fly up over the top of the wing, and smash back on to the runway behind the still accelerating DC-10 as it lifted into the air.

Immediately the controller transmitted: "American 191, do you want to come back? If so, what runway do you want?"

There was no reply – the crew obviously had their hands full for the moment. The aircraft's port wing had dropped slightly as the DC-10 lifted off, but this was quickly picked up and, as the controller watched anxiously, the DC-10 continued to climb out with its wings level. The nose-up attitude of about 14 degrees, as well as the aircraft's heading, appeared stable and it seemed that, despite the loss of its port engine, the DC-10 was responding well to control.

But 10 seconds later, when the DC-10 had climbed to about 300 feet, it began to bank to the left. The bank quickly steepened alarmingly, the nose lowered, and the aircraft began to lose height. At the same time, the bank increased still more. Finally the DC-10's wings were past the vertical and to the appalled controller it was obvious a catastrophe was imminent. At this point the port wingtip

Opened in 1971, the futuristic, 61m high control tower dominates the central terminal building complex at Chicago O'Hare. Beyond it, looking southeast towards the city, a Boeing 727 climbs away from Runway 09R.

struck the ground and the giant aircraft exploded in an enormous flash of flame, a great angry cloud of black smoke mushrooming high into the sky .

Fire and ambulance crews, police and emergency workers who raced to the scene of the horrific accident found there was little they could do. The DC-10 had utterly disintegrated as it hit the ground, fortunately in an open field, but only 90 metres short of the boundary fence of a huge caravan park, packed with caravans and mobile homes. There were no survivors – only the fragmented and charred human remains of the 271 people who had been aboard.

Some of the fiercely burning wreckage had been hurled through the fence into the caravan park, killing two people on the ground, destroying a caravan and several cars, and demolishing an old aircraft hangar used for storage. Two other badly burned bystanders had to be rushed to hospital.

The crash site was close to the property of a man who was standing outside his office building at the time, oblivious from long habit to all the aircraft landing and taking off at nearby O'Hare Airport. Suddenly the building was shaken by a tremendous explosion nearby. "By the time I looked up," he said, "there was a rain of fire falling on me."

For the members of the rescue teams, the tremendous force of the impact and the enormity of the disaster almost defied comprehension. "We didn't see one body intact," one fireman commented later. "Just trunks, hands, arms, heads and parts of legs. And we can't tell whether they

Rotate! Little imagination is needed to visualise the port engine separating at about this point in the takeoff run that fateful May afternoon. The centre main undercarriage leg identifies this American DC-10 as a Series 30 – in fact, N138AA [46911] was formerly Air New Zealand's ZK-NZQ, immediate sistership of the doomed ZK-NZP (see next chapter).

Snapped by an alert photographer at the airport, this dramatic picture of the stricken DC-10 was taken less than five seconds before impact. Note the huge aircraft's angle of sideslip, indicated by the direction of the vaporising fuel streaming from the severed lines in the port wing. (Sygma)

were male or female, or whether they were adult or child, because they were all charred." Another man, one of the first on the scene, said: "It was too hot to touch anybody and I really couldn't tell if they were men or women. Bodies were scattered all over the field."

For those responsible for recovering the bodies, it was a grisly task. "Everywhere we walk, there are the remains of bodies," a volunteer worker declared.

With the burnt wreckage of the DC-10 still smoking and its acrid fumes permeating the air, the teams worked through the night under floodlights to remove all the victims. As the fragmented remains were recovered and matched, they were placed in plastic body bags and carried to police vans which conveyed them to an American Airlines hangar, pressed into service as a temporary morgue.

Of the 273 victims, only about a

dozen bodies were intact. The medical officer in charge of the recovery operation told journalists that, in many cases, dental records would be required because the remains were too badly burned or dismembered. "The situation is such that identification will be extremely difficult," he said. "Some bodies may never be identified."

A senior officer of the Federal Aviation Administration (FAA) who rushed to Chicago from his office in

Seconds afterwards, as the photographer panned his camera to follow the DC-10, it was lost to view behind the buildings of O'Hare's "Hangar Alley". A moment later again it had plunged into the ground and exploded violently in a black and orange fireball. (Sygma)

This aerial view of Chicago O'Hare dates from the late 1960s. Runways 04L-22R (middle) and 09R-27L (foreground) have yet to be built, and propeller driven Douglas and Lockheed aircraft are still the mainline types at many of the terminal gates! Even so, this northwesterly perspective enables the 30 second-flight of the DC-10 to be superimposed (top right) from the upwind end of Runway 32R.

Washington DC described the scene as "overwhelming". "It's hard to tell there was a DC-10 there," he said. Asked to compare the disaster to other major air accidents he had worked on, he commented: "The dimensions here were twice as large – this aircraft was so much bigger."

Wreckage

Chicago O'Hare International Airport is 26km northwest of the city and has seven runways. Its elevation is 650 feet AMSL.

An advance party of investigators from the National Transportation Safety Board (NTSB), led by its vice-chairman, Elwood Driver, arrived from Washington DC as soon as humanly possible later that afternoon for a preliminary survey of the accident site and the scattered wreckage. But it was dawn the following morning before the investigation could begin in earnest.

Two key questions dominated the investigators' minds: What had caused

the engine pylon to break away so unexpectedly from the aircraft's wing under perfectly normal operating conditions? And why had this led to such a complete loss of control? In theory, the DC-10 should certainly have been aerodynamically capable of climbing away successfully after the physical loss of the engine, and returning for a landing at the crew's discretion.

Such was the significance of these questions for the future of DC-10 operations, and such the magnitude of the task facing the NTSB, that no less than 100 investigators began work at the scene of the accident early next morning.

The overall team was made up of nine groups of specialist investigators, each with a particular responsibility. One group sought out the DC-10's "crashproof" Flight Data and Cockpit Voice Recorder units from amongst the scattered wreckage, which they would then analyse and transcribe. Other groups mean-

while examined the recent history of the aircraft and its crew, and interviewed hundreds of witnesses.

Structures and powerplants specialists concentrated on the aircraft's charred wreckage, as well as the No 1 engine and its pylon and attachments, which had fallen onto the runway.

The site of the crash was only about a kilometre northwest of the airport boundary. The port wingtip had gouged into the ground some 1400 metres beyond the end of the runway, pivoting the DC-10 into the ground nose first with enormous impact. The resulting huge ball of fire had erupted from the 60 tonnes of fuel in the DC-10's tanks. Except for the No 1 engine and its pylon, pieces of the engine cowling, and a section of the leading edge of the wing from directly above the pylon, all the wreckage lay within the field and adjoining caravan park. So extensive was the disintegration that little information of significance could be obtained from the main wreckage.

Examination of the main and nose legs and their actuators showed that the undercarriage was still down and locked at impact. The setting of the tailplane jackscrews showed that the tailplane trim was about six degrees noseup – a normal position for takeoff. Recovered hydraulic system components did not reveal any evidence of internal operating distress, but the flightdeck instruments were too severely damaged to disclose any usable information. The Nos 2 and 3 engines were located in the main wreckage. The damage they had sustained indicated they were operating at high rpm at impact.

The No 1 engine and pylon assembly was found on the grass to the right of Runway 32R, 2280 metres from the point where the DC-10 began its takeoff run. Some 38 components of the assembly were found scattered over the runway for 460 metres preceding this point. The engine and pylon had fallen onto the runway 2120 metres from the threshold and three metres to the right of the centreline.

The DC-10's engine pylons are attached to the wing by three self-aligning bearings. Two of these, one above the other in the pylon's front bulkhead, connect to the wing structure forward of the front spar. The third self-aligning bearing, on the upper section of the pylon's rear bulkhead, is connected to a transverse clevis bracket on the underside of the wing. Engine thrust loads are carried separately from the pylon to the aircraft by a fore-and-aft thrust link, mounted behind the front pylon bulkhead and attached to a wing fitting.

The front pylon bulkhead, fabricated from sheet metal, was bent forward about 30 degrees. Its two self-aligning bearings were missing, together with most of the bolts securing the upper plating of the bulkhead. The upper 30cm of the plating was bent forward an additional 10-15 degrees. The thrust link fitting remained attached to the pylon structure, but the thrust link itself was missing, as was its forward bolt and bushing. The structures group, using metal detectors, located the bolt, broken in two, in the grass adjacent to the runway. Its nut was still in place.

The upper and lower self-aligning bearings were later found amongst the main aircraft wreckage, still attached to the fittings securing the forward pylon bulkhead to the wing. The thrust link was also found at the main wreckage site with its forward connection severely bent.

The rear pylon bulkhead, a one-piece forging, had fractured in a number of places, and only minor portions were initially accounted for with the separated pylon or among the fragments scattered along the runway. The greater part of the bulkhead, including its upper two-thirds which had separated from the flanges around its periphery, the rear self-aligning bearing, and the rear clevis assembly still attached to the wing structure, were subsequently found in the main wreckage.

A three metre section of the port wing's leading edge, just forward of where the No 1 engine pylon joins the wing, was torn away with the pylon, severing the hydraulic system's lines for the port wing's outboard slats.

Thirty five of the 36 leading edge slat tracks were subsequently exam-ined, disclosing that, at impact, the port wing's outboard slats were retracted, while its inboard slats, together with the starboard wing's inboard and outboard slats, were in the extended position.

Flight Recorders

The aircraft's Fairchild A-100 Cockpit Voice Recorder was recovered and a transcript prepared, but the recording was found to be incomplete because of a loss of electrical power to the CVR as the aircraft was rotated for takeoff.

The Sundstrand Digital Flight Data Recorder (DFDR) had also been damaged structurally, but there was no fire or heat damage. The recording tape was broken but this was spliced and a readout made.

Correlation of the available DFDR and CVR recordings disclosed that the crew had set the flaps at 10 degrees and made a rolling takeoff. Thrust was stabilised at 80 knots, and left rudder with right aileron used to compensate for the right crosswind. The aircraft accelerated through V_2 speed during rotation before it lifted off. The last stable takeoff thrust reading for No 1 engine was recorded two seconds before liftoff. One second later, the word "damn" was recorded on the CVR, then the CVR ceased operating.

One second before liftoff, and simultaneously with the loss of the CVR and the No 1 engine's readings, the DFDR ceased recording the positions of the port inboard aileron, port inboard elevator, lower rudder, and Nos 2 and 4 port wing leading edge slats. It continued to record all other parameters.

The aircraft became airborne 1830 metres from the start of the takeoff roll, lifting off at V_2 plus six knots, 10 degrees noseup. Two seconds later, the DFDR reading for the No 1 engine's rpm was zero, the No 2 engine's speed was increasing through 101%, and the No 3 engine was at its takeoff setting.

The DC-10 lifted off in a slight port wing low attitude, but application of aileron and rudder restored wings-level flight and the aircraft climbed out at 1150 feet per minute (fpm) in a 14 degree noseup attitude – the target attitude displayed by the flight directors on the pilots' instrument panels for an engine-out climb. The No 2 engine speed then increased gradually from 101% to a final value of 107%, but the No 3 engine did not change appreciably from the takeoff setting. During the initial climb, the aircraft accelerated to a maximum speed of 172 knots, reaching this figure nine seconds after liftoff about 140 feet above the ground.

As the DC-10 continued to climb out at around 1100fpm, the pitch attitude and heading remained stable, right aileron and right rudder being used to maintain control. The aircraft then began to decelerate from 172 knots at a rate of about one knot a second.

Twenty seconds after liftoff, the speed had decreased to 159 knots when, with the aircraft 325 feet above the ground, it began to roll to the left at an increasing rate, despite the crew's application of right aileron. As the roll increased further, even though increasing amounts of opposite rudder and aileron were now being applied, the DC-10 began to yaw to the left as well. As it did so, the pitch attitude began to de-

Firefighters and rescue workers do their utmost, but to no avail. Not only was the DC-10 reduced to smouldering rubble, the remains of the great majority of its 271 occupants almost defied recognition. One of the bigger pieces of fuselage is shown being damped down.

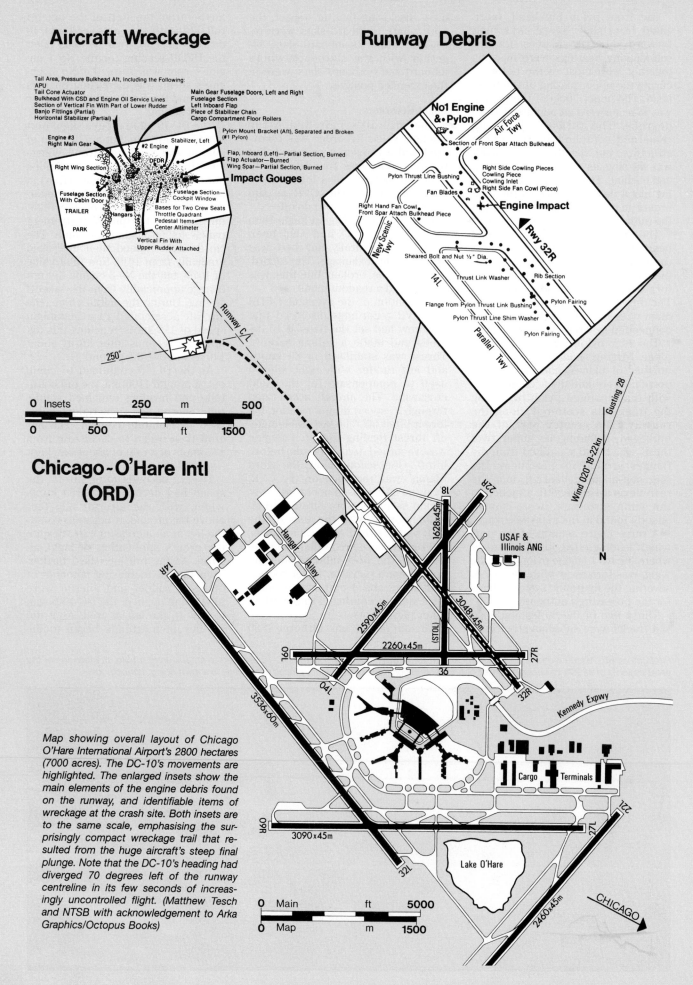

Aircraft Wreckage

Tail Area, Pressure Bulkhead Aft, Including the Following:
APU
Tail Cone Actuator
Bulkhead With CSD and Engine Oil Service Lines
Section of Vertical Fin With Part of Lower Rudder
Banjo Fittings (Partial)
Horizontal Stabilizer (Partial)

Main Gear Fuselage Doors, Left and Right
Fuselage Section
Left Inboard Flap
Piece of Stabilizer Chain
Cargo Compartment Floor Rollers

Engine #3
Right Main Gear

#2 Engine
DFDR
CVR

Stabilizer, Left

Pylon Mount Bracket (Aft), Separated and Broken (#1 Pylon)

Flap, Inboard (Left)—Partial Section, Burned
Flap Actuator—Burned
Wing Spar—Partial Section, Burned

Impact Gouges

Right Wing Section

Trees

Fuselage Section
With Cabin Door

TRAILER

Hangars Fence

PARK

Fuselage Section—
Cockpit Window

Bases for Two Crew Seats
Throttle Quadrant
Pedestal Items
Center Altimeter

Vertical Fin With
Upper Rudder Attached

Runway C/L

250°

0 Insets
0

250   m   500

500   ft   1500

Chicago-O'Hare Intl
(ORD)

Runway Debris

No1 Engine
& Pylon

Air Force Twy

Section of Front Spar Attach Bulkhead

Pylon Thrust Line Bushing

Fan Blades

Right Side Cowling Pieces
Cowling Piece
Cowling Inlet
Right Side Fan Cowl (Piece)

Right Hand Fan Cowl
Front Spar Attach Bulkhead Piece

New Scenic Twy

14L

✛ ← **Engine Impact**

▲ **Rwy 32R**

Sheared Bolt and Nut ½" Dia.

Thrust Link Washer

Rib Section

Flange from Pylon Thrust Link Bushing

Pylon Fairing

Pylon Thrust Line Shim Washer

Pylon Fairing

Parallel Twy

Wind 020° 19-22 kn
Gusting 28

N

18
22R

USAF &
Illinois ANG

1628x45m

Hangar Alley

14R

2590x45m

(STOL)

3048x45m

27R

2260x45m

36

04L

32R

160

Kennedy Expwy

3536x60m

Map showing overall layout of Chicago O'Hare International Airport's 2800 hectares (7000 acres). The DC-10's movements are highlighted. The enlarged insets show the main elements of the engine debris found on the runway, and identifiable items of wreckage at the crash site. Both insets are to the same scale, emphasising the surprisingly compact wreckage trail that resulted from the huge aircraft's steep final plunge. Note that the DC-10's heading had diverged 70 degrees left of the runway centreline in its few seconds of increasingly uncontrolled flight. (Matthew Tesch and NTSB with acknowledgement to Arka Graphics/Octopus Books)

Cargo Terminals

22L

09R

3090x45m

27L

32L

Lake O'Hare

2460x45m

CHICAGO

0 Main   ft   5000
0 Map   m   1500

(above) Pylon and cowling components of the DC-10's No 1 engine litter Runway 32R after the accident. The forklift parked on the grass verge by the Air Force Taxiway intersection is removing the CF6 turbofan engine itself.

(below) General aerial view of the crash site (indicated), looking back over the DC-10's brief flightpath, southeast towards the Chicago City skyline (faintly visible on the horizon over the "32R" key). The extensive caravan park occupies the entire lower half of the picture. The extremely slim margin by which an even more horrific tragedy was averted needs no emphasis. (NTSB)

(below) Looking back southeast from the crash site, this foreshortened drawing sequence identifies the main developments in the DC-10's disastrous takeoff, from engine separation to impact. (Matthew Tesch)

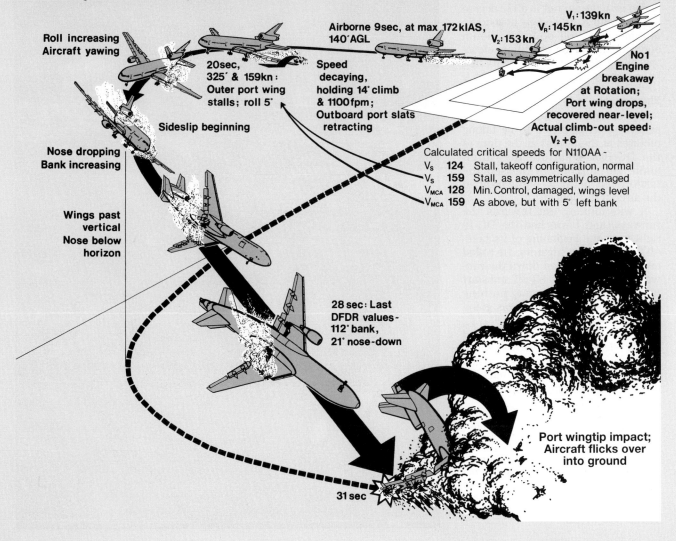

Roll increasing
Aircraft yawing

Airborne 9sec, at max 172 kIAS, 140´AGL

V₁:139kn
V_R:145kn
V₂:153kn

No1 Engine breakaway at Rotation; Port wing drops, recovered near-level; Actual climb-out speed: V₂+6

20sec, 325´ & 159kn: Outer port wing stalls; roll 5°

Speed decaying, holding 14° climb & 1100fpm; Outboard port slats retracting

Sideslip beginning

Calculated critical speeds for N110AA -

V_S 124   Stall, takeoff configuration, normal
V_S 159   Stall, as asymmetrically damaged
V_{MCA} 128   Min. Control, damaged, wings level
V_{MCA} 159   As above, but with 5° left bank

Nose dropping
Bank increasing

Wings past vertical
Nose below horizon

28 sec: Last DFDR values - 112° bank, 21° nose-down

Port wingtip impact; Aircraft flicks over into ground

31 sec

An investigator examines the DC-10's battered No 1 engine after its retrieval from Runway 32R.

crease from 14 degrees noseup, even though up elevator was being increased.

Three seconds before the end of the DFDR tape, the aircraft was in a 90 degree left bank and at a zero pitch attitude. The DFDR recording ended with the aircraft in a 112 degree left roll and a 21 degree nosedown attitude, with full opposite aileron and rudder, and almost full up elevator being applied. The DC-10 had been airborne for only 31 seconds.

Photographs

A photographer who was also a licensed pilot happened to be taking pictures at the airport at the time of the DC-10's departure that afternoon. He not only witnessed the takeoff but actually photographed the aircraft in flight.

"I was looking out towards the runways, and I watched the DC-10 right from the beginning of its takeoff," he told investigators. "It rolled away and accelerated down the runway, then it began to lift off and start its climb. At this point, nothing looked wrong; everything was going just as it should."

He was holding his camera, fitted with a telephoto lens, ready to shoot a picture of another aircraft, when his attention was brought back to the DC-10. "Suddenly the left engine

seemed to explode away from the wing, though there was no smoke or flame.

"I saw the engine come tumbling through the air – tumbling and tum-

bling – to the ground. There was still no flame," he recounted, "but there was a stream of white smoke or vaporising fuel coming from the trailing edge of the wing where the engine was.

"I took my first picture just after the engine was blown off. I took the second after the aircraft started banking very sharply to the left. By that time it was nearly perpendicular to the ground – it had rolled more than 90 degrees and was starting to roll on to its back. The nose was pointing down ..."

The horrified photographer said the DC-10 disappeared from view behind an airport building, then there was a vast ball of flame and black smoke. He snapped another picture as the bright orange flames rose into the sky. "When I saw all that violence and flame, I knew nobody could have got away alive," he concluded.

The DC-10's brief flight was also caught by a camera belonging to a passenger aboard another aircraft which was on final approach to O'Hare's Runway 09R at the time of

(right) The utter destruction of 172 tonnes of trijet and 271 people is abundantly clear from this low level aerial view of the crash site. The dark gouge in the lower foreground marks the impact point of the DC-10's port wingtip. Hurtling debris has almost demolished one of the two old aircraft hangars by the boundary fence of the caravan park. (NTSB)

the ill-fated takeoff. As a result, investigators were able to send a total of five photographs to Lockheed's Palo Alto Research Laboratories for a photo image enhancement study to confirm the positions of the DC-10's flight controls.

The process produced black and white images containing expanded variations of grey shading which, in the absence of the enhancement process, would be too subtle for the eye to distinguish. A study of these images showed that:
• The tail assembly was not damaged;
• The undercarriage remained down during the climbout;
• Spoilers Nos 1, 3, and 5 were extended on the starboard wing;
• The trailing edge of the starboard wing's inboard aileron was up.

Although the position of the slats was difficult to determine, the port wing inboard slats appeared to be extended, and the position of all other control surfaces appeared to be the positions recorded by the DFDR. The pitch and roll attitudes of the aircraft also agreed closely with those recorded by the DFDR.

Investigation

Witness accounts, DFDR readouts, and the distribution of wreckage along the runway provided indisputable evidence that the No 1 engine and pylon separated from the port wing as the DC-10 rotated and lifted into the air.

At this stage, the aircraft was committed to fly, and the crew's decision to continue the takeoff was both logical and proper in light of information available to them. The overall investigation therefore concentrated primarily on two major areas:
• Identifying the structural failure which led to the engine-pylon separation and determining its cause;
• Determining the effects of the structural failure on the aircraft's performance and systems, and what led to the loss of control.

The investigation was also led to probe the vulnerability of the DC-10 as a type to maintenance damage, the adequacy of its systems to cope with unique emergencies, the quality control exercised during its manufacture, and the adequacy of industry maintenance practices, FAA surveillance, and accepted airline operational procedures.

Pylon structural failure

Pieces of the DC-10's pylon rear bulkhead were examined at the NTSB's metallurgical laboratory and disclosed a 25cm fracture of the upper forward flange. The fracture had resulted from overstress, initiated

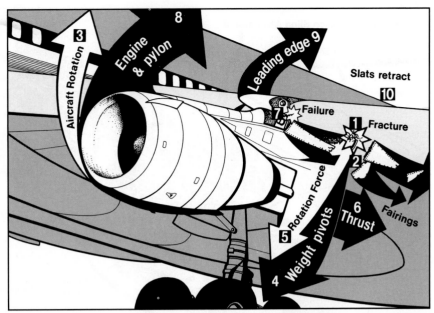

Close-up of N110AA's port wing at the instant of engine separation. The drawing shows the deduced failure sequence of the pylon components and the engine's dramatic trajectory over the top of the wing. (Matthew Tesch)

by a downward bending moment at the centre section of the flange just forward of the fracture. Fatigue cracking was evident at both ends of the fracture, the total length of the fracture and fatigue cracks being about 32cm. The remainder of the bulkhead fractures resulted from overload.

The attachment points of the pylon were also examined. The fractures and deformations in the forward bulkhead and thrust link were all characteristic of overload, and it was clear that the pylon separation had begun when the upper flange of the rear bulkhead failed. Under the thrust of the engine, the rear end of the pylon then pivoted downwards and forwards, before the pylon assembly broke from its front attachments to the wing. After this final separation, clearly evident from the bending of the pylon's front bulkhead, residual engine thrust carried the whole assembly up and over the wing before it fell back onto the runway behind the aircraft.

The separation sequence and movement of the pylon before it broke free were consistent with the loads imposed on it during the aircraft's rotation into the takeoff attitude, the combination of aerodynamic and thrust loads having imposed a downward tensile load on the already cracked rear bulkhead, resulting in its failure.

A crescent shaped deformation on the fracture surface of the upper flange of the bulkhead, the shape of which exactly matched the radius of the wing clevis fitting to which the rear bulkhead was mated, strongly suggested the flange had been

cracked when the pylon was being removed from the wing, or reinstalled, during maintenance.

Enquiries revealed that, about eight weeks before the accident, the No 1 pylon and engine of this DC-10 *had* been removed from the wing to replace the self-aligning bearings in compliance with a McDonnell Douglas Service Bulletin.

As a result of this finding, the FAA took the unprecedented step of grounding all DC-10s on the US register pending fleetwide inspections. The inspections revealed that no less than *six supposedly serviceable* DC-10s had fractures in the upper flanges of their pylon rear bulkheads – four more American Airlines aircraft and two belonging to Continental Airlines. The failure modes were all similar, all were DC-10-10 series aircraft, and all had been subjected to the same maintenance procedures, involving removal and reinstallation of the engines and pylons.

Further corroboration that the cracks were induced during this maintenance came to light when investigators learned that Continental Airlines had, on two previous occasions several months before the Chicago accident, damaged the upper flange on the rear bulkhead as pylons were being removed or reinstalled. In both these instances, the damage was detected, and the bulkheads removed and repaired.

Both American and Continental had devised special procedures to carry out the replacement of the forward and rear bulkheads' self-aligning bearings, as required by the McDonnell Douglas Service Bulletin. Although the manufacturer's service

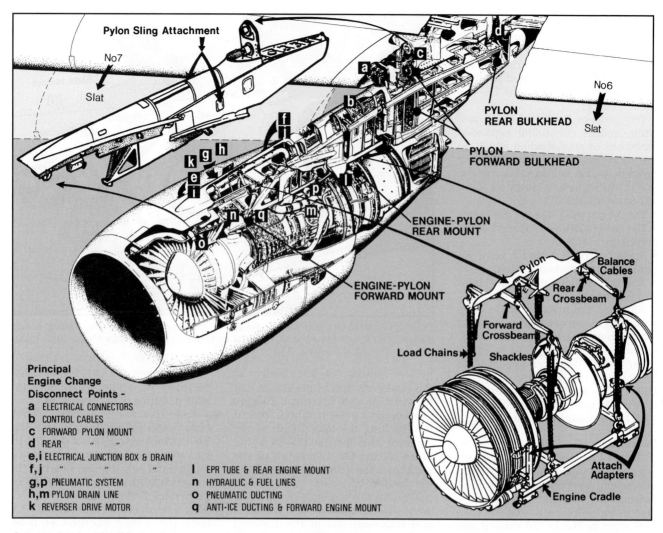

Pylon Sling Attachment

No7

Slat

a ELECTRICAL CONNECTORS
b CONTROL CABLES
c FORWARD PYLON MOUNT
d REAR

PYLON REAR BULKHEAD

No6

Slat

PYLON FORWARD BULKHEAD

ENGINE-PYLON REAR MOUNT

ENGINE-PYLON FORWARD MOUNT

Pylon

Balance Cables

Rear Crossbeam

Forward Crossbeam

Load Chains

Shackles

Attach Adapters

Engine Cradle

Principal Engine Change Disconnect Points -
a ELECTRICAL CONNECTORS
b CONTROL CABLES
c FORWARD PYLON MOUNT
d REAR
e,i ELECTRICAL JUNCTION BOX & DRAIN
f,j " " " "
g,p PNEUMATIC SYSTEM
h,m PYLON DRAIN LINE
k REVERSER DRIVE MOTOR

l EPR TUBE & REAR ENGINE MOUNT
n HYDRAULIC & FUEL LINES
o PNEUMATIC DUCTING
q ANTI-ICE DUCTING & FORWARD ENGINE MOUNT

Cutaway drawing identifying pertinent structural components of a DC-10-10's General Electric CF6 engine and pylon assembly, as hung in the No 1 (port wing) position. Scrap views show the primary pylon structure (top left) for clarity, and the cowling-free engine core (lower right) being lowered from the pylon. (via NTSB, McDonnell Douglas & Matthew Tesch)

bulletin recommended that the engines be removed from the pylons *before* the pylons were removed from the wing, both airlines had individually devised a procedure which they believed to be more efficient than that recommended by McDonnell Douglas – removal of engine and pylon *as a single unit*.

An engine stand and cradle were first affixed to the engine, then the entire weight of the engine and pylon, engine stand and cradle, was taken by a forklift positioned below the centre of gravity of the combined unit. The pylon to wing attachments were removed, and the assembly lowered on the forklift for access to the self-aligning bearings. When these had been replaced, the complete unit was raised again and reattached to the wing fittings.

A close examination of these procedures disclosed numerous possibilities for the upper flange of the rear bulkhead, or more specifically the bolts attaching the spar web to this flange, to be brought into contact with the wing mounted clevis,

and fracture producing loads applied. Because of the close fit between the pylon and wing attachments, maintenance personnel had to be extraordinarily careful when removing or attaching a pylon. A minor misjudgement by the forklift operator could easily damage the rear bulkhead and its upper flange.

The flange could be damaged even more insidiously – the forks could move imperceptibly during pylon removal as a result of a pressure leak in the forklift's hydraulic system. Maintenance engineers who performed the work on the DC-10 involved in the accident told investigators that the whole procedure was "difficult".

Altogether the evidence was compelling that the cracks in the rear bulkhead upper flanges were being introduced as a result of these maintenance practices.

Aircraft and crew performance

By the time the No 1 engine and pylon assembly separated from the wing, the crew of the DC-10 were committed to continuing the takeoff.

Witnesses saw the pylon and engine assembly fly up and over the port wing, and the deformation of the pylon's forward bulkhead was consistent with these observations. The port wing's leading edge skin, forward of the pylon's front bulkhead, was found on the runway, but there was no evidence that the pylon and engine assembly had struck any critical aerodynamic surfaces of the aircraft, or any of its control surfaces.

However, the loss of thrust from the No 1 engine, in combination with the asymmetric drag caused by the leading edge damage, should not have resulted in a loss of control. The investigators therefore sought to determine the effects of the pylon separation on the flight controls, the hydraulic and electrical systems, instrumentation and crew warning systems.

As the No 1 engine separated, accessories driven by this engine were lost. These included the pumps providing pressure to the No 1 hydraulic system, and the No 1 AC generator. During a "normal" emergency, ie when an engine merely ceases to operate, all the services provided by these accessories will remain operational, deriving their power from the remaining engines. But, when the engine *physically separated* from the aircraft, the hydraulic lines connecting the pumps with the system were severed. The separation also severed electrical wiring, resulting in the loss of power to the captain's instrument panel, the stall warning system and its incorporated stickshaker function.

In addition, as the pylon separated from the wing, the forward bulkhead severed four other hydraulic lines and two cables routed through the wing leading edge. These hydraulic lines operated the leading edge slat control valve, located inboard of the pylon, and the actuating cylinders which extend and retract the outboard leading edge slats. Two of these lines were connected to the No 1 hydraulic system and two to the No 3 system, providing backup to cope with a single hydraulic system failure. The severed cables provided feedback from the leading edge slat position, so that the control valve would be nulled when the slat position agreed with the position selected on the flightdeck control.

The severing of the hydraulic lines in the leading edge of the port wing would have eventually resulted in the loss of No 3 hydraulic system because of fluid depletion. But even at the most rapid rate of leakage, the system should have continued to operate throughout this short flight. The extended No 3 spoiler panel on the starboard wing confirmed that this system was in fact operating. Because two of the aircraft's three hydraulic systems were operational, the investigators concluded that, except for the No 2 and No 4 spoiler panels on both wings, which were powered by the No 1 hydraulic systems, all flight controls were functioning. Except for the significant effect that the severing of the No 3 hydraulic system's lines had on the port leading edge slat system therefore, fluid leak did not play any role in the accident.

During the takeoff, the leading edge slats were extended to provide increased aerodynamic lift. With the slats extended and the control valve nulled, hydraulic fluid is trapped in the actuating cylinder and operating lines. The incompressibility of this fluid holds the slats extended and is the only lock provided by the design. Thus, when the lines were severed and the trapped hydraulic fluid lost, air loads forced the port outboard slats to retract.

While other system failures were not critical, the retraction of these leading edge slats had a profound effect on the aerodynamic performance and controllability of the aircraft. With the port outboard slats retracted and all others extended, the lift of the port wing was reduced and its stalling speed increased. Simulator tests showed however that, in this configuration, even with the loss of the No 2 and No 4 spoilers, sufficient lateral control was still available from the ailerons and other spoilers to offset the asymmetric lift at any speed above the stall.

The evidence was conclusive that the aircraft was being flown in accordance with the airline's prescribed engine failure procedures, the consistent 14 degree pitch attitude during the climb indicating that the flight director was being used for pitch attitude guidance. But, because the wing and engine cannot be seen from the flightdeck and the slat position indicating system was inoperative, there would have been no indication to the crew of the slat retraction and its performance penalty. The undetected retraction of the leading edge slats had, however, increased the stalling speed of the port wing to 159 knots. The combined result was that, as the aircraft decelerated during its 14 degree climb, the roll to the left began as the speed reduced to 159 knots (V_2 + 6 knots).

The aircraft configuration was such that there would have been little or no warning of the onset of the stall. The inboard slats were extended and therefore, with the flow

These simplified drawings depict the essential elements of the DC-10-10's pylon-to-wing attachment, while the adjoining photograph, providing a sense of scale with the mechanic's hand, focuses on the thrust link immediately aft of the forward pylon bulkhead. This component carries the engine's thrust loads from its pylon assembly to the aircraft's structure. (via NTSB and Matthew Tesch)

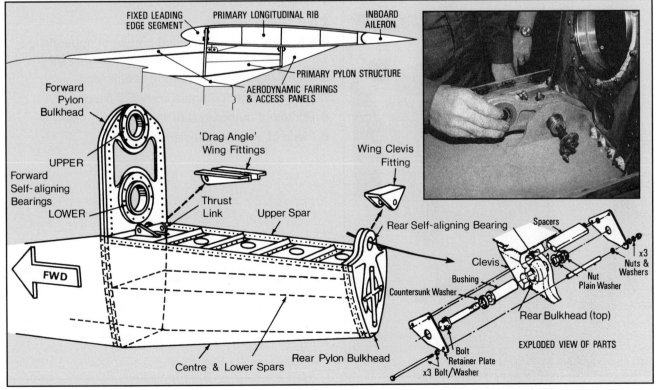

separation from the stall limited to the outboard segment of the port wing, it would not be felt on the port tailplane. For this reason there would have been little or no buffet in the elevator controls. The DFDR also indicated that there was some turbulence, probably produced by the strong gusty wind, which could have masked any aerodynamic buffeting. Because the roll to the left began at $V_2 + 6$ knots and the pilots knew that V_2 was well above the aircraft's stalling speed in the takeoff configuration, they probably did not suspect that the roll indicated a stall. Indeed, the roll probably confused them, especially as the stickshaker did not activate.

The roll was followed by a rapid change of heading. The yaw began at four degrees port wing down at 159 knots, and continued until impact. The abruptness of the roll and yaw indicated that lateral and directional control was lost almost simultaneously with the onset of the stall on the outboard section of the port wing.

Simulator tests showed that the stricken DC-10 could have been flown successfully at speeds above 159 knots. In fact, had the crew recognised the onset of the roll as a stall, they could have lowered the nose, and accelerated the aircraft out of its stalled condition. The simulator tests also showed that the DC-10 could have been landed safely in its accident configuration, using then current American Airlines emergency procedures.

During the simulator tests however, the stall warning system, based on the 159 knot stalling speed, was functioning. Furthermore, the several pilots who were able to recover control after the roll began were all familiar with the circumstances of the accident. Indeed, all the participating pilots agreed that it was not reasonable to have expected the crew, deprived as they were of warning systems, to have recognised the onset of the roll as a stall, or to have recovered from it, in the short time available to them.

The fact remained that the crew's meticulous adherence to the airspeed schedules contained in the company's engine out emergency procedures resulted in the DC-10 entering a stall. Ironically, had the crew maintained excess airspeed, even as little as $V_2 + 10$ knots, the accident might not have occurred.

Because the airspeed schedules contained in American Airlines' emergency procedures were identical to those of other airlines, the investigators believed that speed schedules for engine out climb profiles should be examined to ensure they provided the maximum protection in emergencies.

The loss of control of the DC-10 was thus the result of a combination of three events: the retraction of the port wing's outboard leading edge slats; the loss of the slat disagreement warning system; and the loss of the stall warning system – all consequences of the separation of the engine and pylon assembly. Each on its own would not have resulted in the crew losing control. But together, during a highly critical phase of flight, they posed a problem that gave the crew insufficient time to recognise and correct.

DC-10 design

Other aircraft designs include mechanical locking devices to prevent movement of slats by external loads following a system failure. This feature was not deemed necessary in the DC-10 because it was demonstrated that sufficient lateral control was available to compensate for asymmetrical conditions throughout the aircraft's flight envelope. Analysis of the takeoff regime showed that, with all engines operating, the aircraft would accelerate to and maintain a positive stall margin.

Even so, the analysis showed that if slat retraction, *and* a loss of engine thrust were to occur during takeoff, the aircraft's capability to accelerate to a positive stall margin would be compromised. But be-

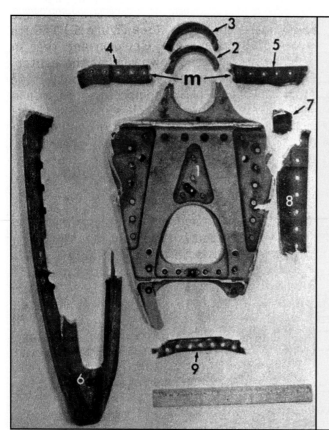

1 Rear bulkhead centre section piece

2 & 3 Upper lug ears

4 & 5 Two pieces of forward portion of upper flange (these mated along fracture indicated by 'm'

6 Side flanges & lower portion of bulkhead

7 Piece of upper outboard corner of flange

8 Portion of outboard side flange

9 Piece of intermediate flange.

The fractured pylon rear bulkhead of N110AA, with recovered pieces placed in correct relative positions. The ring mounting above the main flange in the upper section of the bulkhead carried the pylon's rear self aligning bearing. The fracture of this mounting allowed the whole engine-pylon assembly to pivot down and forward under the thrust of the engine, and finally tear free of the forward bulkhead attachments. (NTSB)

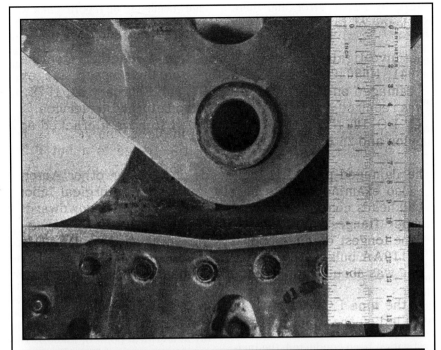

Reassembly of engine pylon rear attachments recovered from wreckage shows how the rear bulkhead was probably cracked. The upper picture shows normal component relationships, with self aligning bearing mounted in upper section of rear bulkhead connected to wing clevis fitting by clevis pin. The lower view shows how inadvertent over-travel, during mating of engine-pylon assembly to wing, could bring base of clevis fitting into contact with upper flange of rear bulkhead, cracking the bulkhead forging. The initial crack can be seen below the flange to the right of centre. (NTSB)

ing system lacked redundancy, there was only one stickshaker motor, and the left and right stall warning computers did not receive crossover information from the applicable slat position sensors on opposite sides of the aircraft.

In summary, the certification of the DC-10 was carried out in accordance with the rules in effect at the time, and with then accepted engineering and aeronautical standards. In retrospect however, the regulations appeared inadequate, in that they did not require manufacturers to allow for multiple malfunctions resulting from a single failure, even though that failure was extremely improbable.

McDonnell Douglas considered the likelihood of the structural failure of a pylon and engine to be of the same magnitude as a failure of a tailplane or wing. The pylon structure was therefore designed to meet and exceed all foreseeable loads in the life of the aircraft.

Maintenance procedures

Although the investigation showed that the design of the pylon was less than optimum in respect of safe and efficient maintenance practices, pylons had been removed from the wing and reinstalled many times without damage. But there was no doubt the procedure required caution and great precision.

McDonnell Douglas was well aware of the precision required, and for this reason specified that engines be detached from pylons before the pylons were removed from the wing. Without the engine, the pylon weighs only about 850kg, and its centre of gravity (CofG) is about a metre forward of the front bulkhead attachments, enabling it to be supported close to the wing attachment points, where relative movement between pylon and wing can be accurately gauged. But the pylon and engine together weigh some 6120kg and their combined CofG is some three metres ahead of the front bulkhead attachments, making adjustment of relative position far more difficult. It was for these reasons that McDonnell Douglas did not encourage removing the engine and pylon assembly as a single unit.

The investigators were therefore concerned with the way in which the airlines developed their own procedures in the interests of efficiency and economy.

American Airlines' engineering staff evidently implemented the procedures without a thorough evaluation to ensure they could be accomplished

cause mathematical probability showed this hazardous combination to be extremely unlikely, the design was accepted as complying with requirements. If the structural loss of a pylon had been included in the probability projection, the vulnerability of the hydraulic lines and slat position feedback cables might have been recognised.

Also, the result of the combined failure of the hydraulic and electri-

cal systems was not considered. When the effect of asymmetric slat settings on controllability was first evaluated, it was presumed that other flight controls would be operable and that the slat disagreement and stall warning systems would be functioning.

In this accident however, the loss of those systems, intended to alert the crew to the need to maintain airspeed, was critical. The stall warn-

without risk to the pylon structure. Furthermore, the company's maintenance personnel evidently did not inform either their engineering or quality control departments about the difficulties they were encountering. Had they done so, the supervising engineers might have examined the operation more closely for the likelihood of damage.

The investigators were also concerned that these shortcomings were not confined to American – a similar situation obviously existed within Continental. The evidence pointed to the need to establish inspection requirements to ensure that any damage sustained during assembly and maintenance was detected before an aircraft returned to service.

Industry communications

Because of limitations in the reporting system, neither the FAA, nor engineering staff at American Airlines, knew until after the Chicago accident that Continental had previously damaged the rear bulkhead flanges on two of its DC-10s.

On January 5, 1979, a month after the first bulkhead was damaged, McDonnell Douglas circulated an Operational Occurrence Report to its DC-10 customers containing a description of pylon rear bulkhead damage inflicted on a Continental DC-10. The report detailed the damage and indicated it occurred during maintenance, but did not mention how it was inflicted. Although American was on McDonnell Douglas' distribution list for Operational Occurrence Reports, the airline's engineering staff responsible for pylon maintenance somehow failed to see it.

Continental personnel discovered the damage to the second bulkhead a month later. As before, the company believed the damage to be

caused by human error, and there was apparently no effort to review the removal and reinstallation procedures. The bulkhead was repaired using the method previously approved by McDonnell Douglas.

Nor did Continental report the bulkhead failures and repairs to the FAA. Indeed, there was no requirement for it to do so, both the FAA and the aviation industry having traditionally interpreted the regulation on Mechanical Reliability Reporting to apply only to *service related* problems.

Nevertheless, the investigators believed Continental had sufficient prompting to conduct a thorough investigation into the procedure being used, particularly after *two* bulkheads had been damaged. Certainly, the possibility that similar damage could occur on other aircraft without detection should have been considered. Had a more thorough investigation been conducted, the incident might have been given more emphasis in McDonnell Douglas' report to other airlines. Action might then have been taken to revise the maintenance procedure and to inspect aircraft that had been exposed to potential damage.

As it was, McDonnell Douglas did not investigate Continental's procedures, accepting its finding that the damage was merely the result of maintenance error. Even when the manufacturer received the report that a second bulkhead had been damaged in an almost identical way, McDonnell Douglas again accepted Continental's evaluation, and did not pursue the matter.

Overall, the Chicago accident investigation showed regulatory reporting procedures to be seriously deficient. Damage to components identified as "structurally significant" needed to be reported in a way that ensured the cause was properly evaluated, and that the findings were disseminated to other aircraft operators and the manufacturer. Damage to such components should be reported – whether incurred during flight, ground operations, or maintenance. The circumstances should then be investigated by the aircraft operator, the manufacturer, and the FAA, and appropriate action taken.

Cause

The National Transportation Safety Board finally determined the cause of the accident to be the asymmetrical stall and ensuing roll of the aircraft because of retraction of the port wing outboard leading edge slats, and the loss of stall warning and slat disagreement indicator systems resulting from the separation of the No 1 engine and pylon assembly at a critical point of takeoff. The separation resulted from damage inflicted by improper maintenance procedures which led to the failure of the pylon structure.

Contributing to the cause were:

• The vulnerability of pylon attachment points to maintenance damage and of the leading edge slat system to the damage which produced asymmetry;

• Deficiencies in the FAA's surveillance and reporting systems in failing to detect improper maintenance procedures;

• Deficiencies in communications between aircraft operators, the manufacturer, and the FAA in failing to disseminate details of previous maintenance damage;

• The inadequacy of prescribed engine failure crew procedures to cope with unique emergencies.

The dos and don'ts of changing DC-10 wing engines, as revealed by the Chicago accident investigation, are summarised by these simplified sequences of drawings. (Matthew Tesch)

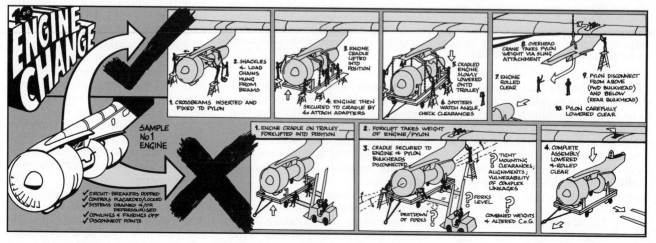

CHAPTER 5

"I don't like this ......"

*– Flight Engineer to crew
26 seconds before impact*

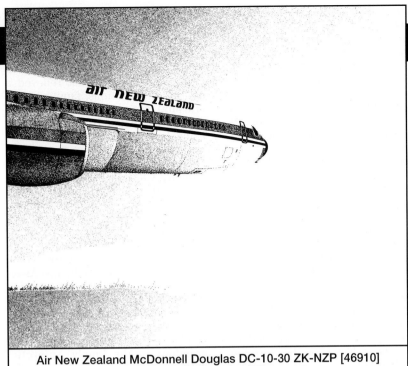

Air New Zealand McDonnell Douglas DC-10-30 ZK-NZP [46910]
– November 28, 1979

The loss of a DC-10 in remote Antarctica generated controversy rivalling that which surrounded the DH Comet disasters in the 1950s. Some of the questions it raised as to who, in this age of computerised operational technology, holds final responsibility for the safety of a flight, remain unresolved even today.

All aboard for Antarctica

Gleaming in Auckland's early morning spring sunlight as it stood nosed in against the international terminal, an immaculate Air New Zealand DC-10 waited at Gate 2 for its complement of passengers.

This in itself was unremarkable – Air New Zealand operated eight of the long range DC-10-30s on its international routes and the giant trijets with the distinctive Maori symbol on their fins were a familiar sight as they came and went at Auckland's Mangere Airport.

The setback to the type's reputation resulting from the Turkish Airlines DC-10 disaster near Paris in 1974 (refer *Air Disaster Vol 1*), and the American DC-10 accident at Chicago only six months earlier, had been felt only indirectly by the New Zealand airline. Small by international airline yardsticks, its maintenance and operational standards were first class. Indeed, as a customer of McDonnell Douglas, Air New Zealand was held up with pride as an example of what an airline operator could be.

What was remarkable on this 28th day of November, 1979, was the route this DC-10, ZK-NZP, would as-

sume after takeoff at 8am Summer Time. For its 237 prospective passengers, milling in the terminal with mounting anticipation, and indeed for the 20 crew members already on board preparing Flight 901 for departure, this was no ordinary trip.

In fact the terminal this morning had an unusual air about it. Though the flight was an international one geographically, most of those booked on it – a 177 strong cross-section of middle class New Zealand society, the majority of them middle-aged to elderly, a party of 24 Japanese tourists, another group of 23 Americans, plus other visitors from the United Kingdom, Australia, Canada, France and Switzerland – were casually dressed as though for a day's outing.

They had brought little luggage, there were neither friends nor relatives to see them off, and there were no last minute purchases from the duty free shop. The New Zealanders carried no passports and, except for the Japanese group whose ultimate destination was Christchurch on the South Island, all their tickets were endorsed "Auckland to Auckland".

All were in high spirits at the prospect ahead; as the time for boarding approached, the collective sense of excitement was unmistakable. For this was a special day – one of Air New Zealand's much sought-after sightseeing return flights to remote Antarctica.

Begun two years before in 1977, the airline's 11-12 hour, 6000nm Antarctic trips had been extensively promoted at home and overseas. "Follow the paths of the great Antarctic explorers across the icy continent," Air New Zealand's advertising proclaimed. "Look down on the lonely land of Scott, Shackleton and Byrd, and their explorer-scientist successors." On a more practical note, the advertisements added: "Don't forget to bring your sunglasses and your camera."

This colourful promotion, the airline's slogan, "Nobody does it better", and the enthusiasm with which those who had previously made the flight and described their experiences to friends, ensured that each Antarctic flight was filled, though purposefully not to capacity. Air New Zealand's DC-10s had seating for 270 passengers but, to allow sightseers room to move about and share viewing from the cabin windows, all the centre seats in the middle five abreast row were deliberately left vacant.

To add authenticity to this glimpse of the globe's awe-inspiringly harsh final frontier, the flights carried experienced guides and commentators. Former mountaineers and polar explorers like Sir Edmund Hillary and Peter Mulgrew, or Dr Bob Thompson, Superintendent of the Antarctic Division of the nation's Department of Scientific and Industrial Research, a veteran of some 50 trips to Scott Base, accompanied the flights, spicing their descriptions with first hand accounts of their own adventures on the ice.

Also, if conditions were favourable, the American air traffic controllers at the US Navy's McMurdo Station, the trip's most southerly turning point, would invite the aircraft to descend for a closer look under radar guidance. Most of the previous flights had descended to 2000 feet or less over the Ross Ice Shelf, to fly low over McMurdo Station and nearby Scott Base, both on the shores of McMurdo Sound, before setting course for the long return flight to New Zealand.

For the passengers, who each paid the reasonable sum of only NZ$329 for such a once in a lifetime opportunity, the daylong flight was as much a party as it was an exciting adventure. With the emphasis on informality and friendliness, visits to the flightdeck were encouraged, and the excellent catering and bar services sought to make the long hauls across the Southern Ocean, during which only occasional island landfalls relieved the monotony of the unending whitecapped seas, as entertaining as possible.

For the crews chosen for the Antarctic trips too, the flights were a much prized "perk" that relieved a routine of repetitious, familiar international stages. Indeed, no one boarding the DC-10 that morning could have been more enthusiastic about seeing Antarctica than its pilot-in-command. Several weeks previously, Captain Jim Collins had been both delighted and surprised when his roster showed he had been assigned to command Flight 901 on November 28.

His keenness had been prompted by his earlier trips over the North Pole as a passenger on the Los Angeles/London interchange service which British Airways operated with Air New Zealand DC-10s. The vastness of the Arctic's icy wilderness had fascinated him, but he knew the grandeur of the lonely Antarctic, with its mountain chains and glaciers, was even greater.

He had not expected his application to fly one of the services to be successful. There were only four Antarctic flights a year and most of them were allocated to senior executive pilots. This one would be the last for the calendar year and rumour had it that spiralling fuel costs might soon put paid to the Antarctic scenic trips for the foreseeable future.

The timing, too, could hardly have been better. With the Antarctic summer only days away, there would be activity at New Zealand's Scott Base and America's nearby McMurdo Station. Teams would be out with dog sleds, and US military transport aircraft would be busy flying in supplies under the 24 hour sunlight. At this time of the year too, the descent towards McMurdo could nearly always be made in clear weather.

Collins, 45, was highly regarded within the airline, having a reputation for professionalism and command judgement. Trained originally in the RNZAF, he had been a pilot for 25 years and a captain with Air New Zealand for 15 years. With a total of 11,000 hours' experience, nearly 3000 of which was on DC-10s, he was also qualified as a flight navigator. Meticulous though he was in his attitude to flying standards, he remained popular with crewmembers who flew with him.

Antarctic briefing

Nearly three weeks earlier, on November 9, Captain Collins, together with First Officer Greg Cassin, one of the two first officers rostered as part of Collins' crew (it was company policy to carry two first officers and two flight engineers on the Antarctic trips to provide crew relief during the long flight), attended an Antarctic briefing at the airline's Route Clearance Unit (RCU), located in the same building as the DC-10 simulator. Other aircrew, rostered for a trip on November 14, also attended the briefing. The RCU's role was familiarisation for pilots about to fly a route that was new to them. Earlier, captains made their first such flights under the supervision of a captain experienced on the route, but the RCU had been developed to replace this requirement.

The Antarctic briefing consisted of an audio visual presentation and a review of a printed briefing sheet, detailing the IFR route to McMurdo, the use of Grid Navigation procedures beyond latitude 60° South, the computerised flightplan used by all Air New Zealand Antarctic flights, and the VMC letdown procedure at the ice airfield for McMurdo Station, located just off the southern coast of Ross Island. No landing was intended, of course, but the approach, letdown and low flying in the area were considered equally critical. The briefing would conclude with a 45 minute "flight" in the DC-10 simulator to enable the pilots to assimilate what had been presented.

The RCU briefing began as a "guided tour" of the route to be flown, with the audiovisual showing views to be seen from the flightdeck as the aircraft flew south. The briefing touched on the route's relationship to Mt Erebus, the 12,450 foot

Pago Pago twilight. One of the most famous travel industry images of its time, this evocative Samoan scene became an Air New Zealand hallmark. With the airline's marketing strategy and emotive advertising indelibly linked to its DC-10s for most of the 1970s, the Erebus disaster, in the context of the type's increasingly tarnished world reputation, was a doubly devastating blow for the small international airline. (Matthew Tesch collection)

active volcano on Ross Island, some 20nm north of McMurdo Station, and pointed out that the minimum IMC altitude for this sector was 16,000 feet.

As the colour slides were projected on the screen, the pilots noted that the latter part of the track lay over the sea ice of the 40nm wide McMurdo Sound, with the high terrain of Ross Island well to the left, and the mountains of the Antarctic mainland to the right. It was the impression they expected. As Mt Erebus loomed into view in its correct place on the left, the taped commentary declared: "Now approaching Erebus at 16,000 feet, the minimum sector altitude. In VMC, a descent to this minimum altitude up to 50 miles before reaching McMurdo will be found advantageous for viewing ..."

There were also slides depicting the Radio Navigation Chart (RNC) of the McMurdo area used by US and NZ military aircraft, a small scale map of the route of the Air New Zealand round trip, via the several en route island reporting points, and Air New Zealand's passenger information map, produced in colour, which also presented the broad detail of the flight. All this briefing material indicated that, after reaching Cape Hallett on the Antarctic continent, the aircraft would continue to the McMurdo area by keeping to the west of Ross Island, avoiding Mt Erebus by flying down the 40nm wide McMurdo Sound.

The presentation pointed out that the McMurdo NDB located at the ice airfield was now "not available". To overcome this deficiency, the descent procedure had been amended to use the DME function of the McMurdo TACAN (Tactical Air Navigation Station) military aid for operations in VMC below 16,000 feet within a closely defined arc over the ice shelf. It was stressed that, if the aircraft was to be taken below the Minimum Safe Altitude (MSA) of 16,000 feet, it must be under strictly visual conditions and with the authority of the USN radar controller at McMurdo.

The minimum altitude after passing overhead McMurdo was then 6000 feet, providing visual conditions existed, there were no snow showers, visibility was in excess of 20 kilometres, and the aircraft's descent was co-ordinated with McMurdo radar. If visual conditions did not exist, the MSA of 16,000 feet was to be maintained.

The question of what height the aircraft might actually descend to in favourable conditions was discussed. Should visibility be clear, crews

Turquoise seas, blue skies, white clouds, sleek, "questing" Maori canoes with flaring sternposts carved with the Koru design: Little was spared to publicise the service entry of ZK-NZL [47846], the first and most photographed of Air New Zealand's eight DC-10s, at the beginning of 1973. In the early 1980s when Air New Zealand finally re-equipped with Boeing 747s, the ill-fated ZK-NZP's seven surviving sisterships found ready buyers around the world. (Matthew Tesch collection)

might well descend lower than 6000 feet at the invitation of the McMurdo radar controllers. Crews on most previous Antarctic flights had taken their aircraft down to 2000 feet or less, and the willingness of the American controllers to co-operate was well known. The practice appeared to have the company's tacit approval – low flying over the ice had been described in a number of publications, including Air New Zealand's own magazine.

But a close watch on fuel would be necessary and the crew would need to ensure they did not linger too long in the viewing area at low altitudes when fuel burn would be excessive. The aircraft would leave Auckland near its maximum all-up weight of 250 tonnes, of which 109 tonnes would be fuel.

Air New Zealand's DC-10s were equipped with an Area Inertial Navigation System (AINS), the most sophisticated available to airline operations. Comprising three independent inertial systems to ensure accuracy, the system also responded to radio navigation aid inputs. Properly programmed, the system had the capability to accurately navigate the aircraft on area navigation routes or great circle tracks from takeoff to final approach anywhere in the world.

On Antarctic flights, the AINS came into its own. The vast Southern Ocean could offer no surface radio navigation aids – only within 40 to 50nm of McMurdo at the southern-

most limit of the trip would any be available.

For Air New Zealand's regular international flights, crews were provided with pre-programmed computerised flightplans in the form of magnetic tape cassettes, which were inserted into the flight data storage unit of the AINS on the flightdeck. Available tapes provided data for most areas in the world, but did not include the lonely latitudes to the south.

For Antarctic flights therefore, crews programmed the latitude and longitude co-ordinates of their flight-plan waypoints directly into the AINS computer. Supplied in the form of a computer printout, this data would be keyed in during the pre-flight checks by the two first officers, then checked by the captain.

The airline had developed two alternative computerised flightplans for the Antarctic flights and these were also discussed at the RCU briefing. Both routes would follow a common track south from New Zealand as far as the Balleny Islands. The primary track then continued to Cape Hallett, followed by a straight leg almost due south from Cape Hallett to McMurdo. But, should a crew learn that weather conditions were unsuitable in the McMurdo area, they would take the secondary westward route from the Balleny Islands to the South Magnetic Pole, via the impressive Ninnis Glacier (see map).

At 60° South the crew would change to Grid Navigation, a system used to overcome problems inherent with normal navigational procedures in polar regions. Towards the poles, meridians of longitude converge increasingly until they all come together at the pole itself. In years gone by, this convergence caused difficulties for navigators because of the progressively diminishing distance between longitudinal points. The nearer the pole, the greater the margin for error, the minutes in each longitudinal degree progressively diminishing to only a few nautical miles – and eventually to a matter of metres! In any case, in regions so close to the magnetic poles, conventional magnetic compasses were useless.

The Grid, laid over the polar areas and centrally aligned on the Greenwich meridian, replaced the normal meridians of longitude and parallels of latitude. At 60° South, therefore, the DC-10 crews would realign their direction indicators with Grid North in accordance with navigational data transmitted from McMurdo.

Within the aircraft's AINS however, the computer, left to its own devices, would continue to fly the aircraft in accordance with the programmed waypoints.

Departure

On the day of the flight the crew were at the airport early, participating in the usual preflight preparations and despatch planning. In addition to Captain Jim Collins and First Officer Greg Cassin, the flight crew comprised First Officer Graham Lucas and Flight Engineers Gordon Brooks and Nick Moloney. Like their captain, Cassin and Lucas had both trained in the RNZAF. Cassin too was a qualified flight navigator.

The distinction of having the longest airline service of any of the crew belonged to Moloney, 49, formerly a ground engineer with the domestic National Airways Corporation. But it was Brooks, 44, a check and training flight engineer, who had the only previous Antarctic flight experience: he had been on a 1977 trip with Air New Zealand's flight operations manager in command.

The flight commentator on today's trip was well known New Zealand adventurer and yachtsman, Peter Mulgrew. In 1958 he had trekked from McMurdo to the South Pole in an expedition led by Sir Edmund Hillary, the first overland Antarctic crossing since that of Captain Scott in 1912.

Knowing the Antarctic continent as well as any man, Mulgrew would join the crew on the flightdeck for the sightseeing part of the trip, using the PA system from the jumpseat immediately behind the captain. He could be counted on to provide a vivid commentary, replete with tales of danger and personal adventure, for the passengers crowding around the cabin windows.

Responsible for the welfare and comfort of the passengers now boarding the DC-10 was the genial Chief Purser, Roy McPherson, 39. He had a young and enthusiastic cabin crew – two pursers, two assistant pursers, a flight hostess, two senior flight stewards (one of whom had been on a previous Antarctic flight), four stewardesses and three stewards.

Shortly before the doors were finally closed, a woman passenger, evidently frightened of flying, was overcome by fear and insisted on leaving the aircraft. Cabin staff did their best to reassure her but to no avail, and she returned to the departure lounge. Here, Air New Zealand

One of the rare published pictures of ZK-NZP. This publicity shot, featuring a representative cabin crew beneath the soaring empennage of "The Big-10", was taken at Auckland's Mangere Airport. (Matthew Tesch collection)

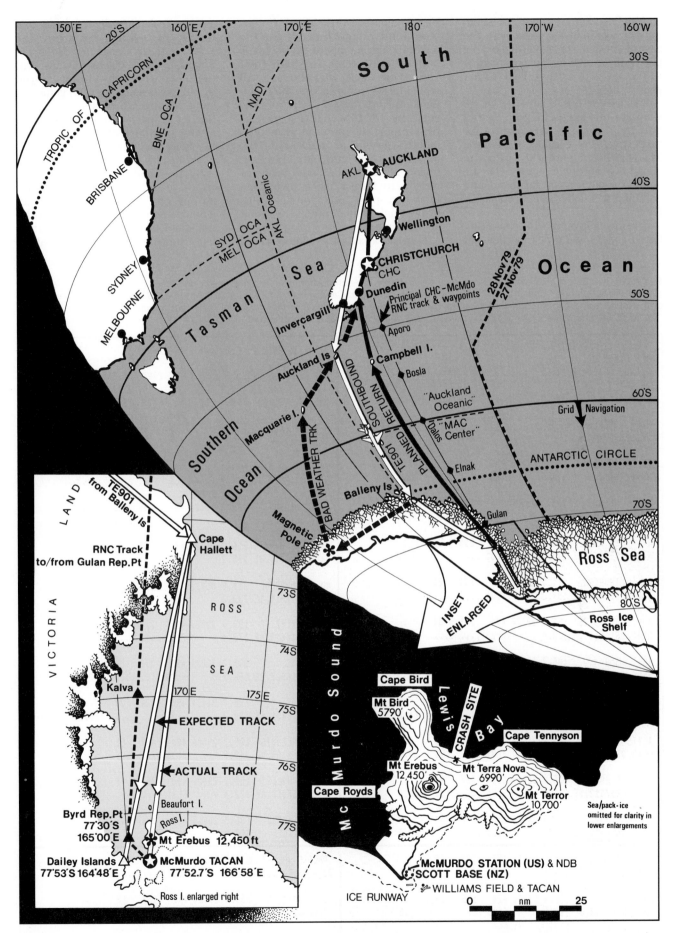

This graphic view of "the bottom of the world", showing the outbound, return, and bad-weather-option tracks featured in Air New Zealand's briefing and publicity material, underlines the remoteness of the Antarctic destination. The inset shows the final stages of the track down the Ross Sea coast of Victoria Land to McMurdo Sound. Significantly, the airline's plotted route did not follow the standard tracks (also included above) on the military RNC chart of the area. Yet all maps provided to the crew – civil and military – showed the final sectors leading down McMurdo Sound to the Byrd Reporting Point west of Ross Island. (Matthew Tesch)

staff calmed her, eventually persuading her to rejoin the flight with the assurance that she would enjoy the trip. Still unsettled, but now willing to try, she was ushered back to her seat.

Because of this delay, the DC-10 was late moving away from Gate 2 but, by 8.17am, it was taxiing for takeoff. A few minutes afterwards ZK-NZP lifted smoothly into the clear sky, setting course over the southern suburbs of Auckland and climbing to Flight Level 350 (35,000 feet).

Cruising above the beaches, timbered valleys and green farmland of New Zealand's North Island, Collins would introduce himself on the cabin PA system, inviting passengers with window seats to share their view with those who did not. All would be welcome to visit the flight-deck during the trip. On its way south the DC-10 would pass over its first reporting point at New Plymouth, the city at the base of the majestic 8260 foot Mt Egmont, thence across to the South Island at Nelson to follow the snowcapped mountain spine of the Southern Alps to the final mainland reporting point at Invercargill.

A lavish breakfast would be served as New Zealand finally fell astern and the DC-10 ventured out across the wild Southern Ocean for McMurdo Sound, nearly 2000nm distant. But the cocooned comfort being enjoyed by the passengers and the generous cabin service would soon allay any fleeting fears there might have been at the prospect of flying into the loneliest and most inhospitable region of the world.

By the time the breakfast trays would be cleared away, the monotony of the heaving grey ocean would be broken by the sight of the Auckland Islands, green and fertile, but 450nm distant from New Zealand

Baffling at first glance, the computer printouts of the first two-thirds of the flightplan become clearer on further inspection. On the left is the plan for the November 7 flight in ZK-NZN; on the right, that issued to Captain Collins for his fateful November 28 trip in ZK-NZP. Comparison of the fourth entry from the bottom (indicated), shows the changed longitude of the McMurdo destination waypoint. (The minor change in "MCMDO" latitude was not relevant to the disaster, reflecting only the move to the McMurdo TACAN.)

```
      CENTRE LANDING GEAR IS EXTENDED FOR TAKE OFF
OPS FLASH
NZN NZAA-NZCH RT NO      /     CAPT DALZIELL    RADIO LOG
06/11/79-1900Z  TRK.T  W/V  G/S  DIST ZEET FUELRM STN
M82  TE 901/07  TRK.M DDUVU FL    ZATA ZETA RQFUEL GMT

NZAA  AUCKLAND                          .  FREQ P
3700.6S17446.9E              S/H ....  101.4      S

NP   NEWPLMTH  193.6      400   123   21
3900.2S17410.9E 174.3     CLB  .... ....   XX.X

NS   NELSON   199.3 23037 448   146   22    .
4117.8S17308.0E 179.3     FL31 .... ....   91.3

RY   MT MARY  216.2 24037 444   208   28    .
4408.2S17016.8E 195.2     FL31 .... ....   86.5

NU   INVRCRGL 211.8 27037 457   163   21    .
4624.8S16819.1E 189.2     FL31 .... ....   83.1

AUKIS AKLND IS 198.4 29078 478   271   34    .
5042.0S16610.0E 173.4     FL29 .... ....   77.5

55S   55S     185.7 29098 497   259   32    .
5500.0S16527.2E 156.2     FL29 .... ....   72.5

60S   60S     185.7 31060 504   302   36    .
6000.0S16431.1E 150.2     FL33 .... ....   66.8

BLYIS BALENYIS 185.7 31053 504  407   48    .
6645.0S16300.0E 349.5     FL31 .... ....   59.6

CPHLT C HALLET 155.9 31063 532  367   41    .
7220.0S17013.0E 322.4     FL31 .... ....   53.6

MCMDO MCMURDO 188.9 34054 517  337   40    .
7753.0S16448.0E 357.4     FL35 .... ....   47.9

CPHLT C HALLET 008.9 34054 425  337   47    .
7220.0S17013.0E 177.4     FL33 .... ....   41.5

70S   70S     358.8 33060 420   139   20    .
7000.0S17003.6E 168.9     FL33 .... ....   38.8

65S   65S     358.8 31068 425   300   42    .
6500.0S16946.6E 168.7     FL33 .... ....   33.2
```

```
ZKNZP ON GATE 2. CLG DOWN FOR DEPARTURE.
OPS FLASH
NZP NZAA-NZCH RT NO      /     CAPT COLLINS    RADIO LOG
27/11/79-1900Z  TRK.T  W/V  G/S  DIST ZEET FUELRM STN
M82  TE 901/28  TRK.M DDUVU FL    ZATA ZETA RQFUEL GMT

NZAA  AUCKLAND                          .  FREQ P
3700.6S17446.9E              S/H ....  100.9      S

NP   NEWPLMTH  193.6      425   123   20
3900.2S17410.9E 174.3     CLB  .... ....   XX.X

NS   NELSON   199.3 30027 486   146   21    .
4117.8S17308.0E 179.3     FL31 .... ....   91.0

RY   MT MARY  216.2 31027 481   208   26    .
4408.2S17016.8E 195.2     FL31 .... ....   86.5

NU   INVRCRGL 211.8 31029 485   163   20    .
4624.8S16819.1E 189.2     FL31 .... ....   83.3

AUKIS AKLND IS 198.4 32029 495   271   33    .
5042.0S16610.0E 173.4     FL29 .... ....   77.9

55S   55S     185.7 31033 498   259   31    .
5500.0S16527.2E 156.2     FL29 .... ....   72.9

60S   60S     185.7 30034 487   302   37    .
5000.0S16431.1E 150.2     FL33 .... ....   66.9

BLYIS BALENYIS 185.7 29026 481  407   51    .
6645.0S16300.0E 349.5     FL31 .... ....   59.3

CPHLT C HALLET 155.9 29021 490  367   45    .
7220.0S17013.0E 322.4     FL31 .... ....   52.8

MCMDO MCMURDO 188.5 24015 463  336   43    .
7752.7S16658.0E 357.0     FL35 .... ....   46.5

CPHLT C HALLET 008.5 24015 483  336   42    .
7220.0S17013.0E 177.0     FL33 .... ....   40.8

70S   70S     358.8 29024 465   139   18    .
7000.0S17003.6E 168.9     FL33 .... ....   38.4

65S   65S     358.8 29024 465   300   39    .
6500.0S16946.6E 168.7     FL33 .... ....   33.3
```

and far too remote in such wild seas for cultivation or grazing. Antarctic educational films would be shown next, with Peter Mulgrew ever ready to answer any questions they might stimulate.

Approach to McMurdo

Shortly after midday, some four hours out from Auckland, excitement would mount as the passengers were treated to their first glimpse of pack ice – white flecks on a now blue sea that were in reality icebergs, stretching south to the horizon as far as the eye could see. Only 15 minutes later, the sight of the bleak Balleny Islands would provide tangible evidence that they were indeed penetrating the Antarctic Circle.

Now the crew, up to this time in touch with Oceanic Control in Auckland, made their first contact, initially on HF, with the USN's Air Traffic Control Centre at McMurdo Station ("Mac Centre") to obtain the latest weather. On the basis of this, Captain Collins had to decide whether to continue towards McMurdo or divert to the secondary scenic route that would take them instead to the South Magnetic Pole.

The reply was not encouraging, the controller reporting "some cloud in the local area, base 3000 feet", with visibility below the cloudbase about 40nm. But, with the coastline of the Antarctic continent near Cape Adare clearly visible in the far distance soon afterwards, Collins evidently decided it was worth continuing.

An hour later at 1.17pm, by which time the DC-10 had crossed the coast of the continent west of Cape Adare, cut across the Admiralty Ranges to Cape Hallett, and was now paralleling the spectacular Victoria Land coast southwards towards McMurdo in clear conditions, the crew again contacted McMurdo for an update on the weather, this time on VHF.

McMurdo replied on HF that there was a low overcast in the area at 2000 feet with some snow, but visibility was still about 40 miles. Switching to HF also, the crew now said "we'd like to descend to FL160." The aircraft was then cleared to "descend and maintain FL180."

Two minutes later McMurdo called the DC-10 to report there were clear areas 75 to 100nm miles to the northwest, but "right over McMurdo we have a pretty extensive low overcast." The controller explained that "within a range of 40 miles we have a radar that can let you down to 1500 feet on vectors," and requested the aircraft's DME distance from McMurdo.

Killer whales frolic near the edge of the pack ice in McMurdo Sound by Ross Island. In this picture, the wide, flat crater of the volcano and the vast spread of its flanking slopes belie Mt Erebus' 12,450 foot height. In Greek mythology, Erebus was the god of darkness, and lord of the limbo regions between upper earth and Hades.

When the crew reported this as "approximately 114", the McMurdo controller requested them to attempt contact on the VHF frequency of 126.2. But nothing was heard from the aircraft and three minutes later the crew called on HF to say their calls had been unanswered. Asked if they had "a good lock on our TACAN channel", the crew answered, "Negative at this point." The controller then instructed the aircraft to "contact Ice Tower [the control tower for McMurdo's ice runway] on 134.1."

Again there was no contact on VHF and three minutes later at 1.27pm the McMurdo controller advised on HF: "Ice Tower is attempting contact on both 134.1 and 126.2. Attempt contact when you're approximately 80 DME."

Shortly before 1.32pm the aircraft reported on HF: "Still nothing on 126.2 or 134.1 – we'd like further descent – or we could orbit in our present position which is approximately 43 miles north?"

McMurdo: "Roger – VMC descent is approved – and keep Mac Centre advised of your altitude." After a further call by the McMurdo controller on VHF failed to get a response, he instructed the aircraft on HF to "Recycle your transponder – squawk 0400."

Again there was no response, but at 1.35pm, Ice Tower suddenly received a VHF transmission: "Mac Tower, this is New Zealand 901 on 134.1 – do you read?

Tower: "New Zealand 901 – you're loud and clear!"

Aircraft: "Roger – you are now loud and clear also – we are presently descending through Flight Level 130 in VMC and our intention at the moment is to descend to 10,000 [feet]."

Tower: "Roger – understand you will be descending to 10,000 VMC – and you are requesting a radar letdown through the cloud?"

Aircraft: "That is affirmative."

The tower's next instruction to the aircraft evoked no response, nor did the controller's five further attempts to re-establish contact on VHF.

But at 1.38 the aircraft again called McMurdo Centre on HF: "We briefly had contact [with the tower] on 134.1 – we've now lost contact," the crew reported. "We're maintaining 10,000 feet presently, 34 miles to the north of McMurdo."

McMurdo: "OK Roger – and keep trying the tower on 126.2 and 134.1 – they heard you too, sir."

Aircraft (three minutes later, still on HF): "New Zealand 901, still negative contact on VHF – we are VMC and we'd like to let down on a grid of 180 [degrees] and proceed visually to McMurdo."

McMurdo: "New Zealand 901 – maintain VMC – keep us advised of your altitude as you approach McMurdo – report 10 DME from McMurdo."

McMurdo (two minutes later – just before 1.45pm): "New Zealand 901 – if possible, give us a tops report on the cloud layers."

Aircraft: "Roger – 50 miles north, the base was 10,000 [feet]."

McMurdo: "Understand bases are at 10,000?"

Aircraft: (at 1.45pm): "Affirmative – we are now at 6000, descending to 2000 and we're VMC."

Five minutes later the McMurdo controller, conscious that the DC-10 had not reported at 2000 feet as expected, called it again. This time there was no reply on HF, so he called on VHF as well. Again there was no reply.

After a number of further abortive calls, he asked US aircraft operating in the area, including a USAF C-141 Starlifter en route from Christchurch to McMurdo less than an hour behind the sightseeing flight, to attempt to make contact with the Air New Zealand DC-10. All their calls were followed only by an ominous silence.

Flight 901 is missing

The first home-based New Zealander to learn that there was concern in far distant Antarctica for the whereabouts of the national airline's sightseeing flight was former airline radio officer Gus Knox.

Knox had originally been a flying boat radio operator with TEAL, Air New Zealand's predecessor. Since retiring from Air New Zealand, he had maintained his keen interest in radio communication as a "ham" operator. One of his frequent contacts was fellow ham Leo Slattery, at present serving with the Antarctic contingent at Scott Base.

Slattery, speaking with Knox shortly after 3pm, told him of the loss of communication with the DC-10 and that a US Navy Hercules and three helicopters from McMurdo "were on the lookout." Slattery immediately telephoned Air New Zealand's Flight Operations office in Auckland. The news was the first indication to the airline of any problem.

Official confirmation that the DC-10 was overdue did not reach Air New Zealand's head office until more than an hour later when, well after 4pm, Oceanic Control in Auckland, acting on advice from McMurdo, declared the Uncertainty phase of Search and Rescue (SAR) procedures.

Dr Bob Thompson, Superintendent of the Antarctic Division, who had acted as commentator on an Antarctic flight only a week previously, also heard the news at about this time. It was telephoned to his Christchurch office by *Operation Deep Freeze*, headquarters of the USN's Support Force Antarctica at Christchurch Airport, the advance base for all US activity on the Antarctic continent. The DC-10 had not arrived overhead McMurdo as expected around 2pm – and there had been no communication from it since.

Could the aircraft have simply suffered a total communications failure?

This was the fervent hope of all – in Antarctica and New Zealand, and indeed within the ATC organisation in Australia – who now knew the DC-10 was unreported for several hours. Such failures were by no means impossible or even unprecedented over the vast distances of the Southern Ocean. Sunspot activity and the influence of the South Magnetic Pole could sometimes play havoc with radio transmissions.

Meanwhile, at Auckland Oceanic Control, SAR procedures had been upgraded to the Alert phase. Yet it was still quite possible that the DC-10 was even now well on its way back to Christchurch. Only time would tell – the DC-10 was due to land there soon after 7pm.

By some extraordinary oversight, no notification reached the Air Accidents Investigation Office at the Ministry of Transport in Wellington, the nation's capital. It was not until 8.50pm that Captain David Eden, Air New Zealand's Director of Flight Operations, telephoned Chief Inspector of Air Accidents Ron Chippindale at his home. It was the first word to

Chippindale that something might have happened to Flight 901.

Eden explained that the DC-10 was now nearly two hours overdue at Christchurch. Chippindale was not only astonished at how little was known of the situation, considering seven hours had elapsed since the last radio transmission, he was justifiably angry he hadn't been advised earlier. It was standard practice to notify his office whenever SAR procedures were instituted. Now, with the DC-10's fuel expiry time finally passed, these had been upgraded to a full Distress phase.

Chippindale realised in those moments that a massive task, far beyond anything he had previously experienced, faced him – with a major investigation that could take him literally to the ends of the earth.

Meanwhile, the same US Starlifter that had flown to McMurdo behind the DC-10 was now returning to Christchurch, following the latter's intended flightpath in the hope of picking up a signal from the missing aircraft. From McMurdo itself, Hercules aircraft and helicopters were continuing to scour the McMurdo Sound area. In New Zealand, an RNZAF Lockheed Orion long range reconnaissance aircraft was preparing to depart from its base at Whenuapai, north of Auckland, to fly south with its sophisticated tracking equipment, seeking any trace of wreckage or survivors in the vast Southern Ocean.

The news, when it reached the media a short time later, that one of Air New Zealand's much vaunted Antarctic flights was missing, stunned the small nation. Across the country, in the North Island as in the South, thousands of people related or con-

The ferocity of the DC-10's 260 knot impact with the 13° slope punched an imprint of its belly four metres deep into the ice. This main impact crater was flanked on either side by gouges left by the aircraft's wing-mounted engines and flap-track fairings. At the instant before impact, the aircraft had been rotated in pitch to about 10° noseup and "go round" power applied, but it had not yet begun to climb. (J T Moehring via Hodder & Stoughton)

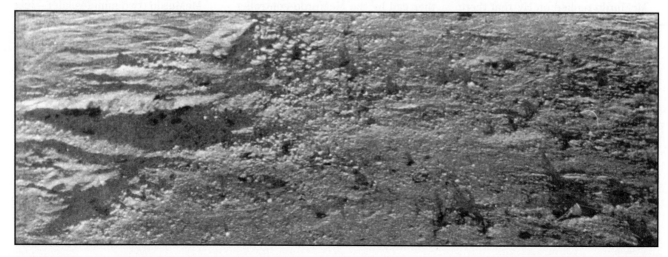

nected in some way to those on board the DC-10, fearful of the worst, hoped and prayed for some glimmer of encouragement.

But Chief Inspector Chippindale, now working into the night back at his office, had come to expect the worst when an aircraft was overdue. With no communication for many hours and fuel known to be exhausted, there could be little real hope. That the aircraft had gone down somewhere was beyond doubt – the outcome was now more a matter of where and why. Tragically, vindication for his view would not be long in coming.

Fearful news

On the morning of Thursday, November 29, the population of New Zealand awoke to headlines on radio, television and in the press that their worst fears had been realised.

Down south in Antarctica at 12.56am, the land of the midnight sun at this time of the year, 11 hours 10 minutes after the last contact with the Air New Zealand DC-10, a USN Hercules searching to the north of Ross Island had called the McMurdo controller with dramatic news: "Mac Centre," the Hercules captain transmitted. "We have located the wreckage. I say again we have located the wreckage of the DC-10. Position 76.26 South, 167.27 East. There appear to be no survivors. I say again there appear to be no survivors."

The report, relayed to *Operation Deep Freeze* in Christchurch and to Auckland Oceanic Control just after 1am, was immediately telephoned to Chief Inspector Chippindale, now planning for what could well prove to be the biggest and most difficult civil aircraft accident investigation ever undertaken in the Southern Hemisphere. It was just four hours since Captain Eden had broken the news to him that the DC-10 was overdue. Though the wreckage was still "unidentified", there could be little doubt of its identity.

For any nation, an air disaster of such magnitude would be mind-numbing. But in New Zealand, with a population of just three million, the horror seemed almost personal. There was hardly anyone in the country who did not know, have some connection with, or was not related to at least one of the victims.

Chippindale and other key personnel had remained at the office throughout the night. There could be no thought of bed – there was far too much to plan and arrange. Chippindale had never been to Antarctica before, nor had he investigated an accident to a heavy airline jet. But there would be no lack of expert assistance.

Offers of help were already pouring in from overseas – from accident investigation authorities in Australia and the UK, from the NTSB, the FAA, McDonnell Douglas and General Electric (the manufacturer of the DC-10's engines) in the USA, as well as from Air New Zealand itself, the police (who would take responsibility for recovering the bodies), and the Airline Pilots' Association.

Elsewhere, the RNZAF, the US *Deep Freeze* base and the Antarctic Division at Christchurch, were working out travel and accommodation requirements for the large contingent that would make up the investigation and recovery team at the accident site. Dr Bob Thompson was assessing the resources available at New Zealand's relatively small Scott Base. As well as accommodating as many as possible at Scott Base, already squeezed by a team of scientists working on summer projects, the whole group would have to be outfitted for polar weather at his Division's Christchurch stores.

Investigation Antarctica

Late the following day, Chief Inspector Chippindale, now at McMurdo Station with the advance members of his team, caught sight of the burnt out wreckage as he approached the crash site in a USN Iroquois helicopter. An alien brown scar amongst the all-pervading Antarctic whiteness on the utterly bleak, windswept northern ice slopes of Ross Island, it was a scene of utter desolation.

All too mindful of the terrible fate that had overtaken the Turkish DC-10 five years before, and that of the American aircraft at Chicago only six months previously, Chippindale studied the strewn wreckage anxiously for telltale patterns.

But, as the Iroquois made a low run, he saw that this accident was different. In the two previous DC-10 calamities, the aircraft had plunged into the ground out of control. In this case, the wreckage distribution left no doubt that the aircraft had flown into the slope in a near level attitude – in other words *under control*. Certainly the degree of disintegration was enormous, but this was only to be expected in an impact at anywhere near cruising speed.

Hovering over the scene of destruction, Chippindale could make out the imprint the huge aircraft had left in the ice and snow on its initial impact. That it occurred at high speed was evident from the length of the wreckage trail. There had obviously been a massive break-up of the structure on impact, followed by a searing fire fed by the many tonnes of fuel still in the aircraft's tanks. Both wing mounted engines lay among the wreckage scatter. The fin mounted engine was also there, its position indicating it had remained at power long enough to propel itself up through the shattered fuselage as the aircraft broke up.

Police Inspector Bob Mitchell, also aboard the Iroquois, looked down at the disaster with different eyes. He had carried out extensive research and conducted police training in recovery and identification procedures, particularly in the wake of major disasters. His major concern was all the bodies – recovering them from the icy slope where the lives of the victims had ended so abruptly, photographing them, labelling them, bagging them and finally dispatching them by air for identification in faraway Auckland.

From above the wreckage, Mitchell could see many frozen bodies sprawling around the remains of the burnt-out fuselage. He was surprised that so many appeared intact. Like Chippindale, he knew the violence of the impact had killed all on board instantly. No one could have possibly survived the forces involved.

After the Iroquois touched down near the wreckage to allow a detailed inspection, they found what they hadn't seen from the hovering helicopter – the victims not thrown clear in the impact. Inside the wreckage of the cabin, beneath twisted metal and blackened interior fittings, were scorched human remains.

Mercifully, Chippindale was too occupied to dwell on the horror. He had the accident site as a whole to examine. After spending several hours on the ice, he came away convinced there had been no structural failure. In at least one area, the McDonnell Douglas representatives in the investigation party would be enormously relieved: the DC-10 had not fallen out of the air as in the two previous major accidents involving the type – Chippindale's examination confirmed it had simply flown into the ice slope, apparently under full control.

But why had it done so? And apparently without warning of any kind? What could have possibly caused the giant, fully serviceable three engined jet, flown by a highly experienced and competent crew, to fly straight into the lower slopes of massive snow covered Mt Erebus at a height of only 1500 feet?

This was the riddle Chippindale

and his expert team had to solve. Somehow they had to find the answer, sifting through the frozen wreckage for vital clues, gathering together every fragment of evidence that might shed light on the reason for the shocking disaster. In particular, somewhere among the shambles of what had been a magnificent aeroplane, they had to find the all important Flight Data Recorder and Cockpit Voice Recorder. The magnitude of the task, particularly in this harsh and hostile environment, was daunting.

Together with USN Flight Surgeon James Goodrum, Chippindale was at the McMurdo ice runway when the helicopters began arriving with their underslung loads of plastic body bags. Bodies provided evidence. The two investigators saw every body that came from the crash site, 114 substantially intact and another 133 bags containing human remains. After being inspected, the bags were crated at the temporary morgue set up in the base's cargo store, ready for transport back to Auckland by RNZAF Hercules.

Film recovered from passengers' cameras, processed at McMurdo Station, provided much valuable information on the weather conditions and visibility encountered by the DC-10 as it neared McMurdo, as well as the track actually flown.

Little movie film survived the shattering impact, but 60% of all colour and black and white still film was processed. Drawing on local knowledge at the bases, in particular that of Dr Bob Thompson, it was possible to identify particular terrain – Beaufort Island and the Ross Island coastline – in the photographs taken from the cabin windows shortly before the crash. From earlier photographs, it was evident that passengers had clear views of Victoria Land's mountain ranges from 33,000 feet before the DC-10 began its descent over the Ross Sea.

Chief Inspector Chippindale interviewed the crews of all the US aircraft flying in the area on the day of the accident, and had long and useful discussions with ATC staff and weather forecasters at McMurdo Centre. American aircrew also provided details of their own training for Antarctic conditions, together with the experiences and insights they had gleaned in actual polar operations.

The deputy leader at nearby Scott Base, Ted Robinson, gave the investigation team an account of his communications with the Air New Zealand DC-10. When the aircraft was about 35 minutes out from McMurdo, Captain Collins had called Scott Base on HF. After Collins had commented that the weather around Cape Adare was excellent, Robinson emphasised to him that conditions at McMurdo and Scott Base were poor, with low cloud enshrouding the area.

He suggested to Collins that it would be inadvisable to continue to McMurdo – the passengers wouldn't see anything. Robinson explained that scientific parties working at Vanda Station had definitely reported clear weather around the Wright and Taylor Valleys. Not only would the passengers get a good view of that area, but the isolated New Zealanders working there would be thrilled to see the DC-10 fly over them.

Travelling at 260 knots, the 200 ton [sic] jet hit with its wings level and its nose up 10 degrees. The DC-10's two underwing engines and the rear underside of the fuselage slammed into the rock hard ice slope with massive force, leaving a twelve foot deep indentation in the shape of the aircraft.

As the lower panels of the fuselage shredded and carved deep into the ice, the wing tanks ruptured. Seventy tonnes of fuel, retaining the inertia of 260 knots, broke free like a hellish rainstorm. It ignited almost simultaneously and balled up the slope engulfing the exploding machine like a shower of napalm bombs.

The ungainly bulk, cracked and gaping at four or five crucial points, lofted over a mound of snow and ice like a helpless, crippled bird. Catapulted from the inferno, the nose section, part of the top of the fuselage, and the tailplane continued on, spinning, rolling and finally coming to a shuddering halt.

The last piece of debris to settle was the tailplane fin containing the rear engine. Even after impact this engine continued for some seconds to deliver full power, ploughing and gouging on, up and into the 13 degree slope for hundreds of metres.

The forces of impact and the air pressure difference between the aircraft's cosy interior and the harsh outside environment combined to break and crumple the fuselage of ZK-NZP as if it were a plastic toy plane. Passengers were blasted out of the two aisled, wide bodied cabin, killed instantly by the deceleration forces. For the few strapped into their seats, the belts provided no restraint from the shock of impact and rush of air. As the nose, flightdeck and front galley section broke off from the main fuselage, the crew and others in the area were ejected, the captain and copilot thrown 200 feet from their cockpit controls. The large main cabin section, with wing roots attached, ended up at the head of the wreckage trail and was rapidly engulfed in an intense, deep seated blaze fed by the jet gas from the adjacent punctured wing tanks. The fuelled fire avoided the flightdeck, already extensively smashed and recognisable only from the mass of dials, wires and columns which were once part of the most sophisticated flight control system in any modern jetliner.

Torn, twisted, blackened pieces scattered over an area of 2000 feet by 500 feet on the ice-and-snow covered terrain, distinguished also by two deep crevasses. The initial distinctive footprint of the plane was at 1465 feet above sea level, about a mile from the rocky coastline of Lewis Bay. Fuel soaked and scarred, the tangled remains spread up to 1900 feet above sea level. Between the crash site and the cloud shrouded volcanic cone of Erebus, another 11,000 feet up, was the menacing, treacherous black rocky face of Fang Ridge.

- Ken Hickson, "Flight 901 to Erebus", and Gordon Vette, "Impact Erebus"

After this communication, neither Robinson nor any of the New Zealand field parties were able to get through to the aircraft. Nor did any of the parties sight the DC-10 in flight.

THE INVESTIGATION REPORT

After two weeks in the Antarctic, Chippindale returned to New Zealand, taking with him various key items recovered from the wreckage. Ahead of him lay almost six more months of intense effort – wider investigation that would take him to the UK and the USA in his probing of all the factors that had combined to destroy a DC-10 and all its occupants in one of the most remote places of the world. And when that was done there would be the writing of the report itself, a document which would not only explain the fate of those who had died but would, in one way or another, affect the lives of many more of the living.

Despite all his efforts to complete the work as soon as possible, there was growing public impatience for Chippindale's report. Politicians, insurance companies, the press, civil aviation management, the airline and its employees, the Airline Pilots' Association, other aviation unions, lawyers, the police, the next-of-kin, friends of those who had lost their lives, and indeed the entire concerned New Zealand general public, were clamouring for some definitive word on the disaster.

The mounting political pressure was such that, on March 10, 1980, only weeks before Chippindale expected to be able to submit his report to the Minister for Transport, the Attorney General announced that a Royal Commission of Inquiry would also be set up to report on the accident. The Royal Commissioner would be the Hon P T Mahon, Judge of the High Court in Auckland.

Chippindale completed his gigantic task and forwarded the report to the Minister on May 31, 1980. It was published three weeks later.

The following is an edited summary of the relevant sections of Chief Inspector Chippindale's report:

Descent

Having been told by McMurdo that Ross Island was under a low overcast, the crew accepted the Centre's offer to let them down to 1500 feet under radar surveillance during their approach. In the event however, it could not be positively established that the aircraft was not located on radar at any time.

The crew then elected to descend in a clear area to the north of Ross

Aerial view of the accident site, looking south towards the summit of Mt Erebus from Lewis Bay. The initial impact mark is faintly visible (lower right), the scorched wreckage trail leading up to the midships section of the fuselage and separated tail fin, (upper left). Just to the right is the investigators' helicopter platform and the line of their tents. (S J Gilpin via NZ Office of Air Accidents Investigation)

Island during two orbits, first to the right and then to the left. Although they were granted a clearance to descend from 10,000 to 2000 feet VMC, on a heading of 180 Grid (013° T) and to proceed "visually" to McMurdo, the aircraft only descended to 8600 feet before it completed a 180 degree left turn to 357G (190° T), during which it descended to 5700 feet. The descent was then continued to 1500 feet on the flight-planned track towards Ross Island.

Shortly after completing this final descent, the aircraft flew into the ground on Ross Island. The Ground Proximity Warning System (GPWS) operated correctly and the crew responded, the engineer calling off 500 and 400 feet heights above ground level, and the captain calling for "go round power". All three engines were at high power and the aircraft had rotated upwards in pitch immediately prior to impact.

The accident occurred in daylight, 10 seconds before 1.50pm, at an elevation of 1465 feet AMSL.

Meteorological information

At the time of the accident, the McMurdo area was under the influence of a low pressure trough. There was a total cloud cover with a base of 3500 feet and layers above, with mountain tops in the area obscured by cloud. The wind at McMurdo Station was 230 Grid at 10 knots. Visibility was good but surface definition was poor and horizon definition only fair.

The crew of a USN Hercules, inbound to McMurdo from the west-northwest at 2pm, said that there was a continuous stratoform layer covering Ross Island with cloud "domes" over Mt Erebus and Mt Terror concealing them from view. A lenticular cap cloud lay over Mt Erebus above the main cloud layer. Visibility was good below the cloud base, but surface definition was poor.

A detailed weather description was also provided by the captain of the USAF C-141 Starlifter following some 45 minutes behind the DC-10.

"As we approached McMurdo, we noted that Ross Island was obscured by cloud and no terrain was visible," the captain said. "Navigating entirely by INS, we maintained 16,000 feet until McMurdo picked us up on radar at 38 DME. We began descent and entered cloud immediately. The cloud cover appeared to be cumulus or stratocumulus and we encountered only light rime icing and light turbulence. Between 12,500 and 11,000 feet we passed between cloud layers. We broke out of the cloud base at about 5000 feet; visibility beneath the ceiling was good. We landed at McMurdo at 2.52pm."

Navigation aids

The DC-10 crew had been briefed that the NDB had been withdrawn, but it was in fact still transmitting, the US Navy having decided not to dismantle it until it failed. Ground based navigation aids available to the DC-10 thus comprised an NDB, a TACAN suitable for interrogation by the DC-10's DME, and a surveillance/precision approach radar installation.

Although the navigation aids were operating normally, the aircraft's DME did not lock onto the TACAN for more than one brief period. It was obvious that the DC-10's low approach had effectively placed Mt Erebus in line of sight between these aids and the aircraft.

The aircraft was equipped with a Bendix RDR 1F radar which had both "weather" and "mapping" modes. Although it was not approved as a navigation aid, crews of earlier Antarctic flights reported that its radar indications of high ground correlated well with the contours they observed visually.

Communications

The crew spent considerable time trying to establish communication with "Ice Tower" and "Ice Radar" on VHF during the last 30 minutes of the flight. Only occasional contact was made on 134.1 and 126.2 MHz. As with the navigation aids, the aircraft was not in line of sight of the VHF transmitters throughout most of this time. HF communications remained satisfactory, the last exchange taking place 4 minutes 42 seconds before the accident.

Impact and fire

The aircraft began breaking up immediately it impacted on the ice slope. Fire erupted and raged in the cabin area of the fuselage after it came to rest.

The terrain at the accident site comprised a solid layer of ice, lightly covered with dry powder snow. The wreckage trail, crossing two deep crevasses, covered an area of some 570m by 120m, aligned on a bearing of 190° True. The uphill slope from the point of impact to the end of the wreckage trail was 13°.

The wreckage trail, impregnated with turbine fuel and coated with soot, was typical of a high speed impact and resulted in extensive fragmentation of the underside of the wing and fuselage. The initial impact with the icy slope had left a clear impression of the fuselage, wing mounted engines and flap hinges, showing that the DC-10 was in a wings level, noseup attitude. Although the noseup attitude had increased and engine power was increasing, the flightpath itself was still essentially straight and level at the instant of impact.

The two wing mounted engines, the underside of the wings, and the underside of the rear fuselage bore the main impact. Debris from each of these sections was left in the impact crater. Both wing engines were stopped immediately by distortion. The fin mounted No 2 engine continued to deliver considerable power for a matter of seconds after the initial impact.

Riding over the mound of ice and snow and displaced by the initial impact, the aircraft, breaking up as it went, continued up the ice slope in a wings level attitude. The progressive destruction of the fuselage would have been aggravated by a pressure differential of about 1.1 psi between the pressure hull and the outside environment. The integrity of the fuselage was broached early in the breakup and the majority of the oc-cupants were ejected before the last of the wreckage came to rest. Most of the remainder were thrown clear in the final impact.

The intense fire was probably fed by residual fuel in the port wing tanks, the only ones to retain their integrity. But the fire did not reach the fuselage interior immediately, many of the ejected victims showing no sign of having been burnt.

Wreckage examination

The biggest remaining portion of the aircraft was the midships section of the fuselage which, though severely damaged by fire, remained attached to the wing centre and inboard sections. The upper forward fuselage, including the flightdeck and front galley, was untouched by fire.

Examination of the wreckage established that the aircraft had been in a normal cruising flight configuration with the undercarriage, flaps and slats retracted. The tailplane jack screws showed that the trim was set two degrees noseup.

Both the DFDR and the CVR capsules were recovered, together with a large number of passengers' cameras, many of them containing relatively undamaged film.

Recovery of victims' remains

An extensive effort by the investigation and recovery team resulted in most of the victims being located. Of these, 213 were identified. Postmortem examinations indicated that all were killed in the initial impact. Very few appeared to have been wearing seat belts. In any case, the decelerations were such that none could have survived.

Flight recorders

A useful transcription was eventually obtained from the tape of the aircraft's Sundstrand Model B CVR, but the task was made unusually difficult by the extra voices on the flightdeck – those of the second flight engineer, the commentator and passengers invited there by the captain.

The aircraft's Sundstrand Model DFDR was not seriously damaged, but the tape was broken. The equipment had performed satisfactorily and all the parameters recorded correctly. All the record required for the investigation was recovered.

The DFDR showed that the aircraft carried out two descending orbits, one to either side of the flightplan track in the Lewis Bay area, then continued descending towards McMurdo before finally levelling out at 1500 feet AMSL. From this point the flight was straight and level with a five degree noseup attitude at 260

ZK-NZP's dismembered fin and centre engine nacelle lying forlornly on their side close to the top of the wreckage trail. The engine itself, torn from its mountings, came to rest some 40m lower down the slope. (Ted Robinson)

knots until immediately before the impact when the aircraft rotated in pitch to about 10° noseup and No 1 engine "spooled up" to 94%. The DFDR sampled each engine's N2 rpm once every four seconds and No 1 engine's rpm was the last to be recorded.

AINS programming

All three of the AINS computer memory modules were recovered from the wreckage and returned to the manufacturer in an attempt to retrieve the flightplan waypoints entered for the flight from Cape Hallett onwards. The data recovered showed that *the flightplan had been entered correctly from the computer printout,* [my italics – author], that no additional waypoints had been inserted in the vicinity of McMurdo, and that no offset from the flightplan track had been flown. It was also established that all three navigation computers were indicating positions within allowable accuracy limits.

Film

Film recovered from passengers' cameras was processed and studied by the Superintendent of New Zealand's Antarctic Division. He was able to determine that the aircraft followed a track over north Victoria Land consistent with the computer flightplan, and approached Ross Island on track. Before crossing the coast of Ross Island east of Beaufort Island however, the aircraft completed some descending turns.

Many of the passengers' last or second last photographs were taken when the aircraft was about six miles east of Beaufort Island, heading south. On other films, the last frames (some snapped only seconds before impact) showed the eastern shoreline of Cape Bird, the northeastern and northwestern coastline of Lewis Bay, and a cloud layer with a base of some 2000 feet, above an unbroken snow covered slope.

The aircraft was within sight of Beaufort Island, which was clearly visible, for some time The sun was shining on the northeastern slopes of Mt Bird, with rocky outcrops and the ice cliff around this section of Lewis Bay clearly visible.

From the photographs, the Superintendent deduced that the weather over north Victoria Land was clear with almost no cloud at any altitude. From about Franklin Island to just north of Beaufort Island, the aircraft flew over continuous cloud layers, and was then able to descend through a break. Several photographs showed a clearly defined cloud base beyond and above the Lewis Bay coastline at something less than 2000 feet.

Preflight briefing inadequacies

An examination of the RCU briefing provided to Captain Collins and First Officer Cassin in preparation for the flight revealed that significant items had not been included:
• The procedure for determining the minimum flight level recognised for the Antarctic area and specifically the McMurdo control area;
• The way in which the Air New Zealand route varied from the usual military route and the reporting points depicted on the Radio Navigation Chart (RNC), particularly on the leg southwards from Cape Hallett;
• Topographical maps for use on the flight. With the exception of a photocopy of a map of Ross Island (1:1,000,000), these were not issued to the crew until the day of the flight, and were of small scale – 1:5,000,000 and 1:3,000,000;
• A comprehensive discussion of the whiteout phenomenon peculiar to the Antarctic, which could be expected with an overcast sky above snow covered terrain;
• The fact that the McMurdo NDB was still operating.

The only "charts" of the area from Cape Hallett to McMurdo available at the initial briefing were:
• The passenger information map (overprint on a 1:16,000,000 chart);
• The McMurdo RNC chart;
• A slide depicting the schematic diagram of the route printed on a passenger brochure.

While these "charts" were not intended for navigation, all three showed a track to the west of Mt Erebus down McMurdo Sound. Crews of earlier Antarctic flights were also of the opinion that the inbound track to McMurdo was over the sea ice of McMurdo Sound to a point to the west of McMurdo Station. Indeed, the commentary that accompanied the audiovisual briefing referred to the military RNC when discussing flight levels.

The two tracks shown on the strip map of the route from Christchurch to McMurdo, issued to the crew on the day of the flight, also both depicted a passage to the west of Ross Island. A track and distance diagram issued at the RCU briefing correctly depicted the intended flightplan track from Cape Hallett to the McMurdo TACAN, but showed no relationship to geographical location or terrain.

The RCU audiovisual presentation included two slides purporting to be of the track between Cape Hallett and the McMurdo TACAN. The first, showing Cape Adare, 73nm northwest of the Cape Hallett waypoint, accompanied the statement: "We are almost 77 degrees south, proceeding from Cape Hallett towards Ross Island at Flight Level 330. Mt Erebus, almost 13,000 feet, ahead. McMurdo Station and Scott Base lie 20 miles beyond the mountain." The second slide accompanied the statement: "Now approaching Erebus at 16,000 feet, the minimum sector altitude. In VMC a descent to this minimum altitude up to 50 miles before McMurdo will be found advantageous for viewing". *This slide gave no indication of the relationship of the track to Mt Erebus, actually showing a view of Mt Erebus from an aircraft heading north.* [my italics – author].

The sample computer flightplan presented at the RCU briefing had been in error for 14 months, showing the destination waypoint for

Members of the on-site recovery team confer beside the burnt out midships section of the DC-10's fuselage. (NZ Police)

McMurdo Station as 2° 10' of longitude to the west of the intended turning point. This error was not corrected in the computer until the day before the accident flight. The flightplan issued on the day of the flight was correct, but the error and its subsequent correction were not mentioned to the crew during their preflight despatch planning.

The RCU audiovisual stated that the "minimum sector altitude", or "company sector safe altitude", for approach to McMurdo was 16,000 feet and that descents to the overall minimum of 6000 feet were only permitted in a sector to the True South of McMurdo in conditions of 20km visibility or better, and only then if there were no snow showers in the area and the descent was co-ordinated with the McMurdo radar controller. The written briefing notes emphasised that "... if VMC cannot be maintained, FL 160 is the Minimum Safe Altitude".

Yet copies of these briefing notes had not been forwarded to McMurdo. US Navy ATC staff there were thus unaware of the Air New Zealand approved minimum altitudes, the approved VMC letdown sector, or conditions specified for VMC letdowns.

Whiteout phenomenon

The US Navy's Support Force Antarctica advised the investigation team that whiteout is an atmospheric effect resulting in loss of depth perception and is especially common in Polar regions. Only two conditions are necessary to produce it – a diffuse shadowless illumination and a mono-coloured white surface. Whiteout is not necessarily associated with precipitation, fog or haze. The condition can occur in a crystal clear atmosphere or under a cloud ceiling with ample comfortable light, and in a visual field filled with trees, huts, oil drums and other small objects.

In Polar regions these conditions occur frequently. Large unbroken expanses of snow, illuminated by a sky overcast with dense, low stratus clouds, blot out all trace of surface texture or shadow, merging snow covered hollows and objects into a flattened white background. Cloud and sky can have the same apparent colour, so that horizon discrimination is lost and the ground plane disappears. Those who have not experienced whiteout are often sceptical about the impossibility of estimating distance under these conditions.

For a person on foot, whiteout may be no more than a nuisance in that he may stumble on ground which appears to be flat but which is in fact undulating. For pilots however, this loss of height and distance perception can be critical. First there is the effect of loss of horizon, when it becomes impossible to separate sky from earth and establish a ground plane. The result during an attempt to land can be misjudgement of the approach – a stall well above the surface, or flying the aircraft into the ground.

In these conditions of course, disorientation is also a major hazard. Another common problem is loss of distance perception, when it becomes difficult to know whether a perceived hill is really a hill in the distance, or a small protrusion only a few feet away.

Investigator's analysis

The initiating factor in this accident was the captain's decision to make a VMC descent below the specified MSA while still to the north of McMurdo.

Although two of the pilots were shown a printout of the erroneous computer flightplan at the RCU briefing before the actual flight, they were not shown on a topographical map that the intended track passed almost directly over Mt Erebus. Yet the military RNC chart for the McMurdo area, plus the three very small scale "maps" of the area between Cape Hallett and McMurdo used in the RCU briefing, all showed a track clear of high ground to the west of the Ross Island mountains. Indeed, so did the small scale strip map of the Christchurch/McMurdo route issued to the crew on the day of the flight.

The flightplan for this and previous Antarctic flights was printed from a computer stored record which, until the night before the accident flight, had the longitude for the McMurdo destination waypoint incorrectly entered as 164° 48'E. The error, which had persisted for 14 months, placed the presumed McMurdo destination near the longitude of the Byrd Reporting Point (165°E and 30nm northwest of McMurdo in McMurdo Sound), which was used by all US and NZ military aircraft. The flightplan error thus aligned the Air New Zealand track closely with that displayed on the military RNC chart.

[This RNC track down the centre of McMurdo Sound to the Byrd reporting point had been developed for military flights with the express purpose of avoiding Mt Erebus and the other mountains on Ross Island. Mt Erebus actually lies on a direct line between Cape Hallett and McMurdo Station. Why the airline did not follow this sound military practice when originally planning the sightseeing flights, electing instead to route the flights on the direct track from Cape Hallett to McMurdo Station – and why it was apparently not realised this would take the flights directly over the summit of the 12,450 foot Mt Erebus – was not addressed in the Chief Inspector's report.]

The error of longitude for the McMurdo destination waypoint in the stored computer flightplan had been discovered two flights earlier [but corrected only hours before the accident flight departed]. Neither the crew of the previous Antarctic flight, nor that of the accident flight, were advised of the error's discovery [nor that its correction would significantly displace the final leg of the flight from that which the crew had been led to expect at the RCU briefing – my italics – author].

The fact that a computer error of over two degrees of longitude could exist for 14 months indicated that the company's RCU briefing officers had not sought to reconcile the intended geographical co-ordinates of the route with the actual topography. And because all previous Air New Zealand Antarctic flights during this period had approached the area in VMC, their crews had elected not to adhere to the flightplan track after reaching Cape Hallett and hence had not detected the error either [my italics – author].

No explanation of horizon and surface definition terms had been given to the crew, either during the RCU briefing or the preflight despatch planning, and only a passing reference had been made to whiteout conditions. The actual weather conditions had a high potential for a "whiteout", and reports from aircraft flying in the area shortly afterwards indicated that surface and horizon definition were poor.

The aircraft's direct flight from Cape Hallett to McMurdo was interrupted some 40nm north of McMurdo to take advantage of a hole in the cloud cover and descend prior to arriving over McMurdo, the captain having been advised that visibility below the cloud was 40nm. When the aircraft requested a clearance to descend from 10,000 to 2000 feet on a heading back towards the north, and then to continue to McMurdo VMC below the cloudbase, there was no reason for the McMurdo controllers to question this. It was from a position to the north of Ross Island, the descent would take the aircraft back out over the sea ice, and the

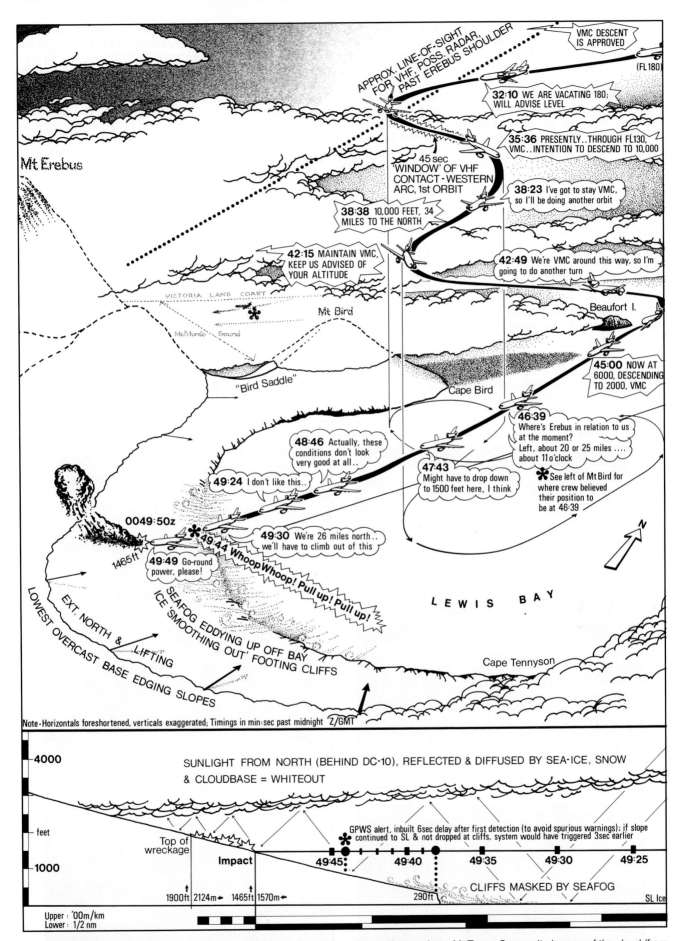

Aerial perspective of Ross Island, Lewis Bay and McMurdo Sound from the southeast, above Mt Terror. Composite images of the cloud (from satellite pictures and local witnesses) are combined in this illustration with a profile of the DC-10's last minutes of flight to show the crew were scrupulous in adhering to VMC procedures in their letdown. They were tragically unaware, however, of how "VMC conditions" in the Antarctic could lead them into the trap of sector whiteout. (Matthew Tesch)

crew had confirmed they would maintain VMC inbound to McMurdo.

But without further advice to McMurdo Centre, the captain reversed the aircraft's descent track and, from 5800 feet, continued the descent to 2000 feet on a heading towards cloud covered high ground. The first officer neither criticised this decision, nor offered any expression of doubt. The captain then descended the aircraft a further 500 feet to get a better view beneath the cloud layer. But, at a height of 1500 feet and at a distance to run of 26 miles, he finally became concerned and said: "We're 26 miles north – we'll have to climb out of this".

After the captain's decision to climb the aircraft out of the area, he and the copilot were in the process of discussing the most suitable climbout path when the Ground Proximity Warning System sounded. The crew responded without hesitation, but coming only six and a half seconds before impact, the warning was too late.

The captain, the first officer and the flight's commentator shared a misconception that their approach path lay over sea ice to the west of Mt Erebus. Although flightdeck discussion indicated they believed they were to the west of Mt Erebus, the two flight engineers voiced queries about the procedure being followed and expressed mounting alarm as the approach continued at low level. The pilots may also have believed they would be able to see any obstruction within 40 miles as soon as they were below the 2000 foot cloud base.

But observed conditions probably resulted in the particular snow slope and the cloud base appearing to the captain as an area of limited visibility, and this whiteout situation may well have been the deciding factor in his announced intention to climb out of the area.

The CVR showed that the pilots' demeanour was composed and confident during the aircraft's approach to the accident area. The apprehension expressed by the flight engineers indicated that they were endeavouring to monitor the flight responsibly, but their suggestions of caution, as with the captain's final decision to climb, were overtaken by events.

Cause

The probable cause of the accident was the decision of the captain to continue the flight at low level towards an area of poor surface and horizon definition when the crew were not certain of their position, and the subsequent inability to detect the rising terrain which intercepted the aircraft's flightpath.

This pair of artist's impressions was presented at the Royal Commission to show how visual cues during the last minutes of flight reinforced what the crew expected to see from their briefing. On the left is the view approaching Lewis Bay, on the right that entering the head of McMurdo Sound. Each top picture shows clear conditions, the centre views add sea fog, and the bottom views further add a low overcast. In the absence of any visual cues of scale, the basalt cliffs of the two northern arms of Ross Island ("actual" view, left) look uncannily like those flanking McMurdo Sound to the west ("expected" view, right). (Geoff Saville & Gordon Vette, via Hodder & Stoughton)

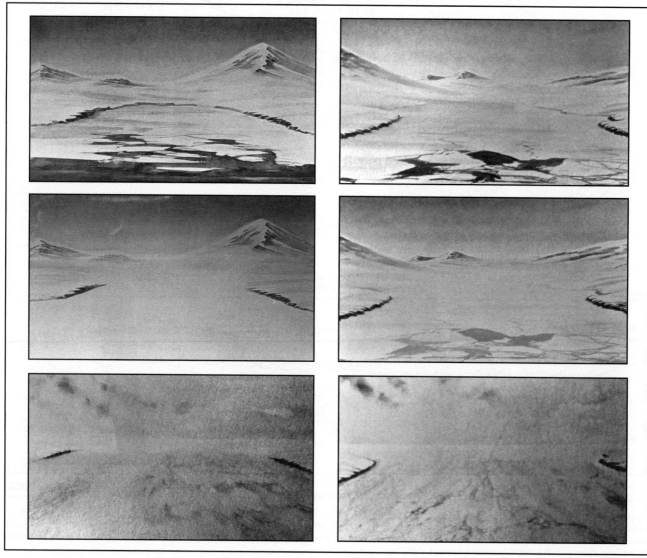

THE ROYAL COMMISSION

The Royal Commission of Inquiry, promised by the Attorney-General before Chief Inspector Chippindale's investigation report was completed, opened in Auckland early in July, 1980.

Assisting the Royal Commissioner, Mr Justice P T Mahon, were barristers Messrs D Baragwanath and G Harrison. All parties involved in the tragedy were legally represented – the Civil Aviation Division, the Office of Air Accidents Investigation, McDonnell Douglas, the Airline Pilots' Association, the families of Captain Collins and First Officer Cassin, and a consortium representing the estates of some of the passengers.

The Royal Commission sat for a total of 75 working days, having obtained four extensions beyond its original October 1980 deadline. During this time, Mr Justice Mahon travelled to the USA, Canada, Britain and Antarctica to seek first hand evidence on which to made his judgements.

The resulting "Mahon Report", with its dramatic and controversial findings, was finally tabled in the NZ Parliament on May 1, 1981, 17 months after the accident.

To the astonishment of the aviation industry throughout the Western world, and in a move almost unprecedented, the Royal Commission completely overturned the findings of the investigation conducted by the Office of Air Accidents Investigation's hard working Chief Inspector, and placed the blame for the tragedy squarely on the airline and its senior management.

The Mahon Report

In the period between the release of the Chief Inspector's Investigation Report and the opening of the Royal Commission, solicitors acting for next-of-kin of the crew objected to the release of the report ahead of the Inquiry. Counsel appointed to assist the Commission also expressed concern at the Minister for Transport's decision to make the report public when he did.

The basis of these objections was the public belief that the findings of the report were entirely predictable. Leaks to the media while the investigation was in progress had led the public to expect blame to be apportioned to the crew, in particular to Captain Collins as pilot-in-command, especially as any possible technical failure had been eliminated.

The matter was taken up after the Inquiry opened, counsel for the estates of the two pilots protesting that the investigation report "gave the impression that, in the Chief Inspec-

tor's opinion, the sole cause of the disaster was pilot error."

"I fully agree that the content of the report led to widespread public misconception," Mr Justice Mahon declared in his findings. "It was popularly supposed, for example, that the aircraft was flying in cloud, and that the aircrew did not know where they were. But the Chief Inspector had not alleged that the aircraft was flying in cloud. Quite the contrary. He had said that the aircraft had been flying towards an area of impaired visibility.

"Nevertheless," the judge said, "I do not think that the Minister's decision to release the investigation report can be criticised. Nearly seven months had passed since the disaster. There had been newspaper criticism of the delay in the release of any information which might throw light on what had occurred. There were hundreds of relatives of deceased passengers who were waiting to hear some official account of what had happened. The Minister's decision to release the report was, in my opinion, correct."

The Royal Commissioner's findings wasted no time in getting to the heart of the matter:

"Whereas McMurdo Centre believed the aircraft was flying down the centre of McMurdo Sound, the DC-10 had, in fact, been flying on a course 27 miles to the east. The captain and copilot must have believed that they were flying down the broad and flat expanse of McMurdo Sound, for otherwise they would not have notified their intention of approaching McMurdo Station at 2000 feet. In addition, the aircraft had informed Mac Centre that it was flying VMC. If that was so, how did the crew fly the aircraft into the side of a 12,450ft mountain? And how did it come to be flying on a course so far distant from McMurdo Sound?"

The crew had not recognised the distant shorelines of Ross Island as Capes Bird and Tennyson, which would have warned them they were over Lewis Bay on a heading for Mt Erebus. Rather, they thought they were, respectively, Cape Bernacchi on the Antarctic mainland, and Cape Royds on Ross Island, features they would expect to see flying down McMurdo Sound (see reproduction illustrations as presented to the Commission).

The DFDR showed that the aircraft had flown on the AINS track from Cape Hallett almost the whole way down to the impact point, except when 40 nautical miles from the destination waypoint, when the captain had made two descending or-

bits. But once the second orbit was completed and the DC-10 was once more on a southerly heading, the captain armed the AINS navigation mode again.

"It was clear, beyond doubt," the judge commented, "that he had been mistaken as to where the navigation track would lead the aircraft. So here was another riddle ... why were the two pilots unaware that the navigation track would guide the DC-10 directly to Mount Erebus?

"As the inquiry developed," he continued, "the answer became readily available. Indeed, the answer had been known to the Flight Operations Division of the airline very shortly after the occurrence of the disaster had been notified. The solution to the riddle was remarkable in the extreme."

Among the documents which Captain Collins and First Officer Cassin were shown when they attended their Antarctic briefing were computer printouts of the flightplan used by previous sightseeing flights. The waypoints were standard, as the pilots knew. The co-ordinates for McMurdo were 164° 48'E and 77° 53'S. Collins noted these co-ordinates – the evidence made that plain – and later plotted them in his own atlas to establish the actual track.

"That track clearly showed it would take the aircraft down the approximate centre of McMurdo Sound towards the final waypoint near the Dailey Islands," the judge said. "When, therefore, the flight crew assembled on the morning of the flight and were handed the flightplan for November 28, 1979, extracted from the ground computer earlier that morning, and when the flight crew inserted into the computer on the aircraft the series of latitude and longitude co-ordinates on that flightplan, they believed ... they were inserting the longstanding co-ordinates always used for flights to Antarctica which they had seen at the briefing 19 days before.

"But, unknown to them, there had been an alteration in the McMurdo co-ordinates [see reproduction of the two plans] ... The figures which were changed were in respect of the longitude of the McMurdo waypoint – the longitude was changed from 164 degrees 48 minutes East to 166 degrees 58 minutes East. This had the effect of moving the destination waypoint 27 miles to the east. Instead of the flightpath taking the aircraft down the *centre* of McMurdo Sound, it would now take the aircraft on a course directly towards Ross Island. Indeed, it would take the aircraft towards a direct colli-

The wreckage of ZK-NZP, taken from the campsite on the northern slope of Mt Erebus, looking northeast towards Cape Tennyson. The coastal edge where the mountain slope meets the pack ice of Lewis Bay can be discerned, but horizon definition in the top background is doubtful.

sion with Mount Erebus so long as the aircraft was flown at any altitude less than 12,000 feet.

"The astonishing fact was then revealed that the flight crew were not told that the destination co-ordinates had been changed. The ground computer co-ordinates had been altered ... at about 1.40am on November 28, 1979. The aircraft left at about 8am with the altered co-ordinates entered into the navigation system.

"No one in the aircraft noticed that two digits had been altered among the mass of digits which represented the flightpath to McMurdo and back. The decision of Captain Collins to maintain his navigation track on the approach to McMurdo was therefore explained ...

"The omission to notify the flight crew of the change in the computer track was, of course, an appalling error. It was the originating and dominating factor behind the disaster," the judge declared.

"It is clear from the text of the investigation report that the Chief Inspector was not satisfied with the written explanation furnished to him by Air New Zealand and the Civil Aviation Division," the judge declared, "and he held that they were in breach of sundry duties which he enumerated. But he did not ascribe any of these breaches of duty as being the cause of the accident."

Why didn't Captain Collins or the other crew members sight Mt Erebus in time to take avoiding action? As the evidence unfolded, the Royal Commissioner began to appreciate that those who have not experienced

the phenomenon of whiteout could not pass judgment on what had happened.

His understanding of the complexity of the Antarctic flight was greatly assisted by a paper prepared by senior Air New Zealand pilot Captain Gordon Vette, instructor, friend, mentor to and colleague of, Captain Collins for 25 years, who knew all the crew members to be extremely able and dedicated professionals.

From his intimate knowledge of DC-10 operations, the route being flown, the voices and exchanges recorded on the CVR, and his familiarity with the personalities themselves, Vette wrote a detailed "reconstruction" of the events on the flightdeck as he believed they had developed in the minutes leading to the disaster. His paper, entitled *Flight to the Ice*, tendered as evidence at the Royal Commission, later became the core chapter of his book *Impact Erebus* (Hodder and Stoughton, 1983).

This condensed extract from Captain Vette's account describes the approach to the unrecognised slopes of Mt Erebus thus:

The two pilots and Brooks noted the altitude warning showed they were approaching 2000 feet. Collins decided there was still plenty of clearance between the aircraft and the overhanging cloud base.

At this point the aircraft had entered the confines of Lewis Bay. The western arm, Mt Bird Peninsula, was beginning to pass astern. To the crew, the flanking coastline looked exactly as they would have expected had they been flying down McMurdo Sound, 28 miles to the west.

They were just three minutes two seconds, and about 15 miles, from the point of impact.

None of the crew, and Mulgrew [in the jumpseat], could have any doubt that Mt Erebus was well masked by the thick cloud beyond the coastline, and they were happy it was passing many miles away to the left. They knew the captain would not consider turning left until they were well past the hidden hump, and under guidance of the radar.

The clean sweeping view ahead of the aircraft contrasted with the cloud build-up to the left. 'It's not too bad,' Cassin said. Collins nodded and decided he would level out at 1500 feet.

Although the two pilots and Mulgrew could feel wholly confident that what they were seeing was what they expected to see, both were becoming aware of the strong contrast in the light intensities from above to below this relatively thin canopy of cloud. Above the cloud layer they had not experienced this peculiar diffusion of the sun's rays. Now they attributed it – correctly – to reflection off the ice. The peculiar thing was that it seemed to give them more light, rather than less as they would have expected.

The trap was now closing on the unsuspecting crew. Not only had a unique set of circumstances invalidated all the careful preflight map preparation by shifting a 13,000 foot mountain in front of them without their knowledge – the layer of cloud they were so carefully avoiding was now insidiously rendering their eyes oblivious to the physical nature of the area they were flying into.

Peter Mulgrew had been looking carefully at the western edge of Ross Island. Placing the map on the pedestal, he pointed well back to the left. 'I reckon Bird's through here.'

Collins noted this, along with the terrain warning light which he cancelled simultaneously as Cassin called: 'Terrain 1500. Alt hold.' (confirming they were 1500 feet over the ice).

Collins detected a slight change in Brooks' voice as the engineer called: 'Hold on both Nav track.' He sensed his old friend was telling him that from where he was sitting he couldn't see anything because of the cockpit coaming.

Collins and Mulgrew resumed their keen surveillance of the cliffs passing to the left. They were looking towards the southernmost end of the cliff face, waiting for a glimpse of the block buildings and fuel tanks of McMurdo Station. From this position they could then make an immediate decision on whether the viewing would be worthwhile over the area. Their scanning was not being rewarded – no sign of the expected scatter of huts.

'Actually, these conditions don't look very good at all,' Collins said thoughtfully.

'No, they don't.' There was disappointment in Mulgrew's response.. He wondered whether it would be worthwhile drawing their attention to Ross Island before they turned away.

Collins turned again to his copilot. 'What's um ... have we got them on the tower?' His tone indicated he was considering abandoning the run over McMurdo.

'No, I'll try again,' Cassin said. He did not sound hopeful, noting they only had about five more miles to go before they were abeam Point Byrd [sic].

Mulgrew chipped in with a confirmatory remark. 'Looks like the edge of Ross Island there.' He was pointing to the cliffs they had been watching to the left. Now they appeared to be edging slightly towards the aircraft's track. As expected, the western coast of the island seemed to have a large hump projecting into the Sound.

Brooks noted the change in tone of the two pilots, and added his own verbal vote: 'I don't like this.' From his position, the cockpit coaming blocked all visual reference to the terrain.

Collins now made up his mind to head back. They still had no radar or VHF contact, which they should have picked up some minutes earlier, unless McMurdo had some power supply problems. There was certainly not much to photograph, except sea ice. 'We're 26 miles north – we'll have to climb out of this,' he said casually, but with regret.

But first there was another option to be weighed up. He knew he still had a lot of clear sea out over to the right over which he could turn and back-track. Cassin noticed Collins looking out to the right in an effort to gauge the distance to the mainland coastline, but the cockpit coaming was masking his view. The copilot assured him it was 'clear on the right'.

Collins was looking out to the left at the cliffs. He decided to reject the right turn, and responded: 'No, negative.' Cassin could see the clear sea ice stretching for about 25 miles across to Cape Bernacchi on the right. He reinforced the right turn option: 'No high ground if you do a 180.'

Collins was about to tell Cassin to call McMurdo on HF to report they would be climbing ahead if they could get clearance. The cloud base seemed to be higher now. It would be good sense to climb towards it at this stage. They should certainly get the radar then. The flat sea ice still stretched reassuringly ahead for miles. He was not to know the apparent increase of the cloud base above them was an illusionary effect of sector whiteout.

Suddenly the radar altimeter dropped to about 700 feet. Almost immediately, the 500 feet terrain warning light blinked on and an urgent electronic voice called: 'Whoop, whoop, pull up, pull up.'

The hands of Collins and Brooks flew almost simultaneously to the power levers. 'Go round power, please,' Collins called. Heaving hard on the control yoke, he peered through the windscreen in disbelief at the unchanging flat surface ahead.

In a calm but urgent voice Brooks called off the ground clearance: 'Five hundred feet ... four hundred feet ...'

Even in these last few seconds of their lives they did not know their eyes had been deceiving them. They must still have believed they were getting a false warning signal. There was no remark about an impending crash. Collins' command for go around power was made in a firm but unworried tone – he did not 'firewall' his engines as he would have done had he seen Erebus ahead.

Mr Justice Mahon, later able to experience these whiteout conditions in the Antarctic for himself, commented:

"So long as the view ahead from the flightdeck of an aircraft flying over snow under a solid overcast does not exhibit any rock or tree or other landmark which can offer a guide as to sloping or uneven ground, then the snow covered terrain ahead will invariably appear to be flat. Slopes and ridges will disappear. The line of vision from the flightdeck towards the horizon (if there is one) will actually portray a white even expanse which is uniformly level."

In these conditions, what the DC-10 crew would have "seen" in front of them, as they levelled out, was a vista of apparently flat snow-covered terrain stretching ahead for miles, with the overcast also extending into the distance. To them it would have appeared to be the distant stretch of ice of McMurdo Sound.

Neither of the New Zealand pilots had any experience of flying low in polar regions, and even the veteran Antarctic explorer travelling on the flightdeck was deceived.

Why did the crew not detect Mt Erebus on the aircraft's radar? Counsel for the Civil Aviation Division posed this question because the Bendix radar had both weather and mapping modes. But, when the judge went to the Avionics Division of the Bendix Corporation in Florida, he learnt that radar returns from rock covered with ice and snow (particularly powdered snow) can be unreliable. Even if the crew had switched to mapping mode (which, at this late stage of their assumed approach to McMurdo, was unlikely), they would not have had a useful radar return.

What about the DC-10's low altitude? The judge took the view that there was no danger in flying at 1500 feet over flat terrain in clear weather – it was higher than the Minimum Safe Altitude prescribed by Regulation 28 of the New Zealand Civil Aviation Regulations.

In practice, the 16,000 foot MSA, with a permitted VMC descent to 6000 feet to the south of McMurdo to allow sightseeing over the ice shelf, had not been observed by Antarctic flights in the two years prior to this one. They were in any case "misconceived", with "no relation to the realities", the judge said. Captain Collins had been briefed to accept the US Navy controller's clearance to any altitude, which in this case was 1500 feet. In the judge's view there was no unauthorised flying at any time.

The Civil Aviation Division came in for the Royal Commissioner's criticism on other counts:
• It had not insisted that pilots-in-command of Air New Zealand Antarctic flights have previous Antarctic experience: "Had Captain Collins flown to Antarctica on a previous occasion, it is very probable that this disaster would not have occurred."
• It had not ensured that pilots-in-command were provided with topographic maps at despatch briefings on which the programmed flightpath of the aircraft had been plotted. This, with Collins' lack of Antarctic experience, had contributed to the disaster.

The judge's view was put into words by one of two counsel assisting the Commission, Mr W D Baragwanath: "While the accident had no single cause, the series of factors giving rise to the accident are [sic] overwhelmingly due to the absence of an adequate company organisation."

While Air New Zealand sought to portray the pilots as the focal point for blame, evidence brought to light during the Commission on the quite incredible measures taken by its staff after the disaster could only be regarded as a condemnation of the airline.

The Flight Operations office realised immediately what had happened for, as soon as the aircraft was reported overdue, printouts of the flightplan for the actual flight and that used at the briefing 19 days beforehand were embargoed. The dismaying truth was plain to Flight Operations staff as soon as McMurdo Centre had signalled the crash site co-ordinates. "And, in particular, it had been reported to the Chief Executive of Air New Zealand, Mr M R Davis," the Royal Commissioner declared.

"The Chief Executive at once saw what would happen if the story of the changed co-ordinates became public – it would generate some of the worst publicity to which an airline had ever been exposed. His reaction was immediate. He determined that no word of this incredible and disastrous blunder was to become public, directing that all documents relating to Antarctic flights – and to this flight in particular – were to be collected and impounded. All those not directly relevant were to be destroyed, while the remainder were to be put on one single file which would remain in strict custody.

"The Chief Executive ... contended that his instructions were that only copies of existing documents were to be destroyed. He said he did not want any surplus document to remain at large in case its contents were released to the news media by some employee of the airline ... He denied any sinister intent ..."

Counsel for the Airline Pilots' Association regarded Mr Davis's explanation with scepticism, if not disbelief. On January 1, 1980, Mr Davis had denied a press report that the destination co-ordinates had been changed without the crew being told, and that this was the main cause of the crash. Mr Davis "asserted that when the aircraft left Auckland, the correct co-ordinates had been inserted into the computer system of the aircraft," the Association's counsel pointed out. "This was in fact true. But the Chief Executive did not divulge the further fact that these co-ordinates had been changed at the last minute without the crew having been told."

Why did Chief Inspector Chippindale not see the changed co-ordinates as the root cause of the problem? Though there was reference to it in his report, the Royal Commissioner said he "did not make it clear that the computer flightpath had been altered before the flight, and that the alteration had not been notified to the aircrew.

"Had that fact been disclosed in the Chief Inspector's report," the judge continued, "then publicity attending the report would undoubtedly have been differently aligned. Instead of headlines featuring only allegations of pilot error, they might well have been dominated by the disclosure that the aircraft had been programmed to fly on a collision course with Mount Erebus, and that the crew had not been told of the change... The news blackout imposed by the Chief Executive was very successful. It was not until the hearings of the Commission that the real magnitude of the mistake was publicly revealed."

The judge said the airline's executive pilots gave one story to the Commission and the non-executive pilots another, the former offering various "ingenious" theories as to how Captain Collins and First Officer Cassin could have sensed the mistake. The non-executive pilots and their Association argued that pilots should be able to trust the printout of the navigation track provided to them.

The judge commented: "So in the end the situation before the Commission developed into something like a union confrontation. The tactics of the management were to nullify, if they could, the effect of the altered co-ordinates as being a factor in the disaster. Consequently the conduct of the dead captain and his

When Mr Justice Mahon, in the course of his Inquiry, visited Antarctica on the first anniversary of the accident, he could not have expected so effective a demonstration of the deception that trapped the crew of ZK-NZP. As his RNZAF Hercules approached McMurdo Sound in clear conditions, the crew, with ATC compliance, diverted left to retrace the final flightpath of ZK-NZP, before breaking away at 1500 feet, about 20 seconds from impact. But the following day, as his Iroquois helicopter repeated the approach to the crash site for touchdown on the ice, sea fog from the pack ice below, and a layer of stratus cloud above, effectively "sandwiched" the Iroquois, though technically its crew "remained visual". This sequence of photos, taken at 30 second intervals during the Iroquois' approach, shows Mt Erebus totally disappearing in sector whiteout!

crew was attacked on every conceivable ground. The ALPA witnesses, in their turn, defended the dead air crew and would not accept that Captain Collins or his crew had committed any error. In this atmosphere, the disappearance through the company's shredder of unknown numbers of documents was a matter to which I was required to give very serious consideration."

He continued: "There was at least one group of documents which certainly were in the possession of the airline as from the day following the disaster, and which have never been seen since ... the flight briefing documents of First officer Cassin. Whereas Captain Collins and First Officer Lucas (who was to fly as spare pilot) brought their briefing documents to the airport on the morning of the flight and took them on the aircraft, it is known ... that First Officer Cassin left his briefing documents at home. They were recovered from his home the day after the disaster by an employee of the airline ... They have never been seen since.

"If the explanation of the Chief Executive is to be accepted, then in the opinion of someone, the briefing documents of First Officer Cassin were thought to be irrelevant to the disaster. Their view would certainly not have been shared by the Chief Inspector, nor is it shared by me. Seeing that the vital question was the extent to which the flight crew had relied upon the original co-ordinates produced at the briefing, it would be of prime importance to see what briefing documents had been in the possession of First Officer Cassin ...

"This was, at the time, the fourth worst disaster in aviation history, and it follows that this direction on the part of the Chief Executive for the destruction of 'irrelevant documents' was one of the most remarkable executive decisions ever to have been made in the corporate affairs of a large New Zealand company."

The Royal Commissioner's findings devoted considerable space to why there had been an error in the original flightplan. He then observed there was an almost total lack of records regarding navigational decisions on computer programming for Antarctic flights between October 1977 and November 1979:

"There is not one memorandum from the Flight Operations Division to the Navigation Section giving instructions for any change, nor is there any written report from the Navigation Section notifying Flight Operations of changes which had been made.

"It was very clearly this absence of written memoranda and settled interdepartmental communications which was responsible for the failure to notify Captain Collins that the destination waypoint on his flightplan had been changed."

The judge's view of the airline's attempts to explain these inadequacies left no room for doubt: "In my opinion, this explanation that the change in the waypoint was thought to be minimal in terms of distance, is a concocted story designed to explain away the fundamental mistake, made by someone, in failing to ensure that Captain Collins was notified ..."

When the Chief Executive was called as a witness, the judge heard that "he controlled the airline on a verbal basis."

"When he communicated with a senior executive officer such as the Director of Flight Operations, then any instructions he gave or any decisions he made were verbally communicated, and no memorandum was drawn up recording any such decision ...

"I said to the Chief Executive that so far as I could ascertain, he had never supplied his board of directors with a report concerning this disaster ... the Chief Executive agreed that this was so, but said that he was in touch from time to time with the Chairman of the Board by telephone. It seemed to me an extraordinary thing ...

"I can only summarise ... by expressing my considerable concern at the haphazard and informal manner in which the Flight Operations Division was conducted in relation to these Antarctic flights."

In regard to this aspect of the airline's *modus operandi*, the Civil Aviation Division did not escape some censure:

"It seems as if the Division adopted as its controlling policy the opinion that the operational proposals of Air New Zealand would always be satisfactory and did not require scrutiny ...

"One of the reasons for the continuation of the loose system of administrative control within the Flight Operations Division might well have been the failure of the [Civil Aviation] inspectors to examine in detail the proposals made to it in regard to this very unusual and unscheduled series of flights. It is even possible that the sheer size of the airline has come to overshadow and dominate the personnel of the Division."

But it was at the airline that the Royal Commissioner aimed his strongest criticism during his summing up:

"... in looking into the communica-

tion lapses which led to the disastrous mistake over the co-ordinates, I have been confronted at every turn with the vague recollections of everyone concerned, unsupported by the slightest vestige of any system of recorded communication ... it was this communications breakdown which in turn amounted to a systems breakdown, which is the true cause of the disaster."

There was more in particular for its Chief Executive:

"There is no doubt that the Chief Executive, shortly after the occurrence of the disaster, adopted the fixed opinion that the flight crew were alone to blame, and that the administrative and operational systems of the airline were nowhere at fault. I have been forced to the opinion that such an attitude, emanating from this very able but evidently autocratic Chief Executive, controlled the ultimate course adopted by witnesses called on behalf of the airline."

The judge concluded his summing up with a vituperative broadside that rang around the world and has since passed into history:

"The palpably false sections of evidence which I heard could not have been the result of mistake, or faulty recollection. They originated, I am compelled to say, in a predetermined plan of deception. They were very clearly part of an attempt to conceal a series of disastrous administrative blunders and so, in regard to the particular items of evidence to which I have referred, I am forced reluctantly to say that I had to listen to an orchestrated litany of lies."

The Royal Commissioner expressed the official cause of the disaster in these terms:

"In my opinion ... the single dominant and effective cause of the disaster was the mistake made by those airline officials who programmed the aircraft to fly directly at Mount Erebus and omitted to tell the aircrew. That mistake is directly attributable, not so much to the persons who made it, but to the incompetent administrative airline procedures, which made the mistake possible.

"In my opinion, neither Captain Collins nor the flight engineers made any error which contributed to the disaster, and were not responsible for its occurrence."

A final editorial comment

Notwithstanding the airline's lamentable role in the many factors that contributed to the accident, and the enormous integrity with which the Royal Commissioner went about his searching Inquiry, did his findings go too far?

Did they overlook fundamental principles of air navigation? The basic terrain-clearance philosophy of IFR flight; and the concept, inherited from generations of seafaring experience, of command responsibility? Will they pose problems of precedent that could one day have far-reaching implications?

For example, how valid can be an opinion, no matter how eminent, whose entire basis and background is essentially legal, on operational judgements made in a highly technical environment? What are we to make of a situation where a professionally qualified government authority, with statutory powers for the safe ordering of air navigation, can have its rulings overturned by legal but technically "lay" arbiters who do not carry that statutory responsibility?

Minimum Safe Altitudes are prescribed for air routes throughout the world to ensure aircraft are not put at risk by descent into areas of high terrain. Both Air New Zealand and the NZ Civil Aviation Division agreed that the MSA for the last 33nm of the route to McMurdo was 16,000 feet.

With terminal conditions at McMurdo poor, the sound navigational procedure would have been to remain at this height until within range of the McMurdo radar, checking over the last portion of the flight that the distance to run on the AINS was of the same order as the DME distance from the McMurdo TACAN.

But, the captain, having spotted a break in the cloud, decided to descend from FL180 when still some 43nm out and not yet identified on McMurdo radar. At this stage the aircraft was only some seven minutes' flying time from the destination waypoint, when the McMurdo aids could have been relied upon for a safe letdown.

The crew thus contravened the MSA requirement by undertaking a descent without corroboration of position from ground based aids. The fact that no VHF transmissions of any sort were being received from McMurdo also did not assume the relevance it might have.

Airline flight crews are constrained by regulatory requirements. If a crew member transgresses those regulations, he can expect to be disciplined. It was thus surprising that the Royal Commissioner condoned the breaking of MSA requirements on the basis of the conduct of previous Antarctic flights, and the perceived need to provide sightseeing passengers with "their money's worth".

Even so, it was the Royal Commissioner who succeeded in uncovering the unpalatable facts about the airline's internal deficiencies and conduct, evidently missed by the technical investigation, which progressively and inexorably painted this unfortunate crew into a corner.

A major, technically complex investigation of this sort, where much hangs on the exact establishment of cause (and, inevitably, the apportioning of blame) is demanding in the extreme. Because of all that is at stake, it can also be subject to subtle but real commercial influences from various "interested parties". Political motives and media pressures for "instant answers" are also brought to bear.

For all these reasons it is plain that such an investigation requires both unfettered technical expertise *and* highly ethical "outside" objectivity – of the standard provided by Mr Justice Mahon's Inquiry – if it is to arrive at the unbiased truth.

But could the Royal Commissioner's findings in this particular case mean that the airline industry might eventually come to the point where the whole basis of command responsibility, as it has been traditionally understood, becomes outmoded? If so, who will then hold the ultimate responsibility for the safe conduct of an airline flight?

In an age when increasingly computerised operational technology is being imposed on the world airline industry – not without serious reservations in some cases – these questions still await answers.

The plain and obvious cause of this massive air crash originated from the concurrent effects of two different factors, the existence of which were not even for one moment suspected by the aircrew.

One was the unannounced alteration to the flight track of the aircraft; the other was the presence of a classic clear air whiteout illusion as the aircraft approached the mountain.

Without the flight track alteration, the whiteout in Lewis Bay would have been of no consequence. The DC-10 would not have been in Lewis Bay.

But even with the flight track alteration, a cloudless sky would have nullified its effect. The aircraft would have approached Lewis Bay with the mountain ahead standing high in its path and the aircrew would have seen, at a range of not less than 100 miles, that they were flying on a computer flightpath widely divergent from the track which was plotted on the map which they had before them.

Without the precise co-ordination in space and time of these two factors, there could have been no disaster.

By a navigational error for which the aircrew was not responsible and about which they were uninformed, an aircraft had flown not into McMurdo Sound but into Lewis Bay, and there the elements of nature had combined, at a fatal coincidence of time and place, to translate an administrative blunder in Auckland into an awesome disaster in Antarctica.

Much has been written and said about the weather hazards of Antarctica, and how they may combine to create a spectacular but hostile terrain, but for my purposes the most definitive illustration of these hidden perils was the wreckage which lay on the mountainside, showing how the forces of nature, if given the chance, can sometimes defeat the flawless technology of man.

For the ultimate key to the tragedy lay here, in the white silence of Lewis Bay, the place to which the airliner had been unerringly guided by its micro electronic navigation system, only to be destroyed, in clear air and without warning, by a malevolent trick of the polar light.

- The late, former Mr Justice, Peter Mahon, "Verdict on Erebus"

CHAPTER 6

"We're going down, Larry!"

– First Officer to Captain

Air Florida Boeing 737-222 N62AF [19556] (F/n 62)
– January 13, 1982

A small, congested midcity airport, freezing conditions in a snowstorm, dense traffic movements, and delays occasioned by temporary closure of the runway, all contributed to the buildup of psychological pressures that were to fatally tax the judgement of a young and relatively inexperienced airline crew.

Departure from Washington DC

January 13, 1982 was a bleak, intensely cold winter's day. Snow was falling and by early afternoon the temperature was only minus five degrees Celsius. With an icy wind from the northeast at 10 knots, the cloud ceiling was less than 400 feet, with visibility was varying between 700 and 1500 metres in snow showers.

Among many aircraft scheduled to fly out of Washington's riverside National Airport that afternoon was Air Florida's Flight 90 – callsign Palm 90 – a Boeing 737 service bound for more equitable southern climes in far off Fort Lauderdale, Florida.

Crewed by Captain Larry Wheaton and First Officer Roger Pettit, two young pilots who had accumulated all their airline experience with the company during the rapid expansion it had experienced as a result of deregulation, the 200 Series Boeing 737 was due to depart at 2.15pm.

But just before 1.40pm, all departures were delayed when a heavy snowfall forced controllers to close the airport. Snowploughs went to work to clear Runway 36, the only instrument runway, of accumulated snow, and it was expected that the airport would reopen at about 2.30pm.

In the meantime, as outbound flights queued to depart, the apron and taxiway areas became increasingly congested.

Washington's National Airport is built on a relatively narrow sand spit on the Virginia side of the Potomac River, immediately to the southeast of the Pentagon building and only 3km south of the White House and the nearby tall Washington Monument (see map). The river in fact provides the noise abatement route for aircraft flying out of this unavoidably cramped airport in the heart of the nation's capital.

At the best of times, the airport's crowded apron, in combination with its short, tight taxiways, limits its ability to cope with high density traffic. In extreme winter weather however, traffic conditions around the cluttered terminal can become chaotic as aircraft wait to be de-iced as late as possible prior to departure. This was the situation on the afternoon of January 13, aggravated even further by delayed flights anxious for a start clearance as soon as the airport re-opened. Meanwhile, having been snowploughed, the runway surface was being swept and sanded.

While waiting, Air Florida's Flight 90 was opened for boarding, and by 2.30pm the aircraft's three flight attendants had shown all 74 passengers to their seats. Meanwhile Captain Wheaton requested that his aircraft be de-iced so that, as soon as a taxi clearance was available, the Boeing 737 could join the departure queue without delay.

The de-icing procedure, to remove ice and snow accumulated on the aircraft while waiting on the ground in subzero temperatures, involves spraying it with a heated solution of 35% glycol and 65% water carried aboard a tank wagon.

About 2.20pm, by which time the Boeing 737 was covered by about 12mm of wet snow, a de-icing tanker drove up to the aircraft and the operator began de-icing the port side of the fuselage. He had covered only a small area when the flight crew received word that there would be a further delay – the airport was not going to be ready by 2.30pm after all. Captain Wheaton also learned that 11 other aircraft had departure priority ahead of his Boeing 737, and that five or six of these would need to depart before the Air Florida flight could even push back from the gate. Wheaton therefore told the de-

Fourth of a batch of seven Model 2T4Adv 737s for Air Florida, N54AF [22055] was accepted from Boeing in January 1980. The blue-over-green livery on the 737s (and later, briefly, on DC-10s and 727-200s) replaced the similarly-styled orange-over-blue colours on Air Florida's DC-9-15s, the airline's first jet equipment. By 1982, the one-time intrastate carrier, in addition to its 14-point Florida network, was serving five other mainland US cities, a dozen ports in the Caribbean and Central America, and, with its leased DC-10s, four European centres.

icing operator to discontinue the work for the time being.

Half an hour later, with the reopening of the airport now imminent, Captain Wheaton requested the de-icing be resumed. It was now snowing heavily but, starting again on the port side, the operator began spraying from the nose rearwards, progressively treating the wing, engine pylon and nacelle, the fuselage, and finally the tail section. A second operator then took over, de-icing the starboard side of the aircraft. No covers or plugs were used during the operation. By the time the work was finished at 3.10pm, there was nearly eight centimetres of snow on the ground.

The Air Florida leadership of former Braniff president Ed Acker, as much as President Carter's Deregulation Act of October 24, 1978, provided the driving force for the Panhandle State airline's rapid expansion. Washington National Airport was in fact Air Florida's first interstate destination, the inaugural service being flown on December 14, 1978, less than six weeks after CAB approval. By Easter 1979, Air Florida had displaced National Airlines as the third largest operator on southern routes from the national capital. Air Florida's 737 fleet (16 plus of a variety of models) was rarely static as cross-leasing deals with such European charter operators as Air Europe and Transavia took advantage of each other's seasonal traffic peaks. In this Gatwick view, N54AF and G-BMSM [22279] wear each other's titles.

Five minutes later, as Air Florida's Washington station manager was about to close the Boeing 737's forward main door and retract the airbridge, Captain Wheaton, in the command seat, asked how much snow was on the aircraft. The station manager said he could see a "light dusting" of snow on the port wing between the engine and the wingtip. Snow was still falling quite heavily.

With a tug now standing by to push the Boeing 737 back from Gate 12, the crew transmitted to Ground Control: "Ground, – Palm 90. We'd like to get in sequence – we're ready."

Ground Control: "Are you ready to push?"

Palm 90: "Affirmative,"

Ground Control: "OK – push approved. [pause] Better still, just hold it right where you are – I'll call you back." But it was not until seven minutes later, at 3.23pm, that Ground again transmitted: "OK, Palm 90, push approved."

The tug, which was not equipped with chains, then attempted to push the aircraft back, but the combination of ice, snow, and glycol on the slightly inclined apron only resulted in wheelspin.

The crew, in contact with the tug driver, then suggested they use reverse engine thrust to push the aircraft back. Although the driver pointed out this was contrary to policy, the crew then started the aircraft's engines and deployed both reversers. Seeing what they intended to do, the driver cautioned them to "use only idle power".

Both engines were then run in reverse thrust for about a minute and a

(opposite) The top portion of the map positions the District of Columbia against the Maryland-Virginia countryside straddling the Potomac River. The enlargement shows the location of National Airport, nearby landmarks, and the Air Florida Boeing 737's fatal, half-minute flight. National Airport has served the capital since June 1941 and its convenience, despite noise and traffic limitations and the lack of space, made something of a mockery of the "showcase" Dulles International Airport after the latter opened in November 1962. Dulles, two-thirds the area of Manhattan with three 3km runways (see inset, top left), lacked nothing except the appeal of its location – 43km northwest of the city. Even as late as 1981, National Airport continued to handle 14.2 million passengers annually – nearly seven times that at Dulles! (Matthew Tesch)

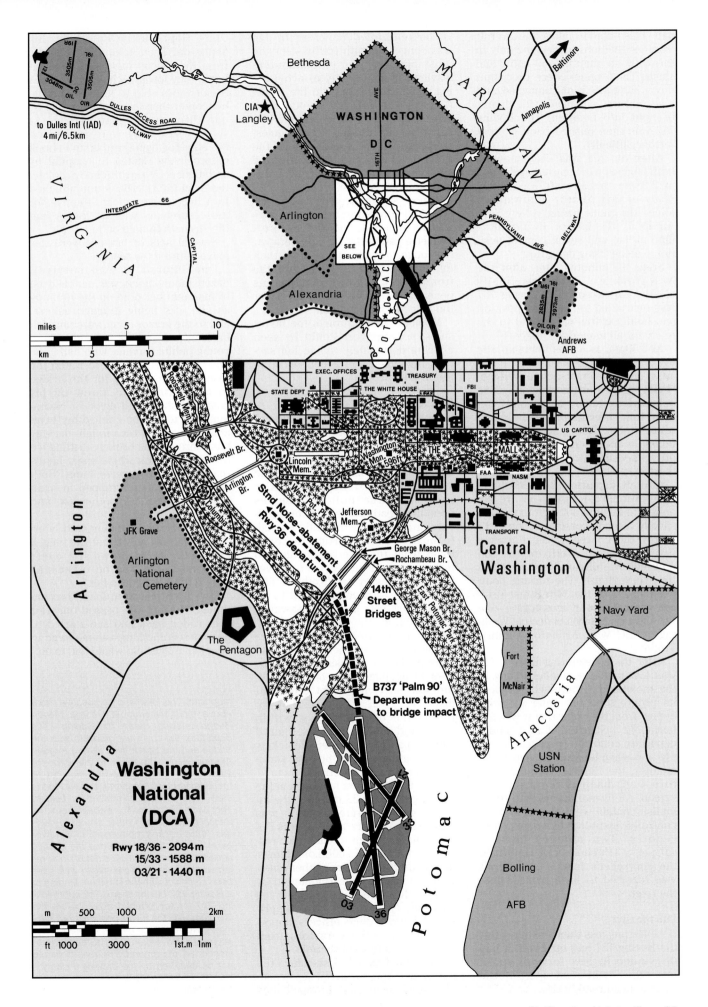

Bethesda

MARYLAND

Baltimore

CIA Langley

WASHINGTON
D C

Annapolis

to Dulles Intl (IAD)
4 mi/6.5km

DULLES ACCESS ROAD & TOLLWAY

V I R G I N I A

INTERSTATE 66

CAPITAL

Arlington

PENNSYLVANIA AVE

BELTWAY

SEE BELOW

Alexandria

P O T O M A C

Andrews AFB

miles   5   10

km   5   10

Roosevelt Mem.

EXEC. OFFICES

TREASURY

STATE DEPT

THE WHITE HOUSE

FBI

Arlington

Roosevelt Br.

Arlington Br.

West Pot. Pk.

Columbia

Lincoln Mem.

Washington Mon. 596ft

THE
MALL

US Capitol

FAA

NASM

JFK Grave

Stnd Noise abatement
Rwy 36 departures

Jefferson Mem.

George Mason Br.
Rochambeau Br.

Central
Washington

Arlington
National
Cemetery

TRANSPORT

East Potomac Park

Navy Yard

14th
Street
Bridges

The Pentagon

Anacostia

Fort
McNair

B737 'Palm 90'
Departure track
to bridge impact

USN
Station

Washington
National
(DCA)

Rwy 18/36 - 2094 m
15/33 - 1588 m
03/21 - 1440 m

A l e x a n d r i a

P o t o m a c

Bolling
AFB

m   500   1000   2km

ft   1000   3000   1st.m 1nm

half. This failed to budge the aircraft from its position, succeeding only in throwing up quantities of snow and slush. The engines were then shut down, the tug was disconnected, and a second tug, equipped with chains, brought into position. The Boeing 737 was then pushed back without further difficulty.

After the tug was disconnected, both engines were started again, and at 3.38pm the aircraft was finally ready to taxi. Shortly afterwards it joined the queue behind a New York Air DC-9, the last of 16 aircraft – nine airline and seven general aviation – all awaiting departure.

Some 15 minutes later, after the New York Air DC-9 was finally cleared for takeoff, the Boeing 737 was instructed to "taxi into position and hold" on Runway 36 and to "be ready for an immediate [takeoff]".

At 3.59pm, as it was lining up, the tower transmitted its takeoff clearance and the crew acknowledged: "Palm 90 cleared for takeoff." This acknowledgement, 14 seconds before 4pm, was to prove their last transmission. Heavy snow was still falling as the Boeing began its takeoff, with visibility now limited to less than 500 metres.

Aircraft departing from Washington National's Runway 36 are required to begin a 40° turn to the left shortly after becoming airborne, to follow the course of the Potomac River and avoid overflying the 596 foot high Washington Monument and the White House. The turning point coincides with the 14th Street Bridges (actually four crossings – one rail and three road) connecting Washington DC with Arlington County, Virginia.

After the accelerating Boeing 737 was lost to the controller's view in the snowfall, he continued to follow its progress on his radar monitor. Seeing from the radar that it was airborne, he instructed it to "contact departure control". There was no reply, and when he again looked at the monitor, the Boeing 737's radar return had disappeared from the screen. All further attempts to re-establish contact were in vain and the controller instituted emergency procedures. Two minutes later at 4.03pm, a telephone call confirmed the controller's fears – an aircraft was reported to have plunged into the river.

Into the river

At 4:01pm, less than a minute after the Boeing 737 had taken off, it had descended at low forward speed into the northbound span of the Rochambeau road bridge.

The reinforced concrete bridge was congested with traffic – for the most part by cars of commuters leaving for home early to avoid being caught in the dark in the snowfall. As the aircraft descended, obviously in a stalled condition, in a steep noseup attitude, the engines, starboard wing, the underside of the rear fuselage and the tailplane struck six slow moving cars and a mobile crane vehicle.

Almost simultaneously, as the aircraft slid across the bridge carriageway, its underside and engines tore a 30 metre gap in the far side parapet. No longer flying, the aircraft then fell nosedown off the bridge into the frozen Potomac River, disappearing beneath the surface ice except for the rear fuselage and tail.

Moments later, through the heavy snow, six survivors could be seen clinging desperately to the tail section, immersed up to their necks in the frigid water.

Rescue operations

Within five minutes, all neighbouring police and fire services were responding to the emergency. But none were equipped to perform a rescue on the frozen river. While the surface ice was sufficiently thick to prevent water police launches breaking a path through to the survivors, it was not nearly solid enough to enable shore parties to reach them from the riverbank only 100 metres away. Firemen on the river bank tried desperately to throw lifelines to the survivors, but all to no avail – they were just too far away.

Meanwhile, the survivors floundering in the freezing water were losing the use of their hands, and were in danger of losing consciousness. Struggling to stay alive herself, the sole surviving flight attendant displayed great selflessness by inflating the only lifejacket within reach and giving it to an injured woman passenger. Other lifejackets were floating nearby, but the survivors were unable to retrieve them.

After the survivors had been in the freezing river for 22 minutes, the increasingly desperate situation was relieved by the arrival of a Parks Police helicopter. Not intended for rescue work, the Bell 206L LongRanger had neither a winch nor other emergency lifesaving gear. Undaunted by this or the hazardous visual flying weather, its crew of two experienced Parks Police officers improvised to save the survivors from certain death by hypothermia.

While pilot Donald Usher hovered low above the survivors, crewman Melvin Windsor first dropped any-

thing floatable he could lay his hands on. Then, taking the lifelines from the rescue party on the riverbank, they lowered the looped ropes to survivors able to grab them. The helicopter then dragged them one by one through the shattered ice to shore where they were treated on the spot for hypothermia and shock before being rushed to hospital by ambulance. A ring lifebuoy, collected from the riverbank and attached to a line, proved most effective for those survivors who no longer had the strength to hold on to a rope.

Several acts of bravery were displayed during the rescue.

One injured woman survivor, dazed and in shock, was unable even to maintain her hold on the lifebuoy as she was being dragged ashore, and to the horror of all watching, fell back into the water. Immediately, a young public servant, who had gone down to the river bank to watch the rescue while waiting for the bridge to reopen to traffic, threw off his coat and shoes and dived in. Swimming out to her, he cradled her head above the water, then fought his way back through the broken, drifting ice to the river bank where eager hands reached out to receive them. Both were immediately wrapped in blankets, treated for hypothermia, and rushed to hospital.

The young man commented later: "When she let go of that life ring, I knew she would drown if I didn't jump in. There was no other way they could have got to her."

"Her body just went limp," he continued. "I think she passed out. Her eyes rolled back and she started to go under. Something told me to go in after her ... I just did what I had to do."

(opposite) This dramatic perspective, from above the northernmost George Mason Bridge crossing, details the Boeing 737's departure, flightpath and impacts with the bridge and the frozen river. Having forgone the opportunities to return to the apron for a further de-ice during the long, slow taxi to the holding point (top right), the Air Florida crew were virtually committed to takeoff. The pace of the traffic, evident from the transcript (tower and other aircraft in capitals, intra-cockpit conversation in lower case) was such that, even had the captain acceded to his first officer's doubts and rejected the takeoff, there might well have been a conflict with the imminent landing of a Boeing 727 behind them. The approaching 727 in fact touched down before the 737 lifted off, the tower controller not having foreseen that the under-powered, snow encrusted 737 would take 45 seconds to stagger off the ground. The reader should not be deceived by the drawing's clarity – visibility at the time was less than 500 metres in falling snow. (Matthew Tesch)

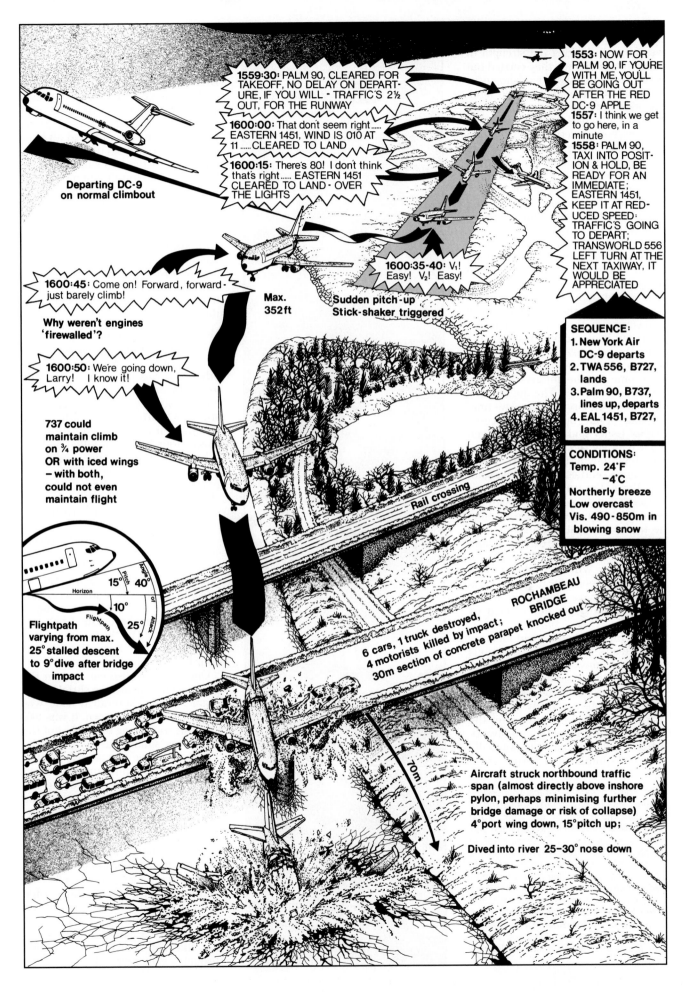

The helicopter crew were also risking their lives. To save another woman, also lacking the strength to hold on to a lifeline, they carried out an extremely dangerous manoeuvre. While Pilot Usher dipped one landing skid into the river, Crewman Windsor climbed out of the cabin and, without safety harness, stood on the skid to physically pull her out of the water. The helicopter then gently deposited her at the door of an ambulance waiting on the bank.

One of the six survivors of the crash forfeited his own life to ensure others were rescued. When the helicopter first dropped a line to him, he placed it around one of the women in the water so that she could be dragged to safety. And each time the line was dropped back to him, he passed it to another. After the other five survivors, three women and two men, had been plucked from the icy river, the helicopter returned to pick him up. But it was too late – finally overcome by the intense cold, he had disappeared. The helicopter crew went on circling for some time looking for him, but without success.

Pilot Usher said he had never seen such courage, not even in Vietnam, where he flew in combat. "He could have gone on the first trip," he said. "We threw the ring to him first, but he passed it to somebody else. We went back five times and each time he kept passing it to someone else. He is the real hero of this whole thing."

Crewman Windsor added: "If I could have seen him under the water, I would have plunged in myself to try to pull him out – dead or alive."

Both officers had a vivid memory of the man's face and were anxious to at least know who he was. Ironically, although the bodies of all the victims were eventually recovered, he could not be positively identified. It was not until 18 months after the accident that a Coast Guard investigation finally concluded he was a 46-year-old bank inspector from

(right) This montage of photos, snapped by an alert spectator, captures something of the desperate efforts by the crew of the Parks Police LongRanger to pluck the survivors from the freezing Potomac River. In the top view, as Crewman Windsor pulls a woman victim on to the starboard skid, Pilot Usher actually has the helicopter's port skid immersed in the icy water. That there were any survivors at all may be attributed to the determination of the helicopter crew, as much as to the Boeing's nose-high, stalled configuration and "pancake" impact with the bridge, which fractured the rear fuselage.

Atlanta. His mother was subsequently awarded the Coast Guard's Gold Lifesaving Medal by President Reagan at a ceremony at the White House.

The five passengers and one flight attendant who, out of the total of 79 people on board, escaped going down with the aircraft, had all been seated in the rear section of the fuselage. One of the two surviving men, boarding the aircraft late because he was parking his car, said afterwards that he took a seat "as far back as you could go." Although a senior colleague, travelling on the same flight with six other of his associates, invited him to join them in the forward section of the cabin, he declined. It was not until after being rescued that he learned all seven had died in the accident.

Meanwhile on the bridge ...

While the rescue drama was being played out on the Potomac River, another one was unfolding in the falling snow on the bridge itself. Of the motorists unfortunate enough to be stuck in traffic in the path of the Boeing as it clawed the air for flying speed, four had been killed and another four injured, one seriously. Screams had been heard above the roaring of the engines and the spine chilling sounds of impact as the near stationary vehicles were crushed by the descending aircraft.

"Some of the cars were flattened, some were without roofs, others were spun around," said the police officer in charge of the rescue. "It looked like the plane just sliced the top off the cars." Rescuers trying to free bodies in the crushed vehicles were frustrated by the fact that some of the cars had been flattened to door level.

One driver whose car was on the bridge said: "I heard the shrieking jet engines ... the [aircraft's] nose was up and the tail was down. It was like the pilot was trying to climb, but the plane was sinking fast ... I saw the tail of the plane tear across the top of the cars, smashing some tops and ripping off others ... Once the tail was across the bridge, the plane seemed to continue sinking very fast ... (and) ... hit the water intact in a combination sinking, ploughing action. I saw the cockpit go under the ice. I got the impression it was skimming under the ice and water."

Another witness on the bridge said: "It went down under the water, nose first. When it hit the ice, it sounded like a pane of glass breaking – like a big rock had been thrown through a giant piece of glass."

INVESTIGATION

Another witness who saw the aircraft's final plunge said the tail section fractured just forward of the rear doors "as if someone had cracked an egg on the side of a dish."

The aptness of his description became clear in the days that followed, after cranes had lifted major sections of the aircraft's wreckage from the river. When laid out as a "reconstruction" on the floor of the Coast Guard hangar at National Airport, National Transportation Safety Board investigators saw that the Boeing 737 had actually begun breaking up before it left the bridge. On impact with the river, the floor of the cabin had collapsed, flinging the occupants, still strapped in their seats, towards the front of the telescoping fuselage.

Deceleration forces far exceeded any requirements for crash restraint that could be imposed on aircraft manufacturers. Postmortem examination of the recovered bodies showed that only 25 had died from drowning, the seat and floor failure accounting for the instantaneous death of the majority. The six survivors of the impact itself had all been seated in the tail section – the part most likely to remain intact in a catastrophic accident – and escaped through the break in the fuselage.

Other ground witnesses, located between the airport and the bridge, enabled investigators to reconstruct the aircraft's flightpath from the start of its takeoff to the point of impact. The fact that witnesses could see it throughout its fatally brief flight meant that the Boeing 737 had not climbed through the low cloud ceiling.

After interviewing more than 200 witnesses, investigators found general agreement that the aircraft was at an unusually low altitude in a noseup attitude of 30° to 40° before it hit the bridge. Four people in one car on the bridge claimed that large sheets of ice fell from the aircraft on to their vehicle.

Crews of other aircraft departing or arriving while the Air Florida Boeing was taxiing for takeoff saw snow or ice on its wings, some of them describing it as "unusually heavy". One crew, taxiing parallel with but in the opposite direction to the Boeing 737, even discussed the amount of snow on its fuselage. That captain had commented: "Look at the junk on that airplane ..." Almost the entire length of the fuselage "had a mottled area of snow and what appeared to be ice ... along the upper part of the fuselage above the cabin

windows ..." The captain could hardly have been deceived, even in the blowing snow and wintry twilight – the snow and ice would contrast vividly with Air Florida's distinctive blue and green fuselage livery.

None of the airport witnesses could identify the point at which the aircraft lifted off because of the restricted visibility, but said it was beyond the intersection of Runways 15 and 36, and that the aircraft's rate of climb was slow as it left the runway.

Ice on the wings could have been partly responsible for the aircraft's failure to remain airborne. But it certainly did not explain the low rate of acceleration during the takeoff. Had the conditions affected the performance of the engines as well?

An answer to this question had to wait until divers located the aircraft's Flight Data Recorder (FDR) and Cockpit Voice Recorder (CVR) amongst the fragmented wreckage on the river bed.

Flight recorders

A total of 82 divers, trained to work in icy waters, were brought to Washington DC from various Navy, Army, and Coast Guard units to conduct the salvage operations. Underwater visibility was only 20cm and the divers had to search for the FDR and CVR using acoustic equipment designed to home in on signals emitted by the recorders. Both recorders were recovered from the river seven days after the crash.

The Fairchild FDR and Sundstrand CVR were only superficially damaged and both were successfully read out.

The FDR showed a gentle rise in the altitude trace, beginning from aircraft rotation at 4.00.31pm. After an initial increase in speed to 147 knots, the aircraft climbed at decreasing airspeed. Fifteen seconds after liftoff, the altitude was 240 feet, but the speed had decreased to 144 knots. During the next seven seconds, the aircraft reached its maximum altitude of 352 feet as the airspeed decreased further to 130 knots, while its heading changed seven degrees to the left. The heading continued to diverge to the left, reaching 354° when the recording ended 7.2 seconds later.

The CVR revealed that, while completing the after start checklist, the captain had responded "off" to the first officer's call for "anti-ice". The enunciation of the word "off" was far from clear, but it seemed possible that the crew had failed to turn on the engine anti-ice system.

The CVR also showed that, during their long wait for takeoff, the cap-

tain and first officer's conversation returned again and again to the subject of ice accumulation on the aircraft. This edited portion of the CVR transcript begins at 3.39pm, soon after the Boeing 737 joined the queue of aircraft waiting to takeoff:

CAPT: (We ought to) go over to the hangar and get de-iced.

F/O: Yeah, definitely – it's been a while since we've been de-iced.

CAPT [tongue in cheek]: I think I'll go home and play ...

F/O: That Citation over there – he's ankle deep in it. (Laughter)

F/O: Hello, Donna.

FLIGHT ATTENDANT [entering flightdeck]: I love it out here!

F/O: It's fun!

FLT ATT: I love it – look at all those neat tyre tracks in the snow ...

F/O: See that Citation over there – looks like he's up to his knees in it.

As the long queue of aircraft continued to move slowly towards the runway holding point, Captain Wheaton positioned the Boeing 737 close behind the DC-9 in front of them in an attempt to use the heat from its tail-mounted engines to remove snow and slush from the Boeing's wings.

14 min to takeoff

CAPT: Tell you what – my windshield will be de-iced; don't know about my wing.

F/O: Well, all we really need is the inside of the wings anyway, the wingtips are gonna ... shuck all that other stuff ...

CAPT: Get your wing now. [A reference to the effect of the jet efflux of the DC-9's engines on the Boeing's starboard wing.]

F/O: Did they get yours? Can you see your wingtip over there?

CAPT: I got a little on mine.

F/O: A little! This one's got about a quarter to half an inch on it all the way ... [now speaking of another aircraft that had just landed]: Look how that ice is just hanging on his back ... see that? It's impressive that these big old planes get in here with the weather this bad ...

11 min to takeoff

F/O: [referring to centre panel engine instruments] See the difference in that left engine and right one?

CAPT: Yeah.

F/O: Don't know why it's different ... unless it's his hot air going into that right one. That must be it – from his exhaust. It was doing that on the chocks awhile ago, but ah ...

GROUND CONTROL: OK, Palm 90 – cross Runway 03 if there's space – then monitor the tower on 119.1 – don't call him, he'll call you.

F/O: Palm 90.

F/O: I'm certainly glad there's people taxiing on the same place I want to go, 'cause I can't see the runway – taxiway ...

F/O [referring again to engine instruments]: This thing's settled down a little bit – might'a been his hot air going over it.

TOWER: Now for Palm 90 – if you're with me, you'll be going out after the red DC-9 Apple [New York Air DC-9].

F/O: Palm 90.

7 min to takeoff

F/O: Boy, this is a losing battle here on trying to de-ice those things. It gives you a false feeling of security, that's all that does.

CAPT: That – ah, satisfies the Feds [FAA requirements]!

As the Boeing 737 edged further ahead on the taxiway until almost next in line for the runway holding point, the pilots prepared to go through the pre-takeoff check list.

2 min to takeoff

F/O: I think we get to go here in a minute ... EPR all the way to 2.04, indicated airspeed bugs are 138, 140, 144 [knots].

CAPT: Set!

F/O: Takeoff briefing: Air Florida standard. Slushy runway – do you want me to do anything special for this [takeoff], or just go for it?

CAPT: Unless you got anything special you'd like to do.

F/O: Unless ... I just lift the nose wheel off early, like a soft field takeoff or something ... I'll take the nose wheel off and then we'll let it fly off ...

TOWER: Palm 90, taxi into position and hold, be ready for an immediate [takeoff].

FLT ATT [on P/A system]: Ladies and gentlemen, we have just been cleared for takeoff, flight attendants please be seated.

F/O: Bleeds?

CAPT: They're off.

F/O: Strobes, external lights?

CAPT: On.

F/O: Antiskid?

CAPT: On.

F/O: Transponder?

CAPT: On.

F/O: Takeoff [checklist] is complete.

TOWER: Palm 90 – cleared for takeoff ... no delay on departure if you will – traffic is two and a half [miles] out for the runway.

Takeoff

CAPT: Your throttles.

F/O: OK.

CAPT: Say if you need the wipers.

CAPT: It's spooled ... really cold here [a reference to instrument indications as aircraft accelerates].

F/O: Got 'em?

CAPT: Real cold ... real cold ...

F/O: God, look at that thing! That don't seem right, does it?

F/O: Ah ... that's not right.

CAPT: Yes it is – there's 80 [knots]!

F/O: No ... I don't think that's right ...

F/O: Ah, maybe it is.

CAPT: 120 [knots].

F/O: I don't know ...

CAPT: V_1!

CAPT [as aircraft suddenly becomes airborne steeply noseup]: Easy!

CAPT: V_2!

(Two seconds later, sound of stall warning stick shaker begins, continuing to impact.)

TOWER: Palm 90, contact Departures Control.

CAPT: Forward! Forward! ... Easy! We only want 500 [feet per minute – fpm]!

CAPT: Come on ... forward ... forward! ... just barely climb!

Lashings bite into the fin leading edge as the mangled empennage of the Boeing 737 is lifted clear of the Potomac River. All the recovered wreckage was taken to a US Coast Guard hangar at Washington National Airport for detailed examination. (Wide World Photos)

F/O: Larry – we're going down, Larry!

CAPT: I know it!

Sound of impact.

Engine operation

Valuable as these insights into the crew's exchanges were to the overall investigation, it was paradoxically not the flightdeck comments, but the sound of the engines that provided the vital CVR clue as to why the aircraft failed to accelerate normally.

Using a sound spectrum analyser, investigators found that the engine note during takeoff, emanating mainly from the 27 bladed, large diameter fans just inside the air intakes of the Pratt & Whitney JT8D-9 turbofan engines, registered a frequency of 3189 cycles per second (cps).

Yet, according to the Boeing Company, the fans at takeoff power should have been emitting a sound of 3545 cps. A reading of only 3189 cps indicated the thrust being developed by the engines was too low.

Why had the crew not detected this low thrust from their instrument indications?

The primary instruments used to set power on Pratt & Whitney JT8D engines are the Engine Pressure Ratio (EPR) gauges, which measure the ratio of the pressure at the engine jetpipe to that at the compressor inlet (see diagram on page 93/ – refer also to cutaway drawing of engine in Chapter 1). For the takeoff on which the accident occurred, the desired EPR setting was 2.04.

Because conditions at the time were conducive to the formation of ice on the compressor inlet pressure probe, tests were conducted to determine the effect this could have on EPR indications. The tests confirmed that an iced up probe would produce a false EPR reading, indicating a higher thrust level than that actually being developed by the engine.

A function of the engine's anti-ice system is to maintain a flow of heated air over the compressor inlet pressure probe to prevent ice formation. The wreckage examination indicated that the engine anti-ice system was off at the time of impact, a finding substantiated by the CVR

evidence that the system had not been switched on during the pre-takeoff checks.

The crew

Captain Larry Wheaton, 34, was promoted to captain on 737s in August 1980, after two years as a first officer on DC-9 and 737 aircraft. A quiet man, Wheaton then received an unsatisfactory grading during a proficiency check in April, 1981, with deficiencies in memory items, knowledge of aircraft systems, and aircraft limitations. Three days later, a recheck proved satisfactory. In October, 1981, a 737 simulator check was also satisfactory.

First Officer Roger Pettit, 31, had begun airline flying on Boeing 737s in November 1981 after three years' experience on F-15 jet fighters. Described as a bright, outgoing individual, he was said to have an excellent grasp of the skills required in a pilot. Those who had flown with him during stressful operations said he remained the same sharp individual "who knew his limitations." He was the type of pilot who "would

Laid out on the hangar floor, the recovered wreckage of the 737 tells its own tragic story. Black paint hurriedly applied to the fin belatedly attempts to conceal the identity of the airline. This post-accident, marketing-driven practice is not without good reason. The Washington accident was estimated to have cost Air Florida around 100,000 reservations. (with acknowledgement to Hank Morgan & Discover magazine)

not hesitate to speak up if he knew something was wrong."

ANALYSIS

The evidence was conclusive that the Boeing 737's acceleration and climb were subnormal. In the existing conditions, the aircraft should have accelerated to liftoff at 145 knots in about 30 seconds, using about 3500 feet of runway. It should then have climbed at more than 2000 fpm. By contrast, it took 45 seconds and 5400 feet of runway to lift off at between 140 and 145 knots. The stick shaker stall warning activated immediately and, at an altitude of between 200 and 300 feet, the airspeed began to decrease, with stall buffet being experienced.

The exchanges between captain and first officer during takeoff indicated the latter was concerned about engine instrument indications. Analysis of the CVR tape disclosed a significant disparity between engine fan speed (technically referred to as N_1) during the takeoff and the N_1 reading to be expected at the target takeoff power setting.

The investigation established that ice on the compressor inlet pressure probe would produce an EPR reading higher than actually being developed. With the pressure probe blocked by ice, an EPR setting of 2.04 would equate to an actual EPR of only 1.70. The expected N_1 speed at this thrust level correlated with the N_1 speeds achieved during takeoff. The evidence showed that the engine anti-ice system had not been switched on before takeoff, and was off at the time of impact.

Airframe Ice

The theoretical performance of a Boeing 737 at the weight of the accident aircraft in the existing conditions was analysed by the Boeing company for the thrust levels indicated by the CVR sound spectrum analysis. The performance theoretically achievable was then compared with the actual flight trajectory to the point of impact to determine whether the aircraft's subnormal performance was attributable solely to reduced takeoff thrust.

The takeoff acceleration, as indicated by airspeed, time, and distance, correlated closely with the performance to be expected at 1.70 EPR, indicating that increases in aerodynamic drag and rolling drag caused by snow or slush had little effect while on the runway. Once airborne however, with a thrust level of 1.70 EPR, the aircraft should have achieved a climb rate of more than 1000 fpm at an airspeed of 145 knots. It was thus obvious that factors other than reduced thrust affected its performance.

Even a small amount of snow or ice on a wing has a significant effect on the smooth flow of air over the surface contour (see illustration). Changes in the shape and roughness of the surface cause the airflow to separate from the wing at lower angles of attack than normal, resulting in a reduction in lift developed at a given angle of attack and a given airspeed. Both the maximum lift, and the angle of attack at which it will be developed, will be reduced. Since the total lift developed is a function of both airspeed and angle of attack, an aircraft with snow or ice on its wings will have a higher than normal angle of attack at a given airspeed – or conversely be required to maintain a higher airspeed for a given angle of attack. Stall buffet and a full stall will also occur at higher than normal airspeeds.

In the case of the Boeing 737 design, the manufacturer found that even a light coating of frost on the leading edge slats could also give the aircraft a tendency to pitch up. Bulletins detailing action pilots could take to deal with the problem had been issued to Boeing 737 operators in 1974, 1979, and 1981.

The stall warning stick shaker in the Boeing 737 is activated when a fuselage mounted vane reaches a preset angle of attack that is a little less than the actual stall angle of attack. The alarm margin is about 10% of the stalling speed. Because the vane is independent of airflow conditions on the wing, the angle of attack at which it will activate is not

(top) NTSB investigators pore over printouts from the 737's FDR (foreground) and CVR. (bottom) A close-up view of the aircraft's CVR and a tracing from its sound spectrum analysis. (with acknowledgement to Discover magazine)

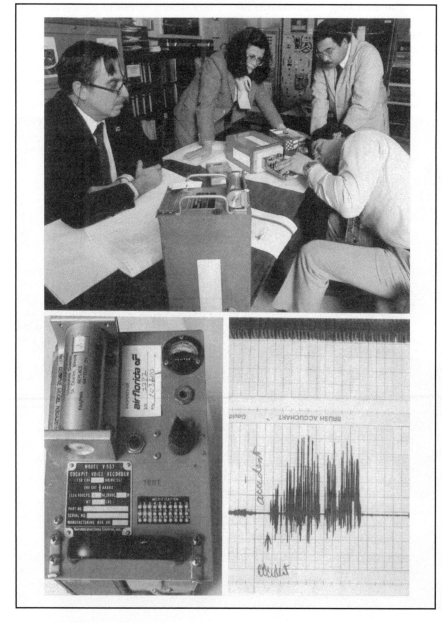

affected by snow or ice on the wing. Thus, if the wing's efficiency is reduced by snow or ice, the stick shaker will activate at a higher than normal airspeed. Furthermore, the margin between stall warning, stall buffet, and the stall itself will be reduced or even eliminated.

The CVR showed that the stick shaker activated almost immediately after liftoff and remained so until impact. The FDR showed that the airspeed after liftoff was 145 knots, about 12 knots above normal stick shaker speed. The FDR's vertical acceleration parameter was consistent with survivor evidence that the aircraft was encountering stall buffet during much of its brief flight. This was positive evidence that snow or ice adhering to the aircraft was degrading its lift.

The next most detrimental effect of snow or ice is the increase in the aircraft's total drag. And the overall effects on lift efficiency and drag are further compounded by the additional weight of the snow or ice. While the lift-producing capability of the wing is diminished, the lift required is greater because of the added weight and, since drag is a function of lift, this too, is increased.

The captain's exclamation, "Easy!", closely following his V_1 call, was a likely reaction to an abnormally abrupt, nose-up aircraft rotation. Based upon the experience of other Boeing 737 operators, the investigators concluded that the snow and ice on the wings produced a noseup pitch during rotation which could not be immediately countered by the first officer, and which aggravated the subsequent deterioration in the aircraft's performance.

The rate of climb achieved immediately after liftoff could be attributed to ground effect and a tradeoff of speed for height. The initial rate of climb probably exceeded 1000 fpm which, together with the stick shaker warning, most likely prompted the captain's utterances, "Forward, forward!", "Easy!" and "We only want 500." The captain undoubtedly meant a rate of climb of 500 fpm but, as ground effect diminished, so did the aircraft's performance. As the airspeed began to decay during the climb, the drag produced by the increasing angle of attack soon exceeded the thrust being developed by the engines. At this point, the aircraft might have been theoretically recoverable with a combined application of full thrust and nosedown pitch. In practice however, recovery within the altitude and time available to the crew was barely possible.

Although illustrating more extreme winter conditions than those prevailing at Washington on the afternoon of January 13, 1982, this picture is nevertheless instructive. Here, a ground crewman uses a "cherry picker" to apply de-icing solution under pressure to remove slabs of ice some 2cm thick from a British Boeing 737. (with acknowledgement to Flight International)

(bottom) This simplified drawing shows how Engine Pressure Ratio is determined by comparing intake and exhaust probe readings. EPR gauge readings are the standard and most efficient means of setting thrust in modern jet engines. (For a more detailed view of a JT8D engine, and the location of its sensors and major components, see the sectional cutaway drawing in Chapter 1.) (below) This graphic of an EPR dial shows the false reading the Boeing 737 crew would have seen (solid arrow) that fateful January afternoon, compared with the much lower actual thrust reading (broken arrow). (Matthew Tesch)

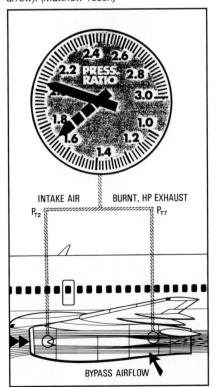

De-icing operations

Until the mid 1950s, the methods used to remove frost, snow, or ice from an aircraft were mechanical – ice was scraped away and snow was swept from the wings and fuselage. But as aircraft became bigger and their aerodynamic surfaces more critical, mechanical techniques became impractical.

By the early 1960s, airlines had accepted the use of de-icing solutions which could be applied to aircraft surfaces more easily and quickly. Initially, these were a mixture of ethylene glycol, propylene glycol and water. The fluids were applied cold using agricultural-type spray apparatus. While this effectively melted frost or ice, time was needed for the glycol to react, and some mechanical effort was also necessary to remove the softened snow or melting ice. Over the years, de-icing solutions were refined and special equipment developed to deliver large volumes of hot fluid at sufficient pressure to remove snow or ice. The resulting refinement in de-icing techniques allows operators to mix water and de-icing solutions and thus adjust the concentration to suit the particular conditions.

Using this equipment, heat melts the ice and snow, and pressure removes it. If conditions are conducive to refreezing of any residual moisture, de-icing solution manufacturers recommend that aircraft surfaces be sprayed with a high concentration solution after the ice and snow has been removed.

Ground operations after de-icing

Although the investigators could not determine whether the aircraft was completely free of snow and ice after its de-icing was completed, the evidence was conclusive that snow subsequently accumulated on the aircraft for nearly 50 minutes before it was cleared for takeoff.

Other departing flights also experienced extensive delays, yet took off without difficulty. However, the exact conditions – temperature and ground accumulation on aprons and taxiways, the length of time the aircraft was exposed to critical wind conditions, and the proximity of the Boeing 737 to the jet effluxes of other aircraft after de-icing – were all factors that could have made the difference between a successful takeoff and an unsuccessful one. While other departing aircraft probably also had some snow on their surfaces, the investigators believed the actions of the Boeing 737's crew during the ground delay increased the risk of dangerous accumulations of ice on the aircraft

Engine anti-ice system

The closed position of the thermal anti-ice valves, as well as the engine speed during the takeoff were explicable only if the anti-ice system was off. The captain's response to "anti-ice" during the after-start checklist was "off" and the crew made no further mention of engine anti-ice.

The FAA-approved Boeing 737 Flight Manual used by Air Florida prescribed that the engine inlet anti-ice system should be on when icing conditions exist or are expected during takeoff and initial climb. As there are no restrictions on its use during ground operations and no significant performance penalty during takeoff and climb, the crew could have been expected to use it. Yet there was no evidence that they even considered it.

About 3.49pm, while the aircraft was in line for departure, the first officer said: "See the difference in that left engine and right one?" And two minutes later: "This thing's settled down a little bit, might'a been his hot air going over it."

The investigators believed he was commenting on an erratic EPR indication, probably as a result of ice forming on the engine inlet probe. Yet even this indication did not prompt either of the crew to question the status of the engine anti-ice system .

Whatever the reason, their failure to use engine anti-ice was a direct cause of the accident. Had the engine probes not been blocked by ice, the correct EPR values would have been indicated when setting takeoff power, and the engines would have developed the correct thrust. Even with the ice and snow on the aircraft, this additional thrust would have provided a performance margin for acceleration and climb.

Aircraft spacing

The CVR indicated that the captain intentionally positioned the Boeing 737 close behind another aircraft in an attempt to use the heat from its jet engines to melt the accumulated snow on the Boeing's wings. This action, which might have contributed to the accident by enabling the moisture to refreeze in more critical places on the airframe, could only be seen as a further example of the captain's lack of familiarity with the flight manual. This categorically warned: "Maintain a greater distance than normal between airplanes when taxiing on ice or snow covered areas."

Takeoff: snow on the aircraft

It was evident the crew believed the accumulation of snow or slush on the wings might have some deteriorating effect, but would not seriously affect the aircraft's takeoff and climb. After the prolonged delay, they were understandably reluctant to forego their takeoff opportunity and return to the apron for another cycle of de-icing and delay, particularly as other aircraft were departing successfully.

Regardless of the many factors influencing the crew however, the investigators believed they should not have begun the takeoff. FAA Regulations specified that "no person may take off an aircraft when frost, snow or ice is adhering to the wings, control surfaces, or propellers ..." The crew's decision to do so was a direct cause of the accident.

Reproduced from an ICAO circular, this graph shows how the Coefficient of Lift for an aerofoil section can vary as a function of both surface contamination and angle-of-attack. Note that a frost-encrusted wing upper surface, which roughly retains its aerofoil section, loses only about 20% of its Lift Coefficient compared to a smooth wing. But an iced-up leading edge, which disturbs the smooth airflow over the wing's upper surface, plays havoc with its capacity to create lift, degrading its performance by some 50%.

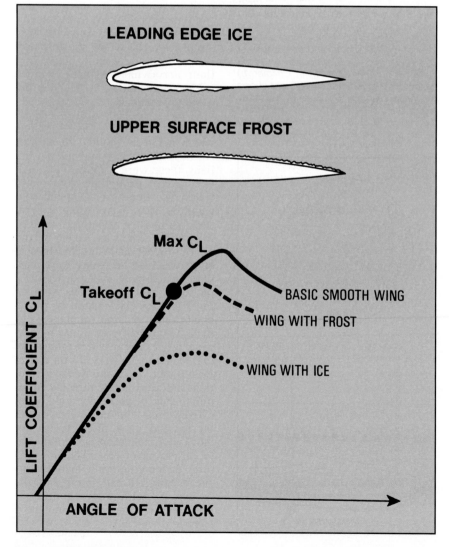

Takeoff: instrument anomalies

Even though the first officer appeared to be seeking advice when he commented, "Slushy runway, do you want me to do anything special for this or just go for it?" the captain's response was noncommittal, and he gave no detailed takeoff briefing.

As the crew awaited their clearance to takeoff, the traffic flow was being sequenced alternately between departing and arriving aircraft. The Boeing 737 was cleared to "taxi into position and hold" as a just-landed aircraft was rolling out, and told to "be ready for an immediate" ahead of the next approaching aircraft.

As the Boeing began to taxi, the crew completed the takeoff checklist. Twenty nine seconds after being cleared into position, they were finally cleared for takeoff, the controller adding: "No delay on departure if you will, traffic's two and a half out for the runway."

The crew began applying power before the aircraft was aligned with the runway heading and, as the first officer brought the power up, the EPR indication probably overshot the 2.04 target value.

The crew's exclamations – "Ho", "Whoo", "Really cold here", "Got 'em", "Real cold", and "God, look at that thing" – were all indicative of an exceptionally rapid increase in EPR as the power levers were advanced. The CVR sound spectrogram study confirmed the engine speed peaked, then was immediately reduced to a value corresponding to an actual EPR of 1.70 – the false reading resulting from the iced engine probe. As the aircraft accelerated, the first officer commented: "That don't seem right does it?" Then: "Ah, that's not right."

The captain's only response was: "Yes it is, there's 80 [knots]". But the first officer again expressed concern: "No – I don't think that's right."

No further comment came from the captain and the takeoff continued. But the first officer continued to show concern as the aircraft accelerated through 120 knots, reaching V_1 41 seconds after the beginning of the takeoff.

Because the captain was the monitoring pilot, he could have been expected to be the more attentive to the instruments and more observant of any anomalies. Instead, it was the first officer who repeatedly expressed uneasiness that something was not right. There was no evidence that the captain tried to evaluate the problem by scanning the other engine instruments. Instead, he apparently ignored the first offic-

er's comments and allowed the takeoff to continue.

The investigators believed the instrument readings were doubtful enough to reject the takeoff while the aircraft was still at relatively low speed. Doubt was clearly expressed by the first officer, and the captain's failure to respond was a direct cause of the accident. Analysis showed that the aircraft could have been brought to a stop from 80 knots in less than 2000 feet even on an extremely slippery runway. In fact, the crew should have been able to stop within the runway length even if the decision had been delayed until 120 knots.

Reaction to stall warning

If the extent to which the aircraft's performance was degraded was not recognised by the crew during the takeoff, it should have been apparent to them immediately the aircraft became airborne.

The crew were surprised as the nose pitched up abruptly during rotation as a result of the trim change caused by wing icing, and the control column force required to lower the nose was probably much higher than expected. They would also have been surprised – and probably confused – when the stick shaker activated at an airspeed well above the stall.

The remedy would have been to immediately apply power and reduce the noseup attitude. But the crew, believing thrust was already at the takeoff limit, confined their actions to correcting the pitch attitude, as evident from the captain's urgings: "Forward, forward!", "Easy!", "We only want 500", "Come on, forward!", and "just barely climb."

In their desperate attempts to remain airborne, the crew then progressively increased the nose attitude. From the continuing stick shaker operation and the decreasing airspeed, it should have been evident that the aircraft was not recovering. Near to stalling at extremely low altitude, the crew should have responded at once with an increase in thrust, regardless of EPR limits. They should also have seen that other engine parameters – N_1, N_2 and exhaust gas temperature – were all well below their limits.

The investigators voiced concern that the pilots were indoctrinated against exceeding engine limitations to such an extent that they withheld available power, rather than use it to save the aircraft from disaster. While pilot training should certainly emphasise the importance of adhering to engine limitations, it should also

stress that available power should be used beyond those limits if the safety of the aircraft is at risk.

Crew experience

Both the airline industry and the public have come to expect the highest degree of professionalism from crews of regular public transport aircraft, particularly from airline captains.

All the captain's jet experience in this case had been gained with Air Florida. This consisted of about 1200 hours as a first officer on DC-9s and Boeing 737s and, since being promoted to captain, another 1100 hours in command on Boeing 737s. During this time he had made only eight takeoffs or landings in falling snow. His flying experience before joining Air Florida was confined to light singles, twins, and turboprops, much of it in the more benign weather of the southern United States.

The first officer's prior experience was gained as a jet fighter pilot. His airline experience consisted of about 1000 hours as a first officer on Boeing 737s. On only two occasions during that period had he conducted operations in icing conditions.

Neither pilot thus had much experience of jet transport operations in snow and icing conditions like those at Washington on the day of the accident. And, as a crew, they had flown together for a total of only 17½ hours.

The investigators concluded that this limited experience was a contributing factor to the accident. Because of the rapid expansion of Air Florida between 1977 and 1981, the captain had missed the extended "seasoning" experience normally accumulated by airline first officers before they gain their first command. An informal survey of major US airlines showed that pilots serve an average of 14 years as first or second officer before being promoted to captain.

The investigators believed that flightcrew training, as well as selection criteria, should include considerations of command decision, resource management, role performance, and assertiveness. As a result of previous accidents in which lack of crew communication was a factor (see Chapter 3), the National Transportation Safety Board recommended crews be trained in principles of flightdeck resource management.

A number of airlines have since developed training programs which include leadership, management skills, human relations, and problem solving in the operational environment.

CHAPTER 7

"I don't believe it – all four have failed!"

– Flight Engineer to Captain

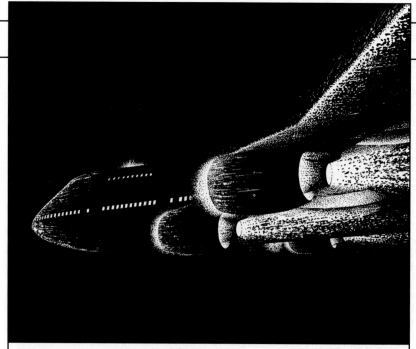

British Airways Boeing 747-236B G-BDXH [21635] "City of Edinburgh" – June 24, 1982

Statistically, the odds against a total, near-simultaneous failure of all four engines on a modern jetliner were so astronomically unlikely as to be considered impossible. Yet one incredulous crew found it actually happening – accompanied by weird visual manifestations utterly beyond their experience ...

Departure from Kuala Lumpur

For the crew of British Airways' Boeing 747 *City of Edinburgh*, operating the third leg of the company's Flight BA009 from London Heathrow through to Auckland, New Zealand, it was just another routine international sector.

The aircraft had left London just after 9pm British Summer Time the previous day with a near capacity load, bound for its first port of call at Bombay. Completing an uneventful flight, it had touched down there on a sunny Indian morning, soon after the passengers had breakfasted.

After refuelling and a change of crew, G-BDXH had continued to Kuala Lumpur, a shorter international leg, this time of less than five hours, arriving early in the sultry Malaysian evening of Thursday, June 24.

Here, at the airport's terminal, Captain Eric Moody and his youthful crew of 15 were waiting to take the aircraft and its load of now travel-weary passengers on to its next call at Perth, a flight southwards over the Indian Ocean that would occupy most of the hours of darkness before making landfall on the lonely coast of Western Australia very early in the morning.

Initially crewing a British Airways flight to Muscat in the Middle East, they had all left London together the previous Saturday. Another flight two days later had brought them to Jakarta, and they arrived in Kuala Lumpur on the Wednesday for a day's rest prior to reporting for duty as scheduled to take over the Kuala Lumpur/Perth stage of Flight BA009 late the following afternoon.

The weather briefing provided to Captain Moody for the Indian Ocean crossing was unremarkable, the Boeing 747 itself had no unserviceabilities of any note, and there was no reason why the flight to Perth should be anything but perfectly normal and routine.

When the doors were closed for departure at 7.45pm local time, there were 247 passengers aboard, including eight infants and a number of older children. The majority had travelled with the aircraft from London, but newcomers included two Malaysian firemen en route to New Zealand to attend a firefighting course, and a tour party of Australians from Perth who had been holidaying in Penang.

At 7.56pm local time a tug pushed the Boeing 747 back from the termi-

nal. Thirteen minutes later it lifted off Kuala Lumpur's main runway, climbing to Flight Level 370 (37,000 feet) as it set heading for its first reporting point at Jakarta, 85 minutes' flying time to the southeast.

Cruising flight

Maintaining a heading of 160° on autopilot, the aircraft crossed the Strait of Malacca to the Indonesian island of Sumatra, following its coast toward Sunda Strait and Jakarta beyond it on the northwest tip of Java. Under the direction of Cabin Service Officer (CSO) Graham Skinner, the cabin crew's first task after the aircraft reached cruising level was to serve drinks, followed by a light evening meal, to the passengers. Many of them, having travelled through from London, were now feeling the effects of fatigue, and were anxious to settle down to sleep as soon as the meal was over, rather than watch the film, *On Golden Pond*, scheduled for screening afterwards.

By 9.30pm, the galaxy of ground lights that was the Indonesian capital of Jakarta lay spread below the aircraft, filling the downward view from the flightdeck windows. Five minutes later the needle of the VOR dial on First Officer Roger Greaves' instrument panel indicated station passage over the beacon at Halim Airport.[1]

In a moment Greaves depressed the transmit button on his control wheel to pass the routine position report: "Jakarta Control – Speedbird Nine. Over Halim at 35 [1335 hours Greenwich Mean Time], Flight Level 370, Estimate TOPAR [the next reporting point off Java's southern coast] at 54 [1354 GMT]."

On the darkened flightdeck, lit only by the glow of the instrument lights and displays, all was well. The air was calm and the night sky clear of cloud, the stars a brilliant canopy above the aircraft. The weather radar screens for each pilot portrayed no significant weather ahead.

Presently Captain Moody handed the monitoring of the flight over to First Officer Greaves, undid his seatbelt, and went back to the crew toilet on the aircraft's upper deck. Finding it occupied, he descended the spiral staircase to use one of the forward toilets near the lower deck First Class cabin.

There were not many First Class passengers aboard and they were all seated in the nose section on the lower deck. Having served them their evening meal, Stewardess Fiona Wright sought a few minutes respite in the unoccupied First Class cabin on the upper deck while she ate her own meal. She had just begun when the intercom telephone rang.

It was First Officer Greaves. "Come look at this," he insisted. "You won't believe your eyes!"

Reluctantly, because she was hungry after the late start from Kuala Lumpur, she got up and walked forward to the flightdeck. As she gazed through the windscreen, her eyes widened in amazement. Myriads of brilliant white sparks were hurtling out of the night towards the front of the aircraft, those actually hitting the windscreen exploding in brighter flashes.

First Officer Greaves and Flight Engineer Townley-Freeman were equally fascinated. In their experience, the only thing remotely resembling the phenomenon was St Elmo's fire – the luminous electrical discharge sometimes visible at the wingtips, nose and windscreen of aircraft flying in the vicinity of a thunderstorm. Inflight, St Elmo's fire can resemble miniature forks of lightning playing around the structure of the aircraft, but what they were now seeing was quite different.

There was still nothing showing on the aircraft's weather radar, but the sky above the aircraft had become obscured – no stars were now visible. Greaves switched on the landing lights for moment and gained the impression they were now flying in thin cloud.

"I don't like the look of this," he told Townley-Freeman as he turned on the cabin Fasten Seatbelt signs. Both crew members put on their shoulder harness, and at Greaves' suggestion Townley-Freeman switched on the engine anti-ice system and the engine igniters as a precautionary measure.

With the aircraft now approaching the southern coast of West Java, the sparks impacting against the windscreen were increasing in intensity. In a moment Greaves turned again to Fiona Wright. "I think you'd better get the captain back up here!" he said quietly.

Smoke ...

In the lower deck cabins, particularly those further aft, some passengers were becoming conscious of an unusual amount of smoke in the air. With the evening meal over and the trays cleared away, a number of passengers had already dozed off to sleep and it seemed strange that those still smoking cigarettes could have produced so much smoke. A woman passenger wondered if someone had dropped a cigarette and it was smouldering on the carpet.

But the smoke was just as noticeable in the non-smoking areas, and passengers were commenting on it. They were not the only ones to notice. Steward Roger MacNicol, making his way back to the rear galley to speak to the Purser, particularly noticed the smoke hanging in the air towards the rear of the lower deck. It certainly seemed excessive.

"Can you see smoke?" he asked Steward Stephen Johns as he passed him, "or is it my imagination?" Johns looked at the haze, wondered if something was smouldering, and went to check the centre toilets.

Further aft in Zone E, the rearmost section of the aircraft, Purser Richard Abrey and Steward Stuart Gray were readying the bulkhead screen for the inflight film. The cigarette haze seemed unusually thick. "Someone must have dropped a cigarette," Gray observed with concern. Abrey agreed and both began unobtrusively checking passenger seats, the galleys, toilets, and anywhere else a small fire could be smouldering.

Unable to find the source of the smoke, Gray then went forward to tell Cabin Service Officer Skinner. Meanwhile, as Steward MacNicol returned to his own forward station, he paused to look back – the rear of the aircraft was now invisible in the smoke.

Other cabin staff were noticing it too. Steward Martin in Galley 2 looked down the cabin and saw smoke moving from the rear of the aircraft towards the front. It smelt acrid. In the forward galley, Stewardess Lorraine Stewart commented to Claire Wickett on "how much the passengers have been smoking down in the back today!" As they looked back towards the tail, the smoke continued to thicken until the rear of the aircraft was obscured.

Fiery particles – eerie pyrotechnics

Stewardess Wright ran down the stairs from the upper deck to find Captain Moody talking to CSO Graham Skinner near the entrance to the First Class section. Interrupting them, she quickly passed the mes-

The now familiar red, white & blue livery adopted for the BOAC/BEA merger (and first displayed by B707 G-AXXY in September 1973) was modified slightly at the end of the decade. In July 1980, the company's third-oldest 747-136B, G-AWNC [19763], appeared at London Heathrow wearing the definitive "British" title statement, subsequently adopted by all the carrier's fixed wing aircraft and divisions, although the proper name continued to include "airways". The full title was reinstated from December 4, 1984 when the current pearl grey livery was introduced. This also marked the disappearance of the traditional "Speedbird" emblem, although crews were reluctant to discontinue the use of the word as the airline's radio callsign prefix. (with acknowledgement to APN/A Halse)

G-BDXH "City of Edinburgh" as it looked at the time of the Jakarta incident. Delivered by Boeing in March 1979, it was the eighth of BA's Rolls-Royce powered 747s and was equipped with RB211-524B/D engines, an uprated version of the L-1011 TriStar's RB211-22Bs, with 20% greater takeoff thrust. The first RB211 powered Boeing 747, G-BDXA [21238] "City of Cardiff", which made its maiden flight on September 3, 1976, established an FAI world record during its certification, taking off at an all-up weight of 381,251kg (more than 375 tons – over 10 tons heavier than any of the 291 747s built to that time). In mid 1989, when new deliveries of Boeing 747-436s began taking the names of principal UK cities, G-BDXH was renamed "City of Elgin". The name "City of Edinburgh" was then allocated to Boeing 747-436 G-BNLB [23909]. (British Airways)

sage that the captain was needed urgently back on the flightdeck.

All three immediately ran back up the stairway. The captain, as he reached the upper deck, was alarmed to see smoke seeping from the floor level ventilation ducts. But this was only a precursor to his reaction as he entered the flightdeck.

Never in his long flying career had he seen anything like the astonishing phenomenon visible through the windscreen – it was if they were flying through a storm of fiery rain. As the myriad glowing particles struck the aircraft, they were producing effects similar to St Elmo's fire, but never had he seen St Elmo's fire quite like this.

Astonished, Moody quickly resumed his seat. Even as he watched, the fantastic display increased in intensity. He had never seen machine gun tracer fire, but the effect was much as he imagined tracer fire would look like – except that there was so much of it.

Behind the flightcrew, Graham Skinner and Fiona Wright stood spellbound, watching in awed silence. As the glowing particles struck the aircraft there were flashes of miniature lightning, forked and zigzag shaped, which seemed to come right through the windscreen.

The darkness of the night ahead seemed to be illuminated by a bright, sparkling light source, much like a headlight seen through heavy rain, from which the glowing particles seemed to be radiating at high speed.

Glancing back through his starboard side window, First Officer Greaves was astonished at the appearance of No 4 engine. In contrast with the blackness of the night, the inside of the nacelle was bathed in a brilliant white light! It seemed to be emanating from somewhere behind the fan, because he could clearly see the blades, the stroboscopic effect making the fan appear to be rotating backwards. Every detail of the fan and spinner was visible and they seemed to be glowing, as though incandescent.

Thoroughly startled by this utterly inexplicable development, he drew the attention of the others to it, including Skinner and Wright. To their amazement, they then saw the other engines were affected in the same way. Moreover, the same glowing white incandescence was now visible on the leading edge of the wings!

Mature and experienced crew members though they were, they all sensed a chill of fear – not the fear generated by ordinary danger, but the uncanny fear associated with something quite outside human experience. It was all so eerie – almost unearthly – and ominous. What could be causing these weird manifestations? What was going to happen to them next?

Cabin Service Officer Skinner and Stewardess Wright hurried back to their stations in the passenger cabins, determined to prepare for whatever emergency was in store.

In the passenger cabins

As she went back into the upper deck cabin Stewardess Wright could detect a musty sort of smell as if something had fused. Quickly she switched off the upper galley electrical equipment, the boilers, the ovens and refrigerators, and stowed and secured the equipment.

Towards the rear of the aircraft, the increasing smoke was concerning a number of passengers. "They should ban smoking on these flights," one man declared aloud. Another, who had been dozing, alerted by comments near him, opened his eyes and saw the smoke. Now he could smell it too. Yet he was in a non-smoking section. "What's all that smoke?" he demanded.

His young son, in the seat alongside him, pressed his face to the win-

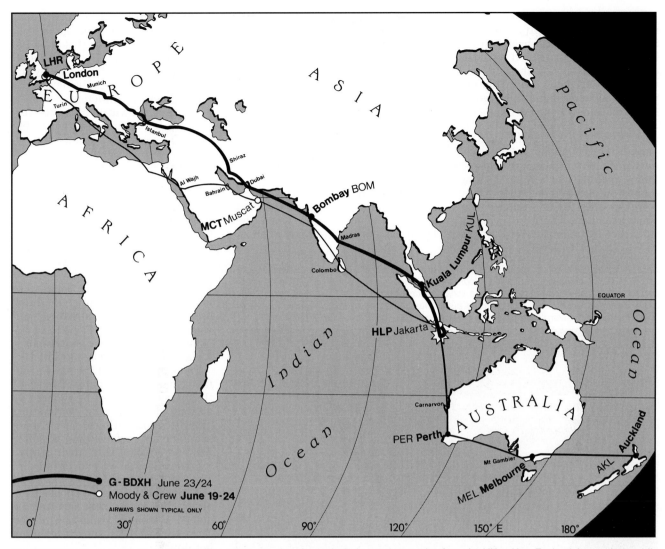

The BA009 route, as it was in June 1982. The only same-aircraft, single flight number service from the UK to New Zealand, it was the world's longest scheduled commercial air service. The supplementary route shows the progressive sectors operated by Captain Eric Moody and his crew prior to their taking over G-BDXH in Kuala Lumpur for the fateful sector on June 24, 1982. (Matthew Tesch)

dow and gasped: "Dad," he called, the urgency plain in his voice. "The engine's on fire!"

Other passengers heard and looked for themselves. Not only the engine nearest to them, but the wing itself appeared have small flames dancing on it.

"We're on fire!" a woman cried out, quickly becoming hysterical.

Immediately her fear communicated itself to others. "My God, we're on fire!" another passenger yelled. "Oh, my God ... look at that!" someone else called out. Somewhere else again, a woman screamed. "Look! There's a fire! There's a fire!" cried someone else. "Be quiet!" another passenger commanded with authority. "We won't hear any announcements!"

Further aft, dark grey smoke was pouring in through the vents above the windows while, above the doors adjacent to the rear galley, thick black smoke was now billowing in clouds. And the sound of the engines seemed to have changed, rumbling

Passenger's-eye view of the RB211 engines hung in the No 3 (inboard) and No 4 (outboard) positions of sistership G-BDXA. (with acknowledgement to Rolls-Royce Ltd & Ian Allan)

and banging noises, accompanied by vibration, now punctuating their former smooth running.

"My God, what's happening?" a young woman exclaimed fearfully, catching sight of masses of glowing particles coming from both engines on her side of the aircraft. A glance at the engines on the other side showed her they were behaving in the same way. Had their flight somehow come under attack? Like the Korean Air Lines Boeing 747 shot down near Japan a year before?

Another woman, glancing across the cabin to the starboard side, saw a spectacle that horrified her. Long, yellowish-white glows, of the same diameter as the engines and several metres in length, were coming from the jet pipes of both starboard engines. They looked just like the rocket propulsion system of the spacecraft in *Star Wars*. Pushing up the blind on her window revealed that the two port engines were producing the same effects!

Purser Abrey was returning to the rear cabin after reporting to CSO Skinner, when a passenger, attracting his attention, pointed out that one of the engines on the port side was streaming flame. Abrey did not waste a moment, immediately going forward again to report to Skinner.

Steward Gray, also on his way back after reporting the smoke, paused for a moment as he passed two of the stewardesses to whisper that something was burning. As they looked out a port side window they were appalled to see flames – or something more like flares – coming from the engine intakes and stream-

ing rearwards around the engine nacelles.

Gray himself did not realise the extent to which "something was burning" until he had returned to the rear cabin. He was stunned then to see that both starboard engines appeared to be on fire. Quickly he cut through the centre toilet complex to look through the windows on the other side. Both port engines also looked to be ablaze, lighting up the area around them!

In the rear galley, Stewardess Susan Glennie had just finished clearing the meal trays when she heard passenger consternation about

something visible through the starboard windows. Looking out herself, she saw to her horror that No 4 engine was glowing, with flames shooting from its jetpipe. Immediately she set about clearing the galley, ready for an emergency briefing.

Another steward, hurrying forward to his assigned station in the First Class cabin, encountered Skinner on the way. Skinner got in first: "I know – don't tell me. Just do what you can. But don't walk fast – walk slowly!"

The rough running of the engines woke another passenger sitting in a port side window seat not far behind the trailing edge of the wing. What he saw as he opened his eyes sent a chill down his spine. Intermittent jets of orange and blue flame were issuing from both port engines, breaking up as they streaked rearwards. The bursts of flame were accompanied by muffled explosions – it was these that had awoken him.

The suddenness of the smoke and fire seemed to have numbed many of the passengers. Most, bewildered by all that was happening, were sitting quietly. From others, there were spontaneous exclamations as shock, fear and doubt assailed their minds.

Somewhere a woman called out: "We're all going to die!"

At once there was a response from another woman: "Shut up! And be quiet!" A steward came and tended the distressed passenger, calming her down.

But the terrifying visual effects continued, as did the grinding and banging noises from the engines ...

On the flightdeck

The smoke haze on the flightdeck had become considerable, and accompanied by the smell of electrical arcing.

Watching his systems instrument panel closely, Flight Engineer Townley-Freeman had checked and rechecked for any indication of fire, but could find nothing. The smoke could be the result of an electrical or airconditioning problem without there actually being any fire, and the smell strongly suggested that it was electrical.

He was about to begin the Airconditioning Smoke Drill procedure when one of the pneumatic supply "VALVE CLOSED" warning lamps began to flicker. A moment later No 4 engine surged and flamed out. In accordance with standard emergency procedures, the Flight Engineer immediately called: "Engine Failure Number Four!"

Captain Moody responded at once with the command: "Fire Action

Same engines, different angle: this apron view, taken at Boeing's Paine Field, Washington, shows G-BDXA being readied for flight (note the extended leading edge flaps). The engineer beneath No 4's open cowlings provides a sense of scale for the RB211 nacelles, themselves easily distinguished by their shorter, more bulky lines compared to the elongated curves of the GE and P&W powerplants. (with acknowledgement to Rolls-Royce Ltd & Ian Allan)

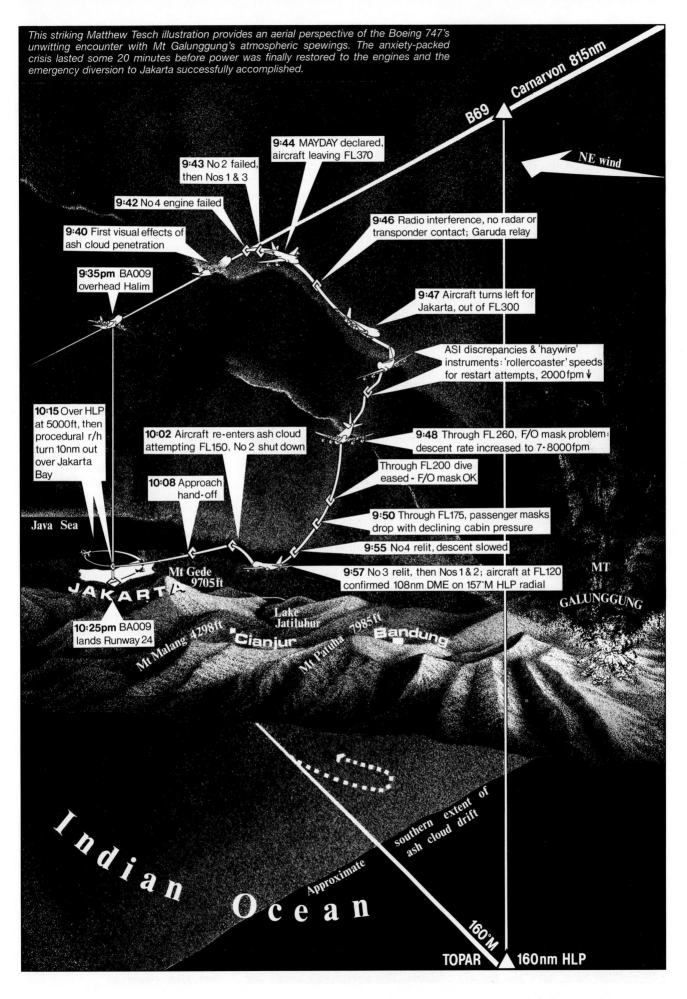

This striking Matthew Tesch illustration provides an aerial perspective of the Boeing 747's unwitting encounter with Mt Galunggung's atmospheric spewings. The anxiety-packed crisis lasted some 20 minutes before power was finally restored to the engines and the emergency diversion to Jakarta successfully accomplished.

B69 Carnarvon 815nm

NE wind

9:44 MAYDAY declared, aircraft leaving FL370

9:43 No 2 failed, then Nos 1 & 3

9:42 No 4 engine failed

9:40 First visual effects of ash cloud penetration

9:46 Radio interference, no radar or transponder contact; Garuda relay

9:35pm BA009 overhead Halim

9:47 Aircraft turns left for Jakarta, out of FL300

ASI discrepancies & 'haywire' instruments: 'rollercoaster' speeds for restart attempts, 2000 fpm ↓

10:15 Over HLP at 5000ft, then procedural r/h turn 10nm out over Jakarta Bay

10:02 Aircraft re-enters ash cloud attempting FL150, No 2 shut down

9:48 Through FL 260, F/O mask problem: descent rate increased to 7·8000fpm

10:08 Approach hand-off

Through FL200 dive eased - F/O mask OK

Java Sea

9:50 Through FL175, passenger masks drop with declining cabin pressure

9:55 No4 relit, descent slowed

Mt Gede 9705ft

9:57 No 3 relit, then Nos 1 & 2; aircraft at FL120 confirmed 108nm DME on 157°M HLP radial

MT GALUNGGUNG

JAKARTA

10:25pm BA009 lands Runway 24

Mt Malang 4298ft

Cianjur

Lake Jatiluhur

Mt Patuha 7985ft

Bandung

Indian Ocean

Approximate southern extent of ash cloud drift

160°M

TOPAR 160nm HLP

Number Four!" He then wound in rudder trim to compensate for the asymmetric thrust.

Together the first officer and flight engineer immediately carried out the memory items of the Engine Fire/Failure Drill emergency shutdown procedure, subsequently confirming their actions from the emergency checklist. They then quickly completed the One Generator Inoperative Drill to ensure that the aircraft's electrical system would not be overloaded

Only a minute later Townley-Freeman suddenly announced a second engine failure. "Number Two's gone!" he called. The failure of a second engine was serious indeed – but the Boeing 747 would still be capable of maintaining flight and diverting for an emergency landing.

But before the crew even had time to begin the emergency shutdown procedure for No 2 engine, the unbelievable occurred – almost simultaneously, the remaining Nos 1 and 3 engines surged and flamed out!

Incredulously, Townley-Freeman called: "I don't believe it – all four have failed!"

The time was now 1344 GMT – 9.44pm Kuala Lumpur time. In the space of minutes, the status of the Boeing 747 had been transformed from that of a fully functioning, highly efficient giant airliner, operating a normal, routine international flight, into that of an unpowered 250 tonne glider – with nowhere to descend but into the sea, invisible in the darkness of the tropical night, 37,000 feet below.

Mayday, Mayday, Mayday!

Immediately the incredulous Captain Moody instructed First Officer Greaves to declare an emergency, and called for the Four Engine Failure drill, a procedure all three crew members had practised from time to time in the airline's simulator, though not one of them ever expected to have occasion to use it.

The odds against the simultaneous failure of all four engines in normal operations were theoretically so astronomical that the possibility could be disregarded. The only conceivable situations in which such a dire emergency could occur were total fuel exhaustion or mishandling of the engines in icing conditions. Yet here, with absolutely no ineptitude on the part of the crew, the unbelievable had actually happened!

"Mayday, Mayday, Mayday – Speedbird Nine," Greaves transmitted grimly. "We have lost all four engines. Out of [Flight Level] 370."

"Speedbird Nine, have you got a problem?" the Jakarta controller enquired blandly.

Controlling his exasperation, Greaves tried again: "Jakarta Control – Speedbird Nine. We have lost all four engines. Now out of 360."

Again Jakarta misunderstood: "Speedbird Nine – you have lost number four engine?"

In the heat of the moment this was too much for Greaves. "The **** wit doesn't understand!" he exploded to Moody. But to Jakarta he transmitted more evenly: "Jakarta Control – Speedbird Nine has lost *all four* engines, repeat *all four* engines! Now descending through Flight Level 350!"

Still Jakarta Control seemed unable to comprehend the urgency of the situation, but a Garuda Indonesian Airways aircraft, having heard and understood the distress call, came to the rescue and relayed the message to Jakarta.

Flight Engineer Townley-Freeman implemented the Loss-of-all-Generators Drill, reducing the electrical load to bare essentials and ensuring that the standby bus-bar was being powered by the battery-operated emergency inverter. He then began the Engines Failed Drill in what was to prove the first of many vain attempts to restart the engines.

Drastic and inexplicable as the situation now was, there was some slight consolation for the hard pressed crew – time and height were still on their side. From 37,000 feet, the descent to sea level would take some 23 minutes, during which the aircraft would cover a distance of 141nm on a glideslope of three degrees.

Meanwhile, Cabin Service Officer Graham Skinner, without knowing the details of the aircraft's plight, had seen enough to know it was serious. The passengers' welfare was of paramount importance and he kept his crew moving quietly and efficiently among them to reassure them. His next priority was to reseat the more able passengers near the elderly and infirm or anyone showing signs of distress.

On the flightdeck Greaves joined Townley-Freeman in further attempts to restart the engines. Fortunately, the windmilling engines were continuing to supply sufficient hydraulic power for the flying controls as well as a surprising amount of electrical power.

Turn back towards Jakarta

When the aircraft had descended to 30,000 feet, still with no success in restarting the engines, Captain Moody decided to turn back towards Jakarta. The lowest safe height for the area over which the aircraft had flown before crossing the southern coast of Java was 11,500 feet.

Again Greaves called Jakarta Control: "Jakarta – Speedbird Nine is turning left back to Halim. Now out of [Flight Level] 300."

Jakarta Control: "Speedbird Nine – radar cannot see you. Squawk Alpha 7700 [the emergency transponder code]."

Greaves: "Jakarta – Speedbird Nine. We are already squawking 7700."

Despite the high mountainous terrain between the aircraft and Jakarta, the aircraft's altitude should have ensured radar identification, but for some reason there was no contact.

It had also become difficult, and sometimes impossible, to read Jakarta Control's transmissions. Not only were the transmissions weak, but there was also massive interference on the frequency. Noisy, with almost continuous "hash", it was assaulting the ears of all three flight-crew through their headsets, a condition almost unknown on VHF bands.

Together Greaves and Townley-Freeman went through the engine restart drill yet again. Again and again they tried, losing count of the number of times. But still all four engines refused to fire. All the while the aircraft continued to descend at close to 2000 fpm.

The indicated airspeed required for an inflight engine relight was between 250 and 270 knots. But Greaves was now startled to see his airspeed indicator reading 320 knots – 50 knots more than recommended.

"Watch the airspeed!" he exclaimed to the captain. "I've got 320 knots my side!"

"Well – I've got 270!" Moody answered.

"Bloody hell! Fifty knots difference!"

Which airspeed indicator was correct? Could they both be giving spurious readings? Was this the reason the engines would not fire?

Moody could no longer be certain of the accuracy of the groundspeed readout on the Inertial Navigation

(opposite) Results of the ash cloud encounter: (top) Eroded compressor blade tips in the Low Pressure section of one of the aircraft's RB211 engines. The damage is particularly apparent at the corners of the third stage blades, third from left. (bottom) Ash samples taken from various points within the No 3 engine. The cutaway diagram shows the locations in which the samples were found. (with acknowledgement to Rolls-Royce Ltd)

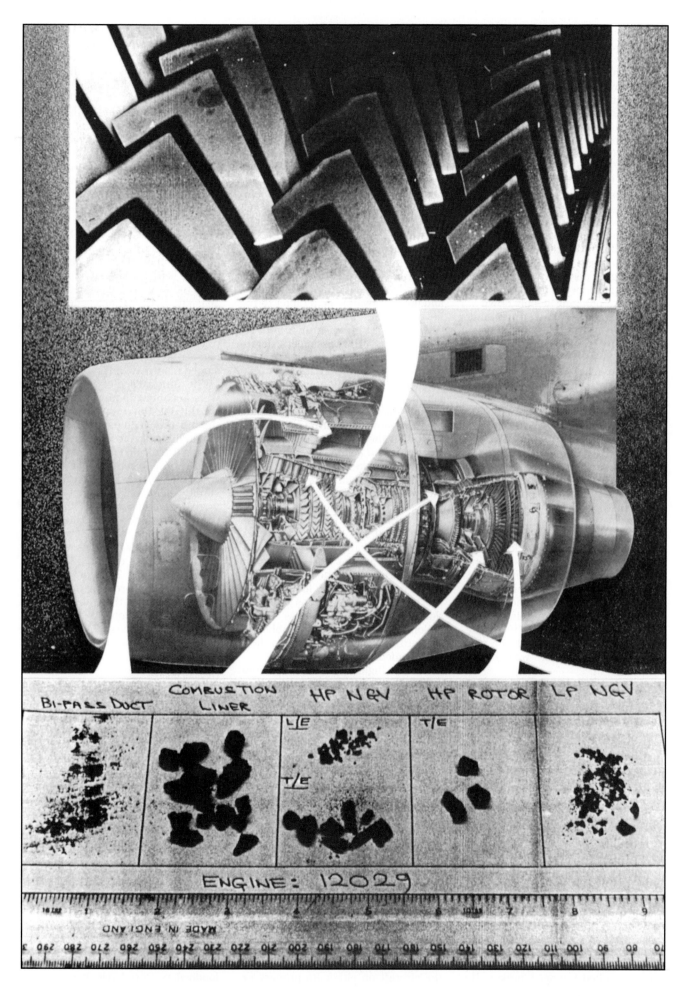

BI-PASS DUCT   COMBUSTION LINER   HP NGV   HP ROTOR   LP NGV

L/E
T/E
T/E

ENGINE: 12029

System (INS) either. It too was giving erratic indications. In an attempt to find an optimum speed for relighting the engines, Moody decided they would have to fly at varying speeds above and below the recommended range of 250-270 knots.

For the passengers and cabin crew, knowing nothing of what was happening on the flightdeck, the overall effects were alarming in the extreme. One minute the passengers were conscious of a floating, almost weightless, sensation, the next a feeling of being pressed down in their seats. Then the aircraft seemed to slow down as if it did not have enough forward momentum. It felt like a "big dipper" – when there was just enough impetus to get it to the top, before plunging steeply down ...

All the cabin crew were continuing to move around, trying to reassure frightened passengers and answer questions about what was happening. The difficulty was they had no idea and, beneath their outward professional calm, they were thoroughly worried themselves. They knew only too well the engines had ceased to function and that the aircraft was going down. How far they had already descended, and how much longer the aircraft could go on gliding, they did not know. But it obviously could not be for long.

Many people were sitting upright, showing no fear. Some sat stiffly as though in a state of shock. Others were clearly frightened and making no attempt to disguise their feelings. Further forward, Stewardess Wright recalled the story about the aircraft that slowed further every time it lost power on another engine. "If we lose another engine," she joked to a passenger in Club Class, "we'll be up here all night!"

Cabin pressurisation

The loss of the engines was having its effect on the cabin pressurisation. Although the outflow valves were closed, without engine power the cabin pressure could not be sustained, and the cabin altitude was progressively "climbing".

On the flightdeck, as the aircraft descended through 26,000 feet, the altitude warning horn suddenly sounded, indicating the cabin altitude had climbed to the equivalent of 10,000 feet. Immediately the flightcrew donned their oxygen masks. But Greaves' mask was malfunctioning. He threw it down impatiently, and carried on without it.

But Captain Moody could not afford to have his first officer disabled by anoxia. Disconnecting the autopilot, he applied the speedbrakes. He decided against lowering the undercarriage in case it became necessary to ditch the aircraft. With the speedbrakes extended and the nose down 10 degrees, he increased the rate of descent to between 7000 and 8000 fpm.

The steep angle of descent and the effect produced by the speedbrakes was immediately evident to the passengers. There was a sudden vibration – nothing like normal turbulence, while the earlier quietness without engine noise was replaced by a rattling sound, with the whole aircraft buffeting alarmingly. Babies and small children began to cry as the pressure change affected their ears. An elderly woman passenger suffered an attack of angina pectoris and quickly swallowed a tablet to relieve the pain.

Graham Skinner continued to move amongst the passengers, determined to minimise their fears by keeping the situation lighthearted, frequently crouching down to talk to people in their seats, rather than making them look up. It was psychologically more reassuring.

Most of the infants were now crying. Some had been startled by being suddenly awakened, removed from their sky-cots and secured on their parents' laps. And now the rapid change in air pressure was hurting their ears. But Skinner believed it better to let the babies cry as this tended to clear their ears.

To make matters worse, the cabin lights, already dimmed, were now flickering on and off, leaving only the balefully lit exit signs over the doors to relieve the darkness .

Somewhere a woman grabbed a steward's arm. "I don't want to die," she pleaded.

On the flightdeck, Townley-Freeman and Greaves were working unceasingly to get the engines restarted. The flight engineer had reviewed all possible fuel problems. Could it be fuel contamination? But the tanks were checked for water after refuelling at Kuala Lumpur. In any case, with modern quality control, water contamination was a virtual impossibility. Yet there seemed no other logical explanation for the simultaneous engine failures – and their consistent refusal to restart.

Strange manifestations

There were other strange manifestations about the flight that were equally perplexing. VHF radio exchanges with Jakarta had become weak and often unreadable, and interference considerable. Jakarta Control had been unable to identify the aircraft on either its primary or secondary radar, and the flightcrew were unable to receive Jakarta's VOR and DME. Yet all these facilities were functioning normally before the weird visual effects began.

And that was not all. The digital readouts of both the DME and the INS were now displaying meaningless symbols, the ADF needles were rotating aimlessly, and the HSI deviation needle was revolving wildly.

Successful communication with Jakarta remained almost impossible. At 9.49pm, Jakarta Control asked a Singapore Airlines flight to relay any messages from Speedbird Nine. "We find Speedbird Nine barely readable," the Singapore Airlines aircraft replied.

As the aircraft descended through 20,000ft, Greaves succeeded in fixing the problem with his oxygen mask and was able to get back on to oxygen. Moody therefore discontinued the steep rate of descent and resumed a normal glide.

The aircraft's electrical systems were becoming increasingly affected by the loss of engine power. Although the engines had continued windmilling, the frequent changes in airspeed had intermittently affected their rpm. For some of the time the rotational speeds were sufficient to supply electrical power, but there were frequent periods when they were not, resulting in the failure of the cabin lighting. Standby power, fed from the aircraft's batteries, was being used to maintain essential systems.

As the Boeing 747's descent continued and its pressurisation problems worsened, the cabin altitude continued to climb. As the aircraft descended towards 17,000 feet, the cabin altitude reached the equivalent of 14,000 feet.

Oxygen masks

Throughout the cabins, passengers suddenly heard what sounded like hail on an iron roof. Looking up they saw that, all through the aircraft, overhead hatches had sprung open – and now dangling from them was a veritable jungle of yellow oxygen masks. Seconds later, hands everywhere were reaching out to take hold of the masks and put them on.

The cabin crew, each with their own portable oxygen equipment, waited for the usual prerecorded announcement advising passengers on the correct use of the masks. But none came. Purser Lea, at her cabin crew station by the main entry door, attempted to make a live announcement, but this also produced no result – the PA system had obviously failed. The crew fell back on the loudhailers, stored in lockers at strategic positions throughout the aircraft.

Moments later a woman ran down one of the aisles calling out: "Please help me!" She was sure her husband was having a heart attack. At once a stewardess went with her to help the man with his oxygen supply.

Cabin Service Officer Skinner, oxygen mask on and loudhailer in hand, continued to move through the cabins, reminding passengers of the correct use of the masks, but doing his best to keep the mood light. It was vital to inform the passengers, but he had to play down any hint that their situation was becoming desperate. "I'm getting so confused that I'm breathing through the megaphone and talking through the oxygen mask!" he joked.

An extremely anxious elderly passenger was throwing his arms about and Stewardess Claire Wickett was almost hit as she bent to talk to him. Gently she calmed his fear and persuaded him to put on his oxygen mask. She understood how he felt – underneath her poised exterior, she was full of fear herself for what the next few minutes held for them all.

As she worked she was conscious of the sea of faces watching her, mentally begging for some reassurance that all would be well. So many were obviously frightened and distressed, none more so than some of the young mothers with babies. Regardless of her own feelings, she resolved to do all she could for them. At that moment Graham Skinner came walking through her cabin with his loudhailer, comforting passengers with a word here, another word there. He looked so calm that it helped her to carry on.

Elsewhere throughout the aircraft, other crew members were also doing all they could to help distressed passengers and keep spirits up generally. Some of the more able and composed passengers were doing the same, comforting those near them, especially the elderly, the very young, and those who were alone.

Moment of truth ...

On the flightdeck, time was running out. There was still not a spark of life from any of the engines, nor any sign they were going to respond. The flightcrew still had no notion of what had caused the engines to flameout so unexpectedly, or what more could be done to start them again. All possible problems had been checked and rechecked again and again. The situation was more than frightening – for a competent, experienced crew, it was intolerably frustrating.

The stark possibility that the en-

gines were not going to restart had now to be faced. But to contemplate gliding all the way back over the mountains to Jakarta's Halim Airport for an unpowered landing was out of the question. Yet there was nowhere else within range to attempt a forced landing in pitch darkness.

The lowest safe height for a return to Halim Airport was 11,500 feet. If the engines had not fired before they were down to 12,000 feet, Captain Moody now decided, they would turn south away from the mountains again and head back out to sea. It would give them five or six more precious minutes during which the engines might start. If they did not, then there would be no alternative but to ditch the aircraft in the sea.

The ditching characteristics of a Boeing 747 were unknown – it had never been attempted. Ditching was an awesome prospect at the best of times, let alone into unknown sea conditions on a black night when it would be impossible to determine the direction of the primary and secondary swells.

CSO Skinner continued to keep a close watch on the passengers, particularly those with problems, and to superintend the use of therapeutic masks for tiny children. Knowing with certainty that the aircraft had been without power for many minutes, he could only wonder, like so

many aboard the flight, how it was all going to end.

Yet he needed to keep up the morale of the cabin crew and the passengers. Offering the standard advice, "Breathe normally into the mask," to many, he recognised the attitude of some of the passengers, and spoke accordingly. To one elderly man he said, "This is really exciting – something to tell your grandchildren!" Of another he asked, "Are you enjoying your flight?" It was his subtle way of complimenting them on their obvious composure.

On the flightdeck the point at which the aircraft would have to turn out to sea again was getting closer. It was time to get a message to the Cabin Service Officer and give him warning of the possibility of having to ditch.

Captain Moody tried the telephone to Skinner's station but the line was dead. He had no choice but to use the public address system. In any case it was time he communicated with the passengers. They were entitled to be told the truth too.

Addressing them for the first time since the emergency started, Moody did not know that the PA system had also been affected. As a result, only some of the passengers heard his message: "Ladies and Gentlemen, this is your Captain speaking. We have a small problem – all four en-

Unlike weather radar, weather satellites do not depend on the presence of moisture to "see" clouds. This satellite photo of Sumatra and Java was taken an hour and a half after the British Airways Boeing 747 had limped into Jakarta. The fan shaped plume of ash emanating from the erupting Mt Galunggung volcano is clearly visible near the centre of the picture. The less distinct inset, taken later the same night, is notable for the fact that the ash cloud has more than tripled in extent. (with acknowledgement to Australian Bureau of Meteorology & US NOAA)

gines have stopped. We are doing our damnedest to get them going again. I trust you are not in too much distress."

Around those who actually heard the masterpiece of understatement, even passengers who already suspected, there were audible gasps of fright and astonishment. Could it really be true? Then the captain spoke again, and this time his message chilled the cabin crew members who heard it: "Will the Cabin Service Officer report to the flightdeck immediately?"

It was ominous and could surely mean only one thing – the flightcrew were preparing to ditch!

Skinner quickly made his way up to the flightdeck, to find a scene of feverish activity. All wearing oxygen masks, the three flightcrew were still desperately trying to get the engines going, apparently also attempting to make radio contact.

When Moody saw the Cabin Service Officer, he pointed to the unwinding altimeter on the panel in front of him. "Do you get the picture?" he shouted through his oxygen mask.

Skinner did not fully understand what the captain said, but it was clear to him the situation was extremely serious. He waited, expecting further directions. When they did not come, he decided against interrupting the crew at such a critical time and left the flightdeck.

As he came down the spiral staircase from the upper deck, several of the cabin crew were waiting for him, their upturned faces anxious. "What's going on?" they asked.

Emergency preparations

Skinner had learnt little from his visit to the flightdeck, but had drawn his own conclusions. They were far from encouraging. But for the time being he would keep that to himself – it was much better to be positive. He made a calculated guess at what the captain would decide to do – assuming the crew succeeded in starting the engines.

"We're diverting to Jakarta – but batten everything down," he told them.

Quickly the word spread to other members of the cabin crew. With renewed enthusiasm they were able to further reassure the passengers. They were certainly in need of it.

Moments later the aircraft shuddered and the cabin lights went out again, vividly emphasising the emergency exit signs.

Suddenly there was a blinding flash along the side of the aircraft. A great streak of fire, 10 to 15 metres

long, had shot out the jetpipe of one of the engines

"Bloody hell!" a passenger called out grimly, "we've had it now!'"

Throughout the aircraft the cabin crew now prepared for a possible emergency evacuation. Again they checked that all their passengers' seatbelts were fastened and there were no small items unstowed.

They also began mentally selecting fit, able bodied male passengers who could help with the evacuation when needed. To their surprise they found some passengers already wearing their lifejackets. "Is there something you know that I don't?" Stewardess Glennie asked lightheartedly. "Are you expecting to go for a swim?"

One steward took the precaution of handing out pillows to his passengers, instructing them to protect their faces as the aircraft touched down. Some of the passengers were clinging to each other or holding hands. A few were crying quietly.

Again the aircraft shuddered from end to end as one of the silent engines spat out flame, and again the cabins were plunged into darkness. Outside was total darkness and it was impossible to know how high the aircraft was above ground or sea.

Skinner was now faced with another problem. With the PA system virtually useless, announcements regarding the donning of lifejackets and adopting the brace position would be impossible. Instructions to the passengers would have to be conveyed with the loudhailers and this would take time.

Moreover, not knowing if the aircraft was above land or sea, whether or not lifejackets would be necessary, or even how high the aircraft was, he had no idea when to start giving passengers instructions in preparation for impact. If he left it too late, there would be insufficient time to reach all the passengers with the loudhailers before the aircraft ditched. A start would have to be made soon.

For the crew on the flightdeck the prospect of having to ditch seemed increasingly likely. They remained mystified as to the reason for the engine failures, nor could they understand why the engines would not relight. They had come to the end of their resources – every conceivable possibility had been checked over and over again. It was difficult to think of anything else they could try. All they could do was to continue to repeat the vain inflight relighting procedure for as long as they had altitude and airspeed to do so.

Unexpected reprieve

But suddenly, as the aircraft descended through 13,500 feet, and without any warning, No 4 engine unexpectedly burst back into life.

To the flightcrew, to the valiant Cabin Service Officer, about to start evacuation briefings with the loudhailers, to his hardpressed cabin crew, and to the passengers who recognised it for what it was, the sound of the engine roaring again was the sweetest of music to their ears – what one passenger described later as the "most wonderful sound we had heard in our lives."

At once Greaves called Jakarta Control: "Jakarta – Speedbird Nine. We've got one engine running – out of 135." This time, for some reason, the VHF radio reception was better.

Theoretically, in ideal circumstances of weight and altitude, a Boeing 747-200 fitted with Rolls-Royce RB211 engines could maintain height on one engine only. But to what extent the engines had been affected or damaged in the present circumstances was unknown. To Moody, prudence in handling his one live engine was now essential – it would need nursing. Taking care not to apply too much power too soon, he succeeded in gradually reducing the aircraft's rate of descent to just over 300 fpm.

It didn't solve the problem but it was a big improvement on 2000 fpm and gave more time for further relight attempts. Already they had descended through 13,000 feet.

Anxiously the flightcrew continued their feverish activity. Another minute and twenty seconds slipped by as the altimeters continued to unwind, more slowly but just as inevitably, towards 12,000 feet. Then, as suddenly and unexpectedly as before, No 3 engine relit, came to life, and developed thrust.

Now treating both live starboard engines with the greatest care, Moody succeeded in re-establishing level flight just above 12,000 feet – more than the lowest safe altitude for a return to Jakarta – if only just!

All at once life took on a new dimension. The aircraft could certainly fly on the two engines, even if it could not climb. With good luck, skilled handling, and careful manoeuvring, they could probably now make it back over the Javanese mountains for a two-engined emergency approach to Jakarta Airport.

But there was more to come. Very soon afterwards, No 1 and No. 2 engines on the port side relit almost simultaneously. Again the great surge of power seemed like magic.

Not only on the flightdeck, but throughout the aircraft, the sense of relief was palpable – all four engines were operational again. For all on board it was a reprieve from certain disaster ...

"Jakarta – Speedbird Nine," Greaves transmitted joyfully. "We're back in business. All four engines running – level at 12,000." On the captain's instruction, he added, "Request higher level." Not only was the radio reception back to normal, the aircraft's radio navigation aids also appeared to be operational again. Kuala Lumpur time was now just before 10pm.

"Speedbird Nine," Jakarta Control replied, "Cleared to Flight Level 150."

Diversion to Jakarta

Captain Moody tried the PA system again and this time, with the aircraft's electrical power fully restored, it worked: "Ladies and Gentlemen, this is the Captain speaking. We seem to have overcome that problem and have managed to start all the engines. We are diverting to Jakarta and expect to land in about 15 minutes."

For Graham Skinner, the announcement conveyed something akin to fulfilment. His "long shot" to the cabin crew had come off! Amongst passengers and cabin crew alike, the sense of elation overflowed. People embraced spontaneously, and talked excitedly – everything was going to be all right after all!

But their high spirits were short-lived. Suddenly, as the Boeing 747 climbed towards its new cruising height of 15,000 feet, the tracer-like visual effects abruptly reappeared. Immediately Captain Moody reduced power to descend from whatever strange phenomena existed at the higher level.

It was not soon enough. In a moment the No 2 engine surged, recovered, then surged again and again. Quickly the crew went through the shutdown drill for No 2.

"Jakarta – Speedbird Nine," Greaves transmitted urgently. Leaving Flight Level 150 for 120. We are now on three engines."

"Roger, Speedbird Nine," acknowledged Jakarta. "Cleared to Flight Level 120. Fly heading 345 degrees."

To the occupants of Zone C, particularly those seated on the port side, the repeated surging of the No 2 engine had presented a sight as daunting as anything they had seen so far. In the pitch darkness, each time the engine surged it seemed to explode into flames, with what looked like a stream of glowing red fireballs spinning away from the jetpipe.

Once again, shocked, white faces, with white knuckled hands gripping seat arms, characterised the mood of the cabin.

Was the problem, whatever it was, starting all over again?

Captain Moody spoke over the PA system again: "Ladies and Gentlemen, this is the Captain again. I have had to shut down No 2 engine as it was rough running. We shall be landing at Jakarta in about 10 minutes."

The captain's voice was reassuring – so calm and matter-of-fact, as if this sort of emergency were an everyday happening. Yet, after all the fear and tension, some passengers found it hard to believe that safety now lay only minutes away.

Cleared by Approach Control for a long, low rate descent, Moody handled the engines carefully, using the speedbrakes against engine power as far as possible to avoid altering the thrust settings and risking another engine's surge.

To the passengers with window seats, the lights of Jakarta in the distance were a welcome sight, but for many the tension continued. Was the aircraft damaged? If so, how would it affect the landing?

The minutes dragged as the gradual descent continued. The aircraft was still carrying more than 30 tonnes of fuel, but it was below its maximum landing weight so it would not be necessary to dump.

"Do you require assistance on arrival?" enquired Jakarta Approach.

"Affirmative – request fire services," replied Greaves.

The duty runway was Runway 24, but the slow, gradual descent dictated by the condition of the engines had left the aircraft too high to join the circuit on a normal left base leg for landing. Moody therefore planned to overfly the airport, continue out over the sea to the northwest to lose height, then make a procedure turn back towards the runway.

Cleared now for this manoeuvre, the crew would be able to acquire the localiser well out from the runway. But the approach controller now added: "Be advised our glide path is unserviceable." The crew would have to judge the descent visually.

Four minutes later, now well beyond the northern coast, Greaves called Approach Control again: "Speedbird Nine is commencing right turn."

Viewing the distant lights of the airport from the northwest as the turn continued, Greaves noticed they appeared extremely misty. Use of the windscreen demister and wipers had no effect. He and Captain Moody then realised the transpar-

Mt Galunggung gained world notoriety in rendering a salutary lesson to the aviation industry on the night of June 24 1982, but its previous history had been far from inactive. Major eruptions occurred in 1822, 1894, and 1918, then were followed by relative quiescence until April 1982, when the mountain again "awoke". Two months later, the triple explosions which rent the Javanese night at 10 to 20 minute intervals just as G-BDXH was becoming airborne at Kuala Lumpur, were the most violent in living memory. This photograph shows the volcano erupting yet again on the morning of September 2, 1982. (with acknowledgement to Captain L Allen, Air New Zealand, via Andre Deutsch/Hutchinson Publishing)

ency of the glass had been affected. The only clear visibility was through a narrow vertical strip on the outboard edge of each windscreen panel. This result was that Captain Moody, trying to sight the airport to his right across the flightdeck, could hardly see it at all.

Talking the captain around, Greaves called Approach Control again. "We're level at 2500. We're 16.5 DME, and intercepting the localiser."

Approach: "OK, Speedbird Nine – cleared for approach to Runway 24."

Using the DME readout, Greaves was cross checking distance against altitude and advising the captain accordingly. The earlier discrepancy in the airspeed indications had disappeared. Both instruments were now giving the same reading. "Could you turn up the runway lights?" Greaves asked the approach controller.

Suddenly the lights appeared dimly through the windscreen. "We have the lights in sight," Greaves reported.

"OK – continue approach – contact tower now, 118.3."

Moody could now see a little through the less affected strip down the outboard edge of his own windscreen panel, but it was like trying to land in fog. Fortunately the runway's VASIS was operating, but he was able to see its lights only hazily, and he repeatedly sought confirmation of their indications from Greaves.

The first officer switched on the landing lights, but nothing appeared to happen. The lights were in fact illuminating normally, but the landing light covers had sustained the same type of surface damage as the windscreens.

Greaves called the Tower: "Speedbird Nine on short final for Runway 24."

"Speedbird Nine – wind calm, cleared to land!"

Passengers close to the cabin windows could see the flashing red lights of the fire tenders lining both sides of the runway. For at least one passenger the accumulated tension was too much. Suddenly he was violently sick.

On the flightdeck, Greaves called the airspeed while Townley-Freeman called the height above the runway on the radio altimeter. Concentrating hard, Moody touched the aircraft down smoothly, selected No 3 engine into idle reverse (to balance the shutdown No 2), then quickly applied symmetrical reverse thrust on No 1 and No 4 engines.

As the aircraft came to a stop on the runway, there was a stunned silence throughout the cabins, as if no one could quite believe it. Then, as the tension was released, wild applause and cheering broke out. People embraced, laughed, shook hands with whoever was in reach, and fought back tears of relief. They were alive – and safe!

Some sat quietly for a moment giving thanks to God for their deliverance. All their fervent prayers had been answered. It was only 40 minutes since the first signs of the drama had begun to manifest themselves though to most it had seemed more like a lifetime.

After the aircraft had finally been towed to the terminal building and the passengers were disembarking, Captain Moody noticed that gritty black dust lay on every horizontal surface. He remarked on it to Greaves and Townley-Freeman.

The flight engineer had been in Jakarta a month previously and remembered reading something about a volcanic eruption in the local newspapers. Suddenly all their weird and traumatic experiences seemed to make sense.

"That's volcanic ash!" he exclaimed. "That's what we must have flown into!"

Mt Galunggung

Confirmation of the crew's suspicions came next day when, after spending the night at a hotel in Jakarta, they returned to the airport to inspect the damage sustained by the Boeing 747.

All the leading edges of the aircraft – wings, tailplane, engine cowlings and spinners, the windscreen and the nose itself – were abraded as though they had been sandblasted. The engines themselves were heavily contaminated with ash, and ash had found its way throughout the cabin pressurisation ducts and into the pitot static system – explaining the discrepancy in airspeed indications before the crew succeeded in restarting the engines.

From Jakarta's Rolls-Royce representative, who was at the airport assessing the condition of the engines, the crew learnt that the previous evening, Mt Galunggung, a 2168m high active volcano near the southern coast of the island of Java, some 175km southeast of Jakarta, had erupted violently, spewing a vast cloud of hot volcanic ash high into the atmosphere. A satellite photograph showed that northeasterly winds had fanned the ash cloud out to the west over the southern coast, and to the southwest over the Indian Ocean for more than 150km.

Because the cloud of hot ash contained no moisture, it remained invisible on the aircraft's weather radar. Cruising in darkness at Flight Level 370, the Boeing 747 flew directly into the unseen ash laden volcanic cloud – with drastic results.

The "smoke" seen entering the cabins early in the development of the drama was, of course, volcanic ash. Similarly, the "engine fires" that caused such consternation in the passenger cabins were not true fires as such, but the electrostatic effects of the ash particles being ingested

This regional map shows air routes closed as a result of the second Mt Galunggung incident – this time involving a Singapore Airlines Boeing 747. (Matthew Tesch)

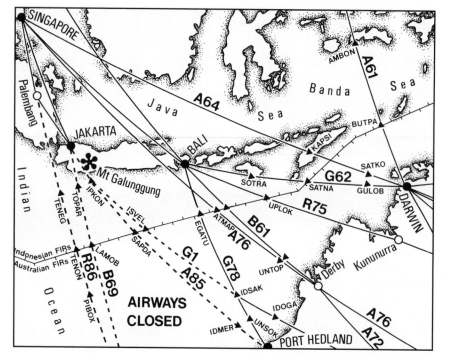

into and discharged from the engines – a related but much more spectacular and frightening version of the weird effects the flightcrew were witnessing on the aircraft's windscreen.

The subsequent spasmodic spurts of flame from the jetpipes of the engines, accompanied by shuddering, which also provoked alarm amongst the passengers, were the result of the crew's continuing attempts to relight the engines while still flying in the ash cloud – occasionally, accumulated fuel being supplied to the "dead" engines would ignite, resulting in the spectacular visual and sound effects.

It was obvious too that the volcanic ash cloud in which the aircraft was flying, possibly because of the electromagnetic charge it was carrying, had acted as a shield against VHF radio transmissions.

Once the aircraft, in the course of its unpowered descent, had emerged from the base of the ash cloud, it not only became possible to relight the engines – all VHF radio propagation, both for communication and navigation, returned to normal.

After extensive checks and a change of three of its four engines at Jakarta, the Boeing 747 was ferried back to London without passengers. Here it underwent major inspection and rectification of all the damage caused by the ash cloud encounter, before being returned to service several weeks later.

The crew themselves were highly commended for their handling of the inflight emergency, their efforts being subsequently recognised by a number of industry awards, including The Queen's Commendation for Valuable Service in the Air, bestowed on Captain Moody and Cabin Service Officer Skinner.

The lessons

As a result of the frightening incident, the Indonesian aviation authorities temporarily closed the airspace in the vicinity of Mt Galunggung, diverting all Australia-bound international flights which would normally overfly the western end of Java further to the east.

Eight days after the incident on July 2 however, because the skies around Mt Galunggung appeared to have remained clear for a week, the affected air routes were reopened to traffic.

It was to prove too soon. Another 11 days later, on July 13, a Singapore Airlines Boeing 747, operating Flight SQ21A from Melbourne to Singapore, encountered inflight problems similar to those experienced by the British Airways aircraft while overflying the same area. This time, thanks to the media and industry publicity given to the earlier incident, the captain recognised the visual and mechanical symptoms and immediately suspected they had flown into an unseen volcanic ash cloud. But even before he could take effective avoiding action, three of the aircraft's engines had overheated. As before, the crew made a successful emergency diversion to Halim Airport, Jakarta.

Mt Galunggung had erupted yet again. Again the airspace was closed – but this time until further notice, all international flights to and from Australia being rerouted to overfly Bali instead of Jakarta, thus avoiding the Mt Galunggung area altogether.

Coming so soon after the earlier serious incident, it was a salutary lesson for the airline industry. A new type of inflight hazard had been identified – one that in future would have to be carefully watched for on weather satellite photographs.

Although there had been instances in the past when aircraft had passed through volcanic ash clouds some distance downwind of a volcanic eruption without serious consequences, these two Boeing 747 incidents were apparently the only recorded cases of aircraft actually flying into an erupting plume of volcanic ash.

The incidents also emphasised the importance of emergency drills, and their frequent practice by flightcrews, even those never expected to be required in actual operations, like British Airways' "Four Engine Failure Drill" exercised in the airline's simulator. Despite the frightening and (at the time) totally inexplicable inflight manifestations encountered by the British Airways crew, it was their disciplined adherence to practised drills, together with their self control and persistence, that finally averted a major aviation catastrophe.

Footnote:

(1) Readers with some knowledge of Jakarta today may wonder at the reference to Halim. The one-time gateway to Jakarta, Kemayoran Airport, in the city's inner northeast towards the coast, was replaced by Halim, to the southeast, for international traffic. But as Jakarta continued to develop as a modern urban centre – and with it the volume of air traffic serving the city – Kemayoran was closed (permanently stranding a number of unserviceable propeller driven airliners), while Halim was itself downgraded to become a base for oil industry support operations and specialist services such as Haj pilgrimage charters. Both these airports were effectively replaced by Soekarno-Hatta International Airport, the modern facility developed for both international and domestic Jakarta traffic at Cengkareng (CGK).

Darken the setting and amend the airline title, and this view of "City of Cardiff" could as well be "City of Edinburgh" rolling out after landing on Jakarta's Runway 24. Note the deployed thrust reverser sleeves (see Chapter 14 for more detailed discussion of a typical reverser system). Captain Moody held his No 3 (inboard engine) at Idle setting only, to compensate for the shutdown No 2.

CHAPTER 8

"Come on back – you're sinking .....!"

– Boeing 727 Captain to First Officer

Pan American World Airways Boeing 727-235 N4737 [19457] (F/n 37)
"Clipper Defiance" – July 9,1982

For an experienced crew, long accustomed to the hot, humid and turbulent summers of the USA's southern Gulf States, a routine en route call at New Orleans on a stormy afternoon was normal. But the fate that awaited them and their 136 passengers was to prove a savage reminder of the respect to be accorded nearby thunderstorm cells – especially in operations close to the ground.

Thunderstorms – but business as usual

The weather at New Orleans, Louisiana, on the afternoon of Friday, July 9, 1982 was hot and humid, with scattered thunderstorms typical of the conditions that prevail across the Gulf Coast States of the USA for nearly half their summer days.

Under the influence of a high pressure area centred in the Gulf of Mexico, conditions throughout the afternoon were expected to be characterised by "scattered clouds, variable to broken at 3000 feet, chance of overcast ceilings at 1000 feet, visibility two miles [3km], thunderstorms, moderate rain showers." There were no fronts or low pressure areas within 100nm of the city.

Certainly, for the Boeing 727 crew of Pan American's Flight 759 ("Clipper 759"), a scheduled service from Miami, Florida, to Las Vegas, Nevada, with an en route stop at New Orleans, we know by now the forecast seemed innocuous enough for the time of the year, especially by comparison with that to which they were accustomed. All from Miami, Captain Kenneth McCullers, 45, First Officer Donald Pierce, 32, and Flight Engineer Leo Noone, 60, had been

long-serving staff of the Miami-based National Airlines, transferring to PanAm when the latter took over National two years earlier in January 1980. All had years of familiarity with the air mass type thunderstorm weather prevailing that day in the New Orleans area.

The first leg of the flight from Miami, cutting northwest across the Gulf of Mexico to New Orleans and lasting a little over an hour, was entirely uneventful, as was the approach and landing itself at the busy Moisant Airport in the suburb of Kenner.

While the Boeing 727 was refuelled and its services replenished for the long 1350nm (2500km) leg on to Las Vegas, Captain McCullers and First Officer Pierce went to PanAm's local operations office, where the flight documents for the New Orleans to Las Vegas leg had been prepared. In addition to the despatch release form, computer flight plan, and preliminary loadsheet, these included the 2.15pm Gulf Coast Aviation Weather Report and the 2.25pm Southwestern States Aviation Weather Report.

Additional weather information

was displayed on clipboards on the operations office's counter, while the New Orleans surface weather observations were available for crews on both a teletype machine and via the operations office's ATIS (Automatic Terminal Information Service) radio receiver.

When all was done, Captain McCullers signed the teletype copy of the despatch release transmitted to New Orleans from the Miami despatch office, signifying he had received all documentation required for the flight.

By the time the pilots returned to the aircraft, the cabin crew – Purser Dennis Donnelly and Flight Attendants James Fijut, Lucille Brown and Vivian Ford, all from Florida – were supervising the seating of the 136 passengers boarding the aircraft for Las Vegas. One non-revenue passenger, a company employee, occupied one of the two jumpseats on the flightdeck, and Flight Engineer Noone had completed his preflight preparations.

The 200 series Boeing 727 was fitted with Pratt & Whitney JT8D-7B engines rated at 14,000lb thrust, and the takeoff computation form prepared by the crew (usually referred to in airline operations as the "bug card") showed the aircraft's gross weight to be 170,000lb (77,180kg); the flap setting 15°, stabiliser trim setting 21.3% MAC (Mean Aerodynamic Chord); the temperature 92°F (33°C); the wind 320° at only three knots; and the altimeter setting 29.98 inches (1015 hPa). The target power settings were 1.9 EPR (see Chapter 6) on Nos 1 and 3 engines, and 1.92 on No 2 engine. V_1 and V_r were one and the same at 138 knots, and V_2 was 151 knots.

At 3.48pm the crew radioed the airport's clearance delivery office and were given their airways clearance to Las Vegas "as filed". The aircraft was to maintain 5000 feet initially, but could expect to be cleared to FL280 (28,000 feet) 10 minutes after departure.

A few minutes later, as a heavy rain shower could be seen approaching the airport from the southwest, the Boeing 727's doors were closed, the rear stairs raised, and a tug pushed the aircraft back from Gate 7. To the consternation of the accompanying ground crew, who were without wet weather clothing, it began to pour with rain on the airport itself as the flight crew were starting the engines.

At 3.58pm the first officer called Moisant Ground Control for a taxi clearance, specifying that, because of their near maximum weight, they would require Runway 10 for takeoff. Ground Control cleared the aircraft to taxi to the holding point for Runway 10 and amended its initial altitude after takeoff to 4000 feet. At this time, the airport's ATIS was transmitting "Information Foxtrot", describing the present weather as "cloud: 2500 [feet] scattered, 2500 [feet] thin broken, visibility six miles in haze, temperature 90°, wind 240° at two knots, winds are calm, altimeter 30.01."

As the first officer read back the amended clearance, he asked: "What is your wind now?" and the ground controller responded: "Wind 040 at eight [knots]".

Moisant Airport, 23km west-northwest of the city and known officially as New Orleans International Airport, has two main runways, oriented at right angles to each other in an L-shaped pattern, extending to the north and west of the main apron and terminal building complex, with parallel taxiways serving their full length. In addition there is a third, shorter runway, intersecting both main runways (see diagram). The airport's elevation is a mere four feet.

The subject Boeing 727 entered service, wearing the orange and "grapefruit" colours of National Airlines' "Sun King" livery, on the last day of January 1968. Earlier sistership N4734 [19454] "Elaine" is shown depicting these colours at Pensacola, Florida, in 1975 (note the natural metal rudder). Eighth of an order for 25 727-235s, N4737 was delivered to Miami and named "Susan" on the same day as "Elaine" began revenue flights. From 1972, National's "Fly Me!" marketing campaign personalised the identities of staff and crew, as well as their aircraft, the latter's names being increased in size, against a splash of the corporate colours, on the forward cabin roof. N4737 "Susan" later became "Erica", while N4734 retained "Elaine" until becoming "Clipper Charmer". (with acknowledgement to Airliners Slides/Airliners Magazine)

A number of other departures and arrivals were in progress as the Boeing 727 taxied north across the apron to join the long taxiway leading westwards to the holding point for Runway 10. A Delta Air Lines DC-9 bound for Washington DC had just lifted off from Runway 10, while two more DC-9s, operated respectively by Republic Airlines and Texas International, were taxiing for Runway 19, as was a Cessna Citation corporate jet following some distance behind them. A Southwest Airlines Boeing 737, which had taxied from the terminal a minute ahead of the PanAm 727, was holding short of the eastern end of Runway 10-28, awaiting a clearance to takeoff in the 28 direction, and a USAir DC-9 behind the PanAm 727 was also taxiing for Runway 10.

With heavy cloud now directly over the airport and rain lashing the locality, the earlier calm had been replaced by gusty, fluctuating wind conditions. As the Boeing 727 was nearing the holding point for Runway 10, with the time now 4.02pm, the still-taxiing Citation asked the ground controller: "What's that wind doing now?"

The controller replied: "Wind 060 degrees at 15, peak gusts to 25, low level windshear alert – northeast quadrant 330° at 10 [knots]; northwest quadrant 130° at three [knots]."

A minute later, as the Boeing 727 reached the Runway 10 holding point, First Officer Pierce also requested another wind check. This time Ground Control replied: "Winds now 070° at 17 – peak gust that was, 23 knots – we have low level windshear alerts in all quadrants – appears the front [sic] is passing overhead right now – we're right in the middle of everything."

At 4.06pm, just after an arriving Boeing 767 had touched down on Runway 10, First Officer Pierce changed frequency and called the Tower to report: "Clipper 759 ready".

The tower controller instructed: "Maintain 2000, fly runway heading – cleared for takeoff," and First Officer Pierce read back the clearance. It was to prove the PanAm aircraft's final transmission.

As the PanAm Boeing 727 was lining up to begin rolling, the tower cleared an inbound Eastern Air Lines flight to land behind it on Runway 10, the controller advising the wind was now 070° at 17 knots and that a "heavy Boeing" (the 767) which had just landed had encountered a 10 knot windshear at about 100 feet on final approach.

To the controllers in the tower, the PanAm Boeing 727's takeoff appeared perfectly normal, the aircraft lifting off cleanly after rotation 50 seconds later and some 7000 feet (2135 metres) down the runway, near the intersection of the centre taxiway. At this stage the controllers turned their attention to other traffic.

But, still visible through the rain, the Boeing's departure was being watched by several people in the airport terminal concourse. After it had climbed to only about 100 feet, they were concerned to see it begin to lose height. The descent continued as they watched with mounting alarm, until the aircraft, still in a noseup attitude of about 10°, finally disappeared from view behind trees beyond the airport boundary. Moments later there was an enormous fiery explosion, and dense black smoke erupted hundreds of feet into the air.

Swathe of destruction

Within minutes, every available emergency vehicle – fire engines, ambulances and police cars – were converging, sirens wailing, on the scene of the disaster from all over the city of New Orleans. With devastating results, the descending Boeing had ploughed into the modern residential suburb which adjoins the eastern side of the airport, cutting a swathe of destruction 150 metres wide and three suburban blocks in extent.

The neighbourhood of neat, brick ranch houses in the path of the aircraft had been instantly reduced to a blazing, smoking sea of scattered bricks, twisted metal, burning cars, and strewn household articles. Of the Boeing 727 itself, little remained that was recognisable, save a section of the fuselage with part of the starboard wing attached, and the blue and white tail fin with the centre engine air intake and the No 2 engine itself. The rest of what had been a fully serviceable three-engined jetliner, carrying 144 people, was no more than a vast scatter of fragmented metal, strewn with the grisly, burnt and dismembered remains of its occupants.

Firemen took two hours to fully extinguish the flames before the grim task of recovering the bodies and assessing the number of those killed on the ground could begin.

Rescue workers found that the aircraft had demolished six houses, setting their remains ablaze, and badly damaged five others. The bodies of eight residents were found amongst the remains of the burnt-out houses. All of them died either in the trauma of the impact, or the fire that followed. Another nine were seriously injured and admitted to hospital. A baby girl of 18 months was found alive and unhurt under the debris of one house in which her mother and sister had been killed.

While a makeshift morgue was set up for the crash victims in an airline hangar at the airport, a team of NTSB investigators led by Board Vice Chairman Patricia Goldman arrived from Washington DC to begin the huge task of determining the cause of this totally unexpected tragedy. Examination of the still smouldering wreckage trail began late the same afternoon.

Wreckage examination

Forced down to a height of only 50 feet, the Boeing 727 had initially struck three trees, part of a row on the east side of Williams Boulevard, running north-south some 700 metres beyond the eastern end of Runway 10. Banked about 6° to the left, the aircraft then struck a second group of trees 100 metres further on at about the same height. Segments of the port wing's leading edge de-

vices and trailing edge flaps were torn off and the aircraft continued to roll to the left until the wing tip struck the ground at a bank angle of about 105°. Demolished by impact, explosion and fire, the wreckage hit more trees and houses before finally coming to rest about 1400 metres from the end of Runway 10. The aircraft had struck the ground in an extreme left wing-down bank, and its disintegration was so extensive that little useful information could be obtained from the wreckage.

Overtaken by events: PanAm's takeover of National Airlines proved not the shrewdest corporate decision in the visionary Clipper history. For years restricted to international and overseas operations as the USA's de facto "chosen instrument", PanAm increasingly hankered after a domestic network. Unsuccessful courtings of TWA and Allegheny, among others, finally led to a stock exchange tussle between PanAm, Texas International and Eastern for the small but strong balance sheet of National. Finally resolved in PanAm's favour between May and December, 1979, the inflated purchase price of US$350m (1979) was being totalled just as President Carter was signing the Deregulation Act – opening the US airline market to all comers! National's 43 727s of various marques were compatible with the total of 78 that PanAm had operated, but National's 16 DC-10s clashed expensively with the dozen short-bodied L1011-500 TriStars PanAm had ordered only months before.

Nevertheless it was determined that the undercarriage was retracted, the trailing edge flaps set to 15°, and the leading edge flaps and slats extended. A static discharge rod which had separated from the trailing edge of the port tailplane was analysed for evidence of lightning strike discharge, but none was found. The EPR gauges, located on the pilots' centre instrument panel, had been damaged by fire, but de-

tailed examination showed that all three had been indicating between 1.97 EPR and 2.0 EPR when the aircraft crashed.

All three engines were found in the main wreckage area. No 2 engine was still attached to the empennage, but No 1 and No 3 engines had separated from their mountings. Damage to the engines indicated that all three were under high power at impact. The engines were dismantled and their components examined, but there was no evidence of any preimpact malfunction.

Flight recorders

The FDR and CVR, both of Sundstrand manufacture, were removed from the wreckage and taken to the NTSB's Washington DC laboratory to be read out.

Although the exterior of the FDR was damaged by impact and fire, the interior sustained only minor damage. All parameters had been clearly recorded, and there was no evidence of any abnormality. The recording began shortly after the Boeing 727 was pushed back from the terminal gate and ended 10 minutes 3.3 seconds later.

The FDR readout showed that, at 1607:57 hours, (4.07:57pm local time), the indicated airspeed began increasing as the takeoff began, and the vertical acceleration trace became active. At 1608:40, the altitude trace began to rise, and at 1608:54.5 had climbed to 95 feet AMSL, the highest altitude recorded. The altitude then decreased, reaching zero feet at 1608:58. The aircraft had maintained a fairly constant magnetic heading of 099° until 1608:41, when it began to swing to the left. By 1608:57, its magnetic heading was 092°.

The CVR recording began before the Boeing 727 was pushed back from its terminal gate and ended with the sound of impact at 1609:05. But the recording was badly distorted, with previously recorded sounds remaining as background noise on the tape. The result was a high-pitched background noise to all the newly recorded sounds. In addition, the noise of the windscreen wipers during the takeoff further masked low level, flightdeck sounds.

Most of the sounds recorded before the wipers were turned on were decipherable by filter adjustment and repeated listening. The final minute of the transcript, recorded after the wipers were turned on, was prepared in the same manner, but because of the poor quality of the recording, its contents could not be deciphered with as much certainty.

PanAm ordered only eight 727-200s from Boeing in its own right, the others being acquired from PSA and Delta during 1983-84, and PEOPLExpress and Lufthansa in 1986. N367PA [22539] "Clipper Matchless" was the fifth such '221, and is shown here just after its entry to service in April 1982. Its livery typifies that worn by "Clipper Defiance" at the time of the New Orleans accident three months later. All the acquired National aircraft took up "Clipper" names from the beginning of 1980, only the absence of a letter suffix to the 727s' registrations hinting at their former National ownership. Not surprisingly, the DC-10s and L1011-500s proved an unhappy dilution of an otherwise all-Boeing PanAm fleet, and were all disposed of by 1984 and 1986, respectively. (with acknowledgement to Flight International)

The CVR transcript showed that the crew completed the takeoff and departure briefings while taxiing to Runway 10, and that the captain and the first officer reviewed the rejected takeoff and fuel dumping procedures. At 1602:34, while the Boeing 727 was still taxiing, Ground Control's advice to the Cessna Citation that there were low level wind shear alerts in the northeast quadrants of the airport was received on the Boeing's radio. A minute later at 1603:33, First Officer Pierce requested another wind check and Ground Control replied: "Winds now 070° at 17 – peak gust that was, 23 knots – we have low level windshear alerts in all quadrants – appears the front [sic] is passing overhead right now – we're right in the middle of everything."

The captain then advised the first officer to "let your airspeed build up on takeoff" and said that they would turn off the air conditioning packs for the takeoff, which would enable them to increase the EPR to 1.92 on both No 1 and 3 engines.

At 1606:22, the first officer informed the tower they were "ready", the tower controller cleared the flight for takeoff, and the first officer acknowledged the clearance.

At 1607:44, as they taxied on to Runway 10 for takeoff, the first officer asked: "Right or left turn after we get out of here?" The captain replied: "I would suggest ... a slight turn over to the left."

At 1607:59, the first officer requested takeoff thrust, and 17 seconds later the captain called "80 knots." At 1608:33, 1608:41, and 1608:43 respectively, he called "V$_r$", "Positive climb", and "V$_2$". Correlation of the FDR and CVR data showed that at these times the re-

corded airspeeds were 78, 138, and 158 knots respectively. As mentioned, the calculated V$_r$ and V$_2$ speeds for the takeoff were 138 and 151 knots.

At 1608:45, the captain called out in an urgent tone: "Come on back – you're sinking, Don ... come on back!" At 1608:57, the Ground Proximity Warning System (GPWS) activated and the warning, "Whoop whoop ... pull up ... whoop", sounded. At this moment, according to the FDR, the aircraft's recorded airspeed and altitude were 149 knots and 55 feet AMSL.

Three seconds later, the sound of the aircraft's first impact with trees was recorded and one of the crew

uttered an expletive. Four seconds after the first there was a second impact, with the final impact occurring another second later as the recording came to an end.

Ground witness evidence

Forty-seven of more than 100 ground witnesses interviewed by investigators provided descriptions of the weather at the time of the accident. Thirty-eight of them saw the Boeing 727 airborne, the fireball on impact, or the smoke cloud after impact, from distances varying between 100 metres and 1600 metres. Only two of them, both airline ground staff, said the rain obscured their view of the aircraft as it passed over the airport's eastern boundary. Two of the only four witnesses who saw lightning said it was not in the area of the accident. Only one witness said she heard thunder.

Of 14 witnesses who were on the airport, six said that, about the time the Boeing took off, the rain was light to moderate; six said it was heavy; and two described the rain as very heavy. Four said the rain increased after the accident.

Of the 33 witnesses outside the airport boundaries, all agreed it was raining at the time, but their opinions varied as to its intensity. Seven who described the rain as "not very intense" said it increased after the accident.

Three witnesses, all driving south on Williams Boulevard when the aircraft struck the line of trees on its east side, said the rain was heavy to

Map of continental USA, showing planned route of Flight PA 759 from Miami to Las Vegas via New Orleans, set against a background of National's route network at the time of its acquisition. National's traditional north-south axis along the eastern seaboard did little to feed traffic to PanAm's intercontinental operations, especially with the opening up of new direct transatlantic services. Nor were National's transcontinental US rights as valuable to PanAm as they seemed, being almost exclusively confined to southern states and missing out on the more lucrative east-west links to the north. National in fact had gained approval beyond Houston (its hitherto westernmost port) only in March 1961, with Las Vegas and the West Coast ports receiving inaugural DC-8 and L-188 Electra services in June that year. (Matthew Tesch, with acknowledgement to R E G Davies)

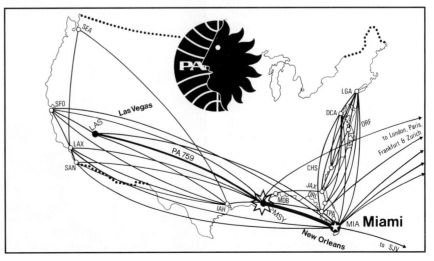

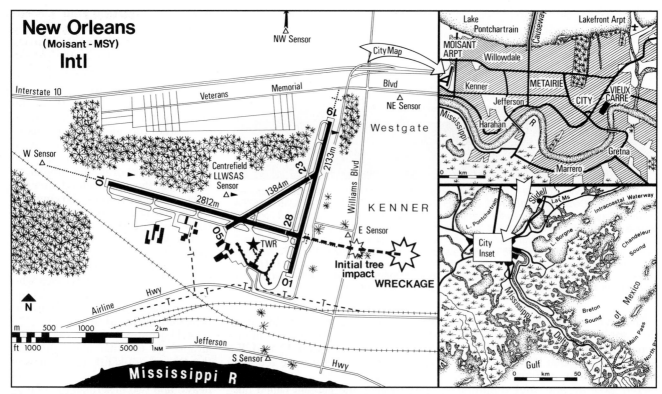

Diagram of New Orleans (Moisant) International Airport, showing locations of sensors for the Low Level Windshear Alert System. The insets show the position of the airport in relation to the city, on the shores of Lake Pontchartrain and the Mississippi Delta, in southeastern Louisiana. (Matthew Tesch, with acknowledgement to NTSB & Rand McNally)

very heavy. One added that the wind was blowing from west to east, and that "whole trees were swaying".

Seven others said it was southerly. Two said it was from the north, and two said there had been a wind change; Some witnesses described the wind as "swirling", "gusty", "strong", or "variable" at the time of the accident.

Flightcrew witness evidence

Between 11 minutes before the accident and 18 minutes after it, four airline aircraft and one corporate Cessna Citation took off. As well, another airline aircraft taxied to Runway 10 but cancelled its departure after the Boeing 727 crashed. The airline types were all fitted with Bendix RDR-1-E monochromatic weather radar, and the Citation with Bendix RDR-1100 X-band colour radar. All their crews used the radar to scan the surrounding weather while awaiting takeoff.

At 3.58pm, when the Washington-bound Delta Air Lines DC-9 took off from Runway 10, its radar showed a storm cell directly over the airport and extending slightly north of Runway 10. It also showed other storm cells 25nm away to the southeast.

The captain of the Republic Airlines DC-9, which departed from Runway 19 three minutes later, used the aircraft's radar to scan the local area while taxiing. There were thun-

derstorms all around the airport – one just east-northeast, with numerous cells to the south, southwest, and west up to 20nm away. The largest radar echo was the one to the east-northeast and the cell contoured when he switched to contour mode. Its gradient "was very steep".

The Republic captain said that during the takeoff the aircraft encountered heavy rain and windshear about halfway down Runway 19 and visibility became very poor. The DC-9

began to drift to the right, continuing to do so even after left rudder was applied. Rather than reject the takeoff, the captain lifted the aircraft off the ground prior to V_1. While the undercarriage was retracting, the stall warning stick shaker activated briefly.

The Republic first officer said the airspeed was fluctuating during the takeoff. V_1 and V_r were 132 knots, V_2 was 140 knots, but the captain actually rotated the aircraft at 121 knots. As they passed over the end of the

Standing on the port elevator, a fireman surveys the only major part of the Boeing 727 still recognisable. The inboard end of the folded-over port tailplane protrudes above the fin and the No 2 engine intake, distinguishable only by the PanAm symbol and the faintly visible aircraft registration. (with acknowledgement to AP/Wide World Photos)

runway, the airspeed went through V_1, V_2, and 160 knots "almost simultaneously." Although the first officer called Departure Control and reported windshear on the runway, his report was apparently not passed on to the tower controller.

The crew of Texas International's DC-9, which also departed from Runway 19, but three minutes later at 4.04pm, observed storm cells five to six nm southwest of the airport. During their takeoff and climbout in light rain, they encountered neither turbulence nor windshear.

The Cessna Citation crew, using their colour radar while holding on Runway 19 awaiting takeoff clearance immediately before the accident, saw two storm cells about two to three nm east of the airport, with another cell about seven nm to the southwest. Each cell was about three to four nm in diameter with sharp-edged red areas outlined in green, indicating they were intense storms. After the accident, the Citation was re-cleared to Runway 01, finally getting airborne eight minutes later. The crew said later they had not considered using Runway 10 for takeoff "because of the weather east of the airport".

The Southwest Airlines Boeing 737 taxied from the terminal at 3.49pm, but stopped on the end of the terminal apron abeam the east end of Runway 10 to await clearance. Its radar showed a storm cell above the airport which was "five to six miles wide, extending two miles east of the airport". A contour was located just to the south of the departure end of Runway 10.

While in this position, the Southwest crew watched the Republic and Texas DC-9s take off, then they were cleared to Runway 01. After they lined up for takeoff, the storm cell was still in the same area – there was "little movement with heavy contour". As the captain was looking out at the weather, he saw the PanAm Boeing 727 climbing out over the departure end of Runway 10. Its undercarriage was retracted and, at the moment he ceased to watch it, it was beginning a turn to the left. The ceiling at the time was about 3,000 feet, it was overcast and raining lightly, and the visibility to the east was about three nm. The Southwest Airlines Boeing 737 finally took off at 4.27pm.

The USAir DC-9 had taxied out behind the PanAm Boeing 727 to Runway 10. While the Boeing 727 was lining up, the DC-9 captain told his first officer: "We'll see how PanAm does, then we'll take a look." After the PanAm Boeing 727 began its takeoff, they continued taxiing towards the runway and, while awaiting clearance to line up, heard the Boeing 727 had crashed. They then shut the engines down to wait until the weather improved. As a result they "didn't get the radar turned around to runway heading to take a good look".

Weather radar observations

At 3.10pm, the Centre Weather Service Unit meteorologist at the Houston ATC Centre had telephoned New Orleans Tower to advise the controller of very strong to intense thunderstorms, with severe turbulence, lightning, and wind gusts, located south and southwest of the airport. He told the controller they were moving northeast towards the airport and to "keep an eye on them".

The meteorologist said he saw the storms on the ATC radar plan view display, and knew from the 2.35pm radar observations at the Slidell National Weather Service station, 30nm

A wider view of the still-smoking wreckage of "Clipper Defiance". The mangled empennage (the focus of the previous picture) lies on the right, with the nose undercarriage in the left foreground. In the centre of the picture, behind the fireman with his back to the camera, the No 2 engine, dislodged from its mounts in the crushed tailcone, has demolished a motor car. (with acknowledgement to UPI/Bettmann)

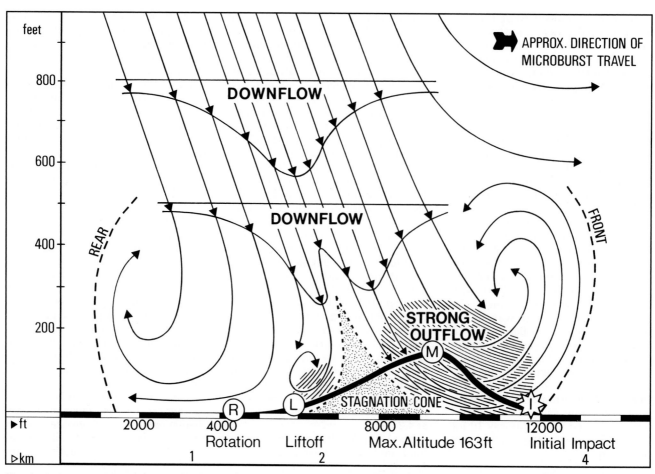

The pioneering work of Dr Theodore Fujita, Professor of Meteorology at the University of Chicago, was introduced to "Air Disaster" readers in Vol 1, Chapter 6. Dr Fujita's expertise was also called upon during the New Orleans investigation. This diagram shows a vertical cross-section of an intense microburst, representative of that affecting Moisant Airport at the time of the accident. The horizontal X-axis reflects the alignment of Runway 10, with the Boeing 727's takeoff profile running from left to right. (Matthew Tesch, with acknowledgement to Dr T Fujita & NTSB)

northeast of New Orleans International Airport, that they were isolated Level 4 and 5 storms. Even so, they did not meet the criteria for the issue of a Centre Weather Advisory. Centre Weather Advisories on thunderstorms are issued only when convective SIGMET criteria are met.

The meteorologist also believed the effect of the weather would be limited to the New Orleans International Airport area and the purpose of his call to New Orleans Tower was to alert the controller to the possibility that the storms might affect arriving and departing traffic, and that the controller could expect requests for route deviations. There was no requirement to broadcast the information on ATC frequencies.

Radar photography by the weather surveillance radar installation at Slidell showed that radar echoes were located in the vicinity of the departure end of Runway 10 before and during the time of the PanAm Boeing 727's takeoff.

A photograph taken at 4.08pm showed a Level 2 echo approximately over the departure end of Runway 10 and another Level 2 echo about four nm east of the airport.

The same photograph showed Level 3 echoes located four nm north, two nm west, and six nm south of the departure end of Runway 10. A Level 2 radar echo indicates a storm cell of moderate intensity, with moderate turbulence and lightning possible. A storm cell producing a Level 3 echo could contain severe turbulence and lightning.

However, the weather radar specialist at Slidell told investigators that none of the radar echoes he observed in the vicinity of New Orleans International Airport before or after the accident met the National Weather Service's severe weather criteria.

Low Level Wind Shear Alert System

At the time of the accident, New Orleans International Airport was equipped with a Low Level Wind Shear Alert System. It comprised a centrefield vector-vane type wind sensor, and five additional sensors located at or near the final approach courses to each runway (see diagram). The sensors provided wind velocity data to a computer and five display units – one located in the tower, and four in the Approach Control centre.

When a peripheral sensor's average wind reading for 30 seconds showed a vector difference of 15 knots or more from that of the centrefield sensor, an aural alarm sounded and the digital information from the affected sensor or sensors began flashing on the display units.

The installation at New Orleans, one of 58 operational throughout the United States at the time, represented state-of-the-art technology in its field. Despite its several limitations, the system provided advisory information (to quote the words of an FAA weather program manager) "to give the pilot ... additional information upon which to make a timely judgement on the approach to the airport or departure from the airport."

ANALYSIS

The investigation established beyond doubt that the accident was in no way attributable to any shortcoming in the aircraft or its maintenance, the crew's qualifications and experience, or the ATC personnel on duty at the airport at the time of the accident.

The thrust of the investigation was therefore directed to the meteorological, aerodynamic and operational factors which could have caused the aircraft to descend while attempting to climbout after takeoff.

Convective weather activity

At the time the PanAm Boeing 727 was preparing for takeoff, convective weather radar echoes, indicating the presence of storm cells, were located over and to the east of the departure end of Runway 10.

The 4.08pm weather radar photograph from Slidell showed a Level 2 echo almost over the departure end of Runway 10 and another Level 2 echo about four nm east of the airport. However, because the intervening rain and clouds would have attenuated the radar beam, the actual intensity of these cells was probably the equivalent of Level 3 echo, indicating intense storms.

Between 4.01 and 4.09pm also, the crews of four aircraft saw three weather cells either over or near the airport on their respective weather radars. One cell was over the departure end of Runway 10, another was two to five nm east-northeast of the airport, and the third cell was five nm southwest. All these cells were Level 3 or higher in intensity.

All this evidence established beyond doubt that Level 3 storm cells were lying over the airport and just east-northeast of the departure end of runway 10 during the Boeing 727's takeoff.

Rainfall rates

A rain gauge installed about a kilometre southeast of the departure end of Runway 10 showed that, between 4.08 and 4.09pm, the rainfall rate increased to about 25mm per hour. But east of the departure end of Runway 10 the rain was probably heavier. Calculations from various sources indicated that the rainfall rates beyond the departure end of Runway 10 during the aircraft's takeoff and climbout were at least 50mm per hour and probably a good deal higher.

Wind direction and speed

Although the investigators had access to meteorological data and witness statements, it was not possible to determine the precise horizontal and vertical wind components affecting the Boeing 727's takeoff. Between 4.07 and 4.09pm, the airport's recording anemometer showed that the average wind was about 16 knots. At 4.04, 4.06, 4.07, and 4.09pm, the tower and ground controllers, using the centrefield sensor, reported winds of 060°/16 knots, 070°/17, 070°/17, and 080°/15.

But about two seconds after the aircraft struck the trees on Williams Boulevard, just after 4.09pm, there was a windshear alert, the ground controller reporting the centrefield wind as 080°/15 knots and the east sensor wind as 310°/6 knots. A wind of 080°/15 knots would have initially provided a 14 knot headwind component on Runway 10, but a wind of 310°/6 knots would result in this backing to become a tailwind com-

Taking their lead from Dr Fujita's research in the 1960s and 1970s, many other research organisations – notably the famous Royal Aircraft Establishment at Farnborough, UK – went to work investigating thunderstorm-related windshear conditions. Airlines too, among them Eastern and American, conducted extensive simulator studies. Shear conditions, and the effect of downdraughts and microbursts during approaches to land were better understood following the investigation of the final approach crash of an Eastern Boeing 727 at New York on June 24, 1975. Similarly, the loss of the PanAm 727 at New Orleans seven years later came to be the archetypal reference for research into microburst encounters on takeoff. This graph shows (top) the effects of downdraughts at 500ft intervals on the Boeing 727's takeoff and climbout profile and (below) wind vector effects on its heading. Note that the most powerful vertical and lateral displacement occurred as the Boeing 727 passed abeam the centre of the microburst, 3000-4000ft after liftoff. The unexpected backing of the winds, accompanied by downdraughts and outflow from the microburst core, less than 1000ft from the aircraft's port side, insidiously affected the takeoff profile, leaving the crew insufficient time to recognise the problem and respond to it before it was too late. (Flight International)

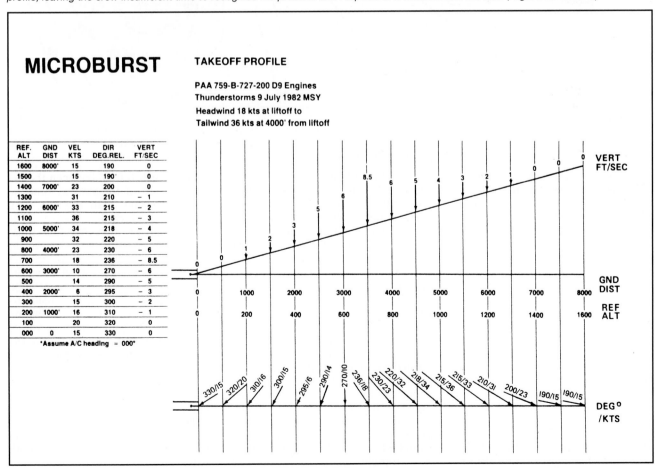

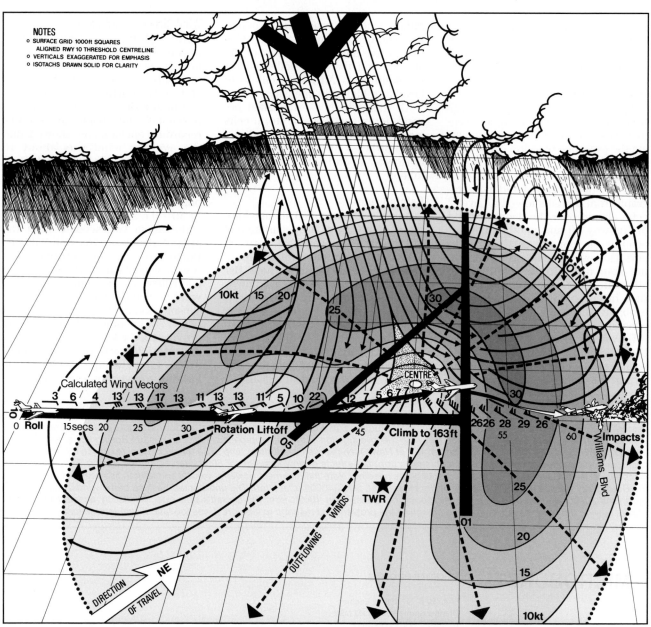

North-facing aerial perspective of New Orleans airport, showing the scale and extent of the microburst which forced the Boeing 727 into the ground. Apart from the effect of downflowing air, the worst windshear in any microburst (see vertical cross-section) will be encountered at the outside (especially the front and rear) "faces" of the microburst, where spreading, boiling air confronts the prevailing air masses and local wind conditions. (Matthew Tesch, with acknowledgement to Dr T Fujita & NTSB)

ponent of five knots. The tree line on Williams Boulevard lay only 100 metres beyond the east sensor, so on this basis alone the aircraft had encountered a 19-knot decreasing headwind shear within a distance of less than one nm.

According to one ground witness however, at the time of the aircraft's initial impact on Williams Boulevard, the wind was blowing strongly from west to east, with "whole trees swaying". This suggested the wind strength was at least 30 knots. If so, the magnitude of the decreasing headwind shear between the centrefield sensor and Williams Boulevard would have been at least 40 knots.

Microburst

Opposing wind velocities of this order are characteristic of a diverg-ing outflow of air produced by a "downburst" or "microburst" from a convective storm cell. Based on expert detailed analysis of all the available meteorological data by Dr T Fujita, Professor of Meteorology at the University of Chicago and a specialist in localised meteorological phenomena, the investigators concluded that the winds emanated from a microburst centred about 640 metres east of the centrefield sensor and 210 metres north of Runway 10 – ie in the centre of the triangle formed by the three intersecting runways. As a result, at a height of about 100 feet after liftoff, the Boeing 727 began encountering a decreasing windshear of *some 48 knots*. At the same time its flightpath would also have been affected by downdraughts of up to 10 feet per second, or 600 fpm, between the departure end of the runway and the initial contact with the trees on Williams Boulevard.

Although an aircraft might theoretically have the performance to penetrate a downburst or microburst without being forced down, its ability to do so was contingent upon the pilot recognising the insidious nature of the hazard and reacting immediately. The pilot's reaction would have to include his perception of the instrument readings as the gradual and continuous wind change took effect, evaluation of these readings, and control column and power lever application.

The time for the aircraft to respond to these control inputs would further modify the aircraft's theoretical performance. In this particular case, the increased drag of the Boeing 727's undercarriage doors, open while the undercarriage was in transit to the retracted position during the most critical part of the microburst encounter, would have further detracted from the aircraft's performance.

Pilot performance

In analysing the pilot's performance leading up to this accident, the investigators considered all the factors that could have affected his reaction times, and the implications of these reaction times on the aircraft attaining its theoretical performance.

The aircraft's takeoff began in light rain, it encountered increasing rain during the takeoff roll, and even heavier rain shortly after liftoff. The calculated rate increased from 25mm per hour to about 50mm per hour, but the rainfall rate east of the runway's end could have approached *as much as 1400mm per hour*. Such heavy rain, as well as directly detracting from the aircraft's aerodynamic performance to a small but nevertheless significant extent, particularly during low speed, high drag flight, would render the crew totally dependent on their instruments to detect and react to the windshear.

The analysis showed that the aircraft climbed for about 11 seconds, after which the pitch attitude decreased from 13° to 5° and a descending flight path developed. The analysis also showed that the pilot reacted to this descent by raising the nose within six seconds of the aircraft beginning to descend. However, the descent itself could not be arrested in time to avoid striking the trees.

From a study undertaken by the University of Southern California, the investigators noted that a pilot already viewing an essential flight instrument would probably require a minimum of 4.25 seconds to respond. This included recognition of the instrument deviation, perceiving its significance, and reacting by applying a force to the control column. Factors such as heavy rain, turbulence and the need to apply an abnormal force to the control column, as well as the need to achieve an unfamiliar pitch manoeuvre, could all adversely affect the pilot's response time. On the other hand, the onset of a Ground Proximity Warning System alert could prompt a pilot to act more positively. The evidence in this case indicated the pilot had already reacted and was applying corrective action when the GPWS sounded.

The performance analysis showed that, by raising the nose attitude to nearly 20° and bringing the airspeed back to about seven knots above the stall, the Boeing 727 could theoretically have maintained an altitude of 95 feet AGL. Physical evidence at the accident site showed that the pilot had been able to arrest the descent rate and even place the aircraft in a slight climb before the initial tree contact at a height of about 50 feet above the ground.

Given the adverse factors which would have delayed the pilot's reactions, and the fact that the altitude difference, between the aircraft's theoretical capability to maintain level flight and its actual performance, was only 45 feet, the investigators concluded that the pilot's response was as prompt as could have been expected in the existing conditions.

The captain and first officer were Miami-based and had flown National Airlines' and PanAm's southern routes since 1965 and 1976 respectively. Considering this, the investigators believed they were experienced in dealing with the convective type weather that prevailed on the day of the accident. They had successfully flown many times in such weather, and they had evaluated its severity using their aircraft weather radar.

The captain's judgement and ability to make proper command decisions were regarded as excellent. His record demonstrated that he performed well under emergency conditions, and his advice to the first officer in this instance to "let your speed build up on takeoff" showed that, based on the windshear information available to him, he was taking precautions to cope with a possible windshear encounter. The direction to turn left after liftoff also showed he had assessed the weather along the takeoff flightpath.

Given the captain's reputation for sound judgement in the exercise of his command responsibilities, and his record over the past 10 years as an airline captain, the investigators believed his decision to take off was a reasonable one.

Remedial action

While the most effective means of preventing this type of accident is of course to avoid critical microburst encounters, the investigators believed action had to be taken to enhance the capability of crews to recover from an encounter when they were unfortunate enough to experience the hazard without warning.

Flight instrumentation needed to be improved. In addition, the scope of simulator training needed to be broadened to increase a crew's knowledge of their aircraft's flight characteristics during windshear encounters. This would not only enable them to recognise the onset of the windshear more quickly, but also to recognise the need to take swift corrective action to prevent a critical loss of altitude.

Both these measures could help to improve pilot response times – and could one day mean the difference between a catastrophic accident and successful microburst penetration.

The National Transportation Safety Board's official report on the accident concluded with no less than 14 detailed recommendations to the Federal Aviation Administration. These included measures for the detection and dissemination of windshear data, the development of operational limitations for aircraft when windshear conditions were known to exist, and training for pilots and air traffic controllers on windshear hazards likely to be encountered in convective weather.

CHAPTER 9

"Excuse me ... there's a fire in the washroom!"

– Flight Attendant to DC-9 Captain

Air Canada McDonnell Douglas DC-9-32 C-FTLU [47196] (F/n 720)
– June 2, 1983

Fire in flight – the secret dread of every pilot from the earliest days of aviation! To those unlucky enough to be faced with this happily rare scourge in modern aviation, the response must be as it ever was – get the aircraft on the ground with the least possible delay!

Among the 40 or so routes that Air Canada, Canada's national airline corporation, was operating into the United States in the northern summer of 1983 was the long distance service connecting Montreal, Quebec, with Dallas, Texas, with an en route stop at Toronto, Ontario.

On June 2, 1983, the late afternoon return service, scheduled to depart from Dallas Fort Worth at 4.25pm (Central Daylight Time), was being flown by the corporation's 100-seat DC-9-32 C-FTLU, under the command of Captain Donald Cameron. Claude Ouimet was his first officer, and the relatively small load of 41 passengers was in the care of flight attendants Sergio Benetti, Laura Kayama and Judith Davidson, all three of them highly experienced Air Canada cabin crew.

The early summer weather was mild and showery, with an almost total overcast at about 8000 feet but, at the aircraft's cruising level of FL330 (33,000 feet), with the exception of one area of towering thunderstorm weather which the aircraft deviated from track to avoid, conditions were calm and clear.

One hour and 20 minutes into the 1070nm leg to Toronto, the aircraft,

in radio contact with Memphis [en route Air Traffic Control] Centre, was over Kentucky, approaching its next waypoint at Louisville.

An interrupted dinner

About 40 minutes of the summer afternoon still remained before sunset, but an evening meal of seafood and steak had been served, and on the flightdeck First Officer Ouimet, in the right hand control seat, was just finishing his meal before taking over the monitoring of the flight while Captain Cameron ate.

But on the flightdeck just after 6.51pm (now Eastern Daylight Time, one hour ahead of CDT), the pilots were startled by three sudden snapping noises in quick succession.

"What was that?" exclaimed Ouimet, looking around to find their source. His eyes fell on the circuit breaker panel mounted on the flightdeck bulkhead behind the captain's seat. Three circuit breakers had "popped". "It's right here – I see it," he told the captain.

CAPT (looking around at panel): Yeah – the DC bus.

F/O: Which one is that?

CAPT: DC bus – the left toilet – the left toilet flushing motor. [The DC-9's

toilet flushing electric motors operate on three-phase alternating current, with each phase incorporating a circuit breaker.] I'd better try it again and push them in.

F/O: Push it one more time, I guess.

But the circuit breakers would not reset, immediately popping out again as the captain attempted to reset them.

CAPT: That's it – they won't take it! Comes out like a machine gun.

F/O: Yeah – zap zap zap!

CAPT: Put it in the book there.

F/O: Log it?

"I want to log it, yes." Captain Cameron decided the flushing motor had seized. "Somebody must have pushed a rag down the toilet or something ... jammed it and it's overheated."

MEMPHIS: "Air Canada 797 – contact Indianapolis now on 137.05."

Ouimet acknowledged the instruction, changed frequency, and called Indianapolis: "This is Air Canada 797 – maintaining 330 [FL330] direct to Louisville on course," he transmitted.

Five minutes later, after one of the cabin crew had come and taken away the first officer's dinner plates, Captain Cameron decided to try to reset the three circuit breakers again. As he pressed each one of them in turn, there was a noise of electrical arcing and the circuit breakers sprang out again.

"Pops as I push it," he observed to Ouimet. "I'd better have dinner here." He pushed the cabin crew call button and Senior Flight Attendant Benetti came to the flightdeck. "Sergio, could I try for my dinner now?" Cameron asked, and Benetti left to bring it.

A DC-9 operator for 30 years, Air Canada was in fact the first foreign customer for the type after Delta's launch order. The second DC-9-14 (and only the 17th built) to wear the Maple Leaf insignia – CF-TLC [45712] shown here – was delivered on January 6, 1966. Two years before, coincident with its move into the jet age, the former Trans-Canada Airlines (TCA) adopted its first livery and name change since the corporation's formation in April 1937. The international requirement for outline painting of all cabin exits was promulgated shortly after this picture was taken. (with acknowledgement to McDonnell Douglas & Jane's)

Thickening smoke

Meanwhile, back in the cabin a passenger, just finishing his dinner in the rearmost row of seats, had drawn Flight Attendant Judith Davidson's attention to the fact that he could smell a strange odour of burning. Looking around, she saw whitish grey smoke seeping from the closed door of the aft toilet on the port side.

Taking a carbon dioxide (CO_2) fire extinguisher from its bracket on the cabin bulkhead, she opened the toilet door a few inches. Light grey smoke was filling the compartment from floor to ceiling, and she was unable to avoid inhaling it. The smoke, which had an acrid, electrical smell, was unpleasant and made her feel dizzy. Quickly she shut the door on it.

Flight Attendant Laura Kayama hurried down the aisle to investigate. "Tell Sergio there's a fire in the toilet!" Davidson gasped at her.

Benetti was still in the galley, immediately behind the flightdeck on the starboard side, preparing the captain's dinner. On being told what was happening, he instructed Kay-ama to inform the captain, then to help Davidson to move all the passengers forward, and to open the air vents over the passenger seats to direct air rearwards. With that, he hurried back to see what he could do to contain the fire.

Flight Attendant Laura Kayama opened the flightdeck door: "Excuse me, Captain – there's a fire in the washroom at the back – they're just going back to put it out."

F/O [to captain]: Want me to go back there?

CAPT: Yeah – go! [then to flight attendant] Leave my dinner for a minute.

As the first officer got up to leave, the captain put on his oxygen mask and selected 100% oxygen on the regulator.

At the rear of the cabin Benetti had picked up the CO_2 extinguisher Davidson had taken from its bracket and opened the toilet door. There were no flames inside, but thick black smoke was now curling from the seams of the walls above the wash basin, and where the wall lining joined the ceiling. Activating the extinguisher, Benetti discharged it into the toilet compartment, using a circular motion as he had been trained, as he aimed it at the seams and then at the waste disposal container. The acrid smoke burned his throat, but he thoroughly doused the places from which the smoke was coming before closing the door.

As Judith Davidson was helping to reseat passengers further forward and reassuring them, First Officer Ouimet came down the aisle to assess the situation. But thick grey smoke had already seeped forward into the cabin over the last three or

Of the 60 plus DC-9s that have appeared on the Canadian register, more than half have been the "standard" Series 32 model, the balance being the early Series 14s & 15Fs. As McDonnell Douglas quickly appreciated the stretch potential of its inaugural marque, so Air Canada was quick to place an order, with CF-TLH [45845] arriving on March 7, 1967. One of four accepted in the last quarter of that year, C-FTLR [47070] is shown inbound to the apron at Toronto in July 1978, wearing the "smartened up" livery modified in 1977. Gone is the massive matt black nose; the cheatline is deeper and continuous (no longer tapered forward nor cut off aft); the Maple Leaf and titles bigger and bolder; and the red now a brighter vermillion. This was the livery C-FTLU carried at the time of its fiery ordeal (see Footnote 1). (with acknowledgement to Russell Brown/APS)

four rows of seats, obscuring the entire rear bulkhead. Ouimet had not brought smoke goggles or a portable oxygen bottle with him, and was unable to reach the toilet door without entering the smoke.

Benetti assured Ouimet he had already discharged the extinguisher into the compartment, and that, although he had not been able to see the source of the smoke before closing the door, he did not believe the fire was in the toilet waste disposal container. Ouimet then returned to the flightdeck, intending to get a pair of smoke goggles.

"Can't get back there," he told the captain. "Smoke's too heavy – I think we'd better go down."

Before Captain Cameron could respond, Benetti also came to the flightdeck to report that all the passengers had been reseated. "You don't have to worry," he continued, "I think the smoke's easing up."

Turning around, Ouimet looked back through the open flightdeck door and saw the smoke had abated at the rear of the cabin. "OK – it's starting to clear now." he told Cameron. "But I'll go back and check – if that's OK?

"Yeah, that's OK – and take the smoke mask."

Grim realisation

The first officer's smoke goggles, in a compartment on the right side of his seat, were inaccessible to him from where he stood. Cameron passed him his own. "Take these goggles," he said, "I'll leave my mask on – go back wherever you can, but don't get yourself incapacitated."

Soon after Ouimet left to go aft again, Flight Attendant Davidson came to the flightdeck with a message from him: "Captain," she began, "Your first officer wanted me to tell you that Sergio has put a big discharge of CO_2 into the washroom and the smoke seems to be subsiding."

But even as she spoke, the master caution light illuminated on the annunciator panel, indicating that the aircraft's left AC and DC electrical systems had lost power. At once Captain Cameron called Indianapolis to report they had an "electrical problem," and that "we may be off communication shortly."

A moment or so later, Benetti looked into the flightdeck again to reassure the captain. "It's getting much better," he said. "I was able to discharge half the CO_2 inside the washroom – even though I couldn't see the source. But it's definitely inside the toilet."

Convinced now that the fire *had*

Strip map showing the (approximate) airway routeing and weather diversion of Flight AC797 being operated by the DC-9 on the afternoon of the accident. Dallas-Fort Worth was one of about a dozen US ports being served by Air Canada in 1983, many of them turnarounds on return services radiating from Toronto. The 38 DC-9-32s on strength that year represented just over a quarter of the total Air Canada fleet (itself an eclectic mix of all three major US manufacturers' types – and subsequently, Airbus Industrie as well!). During 1982-84, in a bid to hold costs and increase capacity, the AC DC-9s were reconfigured with all-Economy seats, complemented by refurbishing with the much-vaunted "widebody interior" look, pending a decision on their replacement. (Matthew Tesch)

been in the toilet's waste disposal container, and that it was being put out, the captain decided not to descend at this stage.

Meanwhile, at the rear of the cabin, the first officer had put on the smoke goggles, intending to open the toilet door to see what the situa-

tion was inside. But finding the door hot to the touch, he decided against it. He was in the process of instructing Benetti not to open the door and to get another extinguisher when he saw Flight Attendant Kayama signalling him to hurry back to the flightdeck.

He did so promptly and, as he slid into his seat, he saw why the captain wanted him – the master warning light and the annunciator lights were now indicating that the emergency AC and DC electrical buses had also lost power and, on the main instrument panel, both the captain's and the first officer's attitude and directional indicators had tumbled.

At the captain's instruction, he immediately activated the emergency power switch, connecting battery power to the emergency AC and DC buses. The attitude and directional indicator gyros began erecting again but, because of the loss of AC power, the stabiliser trim remained inoperative.

"I don't like what's happening," Ouimet declared grimly, "I think we'd better go down."

Benetti, who had followed Ouimet forward, asked if oxygen masks should be made available to the passengers. The captain said no, but told Benetti they would be making an emergency descent, and that he should brief the cabin crew.

Emergency descent

Moments later at 7.08pm, 17 minutes after the first indication of trouble, while Ouimet transmitted a Mayday call to Indianapolis, Cameron pulled the power levers back to their Flight Idle setting and extended the speed brakes, setting up a descent rate of more than 6000fpm at an indicated airspeed of 310 knots.

Benetti called the other two flight attendants to the galley to brief them as instructed and, while they were discussing procedures, one of the pilots shouted back to them to leave the flightdeck door open. It remained open throughout the descent.

Flight Attendants Kayama and Davidson then went down the aisle checking seat belts and briefing passengers on emergency evacuation procedures. They also designated particular passengers to open the overwing exits and to block the aisle so as not to obstruct the crew while the forward cabin doors were being opened.

At the rear of the cabin there had been a sudden thump as the steep descent began, and the smoke increased in intensity. Now black and heavy, with a burning plastic smell, it began to boil progressively forward as the descent continued, filling the upper part of the cabin, billowing around the overhead lockers, and stratifying down towards the floor People began coughing as the smoke and its accompanying heat enveloped them, feeling burning sensations in their nose, throat and chest, and it became increasingly difficult to see. In the galley, the resourceful Judith Davidson began wetting hand towels, which Laura Kayama handed out to passengers to hold over their noses and mouths.

On the ground, the Indianapolis high altitude sector controller, having received the DC-9's Mayday call at 7.08pm, told the crew they were 25nm from Cincinnati. "Can you possibly make Cincinnati?" he asked.

The crew reported they could, and the aircraft was cleared to descend to 5000 feet. At about 25,000 feet, the DC-9 entered the cloud tops, but there was little turbulence and no airframe icing. The crew told the controller they would need to be vectored towards Cincinnati and were now squawking the emergency code 7700 on their transponder. Because of the aircraft's loss of electrical power however, its transponder

was inoperative and the emergency code did not appear on the controllers' radar screens. It also meant there was no indication on the radar that the aircraft was descending.

Approach difficulties

Vectored on to a heading of 060°, the crew were told Greater Cincinnati Airport was at "12 o'clock at 20 miles," and at 7.09pm the Indianapolis low altitude sector controller called Cincinnati Approach to warn of the impending handoff. But when the approach controller accepted the DC-9 only half a minute later, he unknowingly confused it with the radar target of a Continental aircraft westbound at FL350.

Cincinnati Tower, notified that an Air Canada jet with an onboard fire would be landing on Runway 36, positioned the airport's emergency vehicles accordingly. A minute later, when the DC-9 called Cincinnati Approach, it was told to plan for a Runway 36 ILS approach and requested to turn right on to a heading of 090°. Only then did the controller realise he had been watching the wrong target.

"Say type of airplane, number of

people on board, and amount of fuel," the controller asked. *"I'll tell you later,"* the first officer replied. *"I don't have time now!"*

Aboard the DC-9 as it continued its steep descent, the smoke front had moved forward to fill the whole passenger cabin and had finally entered the flightdeck. Captain Cameron donned smoke goggles in addition to his oxygen mask, and First Officer Ouimet put on his mask, setting the oxygen regulator to 100%. Unable to speak directly to each other with their masks on, the pilots communicated with each other by hand signals, and with ATC using a hand microphone and the flightdeck loudspeaker. Neither pilot had any trouble breathing, and Ouimet chose not to use his smoke goggles.

Two minutes later, as the Cincinnati approach controller observed an eastbound primary target on his screen and began monitoring it, the DC-9 called to request the cloud ceiling. The controller responded: "2500 scattered, 8000 feet overcast, visibility 12 miles with light rain."

Deciding that the eastbound target, now about eight nm south of Runway 36's threshold, had to be the

The ghosted image of the burning DC-9 serves as a backdrop to this radar-plotted track of the final minutes of flight over Kentucky. With superimposed edits of actions and conversations, it provides a grim reminder that the DC-9 left the closer haven of Standiford Field, Louisville, well behind before the crew's qualms finally led to the "Mayday" call and emergency descent. (Matthew Tesch, with acknowledgement to the NTSB & The Washington Post)

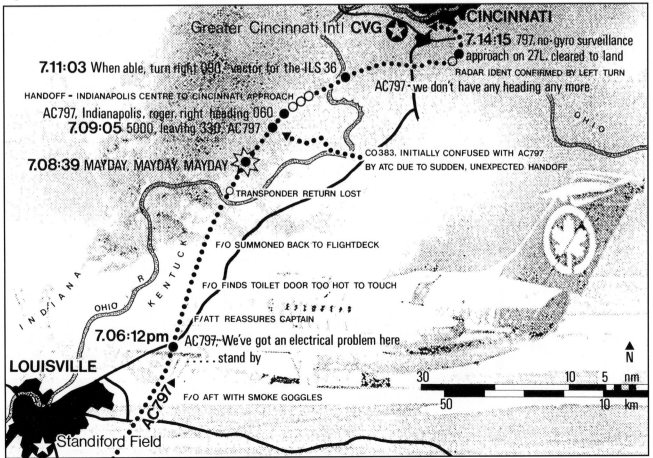

Air Canada aircraft, the approach controller requested: "Say altitude and heading."

F/O: Altitude 8000 – we don't have a heading any more – all we have is a small horizon.

At once the controller saw the aircraft was too high and too fast for a landing on Runway 36 and that he would have to vector it to Runway 27L instead.

APP: If able, turn left.

F/O: Turning left.

APP: Roger, Air Canada – you are now fully identified. This will be a *no gyro*[2] radar approach for Runway 27 Left – descend now to 3500 feet. Your position is 12 miles southeast of the airport – surface wind is 220° at four knots.

Few instruments – less visibility

The descent continued in solid cloud almost until Captain Cameron levelled off at 3500 feet, when he told the first officer to depressurise the cabin in preparation for landing. Ouimet did so and, although not required by the emergency checklist, he also turned off the air conditioning and pressurisation packs. The smoke was still intensifying and he believed the packs were feeding airflow to the fire.

A few moments afterwards he opened his sliding window to clear the smoke from the flightdeck, but had to close it almost immediately because of the high noise level.

Back in the passenger cabin, conditions were deteriorating alarmingly. Visibility was almost zero because of the heavy black smoke, with everyone covered in soot and the heat becoming extremely uncomfortable. It was impossible for passengers to even read their seat pocket emergency cards. Indeed, for those who had failed to heed the flight attendants' safety briefing prior to takeoff from Dallas 90 minutes previously, it was too late to make up for it now.

Finding one passenger particularly distressed, Judith Davidson brought him to the front of the cabin where Sergio Benetti sat him down on the flight attendant's seat and administered oxygen to him. The man, suffering from emphysema, was having difficulty breathing.

Because the smoke was less dense towards the floor, a number of passengers were keeping their heads down to assist their breathing. One passenger was even kneeling between the seats, keeping his face as close to the floor as possible and breathing through a wad of tissues he had in his pocket. Others who had not yet received a wet hand towel were breathing through paper napkins from their dinner trays, head rest covers, and even their jackets. But there was no panic and the passengers' demeanour remained calm and orderly.

Even after levelling off at 3500 feet, the captain found they were still in and out of cloud, so he continued the descent, reporting at 7.15pm that they were level at 2500 feet, and "VFR now".

But because of the smoke, the captain was now having difficulty seeing the instruments and had to lean forward to do so. By this time too, perspiration was fogging his smoke goggles and he had to keep pulling them from his face to clear them. Ouimet too was having difficulty seeing, and from time to time was opening and closing his side window to help clear the smoke.

The approach controller continued to vector the aircraft towards Runway 27L.

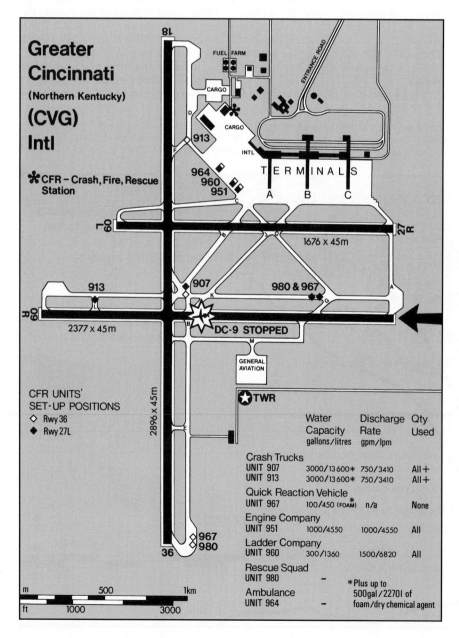

Layout of Greater Cincinnati International Airport. Not unusually for US cities on major waterways providing natural State demarcations, the airport is in a different State to the city it serves! CVG is in northern Kentucky; 12½ miles (20km) by road to the northeast, the urban sprawl of Greater Cincinnati flanks the banks of the Ohio River which separates the State of Ohio from Kentucky. The map also shows the positions of the rescue and firefighting units for the DC-9's anticipated ILS approach to Runway 36, and then for its actual landing on Runway 27 Left. The performance data shown for the CFR equipment do not adequately reflect their efforts to smother the blaze. Thanks to the expeditious connection of the two main vehicles to the airport's underground hydrant system, both ultimately discharged far more water than their onboard capacity of 3000 gallons (13,600 litres).

Greater Cincinnati
(Northern Kentucky)
(CVG) Intl

✳ CFR – Crash, Fire, Rescue Station

FUEL FARM
CARGO
913
CARGO
INTL
T E R M I N A L S
A B C
913
907
980 & 967
1676 × 45m
DC-9 STOPPED
GENERAL AVIATION
964
960
951
ENTRANCE ROAD
2377 × 45m
2896 × 45m
967
980
36

CFR UNITS'
SET-UP POSITIONS
◇ Rwy 36
◆ Rwy 27L

⭐ TWR

	Water Capacity gallons/litres	Discharge Rate gpm/lpm	Qty Used
Crash Trucks			
UNIT 907	3000/13 600*	750/3410	All +
UNIT 913	3000/13 600*	750/3410	All +
Quick Reaction Vehicle			
UNIT 967	100/450 (FOAM)*	n/a	None
Engine Company			
UNIT 951	1000/4550	1000/4550	All
Ladder Company			
UNIT 960	300/1360	1500/6820	All
Rescue Squad			
UNIT 980	–		
Ambulance			
UNIT 964	–		

*Plus up to 500gal/2270l of foam/dry chemical agent

m | 500 | 1km
ft | 1000 | 3000

Dusk at Cincinnati – and the hulk of the DC-9, apparently squatting on its haunches in a sea of foam, still smoulders. Wading knee-deep around the aircraft, firemen have at last been able to prop ladders against the scorched fuselage to continue damping-down. Three standing by the jettisoned tailcone play a hose directly into the gutted rear fuselage. Yet to be removed are the charred remains of the 23 passengers who succumbed to the sudden inferno inside the structurally intact cabin. The fires were not extinguished until an hour after landing.

F/O [anxiously – barely able to see]: Where's the airport?

APP [reassuringly]: Twelve o'clock and eight miles, Air Canada.

F/O: OK, we're trying to locate it – we're going to need fire trucks!

APP: They're standing by for you – can you give me the number of people and amount of fuel?

F/O: We don't have time – it's getting worse here!

APP: Understand, sir – turn left now, you're just half a mile north of final approach.

Even though it was not yet sunset, the approach controller now called for the runway and approach lights to be turned up to full intensity.

F/O: OK – we have the airport!

APP: The tower has you in sight and you are cleared to land.

The landing

As soon as Captain Cameron sighted the runway, he called for the undercarriage to be lowered. Because the stabiliser trim was inoperative, he then had First Officer Ouimet extend the flaps and slats incrementally – allowing the airspeed to stabilise at each flap position as the aircraft slowed – and he flew the final approach at 140 knots.

In the almost pitch darkness of the smoke-filled cabin, Laura Kayama was still handing out wet towels, while Judith Davidson, keeping her head down as much as possible, was also moving through the cabin, telling passengers to breathe through their clothes, and checking their seatbelts. But because the smoke was becoming so thick, she could not go further aft than Row 12.

The flightdeck door was still open and, as the DC-9 approached the runway, First Officer Ouimet, aware there was still movement in the cabin, yelled back: "Sit down!"

Holding a towel to her face and barely able to see, Laura Kayama sat down in a vacant seat in Row 3. Meanwhile Judith Davidson called out: "Everybody fastened?", and sat down on the floor in the aisle. But the smoke prevented her seeing any higher than the passengers' knees and in a moment she got up again and, using the seat backs as a guide, found her way to an empty aisle seat in Row 9. She could barely see the man beside her. Just before touchdown, her voice choking and her eyes watering, she yelled: "Heads on laps, brace for landing!"

The landing itself was smooth and the captain used full braking, spoilers and reverse thrust for a maximum effort stop. Because of the loss of electrical power however, the antiskid system was inoperative and the four main wheel tires blew out.

Blind, groping evacuation

As the pilots hastily completed their emergency shutdown checks, they heard the cabin crew shouting evacuation commands. But as they got up to go back and help, they were confronted by a wall of intense smoke and heat.

Ouimet immediately climbed through his sliding side window, dropped to the ground, and ran round the front of the aircraft towards the main forward door. Through the flightdeck windows he could see Captain Cameron still on board and he yelled at him to jump.

Meanwhile Sergio Benetti had opened the main forward door, deployed the slide, pushed the distressed, emphysemic passenger down it, and shouted at others to follow. Almost simultaneously, Judith Davidson came up the aisle from her seat, opened the starboard front door and deployed the slide. No one else seemed to be moving forward and she began yelling: "Come this way!"

Further back in the cabin, passengers who had been briefed to open the overwing exits were doing so, succeeding in opening the rear exit on the port side and both overwing exits on the starboard side.

Seven fire-rescue vehicles had reached the aircraft as it braked to a stop and, as the doors and overwing exits were opened, firemen saw heavy smoke pouring from them. As passengers and crew began leaving the aircraft, the firecrews doused the fuselage and the ground beneath it with foam to cool the interior and to provide a foam blanket in case of a fuel spill.

Still on the flightdeck, Captain Cameron seemed disoriented, but finally left through his sliding window after Ouimet had repeatedly prompted him to get out. Firemen sprayed him with foam as he did so.

For the hard-pressed and imperilled passengers still inside, the

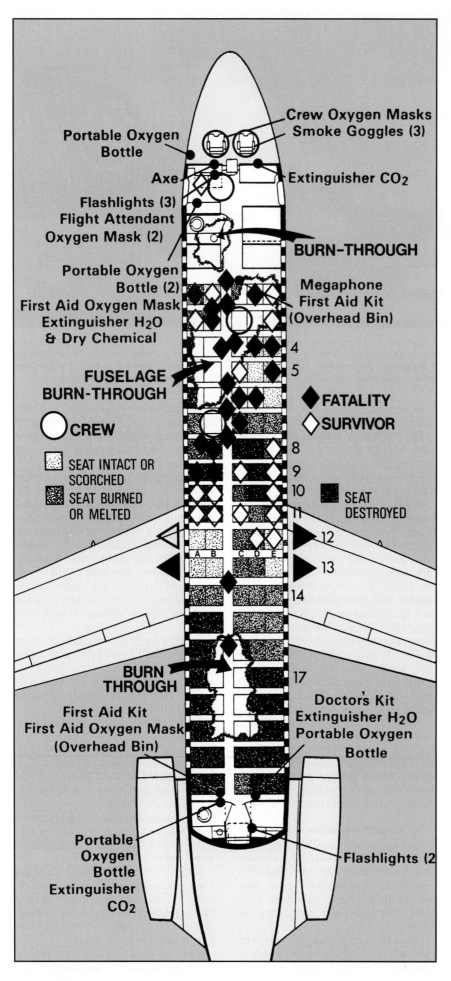

Portable Oxygen Bottle

Crew Oxygen Masks
Smoke Goggles (3)

Axe

Extinguisher CO_2

Flashlights (3)
Flight Attendant
Oxygen Mask (2)

BURN-THROUGH

Portable Oxygen Bottle (2)

Megaphone
First Aid Kit
(Overhead Bin)

First Aid Oxygen Mask
Extinguisher H_2O
& Dry Chemical

4

5

FUSELAGE
BURN-THROUGH

◆ FATALITY

◇ SURVIVOR

○ CREW

8

☐ SEAT INTACT OR
SCORCHED

9

10

☐ SEAT BURNED
OR MELTED

■ SEAT
DESTROYED

11

12

A B C D E

13

14

BURN
THROUGH

17

First Aid Kit
First Aid Oxygen Mask
(Overhead Bin)

Doctor's Kit
Extinguisher H_2O
Portable Oxygen
Bottle

Portable
Oxygen
Bottle
Extinguisher
CO_2

Flashlights (2)

drama was far from over. As soon as the aircraft stopped, the man in seat 2B (Row 2 was the front row of seats in this aircraft), undid his seatbelt and stood across the aisle as instructed by Judith Davidson to hold passengers back while the crew opened the doors.

Engulfed by a blast of hot black smoke that blackened one side of his face and sooted his glasses, he could neither see anything nor feel anyone pushing against him, but he heard coughing and other sounds behind him. After about 30 seconds a male voice called: "Let's go!" and he headed towards the port side front door, the light from which he could see dimly through the smoke. He saw Benetti push Laura Kayama down the slide, and he followed behind her. A woman from seat 2E came next.

Other passengers who left this way included a woman in seat 3A. She had released her seatbelt as soon as the aircraft touched the runway. At first she went aft, bumped into someone, then turned round and went forward. She knew she was only one row from the front and as she reached the door and the slide, Judith Davidson yelled: "Jump!" Another woman following behind her fell forward into the slide and she had to roll out of the way as she reached the ground. She too was immediately sprayed with foam for protection.

In seat 3E, a man paused for a few moments after the landing so he would not knock others down. When he reached across to the aisle seat he found the passenger there had gone. He could feel the heat coming forward, and the overhead lockers were hot to touch. Diving to the floor to avoid the worst of the heat and smoke, he crawled to the doorway on all fours and went down the slide.

A man in seat 5C could see nothing – it was virtually black in the cabin. Heat was coming from behind and he kept his head down to breathe better air. He felt someone's shoulder as he groped forward and the bulkhead was hot as he touched it on his way past. Another man in seat 8E did not encounter anyone as he made his way to the main door.

Interior plan of the DC-9, showing seat configuration and location of emergency equipment. The deduced locations of survivors and fatalities are also shown. One port overwing exit was not used in the evacuation, nor were the rear ventral stairs. The tailcone was removed by fire crews using its external latching control. (Matthew Tesch, with acknowledgement to NTSB)

Judith Davidson had delegated the passenger in seat 9C to open the starboard rear overwing exit, and another in seat 10B to open the forward port overwing exit, but the forward overwing exit on the starboard side was the first to be opened. The passenger sitting alongside it in seat 12E found it opened easily. His wife, sitting alongside him, quickly followed him out on to the wing. Another man, on his own in window seat 10E two rows in front, quickly moved back to Row 12 and followed them out.

The man in seat 9C felt his way back to the starboard rear overwing exit at Row 13 as soon as the aircraft had stopped. There were no passengers in this row, but he had to search for the release handle in the smoke. Having found it, he removed the hatch and climbed out on to the starboard wing.

The passenger from seat 10B found his way back to the port rear overwing exit at Row 13 and opened it without difficulty, except that the tray table of the seat alongside it kept falling down and blocking the way. He had memorised the exit's location before landing and moved towards it immediately the aircraft touched down. A woman who had been sitting alongside him in window seat 10A followed him by holding on to his belt. The smoke was so thick that it prevented her seeing him remove the hatch. They both stepped out on to the wing and at least other two men followed.

A woman in window seat 11E stood up with her purse as soon as the aircraft stopped and she heard the overwing exits being opened. Because she was concerned about wearing her glasses during the emergency landing, she had taken them off. The only voice she heard was that of her travelling companion, in the aisle seat of the same row saying: "I'm still here!" The woman intended leaving through the starboard overwing exit but, as she felt her way back through the smoke, she could not see it. She then felt a breeze on the back of her legs, turned around, and climbed through the port overwing exit.

After the doors and window exits had been opened, the smoke became much worse, the passenger in window seat 9E describing it as a "blast of thick, pitch black smoke that smelt like burning styrofoam." Because of this, he decided against trying to reach the forward door and went back down the aisle to the overwing exits. Holding his breath and bending down, he finally saw light coming from the port exit, and

stepped out on to the wing. It took him about 60 seconds to escape.

By now several passengers were standing on the port wing. Fire vehicles were positioned around the aircraft and firemen were directing foam at the fuselage. From the ground nearby a fireman shouted: "Get off the wing – it's going to blow!" A flight attendant also yelled at them to jump, and they all jumped off the leading edge.

An older woman in aisle seat 11C heard the window exits being opened, but had difficulty releasing her seatbelt, thinking it had a push button release like her car belt. Her companion in window seat 11E pushed past her, apparently unaware she was still seated. She called out: "I'm still here!", picked up her purse and flight bag and moved two rows aft to the starboard rear overwing exit. The cabin was "pitch black" and she did not see or hear anyone else.

As she climbed through the exit, her foot caught on the sill for a moment. Just as she managed to step out on to the wing, the whole interior of the cabin suddenly ignited and flames roared from the open exits. She was immediately hit by a jet of foam which firemen were directing at the fuselage.

Meanwhile, at the port and starboard forward doors, Flight Attendants Benetti and Davidson had been forced to leave via their respective slides. For Benetti the heat became unbearable and, although he saw no flames, he could stand it no longer and went out the port door. Judith Davidson's calls to passengers to "come this way" at the starboard forward door evoked no response. No one came and, finally feeling suffocated, she went down the slide herself. She was the only one to use this exit.

With the interior of the fuselage now fiercely ablaze, five people clustered together near the starboard wing tip. The man who had opened the rear exit jumped off the leading edge. The passenger who had opened the forward exit told those who were left: "We'll have to get off too." Jumping from the trailing edge, he called for his wife to follow him. The older woman followed her and was caught by a fireman on the ground. The remaining passenger also jumped, injuring his left knee.

Soot covered the passengers' faces and clothes, and the paper napkins some of them had been holding over their noses and mouths were black with soot.

Firemen, together with the captain and the crew, assisted the passengers away from the aircraft which, despite being deluged with foam, continued to burn, the cabin fire breaking through the top of the fuselage in several places and releasing boiling columns of black smoke into the air. Six minutes after the DC-9 had landed, the captain radioed Cincinnati Ground Control from one of the emergency vehicles with the melancholy news that 23 passengers had failed to make their escape.

None of passengers, crew, or firemen had seen flames inside the cabin before the survivors escaped from the aircraft. The passenger cabin was gutted before the airport fire services succeeded in extinguishing the fire.

A bus sent out to the aircraft took the survivors to the airport terminal. A number felt dizzy and light-headed and oxygen was administered to them. Several who coughed up black sputum were later admitted to hospital and treated for smoke inhalation.

Painters apparently wasted as little time as the efficient fire crews! Even before the derelict DC-9 had been dragged clear of the runway and towed to a remote apron position, its livery had been de-identified (see hangar photo, Chapter 6). Hosed down to clear remaining foam and slush, the damage and scorching is more evident. Note the still extended flaps. (NTSB)

INVESTIGATION

Wreckage examination

By the time investigators from the National Transportation Safety Board arrived at Greater Cincinnati International Airport, the fire-ravaged DC-9 had been dragged from the runway. Most of the bodies of the 23 passengers who had died in the fire were found still in their seats. Four were on the floor in the aisle, these passengers having apparently been overcome by smoke and heat while trying to reach the exits. Two were well towards the rear of the cabin, evidently having failed to find the overwing exits in the dense smoke.

The entire interior of the passenger cabin had been gutted by fire, only the floor and carpet escaping being consumed or damaged (see diagrams). From behind the main cabin door to just forward of the aft toilet compartment, much of the top of the fuselage was burnt away, and most of the cabin windows were either missing or melted. Below window level the fuselage remained relatively intact. The cabin air dump valve was open, and light soot deposits trailed aft from around its edges.

The forward section of the fuselage, including the forward entry doors, flightdeck, windscreen panels and windows, and the nose, was also intact, but the whole interior of the flightdeck was heavily sooted and there was some heat damage to the overhead switch and circuit breaker panel, and to wire bundles just forward of the flightdeck door.

Neither the wings nor the empennage were damaged by fire or heat and the leading edge slats and trailing edge flaps were fully extended. The nose undercarriage was extended and locked and, except for the fact that all four main wheel tyres had blown out, the extended and locked main undercarriage was also undamaged.

The engines and their cowlings were undamaged, and showed no evidence of exposure to fire, but the engine fire extinguisher bottles had been discharged. Inspection of the hydraulic and fuel systems established that neither had contributed to the fire and there was no evidence of oil or fuel leakage. More than 12,200lbs (5500kg) of Jet-A fuel was subsequently recovered from the intact main wing tanks.

The fuselage skin above the aft toilet remained in place, but a rectangular area corresponding to the compartment's internal proportions had been discoloured and the paint burnt away. Thick soot deposits trailed rearwards along the lower fuselage from the cabin air outflow valve and from around the access door to the toilet service panel. The space inside the service panel access door was covered with soot and a black tar, with the thickest deposits on the inside surface of the access door adjacent to the vent tube and flush-fill pipe outlets.

The aft toilet steel water tank remained attached to its ceiling mounts forward of the aft pressure bulkhead. The ducting behind and above the tank was intact but the ducting and electrical wire bundles routed around the front of the tank were burnt away.

Aft toilet compartment

The Air Canada DC-9's aft toilet compartment was on the port side, just forward of the aft pressure bulkhead, its outboard wall conforming to the shape of the fuselage.

A vanity cabinet, comprising a stainless steel sink and basin, amenities dispensers for paper towels, toilet paper, sanitary napkins and sick bags, and an oxygen mask compartment, extended across the aft wall, with a fresh air outlet mounted on the plastic door of the cabinet below the sink. Behind the sink, a chute led from a waste disposal door down into a container below the sink, with an aluminium shelf installed beneath the container across the whole lower section of the vanity cabinet.

The commode, with its electric flushing pump, was positioned at

Safely clear of Cincinnati's movement areas, C-FTLU awaits the investigators' further attention. Note the replaced tailcone and the rectangular scorch mark on the white crown of the aft fuselage above the No 1 engine, clearly marking the location of the aft toilet compartment. The portside fire damage is clearly visible, and may be related to the profile drawing of the DC-9's starboard side (below). (NTSB & Matthew Tesch)

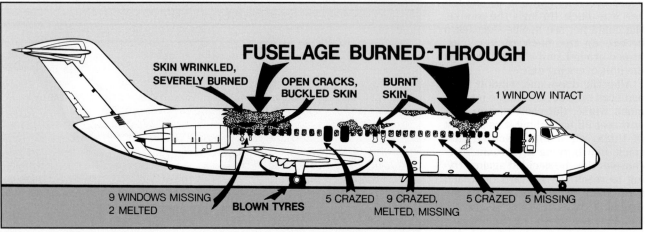

FUSELAGE BURNED-THROUGH

SKIN WRINKLED, SEVERELY BURNED — OPEN CRACKS, BUCKLED SKIN — BURNT SKIN — 1 WINDOW INTACT

9 WINDOWS MISSING 2 MELTED — BLOWN TYRES — 5 CRAZED — 9 CRAZED, MELTED, MISSING — 5 CRAZED — 5 MISSING

right angles to the vanity cabinet against the outboard wall.

Electrical wiring for the commode's flush pump motor, aluminium lines supplying oxygen and cold air, and the sink's stainless steel drain pipe were all routed through the empty space between the underside of the amenities compartments and the aluminium shelf.

The whole toilet compartment was severely damaged by fire. Most of the interior walls had been burned away and the entry door destroyed. The aft pressure bulkhead and fuselage skin, which comprise the outer portions of the compartment enclosure, were buckled and discoloured. The plastic door on the front of the vanity cabinet was burned away, and the cold air outlet nozzle was found amongst the debris on the floor. It was in the closed position.

Except for the top of the waste disposal chute, which had burnt away where it attaches to the waste disposal door, the chute and waste disposal container were intact. The container itself, together with paper rubbish inside it, was scorched, but not burnt. The aluminium shelf below the container was covered with debris, but showed little evidence of heat damage. The floor under the sink was also covered with debris, including a plastic vial and a paper maintenance tag, neither of which were burnt. A Halon automatic fire extinguisher, mounted below the sink, had discharged into the waste disposal chute.

The amenities section was severely fire damaged, with parts of the oxygen mask compartment burnt away. The stainless steel drain pipe was intact, but both the oxygen line and the cold air line had melted near the corner of the pressure bulkhead and the outboard wall.

The plastic lid and shroud of the commode were burnt away, but the commode's fibreglass waste tank was intact and still contained waste matter and water. The flush pump and pump motor were found in pieces in the waste tank. The motor housing had melted and both the rotor and AC wiring were encased in the molten metal. The rotor itself did not appear to be damaged by heat.

A flush and fill line, comprising a flexible hose and a stainless steel pipe, connected the waste tank to a toilet service panel on the outside of the fuselage. The stainless steel pipe leading down from the service panel was intact, but the flexible hose from the pipe to the waste tank had burned away. Soot and tar deposits on the service panel door showed

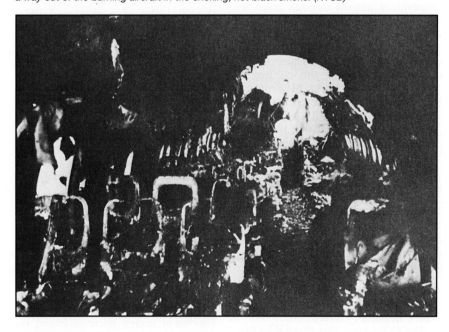

(above) View of the DC-9's cabin looking aft from the flightdeck doorway; the photographer's flash has highlighted the charred ceiling over the galley (left) and its fixtures. The main entry door (right) is out of sight. (below) Halfway down the cabin aisle, only the daylight coming through the open starboard overwing exit (left), the gaping hole in the aft cabin roof, and the faint line of windows each side, provides any visual reference at all. The photograph perhaps conveys a faint impression of the utter lack of visibility which faced passengers trying to find a way out of the burning aircraft in the choking, hot black smoke. (NTSB)

that the pipe had become a conduit for the fire.

The flush pump and filter mechanisms, located below the water line in the waste tank, were in good condition but, above the water line, the plastic housing for the pump and filter had melted.

The flush timer was intact in its normal position on the interior inboard wall of the cabinet below the sink. The timer and connectors showed evidence of external heat damage only. The wiring supplying 3-phase power from the timer to the flush motor was undamaged be-

tween the timer and a point midway into the lower amenities portion of the vanity cabinet. But where the wires leave the vanity cabinet to connect to the motor, the insulation had melted away.

The toilet compartment had been used several times during the flight. The last known passenger to use it, a non smoker, did so some 25 minutes before the smoke was first noticed. She saw nothing unusual but, when she left to return to her seat, a man was waiting to enter. Investigators were unable to determine his identity.

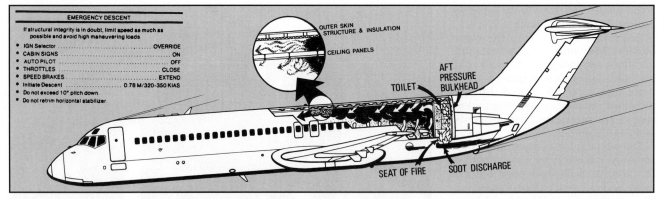

EMERGENCY DESCENT

If structural integrity is in doubt, limit speed as much as possible and avoid high maneuvering loads.

• IGN Selector .... OVERRIDE
• CABIN SIGNS .... ON
• AUTO PILOT .... OFF
• THROTTLES .... CLOSE
• SPEED BRAKES .... EXTEND
• Initiate Descent .... 0.78 M/320-350 KIAS
• Do not exceed 10° pitch down.
• Do not retrim horizontal stabilizer.

One of the popular misconceptions about this accident has been that the fire was burning its way through the cabin before the emergency landing. Apart from crew and survivor evidence, the investigators' examination of the charred fuselage showed this was not so. Propagation took place progressively but unseen in the space between the cabin lining panels and the fuselage skin, as this drawing shows. When the exits were opened, the combination of unlimited oxygen, hot ceiling panels, and large quantities of unburned gases in the upper part of the fuselage interior, produced a flashfire throughout the cabin. (Matthew Tesch)

Rear fuselage and cargo holds

The internal fuselage behind the aft pressure bulkhead was intact with little evidence of heat damage. Except for buckling and discolouration above the toilet compartment's vanity cabinet, the aft pressure bulkhead was intact. However, where the feeder cables from the engine-driven generators passed through holes in the floor beam beneath the aft wall of the toilet, there were clear signs of electrical arcing in addition to heat damage which had melted the nylon conduits for the cables. A small notch, typical of erosion caused by electrical arcing, was found on the lower edge of the floor beam hole through which the right generator cables passed, indicating that one of the cables had been shorting on to the floor beam.

The forward cargo hold exhibited no evidence of fire or heat damage and heat damage to the rear hold was confined to the area immediately below the toilet compartment.

Flight Recorders

The DC-9 was equipped with a Leigh Digital Flight Data Recorder (DFDR) and a Fairchild Cockpit Voice Recorder (CVR).

The CVR casing was affected by fire and smoke, but the tape was undamaged and the quality of the recording was excellent until 1907:41 (EDT) when the CVR ceased to function.

The tape was examined for sounds of electrical arcing which could have been associated with the onset of the fire. A sound of electrical arcing was first recorded at 1848:12, and was repeated at 1848:15, 1851:03, 1851:05, 1851:14, 1851:42, 1859:59 and 1900. At 1905:35, the time when the captain said they had lost the left AC bus, an electrical pulse was recorded simultaneously on both the captain's and first officer's radio channels.

It was determined that the DFDR ceased recording at the same time as the CVR, one hour 42 minutes after departure from Dallas, when the aircraft was in cruising flight at FL330.

Smoke in another DC-9

During the investigation, the circumstances surrounding an incident in which heavy smoke developed in the aft toilet of a chartered DC-9 were also examined. In this case the flush motor had overheated and emitted smoke, but there was no fire. However, during examination of the chartered DC-9's vanity cabinet, identical to that in the Air Canada DC-9, paper debris was found beneath and to one side of the waste disposal container. Toilet paper had accumulated on the shelf beneath the amenities section and the hole through which the flush motor electrical wiring passes was stuffed with paper.

ANALYSIS

The evidence pointed to the fire having originated within the vanity cabinet or the toilet shroud. Possible sources of the fire were a burning cigarette, the toilet flush motor, or the flush motor electrical wiring. Electrical arcing damage found on the feeder cables of the left and right AC generators, routed beneath the floor of the aft toilet, prompted the investigators to also consider this as a possible source of ignition.

Burning cigarette?

The waste disposal container was certainly the most logical place for combustible material to collect and be ignited by a burning cigarette falling down the waste disposal chute. Had a cigarette started a fire in the container however, its only propagation path would have been up the chute. But it was highly unlikely that such a fire could have spread from the top of the chute (which had

burned away where it attached to the sink shroud), down to the flush motor and shorted its wiring – and yet remain undetected for 11 minutes after the circuit breakers popped.

Although there was some evidence of flame damage both in the chute and the container, the automatic Halon fire extinguisher had discharged only into the chute. Evidently, as the container became heated, hot air rose into the chute where the heat-activated discharge nozzle was located, reaching the melting point of the nozzle before the temperature below the sink attained that level, with the result that the entire Halon supply was discharged into the chute. But as there was no evidence of a continuous flame path from the top of the chute down to the intense fire damage under the amenities section of the vanity cabinet, the fire had obviously not originated in the chute – as borne out by the scorched but unburnt paper found in the container.

This area of most intense burning, in the open space in the lowest level of the amenities section, was directly below the failed cold air supply line, the fire melting part of the aluminium bottom shelf. Initially, because the cold air outlet was closed, there would have been no airflow through the line, but once it melted through, air would have been supplied to the fire, causing it to intensify.

Because the amenities section adjoins the waste disposal chute, the investigators sought to determine whether a lighted cigarette could have fallen into the space under the amenities section instead of into the waste disposal container.

An aluminium partition separates this area from the chute and container but, about four inches above the floor there is a square hole through which loose material could pass. Thus, if the fit between the waste disposal door and the chute, or between the chute and container, had not been secure, a lighted cigarette could have fallen from the chute through the hole into the area below the amenities section. That rubbish could enter this area was demonstrated by the waste paper found in the same position in another DC-9. It was possible that the fire had begun in this way.

Overheated flush motor?

The last known person to use the toilet did so 25 minutes before the fire was detected, and the flush motor worked properly at that time. As tests demonstrated that an overheated flush motor would not produce temperatures high enough to ignite adjacent materials, and there was evidence that the flush motor neither failed internally nor was damaged internally by heat, the investigators concluded this was unlikely to have been the source of the fire.

Flush motor wiring?

Another possible source of ignition was the flush motor wiring. The tripping of the three circuit breakers was accompanied by arcing recorded by the CVR at 1851:14. The three circuit breakers tripped almost simultaneously, indicating all three phases shorted at the same time. But the only evidence of wiring damage was where the wiring leaves the vanity cabinet and connects to the motor. The damage at this location could only have been the result of fire that was already burning, and the investigators concluded this was what caused the three circuit breakers to trip

Arcing of generator cables?

From three minutes before the three circuit breakers tripped, numerous electrical arcing sounds were recorded on the CVR. Because of the extensive fire damage, it could not be determined if the cables had been correctly installed or if anything had caused them to chafe against the floor beam. Although the fault protection circuitry eventually tripped the generators off the line, this did not occur until some 15 minutes after fire damage had caused the three circuit breakers of the flush motor wiring to trip. The protective circuitry for the generators operates only when the current differential between generator and bus exceeds some 20-40 amps, so it seemed possible that a current of up to 40 amps, arcing through abraded generator cable insulation, could have provided sufficient heat to ignite the cable's nylon conduit be-

neath the floor of the toilet. The possibility that this was the source of the fire could not be dismissed.

Fire propagation

Regardless of the ignition source, the evidence showed that the fire propagated forward from the lower outboard corner of the toilet's amenities section, burning through the toilet walls and allowing smoke, hot gases, and fumes to rise in the space between the toilet shell and the aircraft's outer skin and aft pressure bulkhead. As the smoke rose, it entered the toilet through the wall and ceiling seams, while the fire itself remained concealed.

As the fire moved forward into the area between the commode shroud and the top of the waste tank, hot gases, smoke, and melted plastic were vented overboard through the toilet compartment vent line. The vent line runs forward beneath the floor and below the generator feeder cables to leave the aircraft through a venturi in the toilet service panel in the side of the fuselage.

The heat melted the aluminium vent tube, thus admitting superhot gases into the floor beam area below the floor and on to the generator cables. As a result, the insulation of both left and right generator feeder cables broke down, and between 1905:35 and 1907:41, the protective circuits tripped them offline. The weight of evidence thus indicated that the arcing of the generator cables *was the result of the fire and not the source of it.*

The flexible connection between the waste tank and its flush and fill pipe was located close to the inlet of the toilet vent line and, when the flexible connection burnt through, this stainless steel pipe also became an overboard vent for the fire. Deposits of soot and tar on the access door of the toilet service panel, and melted rivets in the pipe connector, attested to this.

The momentary abatement of smoke witnessed by First Officer Ouimet and Flight Attendant Benetti at 7.04pm probably resulted from the diluting effect of opening the toilet door, discharging the fire extinguisher into the compartment, and closing the door again, together with the near simultaneous failure of the vent line and flush and fill pipe connections, both of which increased the discharge of smoke and hot gases overboard.

The scorched area on the DC-9's outer skin, coinciding with the position of the toilet compartment within the fuselage, showed that, as the fire consumed the toilet structure, the

airspace between the toilet outboard wall and the aircraft's metal skin became a flue. Superheated gases drawn up this channel then flowed forward between the cabin ceiling lining and the fuselage skin, heating the ceiling panels of the cabin. As a result, smoke, fumes and hot gases poured into the cabin through the ceiling and sidewall liners and began accumulating.

After the aircraft stopped on the runway and the exits were opened, an unlimited amount of oxygen suddenly became available to feed the fire. Within 60 to 90 seconds, the combination of this oxygen, the already hot ceiling panels, and the large quantities of unburned gases collected in the upper part of the cabin, produced a flashfire.

Although the precise origin of the fire in the toilet could not be finally determined, there was no doubt it had spread from the lower part of the toilet compartment's vanity cabinet. But because of the direction of the airflow within the compartment, the smoke, fumes, and hot gases were vented overboard, allowing the fire to burn undetected for almost 15 minutes before the first smoke was noticed.

Neither the captain nor first officer heard the arcing recorded on the CVR. The DFDR showed that they were accompanied by voltage excursions on the right AC bus and, in view of the proximity of the CVR wiring to the generator cables, the investigators concluded the arcing sounds were electromagnetically induced. They were therefore inaudible, and the tripping of the flush motor's three circuit breakers at 6.51pm was thus the first indication to the crew of the developing danger.

Air Canada crews were instructed that a tripped circuit breaker denoted the circuit was no longer powered. Tripping of circuit breakers in flight is not uncommon, and pilots were required only to allow the circuit time to cool, and then to limit themselves to one reset attempt. If the circuit breaker could not be reset, they could assume the component was safely shut down. While it could be argued that the captain could have asked a flight attendant to check the toilet to seek the reason for the flush motor's failure, this was a matter for his judgement at the time. With the benefit of hindsight, his decision not to do so was probably unfortunate.

About five and a half minutes elapsed between the time Flight Attendant Kayama told the captain there was a fire in the toilet and his decision to begin the emergency descent. While there is a need to evaluate a situation before deciding on emergency action, the time to make this decision seemed excessive in the circumstances. The investigators believed a precautionary emergency descent should have begun as soon as it was evident that the fire could not be directly attacked with an extinguisher. Had the descent started at this time, the DC-9 could have landed at Louisville nearly five minutes earlier than it did at Cincinnati.

By the time the captain did declare an emergency, the DC-9 was closer to Cincinnati than Louisville and, although there was a faulty ATC handoff, this did not delay the landing appreciably.

It was not possible to know if the shortened flight time would have delayed or prevented the flashfire, but the lesser exposure to toxic fumes and thick smoke would certainly have enhanced the passengers' capacity to escape after the exits were opened.

With the loss of the aircraft's electrical power, the augmentation valves in the pressurisation system had closed and the smoke was no longer being purged overboard as quickly as it had been. On top of this, when engine power was retarded to Flight Idle for the descent, high pressure bleed air was no longer available to the cabin. As a result, the rate at which smoke and fumes were accumulating in the cabin and flightdeck greatly increased.

The captain's difficulties were compounded by the failure of most of his flight instruments. At about 8000 feet during the descent, the emergency inverter was lost, with the loss of the emergency AC bus, leaving the small emergency standby ADI as the only available attitude instrument. The captain flew the remainder of the descent, the traffic pattern, and the landing using only this standby ADI and his airspeed indicator. And with smoke now filling the flightdeck, he had difficulty seeing even these instruments.

After descending through 3000 feet, the captain told the first officer to depressurise the aircraft in preparation for landing and to ensure the doors and overwing exits could be opened. The first officer did so, but also turned off the air conditioning and pressurisation packs which, powered by the emergency DC bus, were still operating. He thought that the packs were feeding the fire.

Had he not done this, the bleed air supply to the cabin would have been restored when the aircraft levelled out and engine power was applied again and, in the four minutes before the aircraft landed, two complete

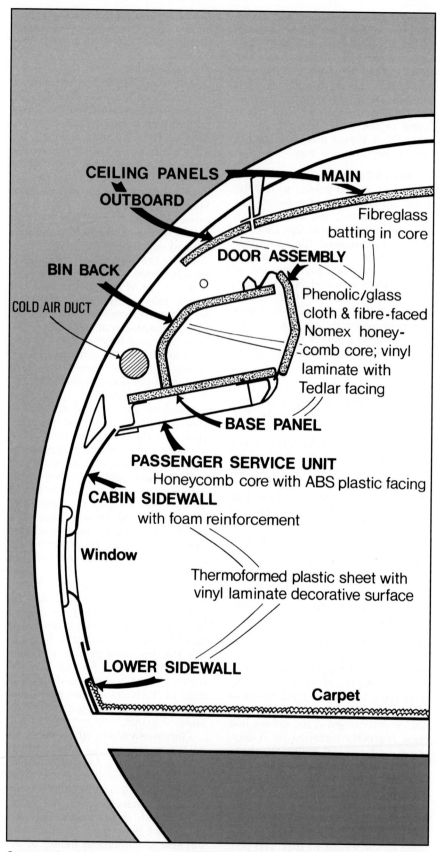

Cross section (sans seating) of a typical Air Canada DC-9 after the "widebody" interior refurbishment undertaken during 1982-84. Lightweight, strong, decorative – and utterly lethal when ignited! Technological advances in composites and fibre-reinforced materials for cabin furnishings, with enhanced "fireblocking" retardants, have still failed to avoid the widespread use of plastics in aircraft interiors. (Matthew Tesch, with acknowledgement to Heath Tecna).

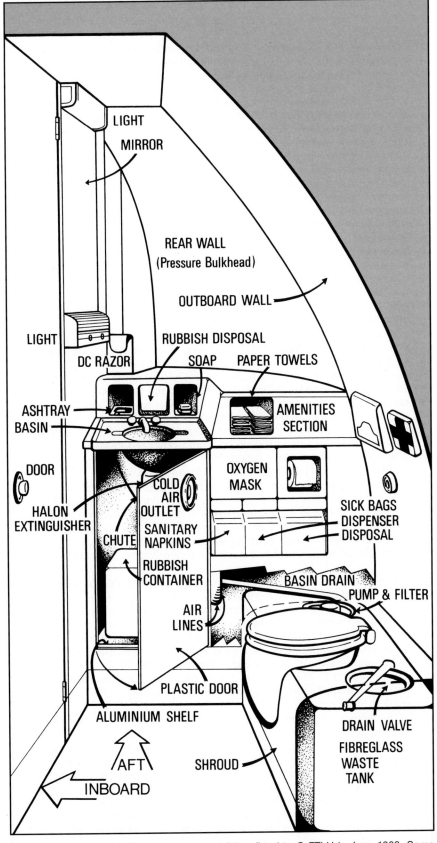

LIGHT

MIRROR

REAR WALL
(Pressure Bulkhead)

OUTBOARD WALL

LIGHT

RUBBISH DISPOSAL

DC RAZOR

SOAP   PAPER TOWELS

ASHTRAY
BASIN

AMENITIES
SECTION

DOOR

OXYGEN
MASK

HALON
EXTINGUISHER

COLD
AIR
OUTLET
SANITARY
NAPKINS

SICK BAGS
DISPENSER
DISPOSAL

CHUTE

RUBBISH
CONTAINER

BASIN DRAIN

PUMP & FILTER

AIR
LINES

PLASTIC DOOR

ALUMINIUM SHELF

DRAIN VALVE

AFT

SHROUD

FIBREGLASS
WASTE
TANK

INBOARD

Layout of portside aft toilet, representative of that fitted to C-FTLU in June 1983. Some fittings are shown open or cut away to expose pertinent equipment. Largely hidden, however, is the toilet pump-and-filter assembly, in this view beneath the covering shroud and behind the bowl. Note that the term "outboard wall" refers only to the interior panel – not the exterior metal skin of the aircraft. (Matthew Tesch, with acknowledgement to NTSB & McDonnell Douglas)

changes of cabin air would have taken place.

In the conditions existing in the cabin during the descent, the first officer's reasoning was understandable. But with the cabin ram air valve also in the closed position, there was now no fresh air being admitted to the cabin at all. As smoke continued to accumulate, it began to build down further towards the floor and the toxicity of the air increased. Moreover, with the buildup of heat and combustible gases in the upper levels of the cabin, conditions conducive to a flashfire increased.

Aircraft control

Despite this hostile environment, the loss of engine and flight instruments, and an inoperative stabiliser trim, the captain somehow maintained his concentration. With the help of the first officer, he configured the aircraft for landing, slowed it to flap extension speeds and, despite heavy control forces resulting from its out of trim condition, touched down smoothly. Considering the near-impossible conditions, the captain's airmanship in bringing the aircraft down safely was outstanding.

The experienced approach controller, a Mr Gregory Karam, had also been instrumental in bringing the flight to a safe landing. The captain himself said later: "We were steered to the airport by the most capable controller I have ever heard."

Evacuation

When the aircraft finally landed, visibility in the cabin was virtually nil and, with passengers and cabin crew already exposed to constantly increasing smoke and toxic gases during the descent and landing, prompt evacuation of the aircraft became extremely difficult.

The flight attendants' action in selecting able-bodied passengers to open the four overwing exits was successful in that three of them were opened and used by surviving passengers. The flight attendants also tried to brief passengers on other emergency procedures, but because of the smoke they had great difficulty communicating their instructions.

Virtually all the survivors had covered their mouths and noses with towels or articles of clothing as instructed by the flight attendants. Wet towels will filter out smoke particles, and gases such as hydrogen chloride, hydrogen fluoride, and hydrogen cyanide. Breathing through items of clothing will also filter out smoke particles, but is less effective in filtering out the gases, and neither will reduce the carbon monoxide concentration. The flight attendants' initiative in distributing wet towels, and instructing passengers to breathe through them or items of clothing, undoubtedly contributed to their survival.

Even so, conditions severely limited the success of the evacuation, and the flight attendants who opened the forward doors were not able to make themselves heard. The location of the victims' bodies after the cabin fire had been subdued, most of them still in their seats, suggested they were either incapacitated even before the exits were opened, or were overcome as they tried to move towards an exit.

Survivors who did succeed in escaping through the overwing exits said they barely had the strength – or the presence of mind – to negotiate these exits. Visibility in this midships part of the cabin was worse than further forward. Many of the survivors found they were able to see a little better by bending forward or crawling, but those who moved back to reach the overwing exits only found them because they had memorised the number of rows between their seats and the exits, and they counted by feeling the seatbacks.

The cabin environment obviously deteriorated very quickly after the exits were opened. Although all the passengers were seated forward of Row 13 when the aircraft stopped, two of the victims were found in the aisle at Rows 14 and 16. Making their way back to find the overwing exits, they apparently bypassed them because of the complete lack of visibility, and were caught by the flashfire.

It can only be regarded as fortuitous that the DC-9 was carrying less than half its normal passenger load. Even so, less than half of these succeeded in making their escape before the cabin became an inferno. Had the aircraft's 100 passenger seats been occupied, the scale of the tragedy would inevitably have been far greater.

Recommendations

As a result of earlier inflight fire investigations, the NTSB had recommended to the FAA that all turbine-powered, airline aircraft be equipped with systems such as smoke detectors for early detection of toilet compartment fires, and that emergency oxygen bottles, with full face masks, be available for each cabin attendant to enable them to fight such fires. Had this DC-9 been so equipped, the NTSB believed that the severity of the fire's outcome could have been lessened.

HOW *DID* THE FIRE START?

Because the exhaustive tests and research conducted during the typically meticulous NTSB investigation failed to finally pinpoint the source of this fire, speculation about its precise cause continues to this day. There remain four possible hypotheses:

The first concerns an incident to the aircraft nearly four years before. As C-FTLU levelled out at FL250 on departure from Boston, Massachusetts on September 17, 1979, its rear pressure bulkhead failed, and there was an explosive depressurisation of the cabin. The badly damaged DC-9 was nursed back to Logan International Airport with some engine and flight controls disabled and its FDR connections severed.

During the two months required to repair the aircraft in a Boston hangar, "numerous wire bundles were cut in order to examine the airplane and to facilitate the removal of damaged structure and reinstallation of replacement structure" (NTSB). Many wires had to be spliced through the rear pressure bulkhead. Air Canada approved the McDonnell Douglas repairs and ferried the aircraft back to the company base at Montreal's Dorval Airport for replacement of the rear toilets (then two – port and starboard) and cabin furnishings, before the DC-9 returned to service. NTSB investigators at Cincinnati reportedly examined all the spliced wiring and repairs and found "no evidence of arcing or short circuiting".

The second hypothesis involved the DC-9's reconfiguration to an all-Economy 100-seat layout, concurrent with a complete refurbishment of all fittings, seats and wall and ceiling panels, a year before the inflight fire. As part of an Air Canada fleetwide DC-9 upgrade program using 'kits' made by the Heath Tecna Corporation, the work on C-FTLU was carried out during June 1982. Enclosed overhead lockers were installed, and the aft starboard toilet was replaced by a coat cupboard. But all fabric, plastic and composite fibre materials used in the refurbishment met applicable flammability and other requirements in force at the time, and enquiries established there could be no question of the work having a bearing on the Cincinnati accident.

A third line of enquiry reviewed the recent maintenance history of C-FTLU. The aircraft's two engine-driven generators and its APU appeared to have been recurring irritants in the 12 months preceding the Cincinnati fire. No less than 76 logbook 'write-ups' were noted by NTSB investigators, half of them in the month prior to June 2, 1983 alone. But all were found to have been properly dealt with and signed off.

Three years of logbook entries regarding the rear toilet/s were also checked, indicating only normal service equipment malfunctions and component changes in the pump and flushing systems. However, exactly four weeks before the fateful flight, a scheduled major maintenance check of C-FTLU evidently turned up an unexpected problem. NTSB investigators found a job card written-up: "Insulation at bottom of pressure bulkhead in rear cargo (compartment) soaked with toilet detergent liquid". The item had been signed off with the note: "Connectors checked and tightened; also, insulation replaced where needed."

This review of otherwise historical trivia is typical of the kind of far-ranging detective work carried out in the course of air accident investigation. Even in the absence of evidence of human, mechanical or electrical error, it was obvious that the aft end of this particular DC-9 had quite a hard life, and a lot of work had been devoted to it. While readers are urged not to draw inferences which the NTSB investigators themselves quite properly did not make, they are reminded of the "thread" running through so many of these *Air Disaster* chapters – that a cumulative chain of seemingly inconsequential incidents can, given certain unfortunate twists in space and time, ultimately lead to a major accident.

So does the most simple explanation proposed by the investigators deserve more credence? That the unknown male passenger, reportedly the last to use the rear toilet before the "commotion", carelessly disposed of a smouldering cigarette? If so, was he the actual *cause* of the fire – or just the *final link* in the chain?

A smoke detector would have alerted the crew to the existence of the smoke before it was actually discovered. Furthermore, had an oxygen bottle with a full-face smoke mask been available, it might have enabled the senior attendant to take immediate action to locate the source of the smoke, if necessary with the fire axe carried on board, and to extinguish the fire. At the very least, earlier detection of the fire would have prompted an earlier decision to descend and land.

In the light of this latest fire-in-flight tragedy, the NTSB issued several additional recommendations to the FAA aimed at preventing the recurrence of a fire similar to that which, apparently innocuous when first discovered, eventually destroyed the Air Canada DC-9 and cost 23 lives:

• Require flightcrews to take immediate action to determine the source and severity of any cabin fire, and to begin an emergency descent if this cannot be quickly determined, or if prompt extinguishing of the fire is not assured.

• Ensure that flight attendants understand the urgency of informing flightcrews of the location, source, and severity of any fire or smoke within the cabin.

• Require all aircrew to be trained in methods of attacking a cabin fire, including donning of breathing equipment, use of the fire axe to gain access to the source of the fire through interior panels, and the discharge of hand fire extinguishers.

• Require that interior cabin panels, including those in toilet and galleys, which can be penetrated with a fire axe without risk to essential aircraft structure, be marked with a standardised identification.

This indistinct view of the DC-9's lower rear fuselage beneath the No 1 (port) engine is noteworthy for only one reason – it shows the stark black trail of scorching soot which was streaming aft from the toilet service panel even as the first officer was tucking into his evening meal over the Kentucky border. (NTSB)

Footnotes:

(1) The ill-fated C-FTLU was in unfortunate company: of the batch of six DC-9-32s accepted by Air Canada between March and July 1968, no less than three were subsequently lost. C-FTLV [47197] barely made it past its 10th birthday before an accident at Toronto, and C-FTLY [47200] was written-off at Montreal in June 1982. Alert readers will have noted the change in the aircraft's national prefix – from CF-xxx to C-(F)xxx – during the early 1970s. This was undoubtedly to free up additional registrations, but this once rare practice has

become increasingly common – sometimes of necessity (as with nationalistic developments in eastern Europe and the former USSR), sometimes more indulgently (as in the case of the former East Germany's change from DM-xxx to the more apt DDR-xxx).

(2) No gyro approach vector: a radar vector provided in the case of a malfunctioning gyro compass or directional gyro. Instead of instructing the pilot to fly specific compass headings, the controller observes the aircraft's radar track and issues directions – "turn right/ left" or "stop turn" – as appropriate.

CHAPTER 10

"JL123 – Uncontrollable!"

*– Boeing 747 crew
to Tokyo ATC*

Japan Air Lines Boeing 747SR-46 JA8119 [20783] (F/n 230)
– August 12, 1985

The domestic widebody, like others in the hardworking fleet, was far from new. But it had been meticulously maintained and there was no reason whatever to doubt its structural integrity. So who could have suspected that an ill-accomplished fuselage repair more than seven years before was in effect a time bomb – waiting to go off?

Domestic Boeing 747s

Japan is notable for its use of Boeing 747s on regular internal services. Two of the country's three airlines, All Nippon Airways and Japan Air Lines, operate fleets of a specially developed domestic variant of the original 100 Series wide-bodied airliner.

Designated by Boeing as the 747SR (Short Range), the version is designed to seat up to 550 passengers and carry a cabin crew of 12 on the relatively short stage lengths that typify Japan's intercity domestic air routes. In addition to its high density seating, the design incorporates modifications to the basic structure, including strengthened wing and undercarriage attachments, to better enable the type to withstand the far more frequent takeoffs and landings demanded of it in short-haul operations, by comparison with long range flying normally undertaken by Boeing 747 aircraft on international routes.

For Japan Air Lines' 528-passenger Boeing 747SR JA8119, one of nine SRs operated by JAL throughout the island nation, Monday, August 12, 1985 began no differently

from most days in the aircraft's eleven years of service, promising the usual busy schedule of flights. JAL was in fact the largest operator of Boeing 747s in the world, its extensive network of worldwide international, as well as domestic routes being serviced by no less than another 37 747 aircraft of various long range marques.

Completing four uneventful services throughout the day, the last of which, Flight JL366, had carried the Minister for Transport, Mr T Yamashita, back from the southern city of Fukuoka on the island of Kyushu, the aircraft arrived back at Tokyo's Haneda International Airport at 5.17pm.

Departure for Osaka

Directed to the JAL domestic terminal's Gate 18, the aircraft was then fuelled and refurbished for its next scheduled service, to be under the command of a senior training captain supervising the upgrading of a former 747 first officer to command status. Except for the two pilots however, the same crew remained aboard, ready to tend the needs of the passengers waiting to board the

aircraft for Flight JL123 to the industrial city of Osaka, 215nm (400km) southwest of Tokyo, departing at 6pm.

The character of this near capacity load of late afternoon travellers was noticeably different to that of the passengers who had occupied the aircraft's seats on flights throughout the day, the majority of whom had been conservatively suited businessmen going about their daily affairs. Undaunted by the late afternoon heat and humidity that was testing the endurance of the terminal building's air conditioning, the jostling, casually dressed crowd that now thronged the departure halls was obviously in a high-spirited, holiday mood. For this was the eve of Bon, a joyful, keenly anticipated three-day Japanese festival, when people traditionally return to their place of birth for family reunions and to pay homage to departed ancestors.

Despite the numerous late afternoon departures, with most flights filled to capacity, Flight 123 was ready to be pushed back almost on schedule and, at 6.04pm, with a total of 509 passengers including 12 small children, the Boeing 747SR taxied away from Gate 18, cleared to the holding point for Runway 15L. Training Captain Masami Takahama, 49, with 19 years' service and a total of some 12,500 hours with JAL, mostly on its international routes, occupied the right hand control seat, with the captain-under-training flying the aircraft under supervision from the left hand seat.

The flight planned route was via the radio navigation aids on the island of Oshima, 50nm southwest of Tokyo, then west-southwest towards Osaka via several nominated waypoints, cruising at FL240 (24,000 feet), with a time interval of 54 minutes. The aircraft carried fuel for three hours 15 minutes.

At 6.12pm the Boeing 747 lifted off normally from Runway 15L. Five minutes later, while climbing on track to FL240 in visual conditions, the aircraft called Tokyo Control to request an amended clearance for a more direct flight to Osaka, bypassing two of the planned waypoints, and at 6.19pm Tokyo Control approved the request. As usual, the radio exchanges were all in English, the international language of Air Traffic Control.

Emergency code

Six minutes later at 6.25, the Tokyo controller, tracking the Boeing 747's target on his radar screen, could see that the aircraft, now cruising at FL240 on a heading of 253°M, was approaching the eastern coast of the Izu Peninsula. But suddenly the emergency code 7700 appeared beside the target on his screen, indicating the Boeing 747's crew had selected this code on their transponder. Seconds later the aircraft called Tokyo Control again, this time with a note of urgency:

Aircraft: "Tokyo – JL123. Request immediate ... ah ... trouble. Request return back to Haneda ... descend and maintain FL220."

Controller: "Roger – approved as you requested."

Aircraft: "Radar vector to Oshima, please."

Controller: "Turn right, heading 090 – radar vector to Oshima."

But to the consternation of the radar controller, instead of making the expected 177° turn back towards Oshima Island, the aircraft made only a gradual turn to the right of about 50°. Crossing the Izu Peninsula and leaving it astern, it then headed out over Suruga Bay in a northwesterly direction.

Controller: "Negative, negative, negative ... confirm you are declare [sic] emergency – that's right?"

Aircraft: "That's affirmative!"

Controller: "Request your nature of emergency?"

There was no immediate reply and the controller saw the target continuing to maintain a northwesterly heading, with its height varying above and below FL240 by several hundred feet.

Controller: "JL123 – fly heading 090 radar vector to Oshima."

Aircraft [tensely]: "But now uncontrol [sic]!"

Controller: "Roger – understood!"

Controller (still watching aircraft's target half a minute later): "If possible, squawk 2072."

Again there was no response. Two minutes later, the controller, seeing the aircraft had reached the western side of Suruga Bay, called the aircraft again.

Controller: "JL123 – can you descend?"

Aircraft: "Roger – now descending."

Controller: "All right – say altitude now."

Aircraft: "FL240."

Controller: "Right – your position 72 miles to Nagoya. Can you land to [sic] Nagoya?"

Aircraft: "Negative – request back to Haneda."

Up to this point, the radio exchanges had continued in English. But because of the obvious tension on the flightdeck, and its effect on clear communication, the controller reverted to Japanese.

Controller: "All right – from now on you may speak in Japanese."

Aircraft: "Hai, hai! [Yes – yes!]"

JAL Boeing 747s docked at Tokyo's Narita International Airport. With ongoing development in customer configurations, upper deck windows are no longer the marque determinant they once were – both JA8108 [20333] (background, 3 windows) and JA8127 [21031] (foreground, 8 windows) are Model 246Bs. In late 1985, JAL's 46-strong 747 fleet (plus 6 on order) included examples of all models except the 747SP. Added flexibility was provided by the 747SRs retaining the fuel tankage of the '100, enabling their deployment on other than domestic trunk routes if required. The successor to the 747SR is Boeing's development, again at Japanese request, of the 747-400(D). This 'domestic' version of the Model 400 omits the distinctive winglets, and is virtually indistinguishable from the '300, save for features such as the '400's aerodynamically refined leading edge wingroots. (with acknowledgement to Flight International/Janice Lowe)

News that the late afternoon Japan Air Lines flight from Tokyo to Osaka was in difficulties had leaked almost at once to the media and, losing no time, the Japanese television network NHK conducted a live-to-air telephone interview with an eyewitness who happened to be watching the Boeing 747 soon after its emergency call. The witness told viewers the aircraft "was wavering and having trouble keeping to its flight path".

Meanwhile, still above 21,000 feet, the aircraft had turned towards the north in the direction of the mountain ranges that form a spine along the north-south axis of the main Japanese island of Honshu.

News of the emergency had also reached Japan Air Lines' headquarters in Tokyo and at 6.34pm the company's radio operations network made contact with the Boeing 747's crew.

JAL (on company frequency in Japanese): "JL123 – this is Japan Air. Tokyo Control received an emergency call [from you] 30 miles west of Oshima Island at –"

Aircraft [flight engineer's voice – obviously under pressure]: "Ah ... the R5 [cabin] door is broken. Ah ... we are descending now ..."

JAL: "Roger – does the captain intend to return to Tokyo?"

Flight Engineer: "What?"

JAL: "Do you wish to return to Haneda?"

Flight Engineer [anxiously and somewhat incoherently]: "Ah ... just a moment ... we are making an emergency descent ... we'll contact you again. Ah ... keep monitoring."

JAL: "Roger."

Out of control!

In the nine minutes that had elapsed since Tokyo ATC's previous call, the Boeing 747 had continued north for about 25nm until it was some 15nm due west of Mt Fuji. It then began a gradual turn on to a northeasterly heading in the direction of the US Air Force Base at Yokota, 77nm distant on the northwestern outskirts of Greater Tokyo. The aircraft was still over mountainous country, maintaining around 22,000 feet above scattered thunderstorms and rain showers. Tokyo Control, still tracking its progress on radar, now called it again in Japanese.

Controller: "JL123 – can you switch the frequency to 134.0?"

Controller: "JL123, JL123 – if you read me, please?"

The American Approach Controller at Yokota now also called the Boeing 747, but in English: "JL123 – Yokota Approach. If you read me, contact Yokota ..."

The aircraft, still heading northeast and over the inland town of Otsuki in mountainous country 45nm west of Haneda Airport, now entered a descending turn to the right. Completing a full circle of something less than a five nm radius in about three minutes, it straightened out on an easterly heading at a height of 17,000 feet.

But the descent continued and, at 13,500 feet on this heading, one of the crew called in an agitated voice: "JL123, JL123 – uncontrollable!"

Tokyo Control: "Roger – understood. Do you wish to contact Haneda [Approach]?"

Aircraft: "Stay with us!"

Tokyo Control: "Do you wish to contact –?"

Aircraft [frantically]: "Ah ... stay with us!"

Yokota Approach (in English): "JL123, JL123 – Yokota Approach on guard. If you hear me, squawk 5423 ..."

Aircraft [now down to 9000 feet]: "JL123 – request radar vector to Haneda!"

Tokyo Control: "Roger – I understand. Since it is Runway 22, maintain [your] heading 090°."

Instead of complying with this instruction, the Boeing 747, still descending, though less steeply than during the 360° turn, now made another more gradual turn, this time to the left, straightening out on a heading of about 340° at a height of 6800 feet – less than that of some of the mountain peaks that now lay in its path.

Yokota Approach (in English): "JL123 – Yokota Approach. If you hear me, [contact] Yokota 129.4."

Fifth of JAL's burgeoning 747 fleet, and only the second 747-246B to be built, JA8105 [19824] lifts off from Narita. The livery is that worn by JA8119 at the time of its loss and, indeed, by the whole JAL fleet for more than 20 years. In the three principal colour schemes of JAL's postwar history, the "flying crane" has remained a consistent insignia. The use of Boeing 747s on domestic services by JAL and its competitor, the once exclusively domestic carrier All Nippon, is not altogether unique – American transcontinental routes come to mind, as do ad hoc traffic needs in Australia and possibly, in Canada and China. But what distinguishes the Japanese 747SRs' operations is their geographical "intensity". A population of more than 120 million occupying four contiguous homeland islands, the area of which would fit comfortably into the state of California, results in trunk sectors of only an hour or less between relatively few major cities.

Tokyo Control (Japanese): "Can you control now?"

Aircraft [desperately]: "JL123 – Uncontrollable!"

Yokota Approach (in English, a minute and a half later at 6.49pm): "JL123 – this is Yokota Approach on guard – how do you hear me? Contact Yokota Approach on 129.4."

Aircraft [desperately in English as aircraft's altitude readout slowly recovered to 9000 feet]: "JL123 – ah uncontrol. JL123, uncontrol."

Tokyo Control (urgently in Japanese): "JL123, JL123, JL123 – change your radio frequency to 119.7 – 119.7, please!"

Tokyo Control (10 seconds later): "JL123 – change frequency to 119.7 if you can."

Tokyo Approach (English): "If you read, come up 119.7 – we are all ready."

Aircraft (tensely in Japanese): "JL123 – yes, I have selected 119.7. Request position!"

Tokyo Approach (English): "Your position ... ah ... 45 miles northwest of Haneda."

Aircraft (anxiously in English, with altitude readout now indicating 13,000 feet): "Northwest of Haneda – ah – [lapses into Japanese] how many miles?"

Tokyo Approach (English): "Yes – that's right. According to our radar, 55 miles northwest ... ah ... 25 miles to Kumagaya."

Tokyo Approach: "I will talk in Japanese – we are ready for your approach anytime. Also Yokota landing is available – let us know your intentions."

Yokota Approach (English): "JL123 – Yokota Approach on guard."

Yokota Approach: "JL123, JL123 – Yokota Approach Control – how do you read?"

Yokota Approach: "JL123, JL123 – Yokota Approach Control on guard – if you hear me come up on 121.5."

There was no reply to any of these calls, but the Boeing 747's height was now decreasing again and, by 6.54pm, its altitude readout on the Tokyo controller's screen was indicating 11,000 feet.

Tokyo Approach Control now also called the aircraft again in English, advising that its radar position was "50 miles – correction 60 miles" northwest of Haneda Airport. But again there was no response.

Having continued northwest at much the same altitude for another minute, the aircraft's radar target suddenly deviated 90° to the right and, as the altitude readout rapidly decreased, it entered a tight turn of less than two nm radius. A minute later at 6.56pm, as its altitude read-

As eloquent a marketing image as that of Air New Zealand's Samoan DC-10 (Chapter 5), this background view of Mt Fuji features the third of JAL's initial order for 16 747s: Model 146 JA8103 [19727] was delivered June 26, 1970. JAL 747 services, inaugurated on the Tokyo-Honolulu route in July 1970, were later extended to the West Coast. Transpolar and trans-Siberian flights to London and Europe began three years later. As delivered, JAL's 747 "Garden Jets" seated 361 passengers, 40 First Class in the "Garden of Wisteria", with the "Teahouse of the Sky" lounge above, and 321 Economy in the Gardens of "Pine", "Wild Orange" and "Red Maple". By contrast, JA8117 [20781], the first 747SR-46 (September 1973), squeezed in 498 all-Economy seats. Space was subsequently found for another 30 passenger seats!

out fell to 8400 feet, the controller was horrified to see the target vanish from the radar screen.

Further radio calls to the Boeing 747 from Tokyo Control, Tokyo Approach and Yokota Approach all went unanswered. Only a minute later the controllers' worst fears were confirmed – a transmission from a Japanese military jet reported "a huge burst of flame in the Nagano Mountains".

Impact in the mountains

It was already after sunset when radio contact was lost with the Boeing 747 and, by the time two search helicopters from the Japanese Air Self-Defence Force had flown through showery weather under overcast skies to scour the area in which the airliner had disappeared, it was dark.

Even so, attracted by a fire blazing near the top of the 5400 foot Mt Osutaka, one of a number of granite peaks in rugged and inaccessible ranges on the border between the Gumma and Nagano Prefectures, about 100km west of Tokyo's Haneda Airport, a helicopter flown by Captain Izumi Omori succeeded in pinpointing the site of the crash.

Making a low pass over the burning wreckage, Captain Omori reported flames "in about 10 spots over an area about 300 metres square", but saw nothing to suggest there could be any possibility of survivors. Much of the wreckage ap-

peared to have spilled down the mountain's near-45° northern slope, and there was nowhere for even a helicopter to land safely in the dark. In the darkness and rain, Captain Omori had no alternative but to defer further searching until first light the following morning.

Meanwhile, reports were being received from police stations along the flight path followed by the Boeing 747, and in the area of the accident.

A witness in a remote mountain village, surprised at the time by the unusual sound of an airliner above his home, vividly described its erratic progress. "All of a sudden, a big aeroplane appeared from between mountains, just like out of nowhere," he told police. "Four times it leaned to the left, and each time it tried to recover its balance to the right. It was flying just like a staggering drunk."

Nagano Prefecture police reported there was heavy cloud and storms over the mountains when local residents sighted a large aircraft flying low. Shortly afterwards a red flash lit the darkening sky and a column of smoke rose above the mountains.

A resident of a hamlet, three to four kilometres southwest of where Captain Omori's helicopter had located the wreckage, told police the Boeing 747 had "limped in at low altitude at a low speed from the direction of Okutama [ESE], with the nose of the aircraft pointing slightly upwards and the engines making an extremely loud noise."

The witness continued: "It flew overhead then, just before it reached Mt Senbira [5576ft] to the northwest, it suddenly turned right and took a northeasterly course towards Mt Sangoku [5989ft]. Just as I thought it had flown over Mt Sangoku, it suddenly turned again and came down very quickly behind the mountain, so that we could no longer see it. It was coming down at a steep angle and after that we saw smoke and flames rising from the direction in which it had disappeared".

A farmer working his land in a valley not far from the crash site told police: "I was looking up in wonder when the aeroplane started to nose-dive. Then there was a big crashing sound like a thunderbolt and then a flash, after which a mushroom cloud of smoke rose from behind the mountain."

From the witness evidence, police estimated that the impact had occurred at 6.56pm.

Search and rescue

Meanwhile, ground parties of police and Japanese Self-Defence Force personnel were already on their way to the area by road. But nightfall and the inaccessibility of the mountain terrain precluded the planning of any major effort to reach the actual crash site that night.

Expecting no survivors, most of the searchers spent the rainy night setting up a base in the mountain village of Ueno, some distance to the north of the crash site. Area fire services and the Ministry of Transport had also mobilised search parties, but the narrow mountain roads and tracks winding up from villages and hamlets in the valleys ended well below where the wreckage lay high on the mountainside. Nonetheless, some of the parties set out on foot during the night to clamber up through the rain and mist towards the scene of the accident.

At first light at 5am the following day, despite poor visibility in drizzle and mist, and before any of the ground parties had reached the site, helicopters again flew over the scene of the crash. This time, the nature of the disaster was plain to see. Flying a westerly heading, the Boeing 747 had descended into a pine forest near the top of the northern face of Mt Osutaka, actually a narrow steep-sided mountain ridge oriented east-west, exploding into flames and breaking up as it bounced and slid along the ridge line.

The empennage and the No 1 engine had been torn off in the initial impact with the trees, and the aircraft had apparently then become airborne again, striking the ridge line for a second time 650 metres further west and uprooting numbers of trees. This catastrophic impact had torn off the port wing and demolished the nose section as far back as the leading edge of the wing, scattering burning wreckage over a distance of about 150 metres. Stripped and blackened trees that remained standing amid the fragmented, scattered wreckage were still smouldering. The No 2 engine had been hurled over the ridge itself to fall into the gorge on its southern side.

The main wreckage of the fuselage, with the two starboard side engines, had spilled down the steep northern slope for some 250 metres. As expected, the helicopter crews could discern no sign of life. Nor were any bodies visible from the air.

In Tokyo, the fearful news was confirmed to a waiting international media corps – the JAL Boeing 747 disaster had resulted in the highest death toll ever to occur in a single-aircraft accident – an outcome second only to that of the horrific collision between two giant aircraft of the same type on the Spanish island of Tenerife, eight years earlier (fully described in *Air Disaster*, Volume 1, Chapter 18).

Because of the extremely inaccessible nature of the mountainous area where the wreckage lay (known locally as the Nagano Prefecture's "Tibet"), it was not until around 9am, more than 14 hours after the Boeing 747 had disappeared from the controllers' radar screens, that firemen and civil defence workers from villages in the nearby valleys finally succeeded in reaching the crash site after a difficult climb.

Map showing flightplanned route of JL123, skirting the Chubu-Kinki Restricted (training) Areas over Enshu Bay along Airway W27, then turning over the VOR/NDB at Kushimoto to pick up V55 into Osaka. In the event, the Boeing 747 was cleared to "cut the corner", passing some 10nm north of Oshima Island's VORTAC/NDB to join W27 at reporting point SEAPERCH. The aircraft had scarcely bypassed the island when its rear pressure bulkhead failed, and the subsequent track shows its remaining 32 minutes of erratic flight to the point of impact. (Matthew Tesch, with acknowledgement to the Japan MoT)

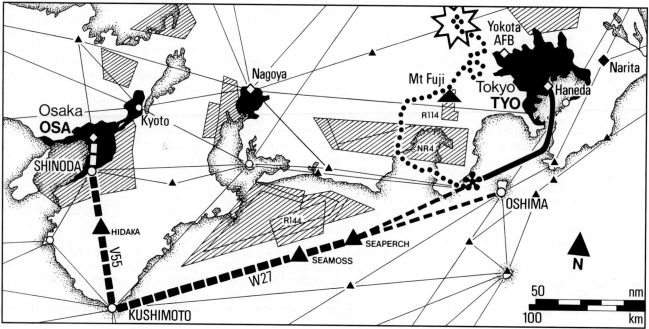

Deteriorating visibility in fog on the mountains was now making helicopter operations into the crash site dangerous, forcing their temporary suspension. But when conditions improved and flying resumed later in the morning, numbers of army paratroopers were able to fly into the site aboard troop carrying Chinook helicopters and, using rappelling gear while the helicopters hovered, literally drop down to where wreckage lay.

Meanwhile, at Haneda Airport, some 320 relatives of passengers on the ill-fated aircraft were boarding eight chartered buses to travel to the town of Fujioka in the Nagano mountains northeast of Mount Osutaka, to await further news.

From Japan Air Lines too, more than 1000 employees were preparing to go to the crash site to assist with the enormous task of recovering more than 500 bodies. And the company itself was making ready to provide food and clothing for this veritable army of rescuers.

On the mountain as the morning wore on, civil defence and army personnel, steeling themselves against the sickening human tragedies that caught their eye wherever they looked, progressively explored the vast amount of widely scattered wreckage. Some of it, reduced almost to ashes, was still smouldering, but in other places, particularly the wreckage that had slid furthest down the mountain slope, it was quite untouched by fire. Even so, the stench of burning hung oppressively over it all, and seemingly countless broken bodies littered the remains of what had been the fuselage structure.

Well down the mountain face from the main impact point, a fireman stood on the steep slope surveying unburnt wreckage, apparently from the rear section of the fuselage, that had slid into a ravine below him. Suddenly he saw something scarcely believable. It looked like an arm waving! "There's something moving down there!" he shouted.

Sure enough, a young woman, badly injured but alive and conscious, was lying pinned between two sets of passenger seats. Within minutes she had been released and tenderly lifted on to a makeshift stretcher, ready to be carried up to a position where one of the military helicopters could winch her up for evacuation to hospital. Suffering a broken pelvis and a fractured arm, she gave her name as Yumi Ochiai.

Not long afterwards there was more unbelievably good news in the ravine – a 12 year old schoolgirl, Keiko Kawakami, was found wedged in the branches of a nearby tree, suffering nothing more serious than cuts and bruises and torn muscles!

And there was even more to come! Rescuers discovered yet another young woman, Hiroko Yoshizaki, 34, and her daughter Mikiko, 8, both of them alive and conscious, but hidden from view by wreckage of the cabin that had fallen on top of them. Both had sustained various fractures.

The two children were winched up into a helicopter in the arms of paratroopers hanging from horse-collar slings. The women were winched up secured to stretchers. All four surviving passengers had been in the rear cabin, one of them on the port side, and the others in the centre block of seats. All of them were seated amongst the last seven rows of seats.

When this unexpected news of survival reached the many relatives and friends, now assembled in the high school gymnasium in the small valley town of Fujioka, where they had been offered seating while they anxiously awaited developments, there was jubilation and renewed hope. Perhaps other survivors

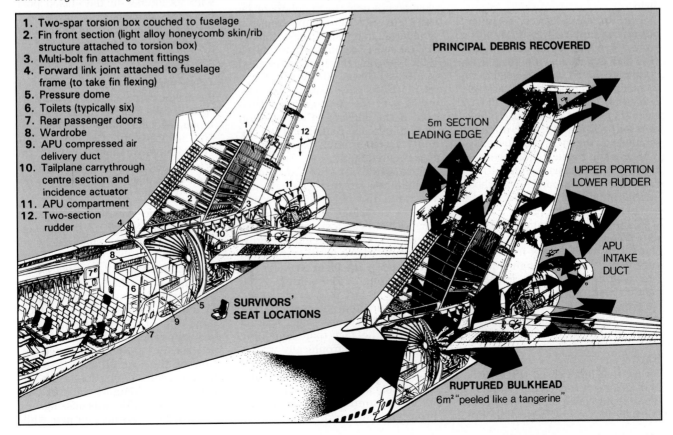

Catastrophe inevitable! Although the rupture of the aft pressure bulkhead did not destroy the aircraft, it rendered the crew literally powerless to control it. The pressurised cabin air which exploded into the tailcone and tail surfaces not only fractured the fin and lower rudder, but effectively carried away all four independent hydraulic systems powering the primary flight controls. (Matthew Tesch, with acknowledgement to Flight International/John Marsden & Time magazine/Joe Lertola)

1. Two-spar torsion box couched to fuselage
2. Fin front section (light alloy honeycomb skin/rib structure attached to torsion box)
3. Multi-bolt fin attachment fittings
4. Forward link joint attached to fuselage frame (to take fin flexing)
5. Pressure dome
6. Toilets (typically six)
7. Rear passenger doors
8. Wardrobe
9. APU compressed air delivery duct
10. Tailplane carrythrough centre section and incidence actuator
11. APU compartment
12. Two-section rudder

PRINCIPAL DEBRIS RECOVERED

5m SECTION LEADING EDGE

UPPER PORTION LOWER RUDDER

APU INTAKE DUCT

SURVIVORS' SEAT LOCATIONS

RUPTURED BULKHEAD
6m² "peeled like a tangerine"

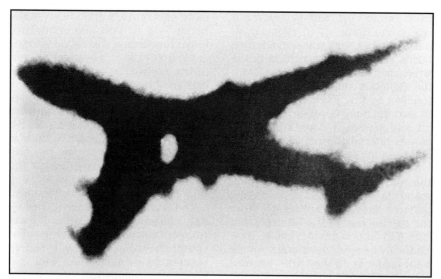

This chance photograph was snapped by an alert ground witness during the latter part of the JAL crew's desperate fight to keep the crippled 747 airborne. The blurred silhouette not only suggests a grossly enlarged image, but also one that is real and un-retouched. The only hints of remaining fin structure at this stage of the flight are the fuzzy, jagged protuberances at its base and the flex-absorbing fairings at the foot of the leading edge. It thus seems likely that inflight aerodynamic loads finished what the bulkhead rupture began, progressively removing the remainder of the fin structure after its leading edge had been blown off by the explosive decompression. The two shadows beneath the aircraft's belly indicate part of the extended main undercarriage, while the lighter patch above them is almost certainly the aircraft's underside anti-collision beacon – flashing at the moment the photographer pressed his shutter button. (with acknowledgement to Arrow Books/Associated Press)

would soon be found – indeed, perhaps after all, the accident was not the utter disaster they had been led to believe.

But as the hours dragged on with no further encouraging news, their optimistic expectations gradually faded. No other survivors could be found amongst the multitude of the dead.

Some of the relatives, becoming impatient and tiring of the long hours of inactivity in the hot and crowded gymnasium building, with nothing to do but wait, decided to try to reach the crash site themselves. Travelling as far as they could by road, they defied police road blocks to tackle the long and difficult scramble up the rocky mountainside.

Meanwhile medical staff, working amongst the teams helping to recover the bodies, found some whose injuries might not have been fatal had help come more quickly.

"If the rescue operation had started 10 hours earlier," one doctor declared, "we would have found more survivors." Some, though injured, had clearly survived the actual impact but, wearing only light summer clothing, had died of shock and exposure in the near-zero temperatures on the mountaintop during the night.

Why?

But what had caused this horrific and utterly unforeseen tragedy? What could have possibly overtaken the fully serviceable airline aircraft,

operating a normal intercity service in well nigh perfect flying conditions? It was evident that, for some reason yet unclear, the crew had suddenly been deprived of control not long after the Boeing 747 reached cruising level on its relatively short stage to Osaka. But why?

This was the question that now plagued not only the members of Japan's Air Accidents Investigation Committee, a division of its Ministry of Transport (established in March 1966 following the inflight breakup of a BOAC Boeing 707 over Mt Fuji – refer *Air Disaster*, Volume 1, Chapter 5), and the Airworthiness Division of the Japanese Civil Aviation Bureau, but also Boeing and the National Transportation Safety Board in the United States.

Throughout the world, media attention too was focused on the disaster and the mysterious circumstances in which control of the aircraft had been lost with no warning of any kind. Speculation grew concerning the rear door problem mentioned by the flight engineer, the only faint hint as to the origin of the tragedy.

Quite apart from the consequences for JAL and Japanese civil aviation generally, the fact that something could go so catastrophically wrong, apparently without any warning of impending danger, could have frightening implications for the hundreds of other Boeing 747s operating throughout the world.

As a type, the Boeing 747 had been in service for 16 years and more than 600 were flying with the world's airlines. In all this time there had been no instance of a fatigue-induced structural failure affecting the safety of the aircraft in flight.

But JAL's Boeing 747SR JA8119 was far from new and had been worked hard throughout its 11 years of life, having flown a total of 25,000 hours in the course of 18,800 cycles (takeoffs, flights and landings). Was this high and demanding utilisation now showing up some hitherto unknown flaw in the aircraft's design?

So far, the only clue to the loss of control was the flight engineer's tense radio transmission to JAL on the company frequency, 10 minutes after the onset of the emergency, to the effect that the 5R cabin door – the rearmost fuselage door on the starboard side – was "broken".

It seemed possible that, if the door had broken away in flight and struck the tail of the aircraft, the multiple hydraulic systems that actuate the aircraft's massive control surfaces could have been disrupted, depriving the pilots of their primary controls.

At this stage however, any such theory was no more than speculation. And the discovery by the Air Accidents Investigation Committee investigators later in the day that the door in question was in fact amongst the wreckage of the rear fuselage on Mt Osutaka, still firmly attached with its latches in the closed position, only deepened the mystery. If the door was closed and latched before the crash occurred, why had the flight engineer referred to it as "broken"?

Speculation only increased when the airline received two separate telephone calls from terrorist groups in Japan, each claiming responsibility for the destruction of the aircraft. The company responded with the press statement: "Terrorism has not been ruled out, though it is not considered likely."

A photograph – and floating debris

But a photograph of the stricken aircraft in the air, snapped by an alert amateur photographer from a mountain village not long before the Boeing 747 crashed to destruction, now provided new and dramatic evidence. Examination of an enlargement of the photograph by investigators appeared to indicate that at least the upper leading edge section of the aircraft's vertical fin, together with the portion of the tailcone which contains the Auxiliary Power Unit (APU), was missing.

Early the following morning, while

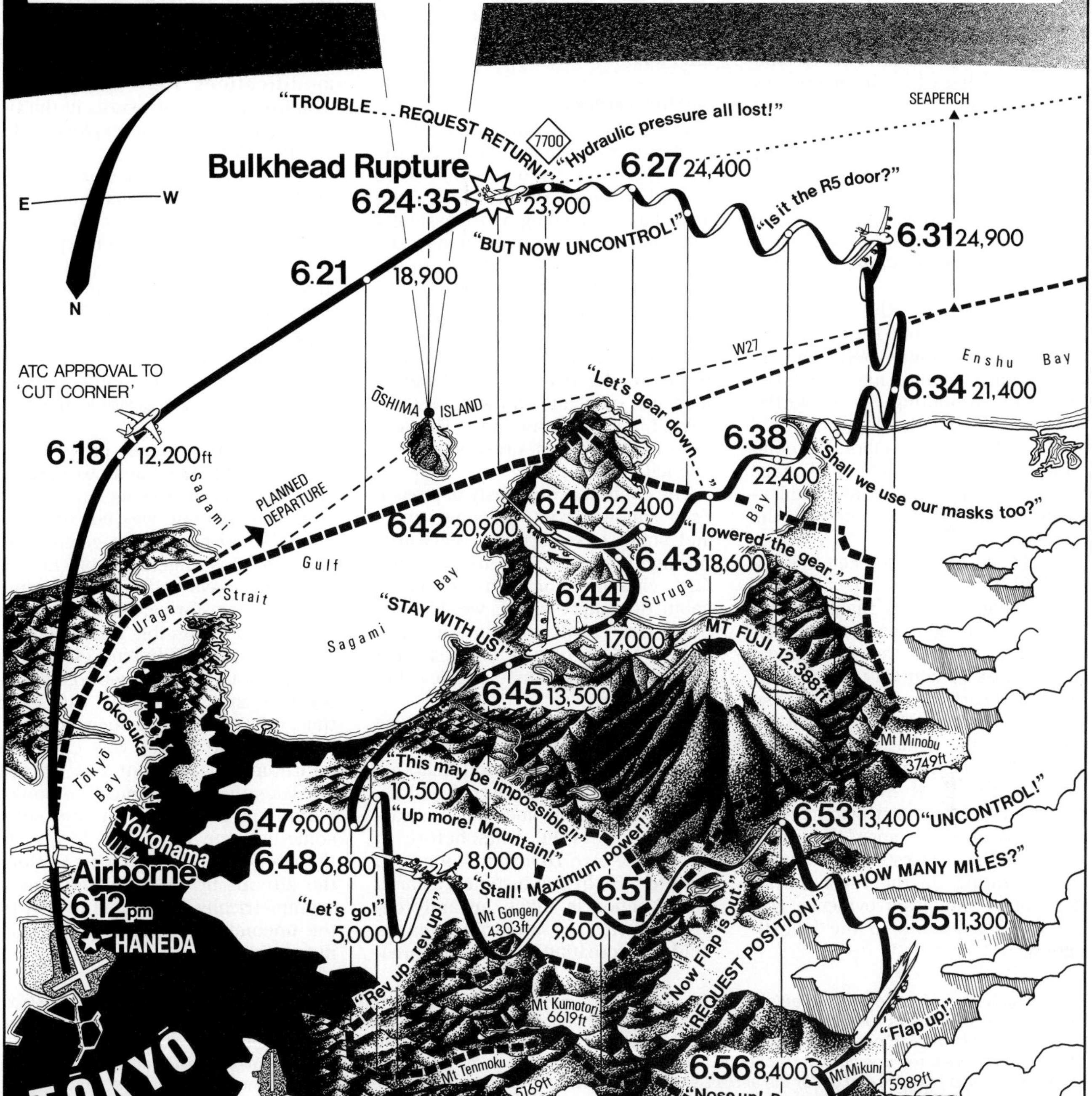

A bland track chart (see previous route map) does little justice to the ordeal to which the crew and passengers of the Boeing 747 were subjected. The height perspective introduced in this spectacular Matthew Tesch illustration, reveals something of the torture endured by 524 people – and of the desperate but vain struggle by the three on the flightdeck to bring the wallowing juggernaut under control. (The continuous line in this perspective view delineates the aircraft's erratic flightpath in both the horizontal and vertical planes, while the broken line "beneath" it marks the aircraft's track over the ground). Twice, at 6.40pm and 6.45pm, the crew succeeded in inching the Boeing 747 around on to an easterly heading towards Haneda Airport. But frustratingly on each occasion, after a minute or so of relative stability, the nose fell away again, first into the 360° right-hand orbit, then into the fatal left turn towards the mountainous terrain to the northwest. When the latter occurred at 6.46pm, the descending aircraft was barely 30nm west of Haneda's Runway 22. (Matthew Tesch, with acknowledgement to Japan MoT)

SEAPERCH

"TROUBLE...REQUEST RETURN!" "Hydraulic pressure all lost!"

7700

Bulkhead Rupture 6.27 24,400 "Is it the R5 door?"
6.24:35 23,900

E — W 6.31 24,900

6.21 18,900 "BUT NOW UNCONTROL!"

N

W27 Enshu Bay

ATC APPROVAL TO
'CUT CORNER' "Let's gear down" 6.34 21,400

ŌSHIMA ISLAND 6.38
6.18 12,200ft 22,400 "Shall we use our masks too?"

PLANNED 6.40 22,400
DEPARTURE "I lowered the gear."
6.42 20,900 6.43 18,600

Sagami 6.44 Suruga
Gulf 17000 Bay
Strait "STAY WITH US!" MT FUJI 12,388ft

Uraga Sagami Bay 6.45 13,500

Yokosuka Mt Minobu
Tōkyō "This may be 3749ft
Bay impossible!!"
10,500 6.53 13,400 "UNCONTROL!"
Yokohama "Up more! Mountain!"
6.47 9,000 8,000 "HOW MANY MILES?"
Airborne 6.48 6,800 "Stall! Maximum power!" 6.55 11,300
6.12pm "Let's go!" 6.51
★ HANEDA 5,000 Mt Gongen 9,600
"Rev up–rev up!" 4303ft "Now Flap is out." "Flap up!"
"REQUEST POSITION!"
TŌKYŌ Mt Kumotori 6.56 8,400 Mt Mikuni
6619ft 5989ft
YOKOTA "Nose up! Power!"
AFB (US) Mt Tenmoku **Crash 6.56:28** 5,400ft
5169ft Mt Osutaka Nagano

Mt Mikabo 4218ft Saitama Gumma Ueno

Kawagoe

Fujioka

engineers and investigators from Boeing and the NTSB were on their way to Tokyo from Seattle and Washington DC to join the Japanese team, the photographic evidence was confirmed beyond all doubt when a Japan Maritime Self-Defence Force destroyer, steaming across Sagami Bay, came upon a 5m section of the aircraft's fin afloat on the water. The wreckage was drifting in the general area over which the aircraft had been flying when the emergency first developed.

Further concentrated searches of the bay and its shores subsequently located numerous pieces from the aircraft's tail section, including a 3m portion of the lower rudder, and a large, 50kg fibreglass duct which had been attached to the APU inside the tailcone.

Examination of the recovered components showed they had sustained severe damage before breaking away from the aircraft's structure, prompting the Airworthiness Division of the Japanese Civil Aviation Board to declare: "Circumstances seem to indicate the damage to the vertical stabiliser and rudders might be the starting point for the accident."

Could the APU have been the culprit? Could this small gas turbine have disintegrated in flight, rupturing the hydraulic lines to the rudder and elevators, and thereby producing the loss of control provisionally attributed earlier to the failure of the rear fuselage door? The result would have been the same, depriving the pilots of their primary controls.

While the Civil Aviation Board prepared to order airworthiness inspections of all Boeing 747 aircraft of all marques registered in Japan, concentrating on the fin and rudders, other important evidence was becoming available to the investigation.

From her hospital bed, one of the surviving passengers was able to provide a firsthand account of what had taken place in the rear passenger cabin up to the time of impact. And, back on the mountain, both the Flight Data Recorder and Cockpit Voice Recorder had been located amongst the wreckage. Both had been damaged in the impact but their recording mediums were not affected.

Survivor's account

The passenger who provided the evidence was Yumi Ochiai, 26, the first survivor to be found, who proved to be an off-duty JAL flight attendant. Travelling as a passenger to Osaka for the festival holiday, she was sitting only four rows from the rear of the cabin, next but one to a port side window seat.

"There was a sudden loud noise," she told investigators. "It was somewhere to the rear and overhead. It hurt my ears and immediately the cabin filled with white mist. The vent hole at the cabin crew seat also opened."

The cabin had obviously depressurised somewhere aft, whipping papers and small loose articles rearwards through the cabin. The instant white mist, characteristic of most sudden cabin decompressions, would have been the result of condensation caused by the rush of cold external air into the previously warm cabin atmosphere.

The "vent hole" in the cabin crew seat to which Ochiai referred was one of a number of modifications made to widebodied aircraft following the Turkish Airlines DC-10 disaster near Paris 11 years before in 1974. (See *Air Disaster*, Volume 1, Chapter 15.) In that instance, a cargo door opened in flight, instantly depressurising the underfloor cargo hold and creating a powerful pressure differential between the hold and the passenger cabin above it. Under the load suddenly imposed on the cabin floor, its support structure failed and the floor collapsed onto the primary control cables running aft from the flightdeck. Longitudinal control of the aircraft was lost and it plunged to the ground at high speed with the loss of all 346 on board – the worst civil aviation disaster in the world to that date. The vent hole modifications were designed to equalise internal pressures in the fuselage in any similar explosive decompression.

"There was no actual sound of any explosion," Yumi Ochiai continued, "But the ceiling panels above the rear toilets fell off. Then the passengers' oxygen masks dropped down, and at the same time the recorded announcement on use of the masks began."

She then felt the aircraft going into what she called a "hira-hira", a Japanese expression describing the falling of a leaf.

The aircraft's purser immediately made an announcement to passengers that there was an emergency and, although she was not on duty, Yumi Ochiai helped the cabin crew brief the passengers on putting on their lifejackets and how to assume a head-down, forward-leaning brace position for a possible crash landing.

By this time the Boeing 747 was in a continuous complex motion, pitching fore and aft and, at the same time, rolling to one side then the other.

The engine power was changing continuously too, but not always consistently – sometimes the power would be increased on one side, sometimes on the other. It was as though the crew were trying to steer the aircraft by using engine power asymmetrically. It seemed to add to the uncomfortable yawing and rolling motion.

This reproduction of part of the aircraft's FDR readout enlarges upon the aircraft motion indicated in the previous drawing. The graph's X-axis (base) linearly marks five minute intervals from takeoff (left) to impact (right). The vertical Y-axis records both speed and height and, superimposed in the 6.35pm-6.40pm section, sample pitch and bank angle excursions are shown. Note the onset of the problems shortly after 6.24pm, when the Boeing 747 reached FL240. Interpreting any one of the graph's traces, it is a straightforward enough exercise to envisage a single plane of motion for the aircraft at any given moment. A composite mental picture that incorporates all the simultaneous excursions, however, is mind-numbing even to contemplate. Not only was the nose pitching from 15° up to 5° down in an average oscillation cycle of about 90 seconds (with drastic effects on speed and height), the aircraft was also "Dutch rolling" (ie, yawing left and right of heading and simultaneously banking left and right through an arc of about 100°) in an average cycle of only about 12 seconds. (with acknowledgement to Flight International & Japan MoT)

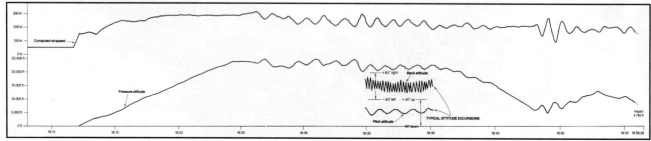

About 15 minutes after the onset of the emergency, Yumi Ochiai was surprised to sight Mt Fuji through the port side cabin window. "I'd thought we were heading back to Haneda Airport," she said. This was about the time the radar controller saw the aircraft's target make a full 360° turn near the inland city of Otsuki.

They were descending now and, within another 10 minutes, the aircraft was clearly below the height of the mountain peaks that loomed ahead. Yumi Ochiai resumed her seat and fastened her seatbelt as they flew on towards the mountains, visible between the banks of cloud and rain showers. Engine power was now varying widely, and with it the fore and aft attitude of the aircraft. But despite the rolling motion that was continuous, they seemed to be gradually climbing again.

Around her in the crowded rear cabin, many of the passengers were clearly terrified, not knowing what was going to happen to them. Others, fearful but outwardly calmer, realising all too well the aircraft was in grave difficulties, began scribbling farewell notes to their families on the back of their flight tickets, or any scrap of paper on which they could lay their hands.

In a few minutes more, after some particularly abrupt changes of engine power and aircraft attitude, the aircraft entered another steep descending turn, then fell into a dive.

"The plane started dropping at a sharp angle, almost vertically," Yumi Ochiai recalled. "Soon afterwards there were two or three very severe impacts. Cabin seats and cushions all around me broke loose, then came tumbling down on top of me. I was pinned under some of the cabin seats, and suddenly there was a piercing pain in my stomach, Finally, when all the noise and confusion of impact had stopped, I was able to unfasten my seatbelt. But then I found I was trapped between the seats and couldn't move at all."

Somewhere amongst the wreckage around her, she could hear children crying. Their cries were quite loud at first, but gradually they became weaker and weaker, and finally there was only silence. After night fell she heard the sound of a helicopter overhead, but it went away and she lapsed into sleep.

Investigation – and frustration!

The arrival of a nine-man expert team of investigators from the United States – five from Boeing and two each from the NTSB and the FAA – failed to produce the timely

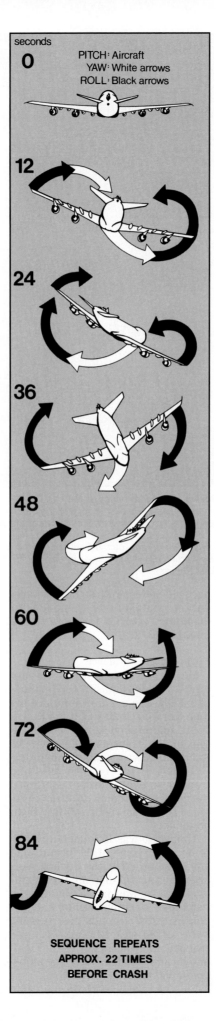

seconds

0

PITCH: Aircraft
YAW: White arrows
ROLL: Black arrows

12

24

36

48

60

72

84

SEQUENCE REPEATS APPROX. 22 TIMES BEFORE CRASH

progress that might have been expected, as differences in the form of Western versus Eastern cultural priorities manifested themselves .

The airline's administration, usually so efficient in the Japanese business tradition, had been thrown into chaos by the disaster. Under the pressures of the rescue operation, with more than five per cent of its total workforce at the accident site, and the company's attempts to care for the bereaved, day-to-day JAL management ground almost to a standstill.

For more than a week, recovery of the victims' bodies remained the top Japanese concern, with the on-site technical investigation relegated to second place. As well as the 1000 plus employees who rushed to the crash site to help with the rescue operation, and the food and clothing provided for the rescue army, a company department was established to comfort the bereaved with an individual staff member assigned to each family. Decision making was disrupted by the calls upon senior executives' time and, without admitting liability, the company paid out 780 million Yen to relatives of victims as "condolence money". At least one member of JAL's Board attended each funeral.

Feelings in the community ran high as personal responsibility was sheeted home to individual JAL staff members. Some staff assigned to mourning families were physically assaulted. JAL workers in Tokyo found themselves abused, spat upon, and thrown out of shops and restaurants if they appeared in company uniform. The suicide of a JAL maintenance manager at Haneda Airport to "apologise" for the disaster provoked a comment from one of the bereaved relatives that one of Boeing's officials should "apologise" in the same way!

In this highly emotional climate, the US investigation team had difficulty even gaining access to the mountain crash site and, by the time they finally succeeded in doing so,

Seeking to visualise the complex motion recorded by the FDR will assist an understanding of the enormous challenge that faced the 747's crew. With the aircraft wallowing wildly about all three axes, the crew's efforts even to orientate themselves would have been demanding in the extreme – let alone trying to anticipate corrections with the extremely limited control afforded by the power levers! As these drawings attempt to depict, in the course of just one 90sec/20° phugoid cycle, the giant aircraft would have Dutch rolled no less than seven or eight times. (Matthew Tesch)

(left) A Kawasaki licence-built KV-107/II (the Boeing Vertol forerunner of the capable Chinook) hovers above the havoc wrought in the mountain forest by the aircraft's second, major impact. The 747's port wing, and the patch of exposed earth on which it lies, point towards the smoking debris of the aircraft on the far side of the ridge. (right) This close-up of the wing shows where the No 1 engine pylon was removed in the first impact, tearing through the "J" of the JAL logotype and taking its adjoining "Hino-maru" ('Rising Sun') symbol from the upper surface. The outboard section was apparently held on only by the front spar of the wing box. A second gaping tear, just beyond the tree trunk which stopped the wing from sliding further down the slope, betrays a like removal of the No 2 engine and pylon. (with acknowledgement to Time magazine & Wide World Photos)

some critical wreckage evidence had been disrupted by the rescue workers.

A further complication was the insistence of the local police that, as the accident had taken place within their area, they, and not the aviation authorities, were primarily responsible for its investigation. Japanese air safety investigators were in fact prevented from using heavy-lift helicopters to carry items of wreckage to a central inspection facility in Tokyo.

Although a senior official in the Ministry of Transport was critical of the police for treating the crash as though it were a road accident, Japanese regulations actually prescribed that all wreckage be seized and controlled by local police. The Air Accidents Investigation Committee, set up by the Ministry of Transport, could only "borrow" the wreckage from the prefecture. For their part, the police in Gumma Prefecture insisted they were required to carry out their own investigation into whether any criminal action had led to the crash.

As a result, items from the wreck-age which required detailed examination could not be removed for laboratory analysis for more than a month.

Flight recorder evidence

Meanwhile a readout of the aircraft's Sundstrand 537A 69-parameter FDR, and a transcription of the tape from its Collins 642C CVR, was being undertaken at the headquarters of the Transport Ministry's Air Accidents Investigation Committee. Correlating the results obtained from these two recorders confirmed much of the account of events provided by the surviving off-duty flight attendant.

Though it was extremely difficult to decipher some of the sounds and voices recorded by the Cockpit Area Microphone (CAM) on the flight-deck, there was no doubt that an explosive decompression had occurred a few seconds past 6.24pm, soon after the Boeing 747 had reached its cruising level of FL240 and its airspeed had stabilised at just under 300 knots.

This had triggered both the cabin decompression alarm and the automatic prerecorded announcement over the aircraft's PA system, enjoining passengers to wear their oxygen masks and to fasten their seatbelts. A personal PA announcement by the purser or a steward followed.

On the flightdeck, the captain ordered the aircraft's transponder to be selected to the emergency code. At 6.26pm, after the crew were given ATC approval to return to Haneda and had requested a radar vector to Oshima, the captain suddenly exclaimed: "What's this – hydraulic pressure has dropped!"

Comments that hydraulic pressure was continuing to fall, and that the amber warning light was on, followed. Nine seconds later an aural warning signal began sounding, and another voice, probably the trainee captain's, said: "Hydraulic pressure all lost ... contact the company!"

With hydraulic pressure gone and the consequent total failure of the 747's multiple-redundant hydraulic control system, *the crew were deprived of all three primary aerodynamic controls – elevators, ailerons and rudder.* Stabiliser and aileron trim were also rendered useless, and of course the yaw damper was no longer effective. With the aircraft's inherent stability seriously impaired by the loss of a substantial part of its fin, it began uncomfortable combined "phugoid"[1] and "Dutch roll" oscillations, settling into pitching, yawing, and rolling cycles of motion akin to a ship in a wild sea.

The pitching or phugoid oscillation, in cycles of about 90 seconds, was taking the aircraft from about 15° nose-up to 5° nose-down, with vertical accelerations varying between +1.4g and -0.4g. Variations in airspeed and altitude during the cycles were averaging around 70 knots and 3000 feet, with peaks of as much as 100 knots and 5000 feet about five minutes after the loss of control. The yawing and rolling motion was much faster, the aircraft alternately rolling some 50° either side of a wings-level attitude in cycles of about 12 seconds.

With the engines now the only remaining means of control, the crew began varying the power lever settings to assess the aircraft's response.

Holding the aircraft's attitude by increasing and decreasing power as required, the crew were also accomplishing limited directional control by applying it asymmetrically. At 6.29pm, as the aircraft approached the western side of Suruga Bay, they succeeded in inducing a sideslip to achieve a bank to the right, turning the aircraft on to a northerly heading while maintaining an altitude between 23,000 and 25,000 feet.

But with the aircraft continuously pitching, rolling and yawing to such an extent, this obviously required extremely delicate handling and was severely demanding of the crew's judgement and timing.

It was clear from the CVR that the crew were still uncertain as to what had happened to the aircraft. At 6.30pm, an interphone call to the flightdeck from one of the cabin crew, answered by the flight engineer, advised that the cabin oxygen masks had dropped. A brief but unclear exchange about cabin pressure followed.

A minute later, after the captain had rejected ATC's offer to be vectored to Nagoya and had requested to return to Haneda instead, the flightdeck interphone chimed again.

Flight engineer [answering telephone tersely]: "Yes – what is it? What is broken?"

Unfortunately the words of the caller in the passenger cabin were not recorded on the CVR, but the content of the conversation was evident from the flight engineer's remarks.

Flight Engineer [speaking on interphone]: "Ah – it is around the baggage hold, is it? The rearmost? Yes, I understand. The baggage hold – the baggage area has collapsed? It might be better to descend ... everybody is now using their mask? Is it the R5 door? Yes, I understand [interphone discussion ends]."

Flight engineer [to captain]: "The R5 door – emergency descent may be advisable."

With the time now 6.34pm, the phugoid motion and the progressively increasing altitude excursions reached a peak, the nose pitching down to the extent that the aircraft dived from 25,000 to 20,000 feet in a little over half a minute, as the airspeed rose from 200 to 300 knots. Just as quickly the motion then reversed, the speed falling off again to 200 knots as the nose rose and the aircraft began climbing again. But the pilots now succeeded in checking the climb before the altitude reached 23,000 feet.

Flight Engineer [to captain]: "Shall we use our [oxygen] masks too?"

Captain: "Yes – that will be better."

Probably because of their preoccupation with trying to maintain control, the flight crew had overlooked the need to don their oxygen masks. Nearly 10 minutes had passed since the decompression and, at the altitudes at which they were flying, they would undoubtedly have been suffering to some degree from hypoxia, resulting in a deterioration in their judgement and ability to cope with the bewildering emergency.

Apparently the oxygen quickly took effect, for the pilots were now able to limit the pitching motion excursions to about 2000 feet in altitude and 60 knots in airspeed. But they were able to do nothing to mitigate the continuous and disturbing rolling from side to side.

As the aircraft continued in a generally northerly direction to the west of Mt Fuji, the flight engineer was engaged for a minute and a half from 6.34pm in a somewhat confused radio conversation with JAL company operations at Haneda Airport. Obviously very tense, the flight engineer reported the starboard rear door was "broken" and that they were making an emergency descent. At this stage however, the aircraft's altitude was still fluctuating between 20,000 and 22,000 feet and the FDR showed no sign yet that the crew were attempting a controlled descent.

Comments on the CVR now reflected the pilots' increasingly desperate efforts to control the aircraft's pitching motion. At intervals varying from 25 seconds to a minute and a half, the captain told the copilot, over and over again, to "lower the nose", all apparently to little avail. The crew's voices were highly agitated and it was obvious that they were under a great deal of stress. Twice too during this time, the captain told the crew to ignore radio transmissions from Tokyo ATC.

Just before 6.39pm, the flight engineer suggested lowering the undercarriage, evidently to help stabilise the motion of the aircraft, but both the captain and the copilot countered: "We cannot decrease the speed!"

A hint of the enormity of the disaster – the world's worst involving a single aircraft – is conveyed by this cheerless scene inside the high school gymnasium at Fujioka (the town nearest to the site of the accident), as the victims' relatives pass anxious, weary hours waiting and hoping for news from the mountainside. Some, no longer able to endure their enforced idleness in such trying circumstances, attempted their own difficult ascent of the mountain in the early morning darkness of August 14. (with acknowledgement to Time/Davis-Blackstar)

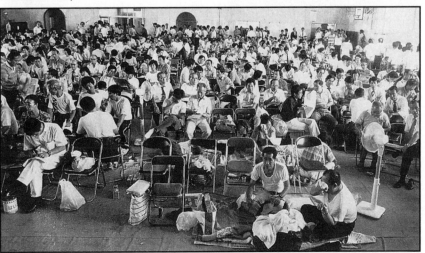

Shortly after 6.40pm, with the pitch oscillations now reduced to about half the peak excursions of five minutes before, the pilots evidently succeeded, again using a sideslipping technique, in turning the aircraft on to an easterly heading directly towards Haneda Airport, 42nm distant. As they did so, the flight engineer, evidently acting on his own judgement, and seizing the opportunity as the airspeed fell below 200 knots at the top of a pitch-up, selected the undercarriage down.

Although the resulting change of longitudinal trim required an immediate counteracting increase in engine power, the drag of the undercarriage quickly had a dampening effect on the pitching motion, gradually reducing the amplitude of the airspeed and altitude excursions, as the aircraft entered a descent of about 3000 fpm.

But the drag of the undercarriage also apparently dampened the aircraft's response to directional control using asymmetrical thrust from the engines. For instead of continuing towards Haneda Airport the Boeing 747, still descending and evidently now out of the pilots' control directionally, entered a turn to the right.

After turning through a full 360°, the pilots appeared to regain some measure of directional control and, now down to 15,000 feet with the pitching motion almost eliminated and the descent rate steady despite the continuous side to side rolling, the aircraft resumed its heading towards Haneda Airport, now only 35nm away.

The mood on the flightdeck was now a little calmer.

Copilot (COPT) [to captain]: What shall I do with the flap – put it down?

CAPT: Too early to do that.

COPT [questioningly]: Not yet?

CAPT: Not yet – not yet. Is the gear down?

COPT: The gear is down.

CAPT: OK.

At about the same time the Assistant Purser was making a PA announcement to the passengers: "Your attention please ... quite soon we will be making an emergency landing. Those who are carrying babies, rest your heads against the back of the seats. Please hold the babies tight. Have you fastened your seat belts? Have you put back your tables? Please check that you have done this ... We are now are now in contact with the ground."

But the apparent reprieve was shortlived. Despite the pilots' efforts to continue guiding the descending aircraft towards Haneda, it now began turning again, this time to the left.

CAPT: This may be impossible!

F/E: Will you contact ...?

CAPT [on radio]: Request radar vector to Haneda.

Tokyo Control: Roger ... since it is Runway 22, maintain heading 090°.

As the turn to the left continued, there were more flightdeck comments about the loss of hydraulic pressure to the flying controls. Half a minute after 6.47pm, the aircraft, now below 9000 feet and still descending, was heading north, again towards mountainous country.

CAPT [anxiously]: Hey – there's a mountain – up more! Mountain! Turn to the right!

The copilot carefully applied more power, evidently trying to juggle the aircraft's attitude at the same time. But with the undercarriage extended, this failed to check the aircraft's descent.

CAPT: Turn right! Up! We'll crash into a mountain!

With the application of more power, the aircraft suddenly pitched nose-up, quickly gaining 2000 feet, while the airspeed fell rapidly from 210 to 120 knots.

CAPT [urgently]: Maximum power!

COPT [acknowledging and pushing power levers forward]: Maximum power!

CAPT: Keep trying!

The coarse application of power had disrupted the relatively stabilised flight the crew had achieved, triggering the phugoid oscillation again.

CAPT: Nose down ... nose down!

As the copilot reduced power again, the nose did indeed pitch down, the aircraft plunging to below 5000 feet with the airspeed rising quickly to around 280 knots, before recovering from the dive at a loading of 1.85g.

CAPT [endeavouring to anticipate and dampen the loss of airspeed during the following pitch up]: Let's go!

F/E [spontaneously attempting to assist the pilots' efforts to stabilise the airspeed again]: Shall I rev it up?

CAPT [urgently]: Rev up – rev up!

CAPT [two seconds later as aircraft climbs even more steeply than before to about 8000 feet]: Rev up! Let's rev up! Rev up!

This time, with the airspeed falling even more sharply as the aircraft neared the top of the rapid climb, the stall warning began sounding.

CAPT [dismayed]: Oh no! [then urgently again]: Stall! Maximum power!

The crew's desperate struggle to counteract the pitching motion, now out of phase with their power lever adjustments, and to regain a relatively controllable and stable attitude, continued while the aircraft slowly swung towards the northwest and its average altitude gradually increased again.

Radio calls from Tokyo Control, Tokyo Approach and Yokota Approach were for the most part now ignored as all three crew members fought to prevent the Boeing 747 plunging completely out of control. It was a losing battle.

At 6.51pm when the aircraft, heading northwest, was 15nm from the point where it ultimately crashed, at a height approaching 10,000 feet, the

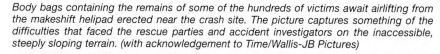

Body bags containing the remains of some of the hundreds of victims await airlifting from the makeshift helipad erected near the crash site. The picture captures something of the difficulties that faced the rescue parties and accident investigators on the inaccessible, steeply sloping terrain. (with acknowledgement to Time/Wallis-JB Pictures)

captain tried to lower some flap to assist in regaining a measure of control.

CAPT: It won't go down!

COPT: No – try alternate.

F/E: We'll descend on 'alternate'.

CAPT: Nose down!

F/E: I'll up the power.

CAPT: Nose down!

F/E: Now flap is out on 'alternate'.

CAPT: Nose down! [repeated twice], then: Nose up!

F/E: Power up!

CAPT [transmitting to Tokyo Control in English at 6.53pm as the aircraft climbed again to a peak of 12,000 feet]: JL123, ah uncontrol! JL123, uncontrol!

A minute later, as they descended through 10,000 feet, there were two urgently worded requests from Tokyo Control to change frequency to Tokyo Approach. The flight engineer did so, then himself transmitted: "JL123 – yes, I have selected 119.7."

CAPT [to flight engineer]: Request position!

F/E [transmitting in English]: JL123 – request position.

Tokyo Approach (APP): Your position ... ah ... 45 miles northwest of Haneda.

F/E: Northwest of Haneda – ah – [lapses into Japanese] how many miles?

APP (English): Yes – that's right. According to our radar, 55 miles northwest ...

APP: I will talk in Japanese – we are ready for your approach anytime. Also Yokota landing is available – let us know your intention.

The crew made no attempt to reply. Indeed, the flight engineer's question concerning the aircraft's distance northwest of Haneda just before 6.55pm was to prove the Boeing 747's final radio transmission. Although Yokota Approach made four more calls to the aircraft over the following 73 seconds, the CVR shows that they were all disregarded, simply because of the crew's compounding difficulties in maintaining control.

The following excerpt from the CVR transcript, containing the increasingly frantic crew exchanges from the time of this final radio transmission until the aircraft crashed to destruction less than two minutes later at 6.56pm plus 28 seconds, speaks for itself. Seconds to impact with the ground are shown in italics in brackets before each exchange:

(108): CAPT: Nose up! (aircraft climbs once more, this time to a peak of just over 10,000 feet – airspeed falls off to 160 knots)

(101): CAPT: Nose down! ... down to the limit!

(93): CAPT: Flap all!

(84): COPT: Yes – Flap Ten!

(73): CAPT: Nose up! (as aircraft enters steepening descending turn to the right and airspeed increases to 200 knots)

(71): CAPT: Nose up!

(69): CAPT: Nose up! (steep turn continues – aircraft now descending steadily at around 2000 fpm)

(63): CAPT: Nose up!.

(46): CAPT: Hey – halt the flap! (airspeed is falling sharply again)

(40): CAPT: Ah ... don' t lower the flap so much.

(38): CAPT: Flap up ... flap up ... flap up!

(36): F/E: : Flap up!

Mountaintop miracle! Twelve year-old survivor Keiko Kawakami, tightly clasped by a rescue party paratrooper, is winched to safety aboard a Self-Defence Force helicopter. The young girl, one of only four occupants to survive the 747's impact with the mountain, was found wedged in a tree, having endured a freezing night surrounded by wreckage of the aircraft's fragmented rear fuselage and the sounds of the injured and dying. Incredibly, she suffered only torn muscles and lacerations. The other three survivors were more seriously injured. All four were seated amongst the rearmost seven rows of passenger seats. (with acknowledgement to Time magazine)

(35): CAPT: Flap up!

(34): COPT: Yes

(33): CAPT: Power! power!

(31): CAPT: Flap!

(30): COPT: It's up!

(29): CAPT: Nose up! Nose up ... Power! (aircraft has turned through about 200° to the right – descending turn continues to tighten)

(14): Ground Proximity Warning System (GPWS): Sink rate ...

(13): GPWS: Sink rate ... pull up ... pull up ... pull up ... pull up ... (continues to sound the same warning)

(3): (Sound of aircraft striking treetops) GPWS: Pull up ... pull up ... pull up ...

(0): (Sound of aircraft crashing)

(-2): (End of recording)

At the time of the initial impact, the Boeing 747 was on a westerly heading, banked about 60° to the right, and flying at an indicated airspeed of about 160 knots.

Wreckage examination

From all the evidence uncovered so far, it was clear to both the Japanese and the US investigation teams that the pre-impact damage to the Boeing 747's fin and rudder, the explosive decompression of the cabin, and the loss of all four hydraulic systems powering the primary flight controls, were somehow linked. But what was the link – and what had precipitated it?

As a precautionary measure, the Japanese Civil Aviation Board ordered inspections of all 69 Boeing 747s of all marques on the Japanese register, concentrating on the fin and rudder assemblies and their attachments and adjacent structures. Aircraft which had flown more than 15,000 cycles were to be inspected within their next 100 flying hours; those with less than 15,000 cycles could be inspected within their next 300 flying hours.

The Boeing company, in a telex to all 747 operators concerning the Japanese directive, said that the highest number of cycles flown by any 747 was 22,970, while the highest number of hours logged by any aircraft of the type was 62,698. By comparison, the crashed JAL aircraft had flown 18,830 cycles in 25,025 flying hours. The Boeing telex went on to suggest that operators "may wish to inspect the aft portion of the pressure hull, in addition to the areas itemised by the Japanese Civil Aviation Board."

In Britain, the Civil Aviation Authority went further, issuing an Airworthiness Directive requiring the precautionary inspection within 10 days of all British-registered 747s with more than 5000 landings. As well as the fin and rudder assemblies, the inspection was to include the rear fuselage and rear face of the aft pressure bulkhead, which was known to be subject to corrosion from toilet spillage.

Although the Boeing 747 had no history of decompression incidents resulting from failure of the rear pressure bulkhead, the consequences of a major bulkhead fracture and decompression appeared to fit the established evidence, including the finding of sections of the upper fin beneath the aircraft's flightpath in Sagami Bay.

The manager of maintenance planning at JAL, Mr Hiroaki Kohno, in fact ventured the opinion, supported by calculations, that pressurised air, escaping from the cabin through a fractured rear bulkhead into the rear fuselage and interior of the fin, could burst the fin, blowing off the leading edge.

Lesson from history

A failure of this sort had actually occurred in 1971 in a British European Airways Vickers Vanguard en route from London-Heathrow to Salzburg.

Thirty-five minutes after departure, when the aircraft was over southern Belgium, cruising at FL190, the crew suddenly transmitted: "We are going down!" This was followed by a series of Mayday calls. Garbled transmissions, which included the words "we are going down vertically" and "out of control" followed. Overlaid by increasing propeller and aerodynamic noise, the transmissions ceased abruptly after 54 seconds.

The Vanguard, in normal cruising flight, had suddenly pitched down and dived vertically into the ground. A detailed investigation established that the rear pressure bulkhead had suddenly and catastrophically failed as a result of undetected corrosion at its base, the tailcone and the tailplane had been rapidly pressurised by air escaping from the cabin, and the upper skin of the tailplane had literally been blown off. Flight loads had done the rest, tearing off both tailplanes and elevators.

But as an explanation for the loss of the JAL aircraft, there was by no means general agreement that a similar sequence had been responsible for the fracture of the 747's fin and rudder, and the disruption of its hydraulic flying controls. While airworthiness engineers specialising in 747 structures did not rule out the pressure bulkhead corrosion theory, they believed it to be only one of several possibilities.

Suspicion narrows

But at least one aspect of the mystery was now resolved. It was now obvious to investigators that 5R (the starboard rear door), referred to by the flight engineer during his disjointed radio communications with JAL operations 20 minutes before the aircraft crashed, had played no part in the events that led to the accident. It was possible that the door warning lamp on the flight engineer's instrument panel had illuminated as a result of structural distortion of the fuselage, giving him the impression that this door had opened or failed.

At the on-site investigation on Mt Osutaka, with the removal of the victims' bodies completed, and a more detailed and expert examination of the wreckage finally possible, the fo-

The waters of Sagami Bay to the west of Oshima Island yielded floating wreckage which provided vital clues for the investigators. On the morning of August 13, the day after the accident, a JMSDF destroyer recovered more than 30 pieces of debris from the tail assembly of the aircraft, the most significant a 5m section of the fin. (above) Naval officers display the port side of a section of the 747's lower rudder. The trailing edge is on the right. Note the impact marks, tears, and scoring across the "L" of the flying crane symbol. (below) Also brought ashore was this 50kg piece of fibreglass ducting, one of two flanking the APU installation in the tailcone of the aircraft. (with acknowledgement to Time/Sankei Shimbun & Flight International)

cus of attention increasingly fell on the aircraft's rear pressure bulkhead. As expected, it was badly damaged. But had the damage all been sustained in the impact?

A senior investigator for the Japanese Ministry of Transport, Mr Hiroshi Fujiwara, described the condition of the bulkhead as found at the crash site as "peeled like a tangerine". The rupture had in fact left a hole some two by three metres in the bulkhead structure. It was possible, he said, that if the failure had occurred in flight, the explosive rush of air into the unpressurised tail section could have been enough to blow off the hollow tail fin and sever the hydraulic lines to the flying control surfaces.

But, as Boeing investigators now pointed out in their company's defence, the pressure bulkhead design had been tested to a simulated service life of 20 years, and it exhibited no evidence of any corrosion which could have compromised its integrity and fatigue life. So how could such a well proven design have failed in flight, for no apparent reason?

A startling find

But for the entire Boeing team engaged in the investigation, a profound shock now lay in store.

As the Boeing structures engineer at the accident site was examining some of the scattered wreckage of the rear fuselage, he picked up what appeared to be a broken off spliced section of the rear pressure bulkhead plating. The splice was held together with only one row of rivets – yet his long experience with Boeing design and with the 747's construction told him at once that such a

These diagrams, produced by Flight International staff for the magazine's readers while the investigation was in progress and drawing on material supplied by the Air Accidents Investigation Committee of the Japanese Ministry of Transport, show a plan view (looking forward) and side elevation of the Boeing 747's rear pressure bulkhead. The points where control and hydraulic lines pass through the bulkhead are indicated. The accompanying photograph of the forward face of the domed bulkhead as seen from the cabin when stripped of fittings and furnishings, provides an idea of scale. Also shown are plan and side elevations of the bulkhead segment that was spliced during the repairs to the aircraft's rear fuselage following a heavy tail scrape in 1978. Section CC shows the detail of the original pressure bulkhead section before the damage was incurred, Section AA the repair scheme as planned, and Section BB the repair as it was actually, but incorrectly, carried out. (with acknowledgement to Flight International/John Marsden & Tim Hall)

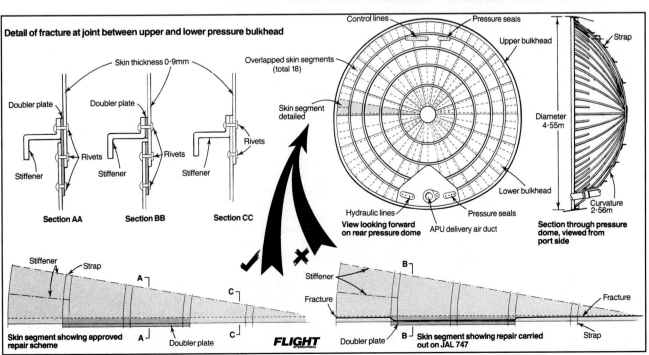

Detail of fracture at joint between upper and lower pressure bulkhead

Skin thickness 0·9mm

Doubler plate

Doubler plate

Rivets

Rivets

Rivets

Stiffener

Stiffener

Stiffener

Section AA **Section BB** **Section CC**

Overlapped skin segments (total 18)

Skin segment detailed

Control lines

Pressure seals

Upper bulkhead

Strap

Diameter 4·55m

Lower bulkhead

Hydraulic lines

Pressure seals

View looking forward on rear pressure dome

APU delivery air duct

Curvature 2·56m

Section through pressure dome, viewed from port side

Stiffener

Strap

A

C

Skin segment showing approved repair scheme

A

Doubler plate

C

Stiffener

Fracture

B

B

Doubler plate

Skin segment showing repair carried out on JAL 747

Fracture

Strap

FLIGHT INTERNATIONAL

splice should have had two rows of rivets!

Subsequent electron microscope photographs of the fracture surfaces of the doubler plate used as reinforcement for the splice revealed striations indicative of metal fatigue. The unexpected discovery now posed two vital questions: What was the reason for the bulkhead having been spliced in the first place? And why had a row of rivets been unaccountably omitted from such a splice? Could this be the solution to the mystery of the bulkhead's inflight failure?

But even worse was to follow for Boeing.

Examination of the maintenance records of this particular Boeing 747 now revealed that its rear fuselage had scraped the ground during an excessively nose-high landing at Osaka seven years before on June 2, 1978. All nosewheel aircraft are of course fitted with a tailskid to absorb the shock of any such mishap, but the impact in this case had been severe enough to remove skin panels from the underside of the rear fuselage and to crack the rear bulkhead of the pressure cabin.

The aircraft had been grounded for a month while Boeing engineers supervised repairs at JAL's maintenance facility. The Boeing repair scheme included the replacement of the lower part of the rear fuselage, and a portion of the lower half of the damaged pressure bulkhead.

The mystery solved

However, from examination of the bulkhead wreckage, it was now evident that, in splicing the repaired portion of the pressure bulkhead to the original, part of the splice had been incorrectly assembled. Over a small section of the splice on the port side of the bulkhead (approximately 17% of the total), two separate doubler plates, instead of one continuous one, were used as reinforcement. The resulting gap in the doubler plating meant in effect that the splice was joined by only a single row of rivets, instead of two rows (see diagram), reducing its resistance to fatigue by some 70%.

According to JAL's maintenance planning manager, Hiroaki Kohno, the Boeing 747's tail assembly and the repairs were examined by the Japanese Civil Aviation Bureau and the aircraft test flown after the work was done, but no shortcoming was detected.

Moreover, in the seven years of operations the aircraft had flown from that time until the accident occurred, no less than six 3000 hourly "C-checks" had been carried out on the airframe. But these checks had found nothing, mainly because the aft side of the rear pressure bulkhead where the splicing had been carried out was inaccessible for visual inspections during such checks. Like so much of the basic aircraft, the design life of the bulkhead was such that no premature fatigue could be expected to develop, provided the structure was maintained free of corrosion, and it was not damaged.

The announcement of the finding came as no great surprise to a highly experienced air safety investigator on the other side of the world. In Britain, the retired Chief Inspector of Accidents, William Tench, formerly head of the Air Accidents Investigation Branch of the UK Department of Transport, knew of instances in which it took three years for a fatigue crack, initiated by an abnormal loading such as a tail scrape or a heavy landing, to become evident during a visual inspection.

One of the reasons why both Japanese and American investigators were initially so reluctant to accept that a failure of the pressure bulkhead had been responsible for the fracture of the fin and rudder *and* the loss of the primary flying controls over Sagami Bay, was the fact that the crew had kept the aircraft flying for more than half an hour afterwards.

Senior pilots of both nations were high in their praise of Captain Takahama's efforts in keeping the stricken Boeing 747 in the air for so long after the loss of control was sustained over Sagami Bay. "In spite of being in such a terrible plight, the aircraft was kept in the air on engine thrust only," declared Captain Mitsuo Nakano, JAL's deputy chief Boeing 747 pilot. "That is an incredible performance."

On the other side of the Pacific, the US Flight Safety Foundation's Captain Homer Mouden, concurred. "The crew exhibited great courage and skill in trying to keep it flying," he said. "But given the very limited amount of control available to them, it seems extremely doubtful that they had any real prospect of bringing the wallowing and porpoising airliner in to a safe landing." As a United Airlines pilot put it more bluntly: "He may have been a goner from the second that fin tore loose."

Remedies for the future – and results

As a result of the JAL disaster, Boeing instituted a production change to its 747 construction, providing for a cover to be placed over the internal access hole in the base of the vertical fin, to prevent the escape of pressurised air into the fin in the event of a massive rupture of the rear bulkhead. At no charge, Boeing also provided similar covers to all operators of the 747 for fitting to aircraft in service. Modifications were also developed to preclude a total loss of hydraulic fluid from the aircraft's four independent hydraulic control systems in the event of the lines being severed, and to provide additional protection for control cables.

Because the tail assembly inspections prompted earlier by the findings of the investigation had revealed a number of non-threatening minor defects – loose and broken bolts, and cracks in metal fixtures – in 747 aircraft which had made more than 15,000 flights, Boeing also replaced the bolts being used in these locations and other primary structural joints with inconel bolts providing greater resistance to stress corrosion. Service letters were sent to all operators urging regular inspections of existing bolts in these locations, and their replacement, if fractured, with the new type bolts.

Overall, for Boeing, the good news from the difficult and demanding investigation was that neither any of its findings, nor the results of the many aircraft inspections the accident prompted, had cast any shadow of doubt whatever on the basic design, manufacture, or structural integrity of Boeing 747 aircraft.

Even so, declared the company, intent upon maintaining its justifiably high reputation for safety and product excellence, it was initiating "programs which would further improve the tolerance of the airplane for extremely remote but possible events". These would include additional fatigue and pressure testing of "domed pressure bulkhead structures to develop more test information on the effect of undetected structural damage."

Unfortunately, the same positive outcome did not hold true for JAL. Despite the fact that the airline was a national institution, part-owned by the Government, and the accident could in no way be sheeted home to any shortcoming on the part of the company or its staff, in the eyes of the Japanese people it became a pariah overnight.

In the Japanese tradition of accepting personal responsibility, regardless of "fault", the airline's President, Mr Yasumoto Takagi, tended his resignation to Prime Minister Yasuhiro Nakasone, and it was accepted without hesitation as the ethical thing to do.

The public also made their feelings clear – domestic loadings dropped by an average of more than a third and, on the Tokyo-Osaka route, passenger numbers plummeted.

Throughout the nation, rumour and suspicion abounded that Boeing's admission of the faulty repair to the bulkhead was no more than a cover-up to protect the honour and commercial well-being of their best 747 customer.

Police sought to bring criminal charges against those responsible for the aircraft's airworthiness inspections, regardless of the findings of the Accident Investigation Committee.

And the press maintained an intense and unrelenting scrutiny, ever ready to humiliate the airline further by making a scandal of any company stumble, be it operational or administrative.

It would take years for JAL to rebuild its shattered morale, win back public confidence, and regain its public image.

Footnote:
1. Phugoid (pronounced foo-goid): This inflight oscillation was discovered by the early English aerodynamicist F W Lanchester (who also founded the Lancaster motor works), and was discussed at length in his 1908 book "Aerodonetics", mainly as an example of the exchange of potential and kinetic energy.

The effect of a short-lived upward gust on the longitudinal motion of an aeroplane in level flight is to leave the machine with its nose slightly down, causing it (unless corrected) to enter a shallow dive, gathering speed as it does so. The

increased speed brings about an increase in lift, which ultimately stops the descent and causes the machine to climb again. At the top of the climb the aircraft has insufficient lift to maintain itself and, if left alone, will fall into a dive again – and so the cycle is repeated.

This is the phugoid oscillation, resulting in a flightpath that is wave-like in profile. The odd-sounding term was coined by Lanchester from the classical Greek for "flight-like", but he erred in using the Greek word implying "flight" in the sense of being a fugitive, and not the flight of a bird! Despite Lanchester's "howler" however, phugoid entered the literature of aerodynamics, probably because it is short and easy to pronounce. (Refer "The Science of Flight", by O G Sutton – Pelican Books, 1955)

Another Narita view of JA8127, this port quarter shot allowing the recovered rudder and APU wreckage from JA8119 (pictures, p150) to be related to their positions on the original aircraft. The aperture beneath the lower rudder is the cooling air exhaust for the APU; its intake is on the starboard side. This picture also highlights the keel area which was so fatefully damaged on JA8119 in its heavy landing at Osaka in 1978. The 747's nose-high angle on its flare-out for touchdown then must have been excessive indeed, the impact forces certainly so on landing. (with acknowledgement to Flight International/ Janice Lowe)

CHAPTER 11

"Aloha 243 – you still up?"

– Maui Tower to Boeing 737

Aloha Airlines Boeing 737-297 N73711 [20209] (F/n 11) "Queen Lilioukalani" (prev. "King Kalaniopuu") – April 28, 1988

For air travellers – whether on holiday or business – the Hawaiian Islands evoke images of tropical sunsets and balmy breezes. But for operators of hard working twinjets used on the short sector interisland shuttles, they pose special operational and environmental problems. Even so, forewarned did not mean forearmed – as 89 passengers learnt to their horror.

For Captain Robert Schornstheimer of Honolulu, Thursday April 28, 1988, began early and predictably. A typically fine and warm, near cloudless mid-Pacific morning, it was to be yet another day of short shuttles between the principal airports of the Hawaiian Islands – a day's work essentially the same as the many hundreds of others he had spent flying the island routes. But though he could not know it, it was to prove one he would be unlikely ever to forget.

The captain had been flying for Aloha Airlines for the past 11 years. One of two major local airlines servicing the various Hawaiian Island airports from Honolulu International Airport on Oahu, where both island companies were based, Aloha operated a fleet of Boeing 737s of various marques in competition with Hawaiian Airlines, which flew McDonnell Douglas DC-9s.

For the crews of both companies, the flying was repetitive and intense, even monotonous at times. Such was the geography of the island network that their ports of call were relatively few and the intervening stage

flights extremely short, particularly for such high performance jet aircraft. Indeed, since the two operators had replaced their former turboprop aircraft with jet equipment, the average stage length for the routes serving six main islands of the group had shrunk to only about 20 minutes.

Yet in the balmy climate of such a sought after island paradise, the parochialism and isolation of the air route structure had many compensations, and few flightcrew of either airline were anxious to exchange their enviable lifestyles, even for a more challenging and diverse aviation assignment.

For Captain Schornstheimer himself, there was further cause to be happy with his lot. Ten months previously, after precisely 10 years as a Boeing 737 first officer with Aloha, and with over 8000 hours in his logbook, he had been promoted to captain. As such, he now enjoyed the privilege of command on his company's constantly busy route schedules with their high tourist and business traveller loadings.

Early departure

Arriving at the Aloha Airlines Operations office at Honolulu International Airport before first light, Captain Schornstheimer familiarised himself as usual at the despatch counter with the flight documents for the day's operations. The Boeing 737 scheduled for the interisland flights he was to command today was N73711, one of the company's older 737s, fitted with Pratt & Whitney JT8D-9A turbojet engines.

There was no reason to suppose that today's trips would be any different in essence to the several he had flown yesterday nor, for that matter, to the many thousands of such flights he had made between the islands in his 11 years with the company. About the only variation from yesterday's schedule was that, back at Honolulu after the first three return flights had been completed, there would be a change in first officer for the remainder of the day's operations.

Completing the pre-departure procedures, Captain Schornstheimer left the operations office and walked down to the Aloha Airlines apron where the aircraft had been standing overnight. His first officer was there already in the predawn darkness, completing a preflight inspection under the apron floodlights.

A few minutes later, satisfied all was in order, the first officer joined Captain Schornstheimer on the flightdeck, reporting the aircraft ready for flight.

The first three round trips for the day, one each from Honolulu to Hilo, Kahului, and Lihue (see map), were uneventful. Throughout all six stages, the aircraft performed faultlessly, and shortly before 11am the Boeing 737 landed back at Honolulu for the third time that morning.

A woman pilot

The first officer who now boarded the aircraft to replace the one going off duty was Madeline Tompkins, one of the company's few women pilots. Aged 37, she had been with the airline for almost nine years and had accumulated some 8000 hours' flying experience, nearly half of it in Boeing 737s.

The cabin crew, consisting of veteran Flight Attendant Clarabelle Lansing, with Flight Attendants Michelle Honda and Jane Sato-Tomita, was unchanged. The three formed an exceptionally experienced cabin crew: Clarabelle Lansing had been flying the company's routes since its DC-3 era in the early postwar years, while the other two had been with the company for 14

and 19 years respectively – testimony perhaps to the unique working environment enjoyed by the airline's staff.

The next flight of the day was scheduled to Kahului, Maui where there would be a midday stopover of about two hours, before continuing to Hilo Airport on the main island of Hawaii. After a brief turnaround at Hilo, the return trip to Honolulu, a distance of 190nm, would be flown direct.

The 20 minute trip from Honolulu to Maui, and then the half hour flight from Maui on to Hilo after the stopover, went to plan. As with earlier flights that day, both were entirely uneventful with no unserviceabilities or abnormalities of any kind.

The scheduled turnaround at Hilo was a brief one and, after shutting down on the airport terminal apron, both pilots remained on the flightdeck while the arriving passengers left the aircraft and the 89 Honolulu-bound passengers were ushered aboard via the terminal aerobridge. An FAA air traffic controller was also returning to Honolulu on the aircraft to begin leave and, at the invitation of the captain, took the centre jumpseat on the flightdeck.

At 1.25pm local time, after a perfectly normal engine start and taxi, and with First Officer Madeline Tompkins flying the aircraft from the right hand seat, the Boeing 737 lifted off from Hilo Airport en route to Honolulu as Flight 243. Handling the aircraft manually, the first officer set

course as she began climbing on track as planned to Flight Level 240 in fine and clear weather.

Twenty minutes later at 1.45pm, when the Boeing 737 was passing abeam the northwestern tip of Hawaii, maintaining its heading towards Honolulu, it reached its planned cruising height and the first officer levelled the aircraft at FL240 (24,000 feet).

Explosive decompression – and emergency descent

Only seconds afterwards, as the captain was discussing the location of a recently established National Weather Service station with the air traffic controller on the flightdeck, there was a loud explosive noise like a clap of thunder somewhere behind them, accompanied by a scream from the passenger cabin and a loud "whooshing" sound. They were followed an instant later by a deafening increase in wind noise and, at the same moment, the flightdeck atmosphere violently decompressed rearwards, jerking all three occupants' heads back, and filling the air with dust, debris and particles of cabin insulation.

Looking around in alarm, Captain Schornstheimer was aghast to see the flightdeck door had been wrenched off, and that he could see blue sky where the ceiling of the First Class cabin had been! The captain immediately took over from First Officer Tompkins, and both the pilots and the air traffic controller in the

This photo of N73711, predating the Maui accident by a year or two, marks the aircraft's first appearance in Aloha's modified livery. The bright pattern of red and yellow flowers overlying an orange upper cheatline gave way to a more muted, twin-stripe orange and gold design, although the sprightly logotype, first used for fuselage titles in 1976/77, was retained. Aloha, formed as Trans-Pacific Airlines at Honolulu in June 1946, formally adopted the Hawaiian word for 'welcome' as its corporate identity in November 1958. Once a DC-3, F27, (and surprisingly) Viscount and BAC 1-11 operator, Aloha came to standardise on Boeing's 737 while its competitor, Hawaiian Airlines, opted for McDonnell Douglas DC-9s.

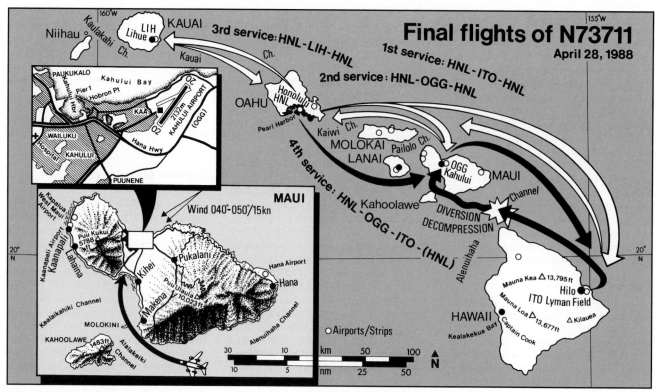

Map of the Hawaiian Islands showing the fateful movements of N73711 (main map) and diversion to Kahului Airport on Maui (enlargement) after the terrifying crossing of the Alenuihaha Channel. The aircraft's earlier flights that day were typical of the takeoff-and-landing poundings endured by Aloha 737s on the tiny, 309nm (572km) network linking six ports on the five main islands. Since the earliest marques entered service in March 1969, the airline's "Funjets" had been flying more than 80 sectors a day. By 1976, they were carrying more than two million passengers a year and, by 1987, averaging more than 15 flight cycles every day – more than 700 a week. (Matthew Tesch)

jumpseat quickly put on their oxygen masks. Although the flight controls did not feel normal and the aircraft itself was slightly unstable in that it was rolling a little from side to side, it still seemed to be responding to control.

Retarding the power levers and extending the speed brakes, the captain began an emergency descent of around 4000 fpm at an airspeed of between 280 and 290 knots, continuing straight ahead towards the island of Maui and its airport at Kahului, less than 40nm distant. Meanwhile the first officer selected the aircraft's transponder to emergency code 7700 and attempted a number of times to call Honolulu [en route Air Traffic Control] Centre to report that they were diverting to Maui. Because of the impossible noise level however, she could not hear any answering radio signals, and was unsure if Honolulu had heard her transmissions. For the same reason, the pilots were now reduced to hand signals for communication with each other.

Although the controller working Flight 243 at Honolulu Centre did not receive any of the first officer's transmissions, he saw the emergency transponder return appear on his radar screen. The aircraft's position at this point appeared to be 23nm south-southeast of Maui's

Kahului Airport. The controller then began calling the aircraft, but without success – there was no apparent response to several calls, though the radar target remained on the screen.

Communication difficulties

Two minutes after the explosive decompression, when the Boeing 737 was descending through 14,000 feet, First Officer Tompkins changed frequency and called Maui Approach Control. When again she could hear no response, she switched to the Tower frequency and went on calling. The radio exchanges now continued with some difficulty, as follows (local pm time is shown in hours, minutes and seconds):

1.48.01: F/O: Maui Tower – Aloha 243?
1.48.11: F/O: Maui Tower – Aloha 243 – we're inbound for landing!
1.48.29: F/O: Maui Tower – Aloha 243?
1.48.34: TWR: Aircraft calling Tower – say again?
1.48.35: F/O: Maui Tower – Aloha 243. We're inbound for landing – we're just ... ah ... to the west of Makena ... to the east of Makena ... descending out of 13 [thousand feet] and we have rapid depress ... we are unpressurised ... declaring an emergency!

At 1.49pm Honolulu Centre called Maui Approach Control to inform

them they had received an emergency code 7700 transponder return that could be an Aloha Boeing 737. "You might be prepared, in case he heads your way," the Honolulu controller advised.

1.49.01: MAUI TWR: Is that Aloha 244 on the emergency?
1.49.02: F/O: Aloha 243!
1.49.03: TWR: Ah – Aloha 246.
1.49.05: F/O: Aloha two four *three*!
1.49.07: TWR: Aloha 243 – say your position.
1.49.08: F/O: We're just ... ah ... to the east of Makena Point ... descending out of 11 thousand [feet] ... request clearance into Maui for landing ... request the [emergency] equipment!
1.49.18: TWR: Aloha 243 – OK the equipment is on the field ... is on the way – squawk 0343.

The requested change to the Maui Sector transponder code was to identify the flight and indicate to other ATC units that it was being handled by Maui ATC. The first officer changed the transponder as requested.

Maui Tower staff then notified the airport's rescue and firefighting personnel, via their direct "hotline", that a Boeing 737 had declared an emergency, was inbound to land, and that the emergency was a decompression. From their understanding of the nature of the emergency, the Tower

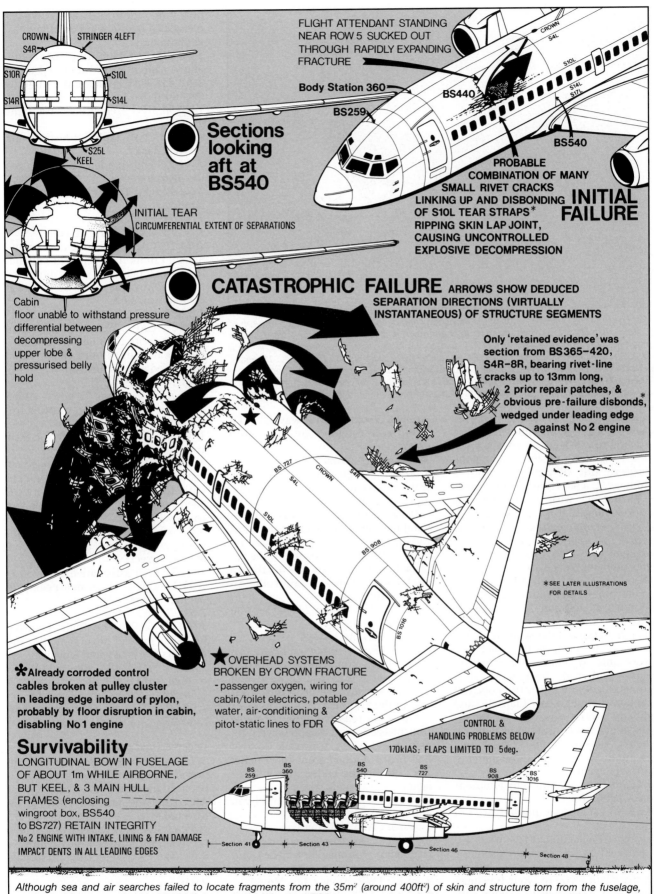

CROWN   STRINGER 4LEFT
S4R
S10R   S10L
S14R   S14L
S25L
KEEL

Sections looking aft at BS540

INITIAL TEAR
CIRCUMFERENTIAL EXTENT OF SEPARATIONS

Cabin floor unable to withstand pressure differential between decompressing upper lobe & pressurised belly hold

FLIGHT ATTENDANT STANDING NEAR ROW 5 SUCKED OUT THROUGH RAPIDLY EXPANDING FRACTURE

Body Station 360
BS259
BS440
BS540

CROWN
S4L
S10L
S14L
S17L

PROBABLE COMBINATION OF MANY SMALL RIVET CRACKS LINKING UP AND DISBONDING OF S10L TEAR STRAPS* RIPPING SKIN LAP JOINT, CAUSING UNCONTROLLED EXPLOSIVE DECOMPRESSION

INITIAL FAILURE

CATASTROPHIC FAILURE ARROWS SHOW DEDUCED SEPARATION DIRECTIONS (VIRTUALLY INSTANTANEOUS) OF STRUCTURE SEGMENTS

Only 'retained evidence' was section from BS365–420, S4R–8R, bearing rivet-line cracks up to 13mm long, 2 prior repair patches, & obvious pre-failure disbonds*, wedged under leading edge against No 2 engine

BS 727
CROWN
S4R
S4L
S10L
BS 908
BS 1016

*SEE LATER ILLUSTRATIONS FOR DETAILS

✱ Already corroded control cables broken at pulley cluster in leading edge inboard of pylon, probably by floor disruption in cabin, disabling No 1 engine

★ OVERHEAD SYSTEMS BROKEN BY CROWN FRACTURE - passenger oxygen, wiring for cabin/toilet electrics, potable water, air-conditioning & pitot-static lines to FDR

CONTROL & HANDLING PROBLEMS BELOW 170kIAS; FLAPS LIMITED TO 5deg.

Survivability
LONGITUDINAL BOW IN FUSELAGE OF ABOUT 1m WHILE AIRBORNE, BUT KEEL, & 3 MAIN HULL FRAMES (enclosing wingroot box, BS540 to BS727) RETAIN INTEGRITY
No 2 ENGINE WITH INTAKE, LINING & FAN DAMAGE IMPACT DENTS IN ALL LEADING EDGES

BS 259
BS 360
BS 540
BS 727
BS 908
BS 1016
Section 41   Section 43   Section 46   Section 48

Although sea and air searches failed to locate fragments from the 35m² (around 400ft²) of skin and structure torn from the fuselage, enough evidence remained in N73711's jagged edges for the NTSB to propound a probable sequence of events. These Matthew Tesch drawings illustrate the deduced primary (cracking) and subsequent (overload) failures which burst open the comfortable cocoon of the cabin and sucked a senior flight attendant to a free-fall death. The fuselage Body Stations referred to in the text are indicated in the profile drawing (bottom) showing the extent of the missing structure and the alarming 1m "droop" in the fuselage that resulted. A bizarre aspect of this condition was the inability of passengers seated towards the rear of the cabin to see anything other than daylight over the tops of seats in front of them. The nose and flightdeck appeared to have been blown off – yet the aircraft was still apparently under control!

Vortices from the outboard ends of the extended flaps become visible in this photograph of Boeing 737 N728AL [22629] on short final approach in crisp morning air. N728AL was a much younger contemporary of N73711, joining the Aloha fleet in February 1982, when it took up the latter's original name. After being "King Kalaniopuu" for nearly 13 years, N73711 was away on sublease to Air California when N728AL arrived new at Honolulu from Boeing. N73711 was renamed "Queen Lilioukalani" when finally bought outright by Aloha in early 1984. (with acknowledgement to "Airliners" magazine and its correspondents)

personnel did not believe it necessary to call for an ambulance. The fire and rescue vehicles left their station to take up positions along the western side of Kahului Airport's Runway 02 a short time afterwards.

Meanwhile, with the aircraft now approaching 10,000 feet as it continued its emergency descent over the Alalakeiki Channel to the south of Makena (see map), the captain began reducing speed to comply with the ATC speed limitation of 250 knots and began a gradual right turn in towards Kahului Airport's Runway 02. As the speed decreased further, he retracted the speed brakes.

Below 10,000 feet, the flightcrew were able to remove their oxygen masks and, with the airspeed now coming back towards 210 knots, the captain motioned for "Flaps 1", and shortly afterwards, for "Flaps 5". The wind noise now somewhat reduced, the crew found that, if they shouted, they could communicate verbally again.

1.49.32: F/O [shouting to jumpseat passenger]: You OK?
1.49.33: Jumpseat passenger: I'm fine.
1.49.47: TWR: Aloha 243 – Wind 040 [degrees] at 15 [knots], altimeter 29.99 [inches of mercury]. Just to verify again – you're [your transmissions are] breaking up – your callsign is 244? Is that correct? Or 243?
1.49.57: F/O: Two four *three* – Aloha two four *three!*
1.49.59: TWR: Aloha 242 [sic] – the equipment is on the roll – plan straight ahead for Runway 02 – I'll keep you advised of any wind change.
1.50.07: F/O: Aloha 243.
1.50.41: F/O [to captain]: Do you want me to call for anything else?
1.50.43: CAPT: No.

Because the aircraft was still beyond the tower controller's radius of radar authority of about 13nm, he requested the crew to switch to the approach frequency of 119.5 MHz to enable the approach controller to monitor the flight.

1.50:58: TWR: Aloha 243 – Can you come up on 119.5?
1.51.04: F/O: Aloha 243.
1.51.07: F/O [having changed frequency]: Can you hear us on 119.5?
1.51.19: F/O: It looks like we've lost a door – we have a hole in this ... left side of the aircraft.

For some reason neither of these transmissions on 119.5 MHz were received and when Approach Control had heard nothing from the Boeing 737, the Tower called the aircraft again.

1.52.12: TWR: Aloha 243 – [are] you still up?
1.52.15: CAPT: Affirmative.

The captain's reply on the tower frequency was also not heard and the tower controller called again.

1.52.17: TWR: Aloha 243 – Maui?
1.52.23: CAPT: ah ... Aloha 243 is ah ...
1.52.23: F/O: Maui Tower – Aloha 243.
1.52.36: TWR: Aloha 243 – if you hear, ident.
1.52.48: TWR: Aloha 243 – Roger. I got your ident straight away – cleared to land – wind 040 [degrees] at 20 [knots].
1.52.56: F/O [shouting to captain above wind noise]: Want the gear?
1.52.57: CAPT [misunderstanding question]: No
1.52.58: F/O [repeating]: Want the gear?
1.52.59: CAPT [still not hearing correctly]: What?
1.53.05: F/O [louder]: Do you want the gear *down*?
1.53.07: CAPT: It will be a flaps 15 landing.
1.53.09: F/O: OK!
1.53.13: CAPT: Here we go!
1.53.16: CAPT [shouting above wind noise]: I think they can hear you, but they can't hear me – tell him [the tower controller] we'll need assistance to evacuate.
1.53.27: F/O: Right!
1.53.29: CAPT: We really can't communicate with the flight attendants – but we'll need ambulances – and we'll need an airstair from Aloha.
1.53.35: F/O: All right.
1.53.40: F/O: Maui Tower – Aloha 243. Can you hear me on tower frequency?
1.53.42: TWR: Aloha 243 – I hear you loud and clear – go ahead.
1.53:44: F/O: We're going to need assistance – we can't communicate with the flight attendants – we'll need assistance for the passengers when we land.
1.53.52: TWR: OK – understand you're going to need an ambulance – is that correct?
1.53.57: F/O: Affirmative.
1.54.14: CAPT [shouting]: Feels like manual reversion!
1.54.17: F/O: What?
1.54.18: CAPT: The flight controls feel like manual reversion. [ie, the controls felt heavy and sluggish]
1.54.25: F/O: Well – we could [be in trouble with] that hole.
1.54.26: CAPT: I know it – yeah!
1.54.30: F/O: Can we maintain altitude OK?

Undercarriage problem?

The aircraft had now reached the normal "gear down" point in the approach pattern, and the captain called for the undercarriage to be lowered.

1.54.31: CAPT: Let's try flying ... let's try flying with the gear down here.
1.54.34: F/O [selecting undercarriage lever down]: All right – you've got it.

Although the main undercarriage immediately indicated down and locked, the nose leg position indicator failed to illuminate. When the first officer pulled the manual extension handle (located beneath an access panel on the floor directly behind the control pedestal), the green indicator light still did not illuminate, but the red "unsafe" indicator light extinguished. After another manual attempt, the undercarriage selector was left down to complete the manual gear extension procedure. The crew made no attempt to use the optical nose undercarriage downlock viewer between the crew seats – it would mean first moving their flightdeck passenger out of the centre jumpseat – and it was obviously vital to continue in to land with the minimum possible delay.

1.54.42: TWR: Aloha 243 – Can you give me your souls on board - and your fuel on board?

1.54.45: CAPT [to F/O]: Do you have a passenger count for the tower?

1.54.47: F/O [on radio]: We have 85 ... 86 plus five crew members.

The first officer did not report their fuel load, and the tower controller did not press the point – even after a further query from the chief of the airport's fire crew.

1.54.52: TWR: OK – and just to verify, you do need an ambulance? Is that correct?

1.54.53: F/O [to Capt with exasperation]: They still don't understand! [then to Tower]: Affirmative!

1.54.59: TWR: Roger – how many do you think are injured?

1.55.00: F/O: We have no idea – we can't communicate with our flight attendant.

1.55.02: TWR: OK – we'll have the ambulance on the way.

1.55.06: F/O: There's a possibility that we ... won't have a nose gear.

1.55.52: CAPT [to F/O]: Tell him we've got such problems, but we are going to land anyway – even without a nose gear. But they should be aware that we don't have a safe nose gear down indication.

1.56.02: TWR: Aloha 243 – wind now 050 – and the [emergency] equipment is in place.

1.56.06: F/O: OK – be advised we have no nose gear – we are landing without the nose gear.

1.56.11: TWR: OK – if you need any other assistance, advise.

1.56.13: F/O: We'll need all the equipment you've got!

On final?

Lined up with Runway 02, the captain established a normal descent profile on a long final approach. In its "Flaps 5" configuration, the aircraft was shaking slightly, still rocking gently from side to side, and felt "springy."[1] But when the first officer selected "Flaps 15" in response to the captain's further request, the

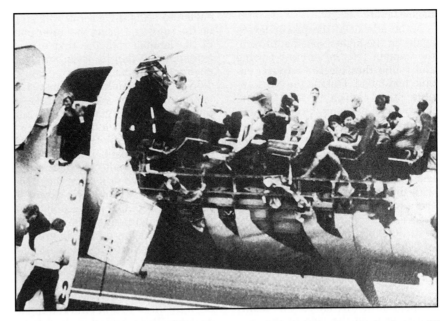

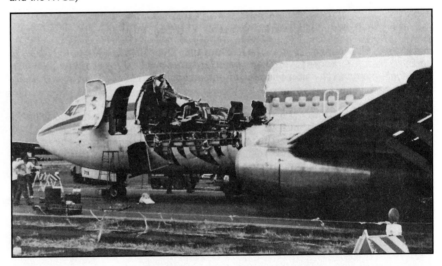

(above) This remarkable and dramatic photograph, taken immediately after the "open air" Boeing 737 came to a stop on Kahului Airport's Runway 02, shows traumatised and injured passengers still huddled in their seats as the evacuation begins. At the cabin door, the female first officer has just pushed a passenger down the partly inflated slide into the arms of a fireman. The captain, rousing shocked passengers, looks over his shoulder. (below) A wider angled view of the aircraft's ravaged nose section clearly shows the skin torn away from the lower lobe of the fuselage. The upward buckling of the floor panels is also evident from the distortion of the seats. (with acknowledgement to Associated Press, Arrow Books and the NTSB)

aircraft became markedly less controllable.

1.56.33: F/O: Is it easier to control with the flaps up?

1.56.35: CAPT: Yeah – put them back to five.

1.56.48: CAPT: Can you give me a V speed for a flaps five landing?

1.57.11: TWR: Kahului Airport wind now 040 at 16.

1.57.36: F/O [hastily consulting flight manual]: Do you want the flaps right down as we land?

1.57.35: CAPT: Yeah – but after we touch down.

1.57.41: TWR: Aloha 243 – wind now 050 at 20.

1.57.56: F/O [reading from flight manual]: V_{ref} 40 plus 30 for Flaps 1 through Flaps 15.

1.57.35: CAPT: So how much is that?

1.58.02: F/O [still consulting flight manual and calculating]: Ah ... V_{ref} 40 is 122 ... ah ... 152 [knots].

1.58.10: CAPT: Right!

But, as the captain began reducing speed towards this target, he found the aircraft becoming less controllable again, once the speed fell below 170 knots. He therefore decided to fly the final approach at 170 knots. Kahului Airport's main 02/20 runway was 6995 feet (2133m) in length and, with this amount of room and the existing wind conditions, stopping was not expected to pose a problem.

1.58.12: TWR: Aloha 243 – just for your information, the gear appears down – the gear appears down.

Engine failure

As he advanced the power levers again for the higher speed approach, the captain felt the aircraft yawing and found that the No 1 (port) engine had failed. Placing the No 1 engine start switch in the "flight" position, he attempted to restart the engine, but it failed to respond.

With the aircraft now only about four nautical miles out on final approach, the first officer attempted to use the PA system to communicate with the flight attendants; but again there was no response.

1.58.23: F/O [anxiously, with aircraft on short final]: Want me to go to Flaps 40 – help you to ...

1.58.25: CAPT: No – on the ground!

An incredible revelation –

At 1.58:42pm, to the utter astonishment of the fire and rescue teams watching from the side of the runway, the Boeing 737, visibly "broken", with the badly damaged forward fuselage bending alarmingly, touched down smoothly at high speed, the apparently defective nose leg holding firm as the captain used the brakes and reverse thrust on No 2 engine to bring the aircraft to a stop on the runway. During the latter part of the landing roll, the first officer extended full flap to assist with the emergency evacuation.

1.58.55: TWR: Aloha 243 – just shut her down where you are – everything's fine ... the gear did it ... and the firetrucks are on the way.

Only when the pilots left the flightdeck to move back into the cabin after quickly completing their emergency shutdown drill were they confronted with the terrifying extent of the explosive decompression damage. And only then did they fully appreciate the incredible degree of structural failure the aircraft had sustained – yet without disintegrating in flight.

– and a horrible realisation

On the floor just behind the flightdeck lay Flight Attendant Jane Sato-Tomita, suffering concussion and severe head lacerations. Standing at the front of the aisle at the time when the decompression tore off the flightdeck door, she had been struck heavily on the head.

Immediately behind the cabin entrance vestibule, not only the roof of the First Class section, but the sides of the cabin down to floor level also, had literally disappeared, leaving the first six rows of passenger seats totally exposed to the elements – and their hapless occupants subjected to the merciless savaging of the extreme wind forces during the emergency descent.

On the starboard side, some of the jagged-edged fuselage structure framing the cabin windows, though shattered and bent out of the way, remained attached to the floor, but on the port side the cabin sides, including the overhead lockers, had completely carried away down to floor level and beyond. On this side also, the cabin floor itself was distorted and buckled upwards, pushing some of the passenger seats into drunken attitudes.

The chaos was by no means confined to the aircraft structure. To the pilots' dismay, passengers still held by their lapstraps to the seats in the six exposed rows were obviously seriously injured and traumatised. Some, having sustained severe head

Ambulance staff tend one of the injured passengers on the grass beside the runway after the miraculous landing. Beyond the gaping cavity in the 737's cabin, treetops bend in the northeasterly breeze, gusting up to 20 knots, into which the aircraft landed. The majority of the passengers suffered at least minor injuries when the cabin structure shattered, while seven passengers and one flight attendant were seriously hurt. A fortunate 29 occupants – including the two pilots – escaped unharmed. Some of the passengers even continued their terrifyingly interrupted trip later that evening. (with acknowledgement to Flight International)

injuries, were unconscious. Others, their heads and faces covered in blood from numerous cuts, were moaning in pain.

Further back in the cabin, in the rows of seats nearest to the break in the fuselage, there were many more who had also sustained varying degrees of injury, for the most part lacerations as a result of being showered with metallic debris when the explosive decompression occurred. Many too were suffering from injuries to their eardrums. Only those seated towards the rear of the cabin seemed relatively unharmed by their traumatic experience.

While First Officer Tompkins quickly opened the main cabin door and deployed its inflatable escape chute for those who were able to move, Captain Schornstheimer sought to help the injured. Of the Boeing 737's two other flight attendants, only Michelle Honda, who had sustained bruising when thrown to the floor, came forward to assist him. Schornstheimer then learnt to his horror that veteran Flight Attendant Clarabelle Lansing, in the aisle in the First Class Section when the cabin burst, had been ejected bodily from the aircraft during the explosive decompression.

After all the passengers capable of walking had left the aircraft via the inflatable chutes and the rear airstairs, crews from the five airport emergency vehicles came aboard to assisted the injured who remained. Within 25 minutes, all had been moved from the aircraft to ambulances summoned to the airport from the town of Kahului, and were en route to the town's hospital.

Injuries

The most seriously injured, with skull and other bone fractures and numerous lacerations, was an 84-year-old woman who had been occupying window seat 5A on the port side. One row in front of her, the passengers in both port and starboard window seats (4A and 4F) had sustained concussion and multiple lacerations to their heads and faces, as did other passengers in rows 5, 6, and 7. But those in the centre and aisle seats of row 4 suffered only lacerations and, after being treated, were released from hospital later that day. Two rows further forward, the passengers in seats 2A and 2C on the port side had been injured by debris and flailing electrical wiring, resulting in multiple lacerations and electrical burns to the faces and hands. The passenger in the window seat 6A, directly beneath the aft end of the cabin fracture, suffered a broken arm, multiple facial lacerations, and blood effusion in both ears.

The majority of passengers in rows 8 to 21 received minor injuries, including lacerations, abrasions, and eardrum injuries They too were released after treatment.

Half an hour after the stricken Boeing 737 landed, a US Coast Guard helicopter, airborne on a training flight, was directed to search the area where the decompression occurred for the body of the missing flight attendant and any floating debris. The Coast Guard cutter *Cape Corwin* was also diverted into the search area, together with a Marine Corps helicopter.

The search effort, supplemented by other ships, helicopters, and fixed wing aircraft was to continue for three days, but without success – not a trace of the wreckage or debris scattered by the explosive decompression nor of the body – could be found.

Fortunately, at the time of the explosive decompression, the seatbelt signs were illuminated and all the passengers were seated with their lapstraps fastened. Passengers in the forward cabin who saw Flight Attendant Lansing ejected from the aircraft said she was standing in the aisle at the time at seat row 5. As the cabin roof failed, they saw her drawn quickly upwards and to the side of the cabin, where she was swept violently out through the jagged hole opening up in the left side of the fuselage. A moment later, the entire cabin structure was carried away. Blood stains on the cushions of seat 5A and on the exterior port side of the aircraft immediately behind the fuselage fracture attested to the passengers' account.

At the same time, three rows further forward, Flight Attendant Sato-Tomita, also standing, was struck violently on the head by flying debris, including the flightdeck door, and thrown to the floor.

Well back in the cabin at about seat row 15, Flight Attendant Michelle Honda also suffered the consequences of the sudden decompression, but happily with less drastic results. Although bruised when thrown violently to the floor, she suffered no serious injuries. Subsequently, during the emergency descent, she was able to crawl up and down the aisle to render assistance to passengers and to try to calm those who were especially distressed.

INVESTIGATION

Fuselage damage

It was quickly obvious to the team of National Transportation Safety Board investigators, who arrived at Kahului Airport from Washington DC at 2pm the following day, that the inflight explosive decompression had damaged the aircraft beyond economical repair.

The major section of fuselage structure which separated in flight extended from slightly aft of the main entrance door, rearward about 18 feet (5.5m) to just forward of the leading edge of the wing, and from floor level on the port side of the cabin to the starboard side windows.

The initial drama over, the aircraft is about to be towed clear of the airport's single runway – but painters have already de-identified the airline title on the 737's fin. De-identification was hardly necessary on the fuselage – the aerial ordeal itself had attended to that! Note the remaining window structure and the relatively clean tear along the floor line on the starboard side of the fuselage. The arrow indicates fuselage fragments lodged between the inboard leading edge flap and the No 2 engine pylon. (NTSB)

The structure from the top of the windows to the floor on the starboard side, though still attached, was severely distorted and bent outwards more than 90°

The basic structure of the Boeing 737-200 fuselage is divided into four sections, each constructed of circumferential frames 20 inches (50.8cm) apart, and longitudinal stringers 10 inches (25.4cm) apart. Each area between adjacent frames and stringers (20 inches by 10 inches) is considered a frame bay, the whole structure supporting the fuselage skin formed of 0.036-inch (0.9mm) thick aluminium panels.

Fuselage Sections 41, 43, and 46, comprising most of the pressure cabin (see drawing of breakup sequence), together with Section 48 at the tail, are butt-joined at the appropriate circumferential frames to form the fuselage as a whole.

Fuselage stringers (S) are identified by numbers left (L) and right (R) from the centreline of the crown of the fuselage, as viewed from the rear, while longitudinal positions on the fuselage, referred to as Body Stations (BS), are specified by their distance in inches from a point near the nose of the aircraft.

Adjoining skin panels are joined longitudinally by overlapping the upper skin panel about three inches (75mm) beyond the edge of the lower panel. The overlap joint is fastened with three rows of countersunk rivets and a bonding process. The centre row of rivets secures the lap joint to a stringer underneath the skin, which in turn, is attached to the circumferential frames by riveted clips. Below the window belt and in the lower lobes of the fuselage sections, the skin is connected to the frames between the stringers using riveted L-shaped brackets called shear ties. To support the cabin floor in Sections 41, 43, and 46, floor beams, spaced 20 inches (50.8cm) apart, run transversely across the fuselage at the S-17 level.

Fuselage Section 43, from BS 360 to BS 540, forms the Boeing 737's forward cabin ahead of the wing. Each skin panel in the upper lobe of Section 43 runs the full length of the section — about 18 feet (5.5m) — with skin panel lap joints at S-4L and S-4R, S-10L and S-10R, and S-14L and S-14R in the upper lobe and at S-19L and S-19R and S-26L and S-26R in the lower lobe.

All the fuselage failures took place in Section 43, the missing structure extending longitudinally from BS 360 back to about BS 540, and circumferentially from just above the floor on the port side of the aircraft at S-15L, across the crown of the fuselage and down the starboard side to a position above the windows at S-10R. In this latter area the skin had peeled off, leaving the frames, stringers, and window forgings in place. Below the floor level on the port side, the skin had peeled off the structure in large arrowhead-shaped gashes.

Five consecutive floor beams at BS 420, 440, 460, 480, and 500 were broken, and the adjacent floor beams at BS 400 and 500A cracked, all of them slightly to the left of the cabin centreline. At these same seven body stations, the fuselage frames had fractured on the port side just below the floor beams. On the same side of the cabin between BS 400 and BS 500, the floor panels were displaced upwards as much as four inches (10cm), the displace-

As the investigation team works its way along the cabin, so the debris of damaged seats, furnishings and wreckage is cleared away for more detailed examination. Protruding from the gaping fuselage opening just forward of the wing root are the two rows of overhead lockers.

ment matching the broken floor beams. Most of the centre floor panels between BS 360 to BS 947 were also displaced upward to some degree, except in the overwing area. The floor panels on the starboard side of the cabin were unaffected.

Detailed examination of the fuselage structure immediately surrounding the failed areas, including skin, rivet, and stringer deformations, showed the following failure patterns:
• Port side, BS 360 to 540: Skin peeled from structure in a downward and rearward direction;
• Starboard side, BS 360 to 540: Skin peeled from structure in a downward and rearward direction, changing to directly rearward near BS 540;
• Circumferential break at BS 360: Fracture of stringers and deformed rivets indicated separating structure was pulled generally rearwards except between S-5L and S-4R, where the direction was about 30° to starboard;
• Circumferential break at BS 540,

port side: From top centre of fuselage to S-10L, the skin fracture was not associated with any rivet line and extended up to 20 inches (50.8cm) forward of BS 540. The fracture then followed the upper rivet line of the skin lap joint to a position about six inches (15.25cm) forward of BS 540, with evidence of fatigue cracking along seven consecutive rivet holes. From S-10L to the floor line, the skin had separated several inches forward of BS 540;
• Circumferential break at BS 540, starboard side: From top centre of fuselage to S-10R, stringer fractures and deformed rivets indicated that separated structure was pulled forward. In the vicinity of S-11R, a small area of structure had been pulled forward and upwards. The skin below S-11R had been torn, but the direction of the tear was unclear.

Pre-existing cracks were found in the S-10L lap joint forward of BS 540, and on each side of a rivet hole in the BS 360 butt strap near S-7R, but all other fractures were the result of overload.

The fracture surfaces and structure around the separation perimeter were generally corrosion free, but areas of corrosion and disbonding were found in circumferential butt joints at BS 360 and 540.

A piece of separated fuselage structure from between BS 365 to BS 420, and S-4R to S-8R, was found wedged between the leading edge flap and inboard side of the starboard engine strut. It was to prove the only significant piece of separated fuselage structure recovered. The piece contained two skin repairs along S-4R, and indications of pre-existing cracks were present in some of the lap joint rivet holes. This piece of structure, together with several samples cut from the remaining fuselage skin, was taken to the National Transportation Safety Board's laboratory for further analysis.

Other damage

Minor impact damage was found on the leading edges of both wings, more extensively on the starboard wing. Both tailplanes and the lower portion of the fin also had random dents in their leading edges.

The inlet cowls of both engines were dented, and several first stage fan blades of both engines were damaged. Remnants of fuselage structure were found lodged against the inlet guide vanes and embedded in the acoustic liner of the starboard engine.

In the port engine control system, cables in the closed loops for the engine power lever and the start lever systems were broken near a pulley cluster in the leading edge of the port wing, immediately inboard of the engine strut. The broken start lever cable prevented movement of the fuel control to the start position, while the broken power lever cable prevented any thrust increase on the engine. The port engine fuel control was found in the "cutoff" position. Both broken cables were badly corroded. The routeing of these cables between the flightdeck and the port engine took them beneath the area of maximum cabin floor distortion at BS 440. The cables were forwarded to the NTSB's Materials Laboratory for further examination.

The loss of the upper fuselage structure resulted in damage to overhead wire bundles and plumbing, and a number of circuit breakers on the flightdeck had tripped. Most but not all were related to passenger service unit and toilet wiring. The pitot-static lines to the Flight Data Recorder were broken, as was the air conditioning ducting. The potable water line was leaking and its conduit broken.

The passenger oxygen manifold was also severed, preventing use of the passenger oxygen system, but the flightcrew oxygen system was undamaged. The engine fire extinguisher switches on the flightdeck had been activated in accordance with emergency evacuation procedures, and both engine fire bottles were empty.

The aircraft's hydraulic system was undamaged. The flaps and leading edge devices were fully extended, the spoilers were retracted,

and the extended undercarriage had locked down normally. Inspection of the nose leg position indicator lamp module revealed that one of its two bulbs had burnt out and the module was slightly loose in its housing.

Pressurisation system

The cabin pressurisation system was examined for any possible malfunction which could have contributed to the explosive decompression. The electrical wiring from the selector panel to the pressure controller, and to the outflow valve, was inspected and found in order. A visual examination of the pressurisation components, including the outflow valve, both relief valves, the controller, and the selector panel

likewise revealed no evidence of any failure. These components were then removed from the aircraft and subjected to the standard acceptance tests for new pressurisation system components. No significant anomalies were found.

Passenger evidence

A woman passenger who had joined N73711 at Hilo for the flight to Honolulu told investigators that, as she was boarding the Boeing 737 through the aerobridge at the main forward door, she noticed a small crack in the side of the fuselage. The crack, which appeared to run through a row of rivets, was just aft of the door – she described its position as about halfway between the cabin door

*The main drawing shows a skin (over)lap joint typical of Boeing 737 construction practice up to production line No 291, in April 1972. The skin segments were about 0.9 of a millimetre thick, and used a cold-bonded adhesive strip to reinforce the triple rows of rivets along the overlap. No problems came to light in the first three years of 737 deliveries but, by May-June 1970, Boeing was receiving reports of joint corrosion and knew of shortcomings in its cold-bonding process. From production line No 292, the lap joints were strengthened with a tapered shim and were fay surface-sealed. Further improvements and an ongoing flurry of Service Bulletins calling for inspections followed – for around the world literally dozens of early 737s could be at risk if the lap joints "disbonded". The failure of the adhesive bonding placed pressurisation stresses directly on the upper row of rivets along such skin joints and, if any of these rivets were propagating otherwise inconsequential fatigue cracks (see lower enlargements), a potentially disastrous situation could develop. Seven of the 10 Boeing 737s flying with Aloha at the beginning of 1988 had come off the production line **before** No 292. (Matthew Tesch, with acknowledgement to NTSB)*

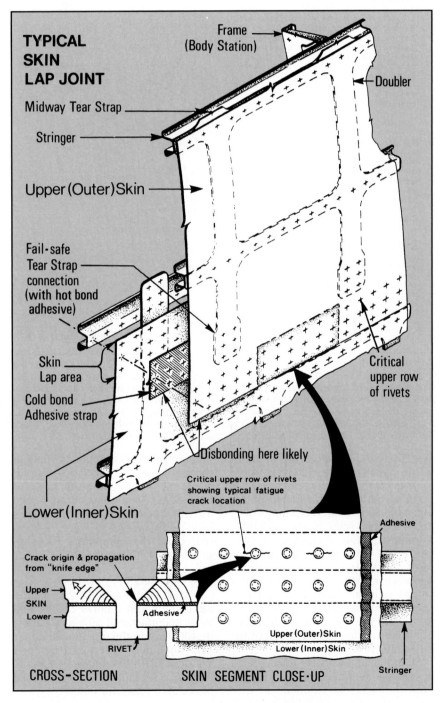

TYPICAL SKIN LAP JOINT

Frame (Body Station)

Doubler

Midway Tear Strap

Stringer

Upper (Outer) Skin

Fail-safe Tear Strap connection (with hot bond adhesive)

Skin Lap area

Cold bond Adhesive strap

Critical upper row of rivets

Disbonding here likely

Lower (Inner) Skin

Critical upper row of rivets showing typical fatigue crack location

Adhesive

Crack origin & propagation from "knife edge"

Upper SKIN
Lower

Adhesive

RIVET

Upper (Outer) Skin

Lower (Inner) Skin

Stringer

CROSS-SECTION

SKIN SEGMENT CLOSE-UP

BOEING 737

SERVICE BULLETIN
SUMMARY

BOEING COMMERCIAL AIRPLANE COMPANY   P.O. BOX 3707 SEATTLE, WASHINGTON 98124

SUBJECT: FUSELAGE - BONDED SKIN PANEL
INSPECTION AND REPAIR

ATA: 5330   NO: 737-53-1076
DATE: October 30, 1986

BACKGROUND

Since 1970, 20 operators have reported 52 occurrences of delamination or corrosion of bonded crown or side skins on 41 airplanes with from 10,100 to 49,100 flight hours and from 7,700 to 46,600 flight cycles. Of these occurrences, 3 were in the forward crown, 14 in the forward side, 10 in the aft crown, 15 in the aft side, 1 in the body crown over the wing center section, and 9 in locations not identified.

Inspection per this bulletin will determine the structural condition of the bonded crown and side skin-doubler assemblies, one belly skin between BS 259.5 to BS 360, and a portion of a belly skin from BS 1016 to BS 1026. Bond separation, corrosion and skin cracking which is not detected could result in expensive repairs, or cabin pressurization difficulties.

ACTION

At the next scheduled D check, or within 4 years from receipt of bulletin, whichever occurs first, accomplish a visual external and internal inspection for corrosion and delamination of bonded skin-doubler assemblies. Selectively inspect per this bulletin the crown and side skins from Body Station (BS) 259.5 to BS 1016, belly skins from BS 259.5 to BS 360, a ten inch strip from BS 1016 to BS 1026, and the edges of the fuselage door cutouts. Reinspect areas at each subsequent D check. Permanent repairs may be accomplished per 737 Structural Repair Manual. Temporary repairs may be accomplished per this service bulletin.

EFFECTIVITY

Line Number 1-464

MANPOWER

Total Man-Hours - 30
(External Inspection Only)

MATERIAL INFORMATION

None

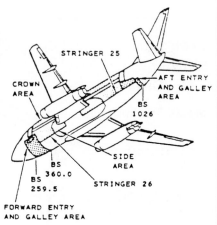

STRINGER 25

CROWN
AREA

AFT ENTRY
AND GALLEY
AREA

BS
1026

SIDE
AREA

BS
360.0

BS
259.5

STRINGER 26

FORWARD ENTRY
AND GALLEY AREA

AREAS OF INSPECTION

Summary Page 1 of 1

Reproduction of Summary Page of Boeing Service Bulletin SB 737-53-1076, issued at the end of October 1986. Between the first doubts, in mid 1970, and the Maui accident at the end of April 1988, Boeing issued more than five Service Bulletins and Revisions, and one Alert Bulletin, in addition to Letters, Reports and Advisories. The FAA was also sufficiently moved by Boeing's Ageing Fleet Evaluation Program, as much as by data collected by its own National Aviation Safety Inspection Program, to issue an Airworthiness Directive, effective November 2, 1987, mandating the contents of Boeing's Service Bulletins. (NTSB)

and the edge of the aerobridge shroud.

The passenger was later taken to look at another Boeing 737 standing at an aerobridge and asked to point out the position and direction of the crack she had seen. It was evidently a small longitudinal crack in the upper row of rivets along the S-10L lap joint. Believing the airline must know what it was doing and that she would only be humoured and regarded with disdain if she "made a fuss about it", she made no mention of it to the airline's ground staff or to the cabin crew.

At the time the first officer conducted the external preflight inspection of N73711 at Honolulu in the

predawn darkness on the morning of the accident, the crack had apparently not progressed sufficiently to be visible. Visual inspections of the aircraft between flights on Aloha's interisland services were not required by the company's FAA approved procedures.

Aircraft history

N73711, a Boeing 737-297, manufacturer's serial number 20209, had been manufactured 19 years earlier in 1969 as production line number 152. Equipped with two Pratt and Whitney JT8D-9A engines, it was delivered to Aloha Airlines, its original operator, on May 10, 1969.

Its maximum certificated takeoff weight was 100,000 pounds (45,360kg), but its actual takeoff weight on departure on the accident flight was calculated at 93,133 pounds (42,245kg). The load distribution was well within the calculated CofG limits for this gross weight.

The Aloha Airlines fleet at the time of the accident consisted of 10 Boeing 737s. Four of these aircraft were considered "high time", having accumulated more than 60,000 flight cycles, and one was the worldwide fleet leader in cycles flown.

At the time of the accident, N73711 had accumulated 35,496 flying hours and 89,680 flight cycles, the second highest number in the worldwide 737 fleet. Because of the short distances over most of the Aloha Airlines routes however, the maximum cabin pressure differential of 7.5 psi was not reached on every flight, and so the number of equivalent full pressurisation cycles accumulated on the aircraft was significantly less.

Examination of N73711's discrepancy log book, the flight attendants' cabin log, the line maintenance activity log, and the dispatch logs for the day of the accident, revealed no significant entries prior to the accident.

A review of 737 accidents and incidents reported to the NTSB, however, showed that N73711 had been involved in one previous mishap. On February 21, 1979, the aircraft had encountered clear air turbulence, resulting in serious injury to two flight attendants, but there was no record of any structural damage.

The review also revealed a fatal accident involving the failure of a Boeing 737 fuselage on August 22, 1981, when 737-200 B-2603, belonging to the Taiwanese airline Far Eastern Air Transport, broke up in flight as the result of an explosive decompression. The accident was investigated by the Civil Aeronautics Administration of the Ministry of Communications, Taiwan, with participation by the NTSB, Boeing, and the FAA. The translated prescription of cause, as determined by the investigation, read:

"... *extensive corrosion damage in the lower fuselage structures ... and in addition, the possible existence of undetected cracks because of the great number of pressurisation cycles of the aircraft (a total of 33,313 landings). Interaction of these defects had so deteriorated* [sic] *that rapid fracture occurred at a certain flight altitude and pressure differential, resulting* [in] *rapid decompression and sudden* break of passenger compartment floor beams and connecting frames, cutting control cables and electrical wiring. And eventually loss of power, loss of control, midair disintegration."

Fail-safe design

Boeing had designed the 737 for an economic service life of 20 years, including 51,000 flying hours and 75,000 cycles. The fail-safe design criteria established by the manufacturer required that the fuselage be capable of withstanding a 40 inch crack without suffering catastrophic failure.

These criteria were derived from an estimate of maximum external fuselage damage to be expected from penetration of fragments from an uncontained engine failure. No consideration was given to the joining up of adjacent cracks which might develop during extended service.

The fail-safe design provided for failure within two frame bays without compromising structural integrity. The design incorporated tear straps at 10 inch (25.4cm) spacings in the fuselage skin in both longitudinal and circumferential directions to redirect cracks resulting from external damage in a direction perpendicular to the crack. The fail-safe concept was based upon the theory that redirecting a progressing crack would cause the fuselage skin to "flap" open, releasing internal pressure in a controlled way without affecting the residual strength of the fuselage as a whole.

No consideration was given to the possibility of disbonding, or the effects of corrosion, on the strength of the fuselage lap joints.

Lap joint bonding

On early model Boeing 737s (to production line No 291), the fuselage skin lap joints were "cold" bonded, using an epoxy impregnated woven "scrim" cloth to join the longitudinal edges of the single thickness 0.036-inch (0.9mm) skin panels together. In addition, the joint was mechanically assembled with three rows of countersunk rivets. The bond cured at room temperature after assembly.

The cold bonding process was intended to provide structural effi-

In the days following the accident, the investigation uncovered this list of previous corrosion or fatigue-related repairs made to the fuselage of the Boeing 737. BS stands for Body Station, the numbers indicating the distance (in inches) of the particular fuselage frames from a point near the nose. The longitudinal Stringers on the Left and Right sides of the aircraft are similarly abbreviated, counting down from the crown (top centreline) of the fuselage. (NTSB)

NATIONAL TRANSPORTATION SAFETY BOARD
Bureau of Technology
Washington, DC 20594

SUMMARY OF PREVIOUS REPAIRS ON N73711

The following summary of existing skin repairs or rework areas was derived from the on-scene examination of the airplane in Kahului, Maui, Hawaii, from April 29 to May 6, 1988.

LEFT SIDE OF AIRPLANE

BS 540 -- Scab patch from S-1 to S-2L, using universal rivets. Replacement of countersunk rivets on forward skin of the butt joint from S-4L to S-4R, and forward along S-4L for the remaining short length (S-4R missing).

BS 580 -- Scab patch with countersunk rivets between S-2L and S-3L.

BS 727A -- Scab patch with countersunk rivets, 6"x 7", just above S-17L

BS 927 -- Scab patch between S-2L and S-3L, universal rivets, 5" long.

BS 1016 -- Scab patch with countersunk rivets above S-19L, 6"x 13".

BS 1121 -- Scab patch with countersunk rivets underneath third vortex generator, 8"x 8".

BS 767 to 818 -- flush patch in top skin of S-20L lap joint, 6" high, countersunk rivets. Repair continued forward under the aft portion of the wing to body fairing.

BS 747 to 1016 -- Top row of rivets at S-25L lap joint were replaced with blind universal rivets.

BS 927 to 947.6 -- Blind universal rivets in the top row of the lap joint at S-20L.

RIGHT SIDE OF AIRPLANE

BS 420 -- Scab patch with universal rivets, 8" long x 6" high, centered over S-17R.

BS 500B -- Scab patch with universal rivets, 7" long x 6" high, centered around S-15R.

BS 727A -- Scab patch with countersunk rivets, 6"x 8", centered about S-15R.

BS 727B -- Scab patch with countersunk rivets along S-17R, 2" aft of frame and 8" forward, 7" high centered around the stringer.

BS 800 -- Scab patch with countersunk rivets in forward frame of aft cargo door, 3"x 5" starting below S-19R.

BS 840 -- Scab patch with countersunk rivets in aft frame of aft cargo door, 1"x 7" starting at S-19R; scab patch with countersunk rivets, 1"x 4", starting above S-23R.

BS 960 -- Scab patch with countersunk rivets at forward edge of aft galley service door, 3"x 4", at S-14R location.

BS 970 -- Scab patch with countersunk rivets at mid-span of aft galley service door aft of the lower door hinge lower corner, 2"x 3", at S-15R location.

BS 1016 -- Scab patch with countersunk rivets in top skin of lap joint at S-16R, 4"x 4", centered about stringer.

BS 1104 -- Scab patch with countersunk rivets under second vortex generator, 8"x 7".

BS 1121 -- Scab patch with countersunk rivets under third vortex generator, 8"x 7".

BS 1121 to 1138 -- Scab patch with countersunk rivets above APU access door hinge line, 9" high.

BS 767 -- three rows of rivets replaced in S-20R lap joint, center row with universal rivets, continued forward under wing to body fairing.

BS 897 to 1016 -- top row of rivets at S-25R replaced by universal head rivets. Replacement started again at BS 767 and continued forward under wing to body fairing.

GENERAL

Several areas of rivets replaced by universal rivets around BS 747 to 807, S-27L and R; S-25R at BS 787.

Model Reg'n [msn]	B737-297 N73712 [20210]	B737-297 N73713 [20242]	B737-2H4 N73717 [20345]
FF Age (end87)	02May69 18½ yrs	11Nov69 18 yrs	20Jan70 18 yrs
AD-87-21-08 checked by Hours Cycles	05Nov87 32,642 87,551	15Dec87 – 83,488	12Jan88 – 67,429
Next Major checked by Hours Cycles	09Apr88 33,676 90,051*	14Apr88 32,026 85,409	27Apr88 39,986 68,954
ACCIDENT	**28Apr88 – B737-297 – N73711 – [20209]**		
Fate	May-Jun88 Found corroded beyond economical repair; reduced to spares; 11Jul88 sold for scrap, broken up	May-Jun88 1984 repair of 19cm (7½in) lap joint crack found; overall condition same as N73712; 11Jul88 sold for scrap, broken up	May-Jun88 WFU HNL & ferried to Mojave, CA; stored pending refurbishment decision; 27Dec91 scrapped

NOTE * Highest number of recorded flight cycles in worldwide 737 fleet

Two years' worth of maintenance records for three of N73711's sisterships were selected for detailed examination by NTSB investigators, with each aircraft subjected to a strip inspection. Data on these 737s – tabled above – provide an insight into the exceptionally demanding character of Aloha's operations. For example, the figures for N73712, in the five months between the mandatory AD inspection and its next major block check, suggest a respectable annual utilisation of around 2500 flying hours – but a whopping 6000 flight cycles! (Matthew Tesch, with acknowledgement to Boeing & NTSB)

ciency, reduced manufacturing costs, and weight reduction compared to traditionally riveted thick skin panels. Circumferential pressurisation loads were designed to be transferred through the bonded joint, rather than through the rivets, allowing the use of lighter, thinner fuselage skin panels.

The early service history of 737s with cold-bonded lap joints (together with early 727 and 747 aircraft using the same construction technique) revealed difficulties with this bonding process. The cleaning and etching process used on the skin panels did not provide a consistent quality surface oxide for the bonding.

Boeing also found bond quality could be degraded if condensation was not removed from the scrim cloth before installation, or if it remained at room temperature too long before use, causing it to cure prematurely. These production difficulties resulted in bonding of low durability, susceptibility to corrosion, and some lap joint areas that did not bond at all. In service, moisture could enter the joint in the areas of disbond, the resulting corrosion in some cases contributing to further disbonding of the joint. As a

result, Boeing discontinued cold bond lap joint production in 1972.

A redesigned smooth, close-fitting, "fay" surface-sealed lap joint, with increased joint thickness, was introduced with 737 production line number 292. This was a riveted joint sealed with a chromated polysulfide compound. The redesigned lap joints were also introduced on Boeing 727 and 747 production lines at this time.

When disbonding occurs in a 737 bonded lap joint, the circumferential pressurisation loads normally transferred through the lap joint are borne by the three rows of countersunk rivets that mechanically fasten the skin panels together. Because of the single thickness skin which the bonded construction permitted, the countersink for the flush rivet heads extended through the entire thickness of the outer sheet. The knife edge thus created concentrated the stresses. These stresses were cyclic with pressurisation loads, leading to fatigue cracking at these points.

In a Boeing 737 fuselage, the circumferential pressurisation stresses are twice the longitudinal stresses and, as fatigue effects take place, cracks propagate longitudinally, perpendicular to the dominant pressuri-

sation loads. The fatigue cracking occurs primarily in the upper row of outer skin lap joint rivet holes because this area carries the greatest stress.

Eddy current inspection

To assess the degree of fatigue cracking present in the skin of N73711, eddy current inspections, as used in ongoing airline maintenance to detect cracks, were conducted on selected sections of remaining fuselage lap joints.

Initially, the skin around 53 rivets showed indications of cracking, some of them apparent from cracks in the paintwork. To make the rivet heads more discernible, the paint was sanded off and the skin inspected again. Twenty-eight of the 53 indications were confirmed as cracks.

In addition, 25 locations were found where previous fuselage skin repairs had been performed. Most of these were external doubler patches at various stringer and frame locations.

Laboratory examination

The selected pieces of fuselage skin and associated structure returned to the NTSB's laboratory for analysis showed evidence of extensive fatigue and corrosion.

The lap joint sample found wedged in the starboard wing contained two external doubler patches. When the patches were removed, extensive fatigue cracking was found in the upper row of rivet holes under and between the patches. The examination found a crack 0.27 inch (7mm) long – one of the longest on the aircraft. This stringer section (S-4R) contained three areas where the tear straps were riveted above the primary lap joint, and there was extensive fatigue cracking in all three. Also, the entire cold-bonded lap joint had disbonded. There was light to moderate corrosion generally, with severe corrosion in some places. Nearly all the tear straps were disbonded in the vicinity of the lap joint.

The lap joint samples, S-4L from BS 727 to BS 747 and from BS 847 to BS 867, each contained 18 columns of rivets. The laboratory examination revealed fatigue cracking in the skin adjacent to nearly every hole in the upper rivet row, with the larger crack lengths in the mid-bay areas (halfway between two adjacent circumferential tear straps).

The laboratory examination found five cracks measuring 0.08 inch (2mm). Yet the eddy current inspection had identified only one of these five. This was at variance with the Boeing Non-Destructive Testing Manual which stated: "This inspec-

C/n [msn]	B737 Marque	A/C Reg'n	FF Date	Age[1] (yrs)	Comm. with Aloha	% of[2] Age	Total Cycles	Total Hours	Av.time/ cycle	Av.cycles/ fl.hr
[19426]	202C	N801AL	18Sep68	19	10Mar86[3]	10%	47,632	39,935	50min	1.2
[20209]	297	N73711[4]	28Mar69	18½	09Apr69	100%	85,300[5]	33,726	24min	2.5
[20210]	297	N73712	02May69	18½	07May69	100%	86,493[5]	32,200	22min	2.7
[20138]	210C	N4906	24May69	18½	04Aug85[3]	15%	47,200	38,995	50min	1.2
[20242]	297	N73713	11Nov69	18	24Nov69	100%	82,336[5]	30,775	22min	2.7
[20345]	2H4	N73717	20Jan70	18	27Jul78	55%	64,551[6]	38,775	36min	1.7
[20206]	2A9C	N803AL	07Apr70	17½	22Dec86[3]	5%	46,374	44,385	57min	1.0
[22148]	2S5CAdv	N802AL	30Apr80	7½	05Dec86	15%	6,527[7]	8,642	80min	0.8
[22629]	297Adv	N728AL	08Feb82	6	23Feb82	100%	29,948	11,598	23min	2.6
[22631]	297Adv	N730AL	06Jul82	5½	21Jul82	100%	28,098	10,830	23min	2.6

NOTES
(1) Age rounded to full/half years as at end of 1987
(2) Proportion of service life (age-years) spent with Aloha, at end 1987, rounded to 5%
(3) Second-hand: prior service with Wien, Markair, Quebecair, in harsh Alaskan/Canadian conditions
(4) Maui accident aircraft, April 28, 1988
(5) Trio with highest flight cycles of *total worldwide Boeing jet transport fleet*
(6) Second-hand: prior Southwest Airlines service on high-density US routes
(7) Second-hand: prior service as corporate transport in Canada & North America

Of the total 26 Boeing 737-200s operated by Aloha Airlines since 1969, no less than 18 were on the books in early 1988. But only 10 were regarded as in the 'active' fleet at the time of Boeing's Maintenance Evaluation visit in November 1987, the others being on various lease arrangements with other operators. The visit by Boeing was but one part of the manufacturer's massive customer support operation (see box). The above data are derived from the Boeing team's findings, only a few months before the Maui accident, with additional research. Ranked in descending order of aircraft age from date of first flight (FF), the figures provide a picture of an exceptionally hard-working fleet. The five 737s which had spent all their service lives with Aloha averaged a scant 23 minutes per flight cycle, and were flying an average of five such sectors every two hours – around 15 cycles and six flying hours every day of the year. Note (5), covering three aircraft, including the ill-fated N73711, makes a particularly dramatic statement. Compare the figures for this half of the fleet with those of the other 737s from different service backgrounds – especially the one-time corporate aircraft, N802AL! As the Maui accident so spectacularly demonstrated, the age of an aircraft can be a good deal less critical than the type and amount of flying it has done. (Matthew Tesch, with acknowledgement to Boeing, & additional research by Mike Clayton)

tion can find cracks 0.040 inches (1mm) or longer beneath the countersunk fastener heads."

One lap joint piece, S-4L, from BS 519 to BS 536, exhibited fatigue cracking from 16 consecutive rivet holes along the upper row of lap joint rivets. The longest single fatigue crack in one direction measured 0.18 inch (4.6mm) from the knife edge of the countersink, while the longest crack length in both directions across a rivet hole measured 0.53 inch (13.5mm). Both the lap joint and the tear straps in this area had disbonded, with light to moderate corrosion present on the previously bonded surfaces.

Fuselage failure

Because so little evidence remained to establish the origin of the failure of the fuselage, it was necessary to determine this by analysing the remaining structure and the airworthiness history of the aircraft.

An examination of the butt joint at the forward edge of fuselage Section 43 (BS 360) showed that the frame was intact, as were the skin and rivets forward of the butt joint's centreline. But the rivets that remained in place aft of the centreline were deformed in a rearward direction, indicating that the skin immediately aft of BS 360 was intact up to the moment of failure. Similarly, the frame at BS 540 was intact with the rivets ahead of its centreline deformed in a forward direction. It was thus clear that the primary failure had occurred somewhere between BS 360 and BS 540, and that the skin at these butt joints had pulled away in tension overload.

The structure along the longitudinal separations of Section 43 was therefore examined in detail for clues to the origin of the failure. On the port side, very little of the structure remained above floor level. All the frames between BS 360 and 540 had broken off at the floor, with a substantial portion of the structure separating outward. This was corroborated by the ingestion damage to the port engine, together with leading edge damage to the port wing and tailplane.

The severely damaged and distorted cabin floor on the port side, with broken and cracked floor beams, contrasting with the starboard side floor panels which were not displaced, also pointed to the origin of the failure being on the port side. As cabin pressure in the upper fuselage lobe was released, pressure in the lower lobe was contained by the cabin floor, resulting in the floor being deflected upwards until the floor panel failure released the pressure.

Studies conducted by McDonnell Douglas following the horrific accident to the THY Turkish Airlines DC-10 near Paris in March 1974, resulting from an underfloor cargo door becoming unlatched during flight (see *Air Disaster*, Volume 1, Chapter 15), showed that, during an explosive decompression, pressure differential distribution peaks at the point of the opening in the fuselage.

The point of maximum floor deflection on the Aloha Boeing 737 occurred to the left of the inboard seat track for the port side seats at seat row 3 (BS 440), and the investigators concluded that the failure occurred on the port side of the fuselage, probably close to BS 440.

The pattern of damage, together with the service history of early 737 lap joints, pointed to the upper lobe lap joint on the port side at S-10L as the most likely source of the failure. At BS 520 in the remaining fuselage structure, fatigue cracks emanated longitudinally from both sides of at least seven adjacent rivet holes in the skin along the lap joint at S-10L. Such cracking was probably indicative of the overall condition of this lap joint (see diagram).

Moreover, the evidence of the passenger who had seen a skin crack while boarding the aircraft at Hilo suggested there was a visible crack at that time in the S-10L lap joint, just aft of BS 360.

Passengers sitting on the port side of the cabin during the flight said that the missing flight attendant was standing in the aisle at seat row 5 immediately before the fuselage failure. During the explosive decompression, she was ejected from the cabin at a position corresponding to S-10L near BS 440.

From all this evidence, the investigators concluded the fuselage most probably failed catastrophically along S-10L, initially near BS 440, allowing the upper fuselage to tear free.

The possible reasons for this catastrophic failure, rather than a fail-safe "flapping" of the skin as designed, were examined in detail.

Fuselage separation sequence

Redirection of a longitudinal fuselage crack, to safely decompress an aircraft cabin, depends on the integrity of the structure ahead of the crack tip. If tear straps disbond, they become ineffective because stiffening is lost, and the crack can propagate as if the tear straps did not exist.

Inspection of the remaining portion of the structure aft of the fuselage separation area revealed multiple fatigue cracks along rivet lines between adjacent circumferential tear straps. Fatigue cracks up to 0.53 inch (13.5mm) in length were evident in the lap joint along S-10L near BS 520, while the piece of structure recovered from the starboard wing leading edge contained numerous fatigue cracks that stemmed from disbonding of the lap joint and tear straps.

The function of the bond in carrying the stress and fatigue loads through the lap joint is lost when the joint disbonds and the rivets have to carry the load instead. The knife edges created by the countersunk rivets then produce stress concentrations that lead to fatigue cracking from the rivet holes. Thus, although a disbonded lap joint can carry the pressurisation load intended to be borne by a properly bonded joint, it becomes more susceptible to fatigue cracking.

The damage discovered on the accident aircraft, damage on other Boeing 737s in the Aloha fleet, and the service history of 737 lap joint disbonding, led the investigators to conclude that numerous fatigue cracks in the lap joint along S-10L finally linked up to cause the catastrophic failure. The extent of tear strap disbonding in the lap joint was evidently sufficient to negate the structure's fail-safe capacity to control the decompression.

Boeing customer visits

Boeing's Ageing Fleet Evaluation Program provided for Boeing survey teams to visit operators to examine selected aircraft and assess their condition. Its objectives were to observe the effectiveness of maintenance programs, corrosion prevention and control, to gather information to ensure the safe and economic operation of ageing aircraft, and to promote improved design in new aircraft. The program also provided Boeing with information on problems encountered by operators.

Aloha Airlines was one of the operators initially selected for a visit by the Boeing team. It was operating the highest flight time and cycle aircraft in the Boeing 737 fleet, and several of its 737s had exceeded 75 percent of the type's design life.

The Boeing team made their first visit to Aloha Airlines in late September, 1987, surveying N73712 while it was in the hangar for a heavy maintenance check. A month later the team returned to survey N73713.

On October 28, 1987, senior Boeing executives met with Aloha's president, vice president (operations), and chief executive officer to discuss of the survey team's findings. The Boeing executives voiced their concern about the corrosion and skin patches found on the two 737s, recommending, among other things, that Aloha Airlines "put present airplanes down for a period of 30 to 60 days and totally strip and upgrade their structures."

Aloha Airlines then requested Boeing to evaluate its maintenance operations. According to Aloha Airlines management, the request was generated by their concern to upgrade and modernise the maintenance program. A Boeing team visited Aloha's maintenance facilities in November, 1987, and their subsequent report contained no less than 37 wide-ranging recommendations (see box).

An "ageing fleet" survey of N73717, similar to that performed on the

other two high-time aircraft, was accomplished in January, 1988, the Boeing team observing the repair of an S-4 lap joint while the aircraft was in for heavy maintenance.

In April, 1988, when Aloha's management again met with Boeing to discuss the findings of this survey and the maintenance evaluation recommendations, Boeing personnel gained the impression that Aloha Airlines was planning to delay the recommended structural overhauls of its high-time aircraft.

Boeing then made the following recommendations to Aloha:
• Reinstate the plan to conduct complete structural inspections on at least the following aircraft: N73711, N73712, N73713 and N73717;
• Conduct a detailed S-4 lap joint inspection on all aircraft with more than 40,000 flight cycles;
• Initiate a belly skin replacement program;
• Immediately reinstate the existing corrosion control program;
• Initiate, when available, the Boeing-developed maintenance program including the recommended corrosion control.

Aloha Airlines maintenance

Several factors in the airline's maintenance program were of particular concern to the investigators.

The airline's structural D-check inspection interval for its 737 fleet was approved by the FAA at 15,000 hours. Although this interval appeared to be more conservative than the 20,000 hour interval recommended by Boeing, because of the consistently short sectors involved in Aloha's interisland shuttles, flight cycle accumulation still exceeded the rate Boeing forecast for the aircraft type generally. Aloha 737s accumulated about three cycles for each flying hour in service, whereas Boeing design life projections were based on accumulating about 1.5 cycles per flying hour. Even with an adjustment for only partial pressurisation on short flights, the accumulation of cycles on Aloha aircraft remained high, continuing to outpace other Boeing 737s in the world fleet.

Flight cycles are the dominant factor in the development of fatigue cracking in pressurised fuselages, and in the development of damage as a result of flight and landing loads. Aloha's maintenance program, based on flying hours alone, did not adequately consider the effect of these factors.

Boeing had stipulated a 6-to-8 year interval for a complete D check cycle, and Aloha's D-check maintenance program required 8 years to complete. But the investigators believed this was too long to permit timely detection of disbonding and corrosion, to provide for damage repair, and to implement effective corrosion control.

The airline's practice of inspecting aircraft in small increments was of further concern. The D-check inspection of its 737 fleet was covered in 52 independent stages. Only limited areas of the aircraft were inspected during each stage, precluding any comprehensive assessment of its overall structural condition. There was also the potential for the checks to be hurried to keep aircraft in service.

Effectiveness of inspections

The effectiveness of the inspection programs was further limited by time and manpower constraints. Because Aloha's schedules involved full utilisation of its fleet in daytime operations, and there were usually no spare aircraft, the majority of Aloha's maintenance was conducted at night. However, as it was important for aircraft to be available for the next day's flying, only a few hours were available in each 24 hour period to complete B, C and D inspection items and to perform any unscheduled maintenance.

Scheduling of this sort forces staff to continually perform under pressure. Indeed, under the intense effort to keep the aircraft flying, maintenance staff were reluctant to keep aircraft in the hangar any longer than absolutely necessary.

Another factor affecting scheduling of this sort is the effect of circadian rhythms on human behaviour. The quality of work can suffer if task scheduling does not take into account the adverse effects of sleep loss and irregular work and rest schedules on the performance of maintenance staff.

For example, one Airworthiness Directive concerning Aloha's early model Boeing 737s required a visual inspection of the lap joints along S-4L and S-4R, with an eddy current inspection of the upper row of lap joint rivets along the entire panel in which defects were found. This imposed considerable physical demands, requiring inspectors to climb scaffolding and move along the upper fuselage carrying a bright light while they made a "close visual inspection" of about 1,300 rivets, with a possible eddy current inspection of about 360 rivets per panel. For eddy current inspections, they also needed a probe and a meter. And when it was necessary to inspect

---

BOEING'S MAINTENANCE EVALUATION VISIT

In late October 1987, Aloha Airlines requested a Maintenance Evaluation visit from Boeing. A four-man team subsequently spent nine days in Honolulu, and their 30 page report, with supporting charts, was delivered to the company by the end of January 1988.

From the contents of Boeing's report (reproduced as an Appendix to the NTSB's investigation report), it appears that both Aloha and Boeing (already conscious of the state of its ageing products around the world), got more than they bargained for.

The Boeing team found seven of Aloha's 10 active 737s were early model aircraft on which the fuselage lap joints had a high risk of disbonding, while three had accumulated more flight cycles than any of the thousands of other Boeing jet airliners elsewhere in the world. Data from maintenance records (tabulated in this chapter) confirmed a very hard-working fleet of very old aircraft while, out of an Aloha staff total of nearly 1,200, barely 200 were maintenance and quality control personnel.

"In comparison with similarly-equipped operators, it appears that Aloha is short of technical personnel in the offices, shops and hangar," declared Boeing as tactfully as it could among the 37 recommendations it put to Aloha's management. But no amount of helpful, supportively deferential language could fully disguise the apprehension obviously felt by Boeing.

There should be "an intense effort" to raise manpower in all departments of the Technical Division "to industry levels", Boeing declared. The appointment of a dedicated Safety Co-ordinator was recommended, as were extra inspectors. More training for inspectors, better recording of labour, time and man-hours to enable better planning and budgeting were also required, and there was a subtle reminder that the Planning & Production Control department needed always to liaise with others. A less subtle nudge sought to "ensure … good rapport between the Flight Operations and Technical Divisions to make sure that each appreciates the other's problems and constraints." The need for improved communication between individuals, positions and departments was a recurring theme of the report.

"Give high priority to revamping the Technical Policies and Procedures Manual," the report declared in another place. It suggested Aloha "institute an aggressive program", to put not only its own Air Carrier Manual in order, but also "all applicable manufacturer and vendor technical manuals and documents." The airline should also "consider initiating the practice of preparing a planning chart to be used by the Maintenance department as a guide in sequencing the items of work to be accomplished."

Day-to-day practical concerns appear to have stretched the patience of the Boeing team even further: "Conduct an inventory exercise" was one specific suggestion of many that might have seemed obvious: "Construct a dust-free, temperature-controlled laboratory"; "Establish better control and accountability of tools"; "Establish a separate area devoted to the shipping and receiving of parts" and the naively explicit: "Consider providing in the hangar a board with slots on which task cards can be grouped by aircraft zone, skills required, and work progress status."

Among concerns more specific to the Boeing 737 fleet, its operational environment and age, was perhaps the most astonishing of all, considering Aloha had been an all-737 operator for nearly 20 years: *"Provide 737 training to all maintenance mechanics who have not received training for this model airplane."*

In Aloha's defence it should be pointed out that the airline, hard pressed to maintain its market share and viability in a geographically-confined and expansion-limited market, had asked for the audit by its principal supplier, and was unstinting in providing information and access to the Boeing team.

The accident occurred only three months after Aloha had received Boeing's report, little progress having been made in the meantime in implementing the manufacturer's recommendations.

---

rivet lines on top of the fuselage, they had to use safety ropes suspended from the rafters of the hangar to guard against falling from the aircraft. Examining the area around one rivet after another for signs of minute cracks under these circumstances was tedious to say the least – and even more difficult with the aircraft skin covered by several layers of paint.

The investigators found that Aloha's technical support for its inspectors was inadequate. Some of the documents detailing lap joint inspections were complicated and subject to interpretation. They needed review and written guidance as to their execution, before being sent to maintenance staff. Aloha's management failed to provide this guidance and, in so doing, contributed to

the cause of this accident.

Exacerbating the difficulties for airline maintenance personnel was the fact that FAA approved training courses contained material that was largely irrelevant. Students were required, for example, to study wooden airframes, airframe fabric repairs, and the application of paint and dope – at a time when the FAA was certificating air transport aircraft with fly-by-wire technology, composite materials construction and computerised monitoring!

The NTSB investigators questioned how such training could equip maintenance personnel for the skills and tasks they were expected to perform in an airline environment today. There was clearly a need for the FAA to examine its requirements governing aviation maintenance schools and the licensing of airframe and powerplant technicians, and to revise them to reflect contemporary aircraft technology.

Corrosion control

Inadequacies in Aloha's maintenance and inspection program significantly affected the control of corrosion in its aircraft. According to maintenance records, when lap joint and other areas of corrosion were detected, corrective action was frequently deferred. Even when maintenance staff found corrosion in the lap joints and tear straps, its significance to lap joint integrity, tear strap function, and overall airworthiness was not recognised. The general condition of Aloha's fleet indicated that pilots and maintenance personnel had come to accept ongoing corrosion damage as a normal operating condition. Economic considerations, lack of structural understanding, high aircraft utilisation, and the lack of spare aircraft, were all factors contributing to this situation.

Engineering services

At the time of the accident, Aloha Airlines, like many small operators, did not have an engineering department. But the condition of Aloha's high-cycle 737's was an example of

---

ALOHA'S FLEET HISTORY

The Boeing and NTSB reports present a picture of an airline with problems – an organisation trying to do too much with too few resources, and with economies that were too tight.

Table 3 (opposite) charts the histories of 25 Boeing 737s which passed through Aloha's hands between 1968 and 1995 – their ages, backgrounds and service lives. Note the numerous aircraft leased in, leased out, subleased in and out, sold and immediately leased back, first leased then bought outright, changes of lessor – not once but several times. Keeping track of all the detail is difficult even for the diligent researcher!

Airlines brokering their own assets – juggling aircraft around other carriers and traffic seasons – are not new phenomena. Indeed, Aloha's management could be commended for its business acumen in squeezing the most out of its every dollar. But given Boeing's concerns about the airline's organisational inadequacies, it is hardly surprising in the circumstances that the maintenance records of individual aircraft left something to be desired.

Additional notes on some of their individual histories may also help in setting the background to the corporate environment in which the Maui accident was able to occur. The 10 737s which were active in the Aloha fleet at the time of Boeing's Maintenance Evaluation are outlined first, then eight nominally with Aloha at the time, but operating elsewhere.

N73711 [20209], the aircraft involved in the accident, leads in the left column. First flown (FF) on March 28, 1969, *King Kalaniopuu* was delivered a fortnight later on a GATX lease to Aloha. Acquisitions of newer 737s in the late 1970s reflect its disposition (and N73712 and N73713 as well), by 1981. From February 1981 to January 1982, N73711 was subleased to Air California (AirCal), then returned to GATX in April. GATX promptly released it directly to AirCal for 14 months, after which, in November 1983, it went back to Aloha on lease again as *Queen Lilioukalani*. Aloha bought it outright four months later.

The next two 737s to be delivered led similar lives, with FFs in May and November 1969. Both were GATX leases, N73712 [20210] as *King Kahekili*, N73713 [20242] as *King Kaumalii* (name changes were endemic in the Aloha fleet and space precludes keeping up with them all here). Both were returned late 1982, re-leased to Aloha at the end of 1983 and both were acquired outright in March 1984. Put under the NTSB microscope after the Maui accident, they were found corroded beyond economical repair, reduced to spares in July 1988, and sold for scrap.

N73715 [20345] (FF January 1970) was to have been Aloha's fourth 737 as *King Kamehameha*, but the first three aircraft were apparently enough at the time. It spent the next seven years on Southwest Airlines' Texan routes, before ITEL leased it to Aloha in July 1978 as N73717 *King Kalamikupule*. Less than a year later, Aloha subleased it to Canada's Nordair for two months, then to AirCal where it remained for three years. It came back to Aloha in July 1982. During the sublease, ITEL sold it to GATX, and by 1986 it had been sold twice more. Further sales after July 1988 were mere "paper changes" because the aircraft, the third Aloha-operated 737 scrutinised by the NTSB, was ferried to Mojave Desert storage and finally scrapped by Christmas 1991.

The next three 737s, all Convertible models, were also "oldtimers" with FFs between September 1968 and April 1970, and their early owners had worked them hard in the harsh Canadian north and in Alaska. Their Aloha tenures were relatively short, their useful lives coming to an end within four years of the Maui accident. N4906 [20138] *Queen Emma Kaleleonalani* was an August 1985 Polaris lease which ended with the delivery of three newer 737s in mid 1990. The aircraft was finally with-

drawn from use while in storage in France in 1994. The "nameless" N801AL [19426] arrived in March 1986 on a CIS lease, but from June 1989 its owner was US Airlease Inc. The third oldest of all, its usefulness had ended by 1992. It spent 1993 parked at Honolulu Airport, but by Easter 1994 it had been returned to the lessor and placed in open storage in Arizona. N803AL [20206] was another of six 737s operated by Aloha not graced with a name. Bought by Aloha just before Christmas 1986, it was resold to Integrated Resources Corp even before it could shed its Pacific Western livery, and was immediately leased back to Aloha. By June 1992 it was being reduced to spares at Honolulu.

Integrated Resources also featured in the Aloha careers of N728AL [22629], the second *King Kalaniopuu*, and N730AL [22631] *King Kalakaua*. Part of a 1982 trio ordered directly from Boeing, Aloha sold these two to Integrated in August 1988, then leased them straight back. N730AL was returned in September 1994, but N728AL remains operational with Aloha at the time of writing. The final member of the fleet at the time of Boeing's Maintenance Evaluation was the statistical oddity, N802AL [22148]. This "young" airframe (FF April 1980) spent its early life as a corporate transport for the mining industry in North America. Aloha, seizing the chance to acquire a low-time, low-cycle 737, bought it in December 1986. It too remains operational with Aloha at the time of writing.

N729AL [22630], the third of the 1982 trio (and the second *King Kahekili*) opens this summary of the eight 737s nominally in Aloha's fleet at the time of Boeing's Maintenance Evaluation. It was delivered with the others but, from August 1985, was leased to America West where it remains today. Another away with America West at the time was the November 1969 vintage N7376F [20364]. Taken by Aloha on sublease from Frontier Airlines and its lessor in June 1986, it was further subleased by Aloha in April 1987. Continental became the prime lessee during this time, the aircraft itself being sold not once, but twice! Back with Aloha in June 1991, reportedly on lease-in, its time was up by July 1993 and it went on to be shuttled about open storage sites in the western USA.

N70721 [21500], the second *King Lunalilo* and N70722 [21501], the second *King Kaumalii* spent their lives almost as twins. The chart sketches a complicated history best left to the reader's own study. Both were ordered new by Aloha, being delivered in August and September 1977; both were also with America West and, by the time both finally left Aloha in 1993, they had been sold three or four times (the only times Aloha saw them after 1987 was as sublessee!). The pair spent more time with Nigeria Airways, Western, Delta and America West than with Aloha.

Another pair – N70723 [21739], the first *Queen Lilioukalani* and N70724 [21740] *Queen Kapiolani* – were out on lease to PanAm between September-October 1983 and July-August 1988, first on Internal German Services under a variety of *Clipper* names. Both were sold within four months of the Maui accident and leased straight back to Aloha where they are still operating. Two more aircraft, ordered a year apart, were also to operate as a pair – N725AL [22051] *Queen Ka'ahumanu* delivered in January 1980, and N726AL [22426] *King Kamehameha II*, which followed in February 1981. Two years later, an abortive lease to the short-lived Pacific Express saw both aircraft placed on an AirCal lease by April 1984, where they spent the next four years. In the upheaval which followed the Maui accident, both were sold to Polaris but still remain operational with Aloha on lease.

(Compiled by Matthew Tesch & Mike Clayton, using APS, ADC and JP products, with special acknowledgment to Roach & Eastwood's Jet Airliner Production List, E&OE)

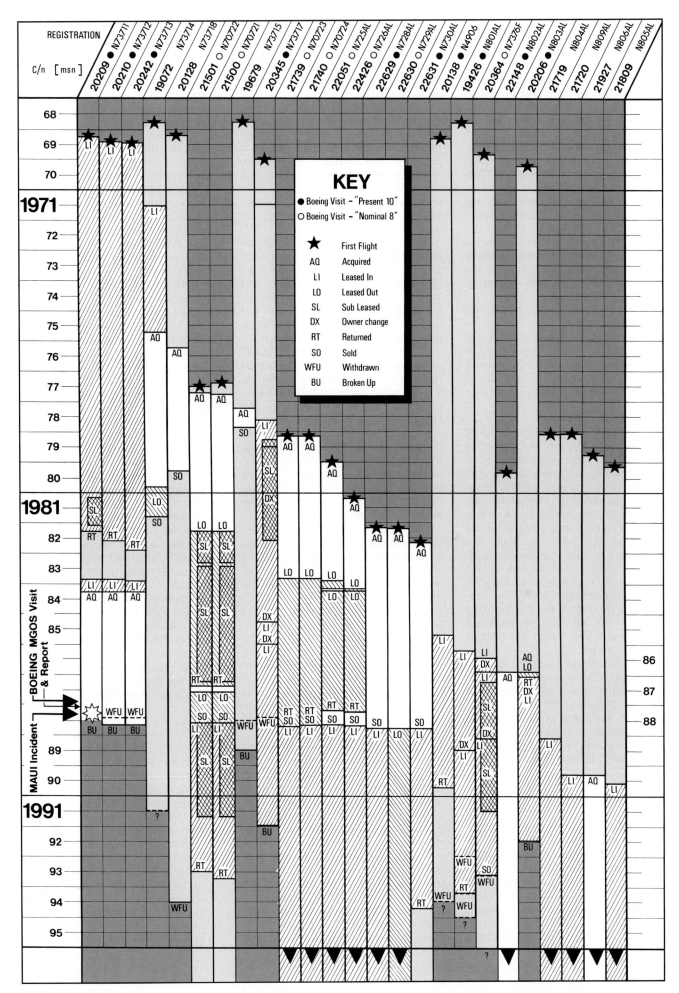

what can occur in a fleet without regular and knowledgeable evaluations of aircraft condition by qualified engineering staff.

The extent and number of skin repairs on the aircraft, and the effect of these repairs on the damage tolerance of the original design, was a further cause for concern. The accident aircraft had over two dozen fuselage repairs; the majority were skin repairs using doubler patches. This condition illustrated the extent to which ageing aircraft could continue to be patched under existing manufacturer's and FAA requirements.

A major repair, or the cumulative effect of numerous small repairs, could jeopardise the capacity of the structure to meet fail-safe or damage tolerant regulations.

Overall, the investigators found that Aloha Airlines' maintenance department did not possess sufficient manpower, technical knowledge, or the required organisation, to ensure the continuing structural integrity of its aircraft fleet.

Boeing 737 Certification

Although the initial certification of the Boeing 737 in 1967 conformed to regulatory requirements then existing, the manufacturer's accelerated fatigue testing schedule did not allow for in-service environmental effects on the bonded lap joints or tear straps. The inadequacy of the testing schedule was partly because the laboratory bonding verification testing available at the time had not yet discovered the problem of long term bonding durability. Indeed, the production problems in the bonding process did not become apparent until several years after the aircraft entered service.

But when the problem did emerge, Boeing addressed it quickly, issuing Service Bulletins to all operators of the type, improving the bonding process, conducting additional fatigue testing, and ultimately eliminating the cold-bond process and redesigning the lap joint on all future production aircraft.

Operational considerations

The enormity of the inflight structural failure far exceeded any situation for which the pilots could have been prepared with simulator training – or indeed any imaginable emergency that could be considered survivable. Even so, they succeeded in managing the multiple emergencies which the explosive decompression triggered, and brought the

aircraft and its passengers to a safe landing. Their coolness and professionalism in the face of such alarming odds spoke extremely well of their training, airmanship and overall ability.

The one flight attendant who was not incapacitated in the accident also performed in a highly commendable manner in the face of a frightening and totally unpredictable situation. Her bravery in moving about the critically damaged cabin to reassure terrified passengers and prepare them for the emergency landing was exemplary.

There was nevertheless one aspect of the way in which the aircraft was handled which the investigators believed was open to criticism, and which, in slightly more adverse circumstances, could have made the difference between a safe emergency landing and a fatal accident.

It was evident from crew statements, as well as the FDR readout, that the pilots began a rapid descent shortly after the explosive decompression. Despite the fact that the flightdeck door had been blown off and that blue sky was now visible to the pilots where formerly the ceiling of the First Class cabin had been, the captain deployed the speed brakes and descended at between 280 and 290 knots without first checking the structural integrity of the aircraft.

The speeds used during the descent certainly minimised the time at altitude during which the passengers would have suffered the effects of anoxia. But they also increased the manoeuvring loads being imposed on the weakened aircraft structure, and exposed the unfortunate passengers in the forward section of the cabin to the ravages of the enormous wind force. The open break in the fuselage was also subjected to extremely high dynamic pressure that could have affected the aircraft's already slim margin of structural integrity.

The Emergency Descent procedure contained in the Boeing 737 Operators' Manual stated that, if structural integrity is in doubt, "limit airspeed as much as possible and avoid high manoeuvring loads." Because proper evaluation of structural integrity and the techniques of emergency descent (target airspeed, configuration changes, and manoeuvring loads) could be critical to the outcome of an inflight emergency, the investigators suggested that the FAA issue an Operations Bulletin reviewing the circumstances of the

Aloha accident and reiterating the need to assess aircraft airworthiness before taking any action that could cause further damage – or even the inflight breakup of a damaged airframe.

One final investigation criticism concerned air traffic control procedures during the emergency. In the course of the aircraft's diversion to Kahului Airport, ATC changed the frequency for primary radio contact. The Boeing 737 was transmitting transponder emergency code 7700 and, after some difficulty, the crew established contact with the airport's Maui Tower.

But after being notified of the emergency, ATC directed that the aircraft change frequency to Maui Approach Control. Later again, the aircraft switched back to Maui Tower for landing instructions. Although the need for such frequency changes during normal operations is well understood, the investigators believed that ATC must make every effort to minimise the workload of a flight crew during an emergency.

In this instance, Maui Tower received both the emergency transponder code and verbal confirmation of a pressurisation emergency before issuing instructions to change frequency. Quite apart from unnecessarily adding to the workload of a crew already under stress, an error during the handoff procedure could result in a loss of contact, with the possibility of losing positive control over the aircraft in the emergency situation.

Addressing the many shortcomings revealed by their investigation of the Aloha Airlines accident, the National Transportation Safety Board forwarded no less than 21 recommendations, intended to overcome these inadequacies, to the Federal Aviation Administration.

Footnote:
(1) The "springy" feel described by the captain was of course the flexing of the nose section forward of the break in the fuselage. Having already drooped about a metre out of alignment with the loss of so much fuselage structure, the nose section ahead of the break was literally "hanging by a thread". It is said unofficially in industry circles that only the additional stiffening provided by the cabin seat rails bridged the difference between the extremely marginal structural integrity that remained, and catastrophic inflight failure.

CHAPTER 12

"Prepare for crash landing!"

– Captain to passengers and crew on PA system

British Midland Airways Boeing 737-4YO G-OBME [23867]
– January 8, 1989

Misidentifying a failed engine and shutting down the "good one" is an operational error as old as the reality of asymmetric flight. That such a basic mistake could still be made by the crew of late model jet equipped with a new technology "glass cockpit" stunned the airline industry throughout the world.

Destination Belfast

For Captain Kevin Hunt of British Midland Airways Ltd, Sunday January 8, 1989 was a normal enough working day. With his first officer and cabin crew of six – flight service manager and five flight attendants – he was rostered that afternoon to operate his company's regular "double shuttle" service between London Heathrow and Belfast's Aldergrove Airport in Northern Ireland.

The aircraft scheduled for the trips was BMA's new 156 passenger Boeing 737-400 G-OBME, a mint condition aircraft that had been granted its Certificate of Airworthiness only two months previously and had so far flown a mere 520 hours. Powered by two CFM56-3C-1 high bypass turbofan engines rated at 23,500lb thrust for takeoff, it was equipped with a new technology "glass" cockpit.

Cathode Ray Tube (CRT) displays replaced the conventional flight instruments for both captain and first officer, while solid-state displays of primary and secondary engine parameters in the centre of the instrument panel replaced the usual electromechanical engine instrument array fitted to earlier marques of the Boeing 737.

The weather over southeastern England for the afternoon of the double shuttle was mild for mid-winter, with only scattered stratus and stratocumulus cloud between 1000 and 3500 feet being produced by a light but moist southwesterly airstream. Freezing level was a high 10,000 feet and surface visibility at Heathrow Airport was six kilometres in occasional light rain.

The aircraft's first trip to Belfast and return was entirely without incident and at 6.45pm G-OBME landed back at Heathrow to be readied for the second return flight, scheduled to depart from Terminal 1 as Flight BD092. This later Sunday evening service was generally popular with British businessmen and civil servants returning to Belfast after having spent the weekend at home in London. On this occasion, 118 Belfast-bound passengers were waiting to board the flight, many of them holidaymakers returning home after the Christmas-New Year break.

At 7.52pm, with the first officer handling the aircraft from the right hand seat, G-OBME took off from Heathrow's Runway 27 Right, climbing initially over Slough to 6000 feet before taking up a north-northwest heading. Six minutes later, London ATC cleared the Boeing 737, now flying under a clear night sky, to climb to FL350 (35,000 feet) on the direct track to the Trent VOR in the Midlands.

Because the 280nm flight to Belfast was of such short duration, the cabin crew began serving passengers their evening meal as soon as the aircraft was established on its cruise climb track.

Engine trouble

But at 8.05pm, when the Boeing 737 was some 25nm south of Derby and passing through FL283 on climb to cruising level, there was a sudden noise like a low repetitive thudding, the aircraft began to vibrate severely, what looked like light smoke poured into the passenger cabin through the airconditioning ducts, and there was a strong smell of burning. At the same time, passengers and three flight attendants in the rear section of the cabin saw what they variously described as "sparks", "bright lights", "flames", "flashes" or "torching" lighting up the night on the port side of the aircraft. They were coming from the jetpipe of the No 1 engine.

On the flightdeck, though the pilots could not hear the noise or see the fiery discharge from the No 1 engine, they felt the sudden airframe vibration and smelt the smoke. No fire warning sounded on the flightdeck, nor was there any other visual or aural warning, but Captain Hunt immediately disengaged the autopilot and took over control from the first officer.

The engine instrument indications appeared to be normal but, as the smoke and fumes on the flightdeck seemed to be coming from the cabin, Hunt's personal understanding of the aircraft's air conditioning system at once suggested to him that the trouble lay with the No 2 engine on the starboard wing. The first officer meanwhile was intently monitoring the engine instrument indications.

"Which engine's giving trouble?" the captain asked, seeking confirmation of his own impression.

"It's the right one," the first officer told him, after a doubtful hesitation.

"Throttle it back!" ordered the captain.

Disengaging the autothrottle, the first officer reduced power on the No 2 engine to idle thrust. This seemed to reduce both the smell and the smoke, and the captain thought the vibration had gone too. The first officer then called London Air Traffic Control to report they had an emergency which "looked like an engine fire," after which Captain Hunt ordered him to "shut it down".

Before the first officer could do so however, Hunt amended this instruction: "Seems to be running all right now," he commented. "Let's see if it comes in."

London ATC then called to confirm the aircraft's position on radar, and asked to which airfield the crew intended to divert. The first officer replied that it looked as if they "would take it to Castle Donington." East Midlands Airport at Castle Donington was the maintenance base for British Midland Airways and, at this point, was only a few minutes' flying time away.

As the first officer began the Engine Failure and Shutdown checklist for the No 2 engine, he commented: "Seems to have stabilised ... but we've still got the smoke."

Diversion to East Midlands

While the captain called the company base at East Midlands Airport to report their situation, the first officer continued with the shutdown procedure for the No 2 engine and started the aircraft's Auxiliary Power Unit (APU). The company base confirmed that the aircraft should indeed divert to East Midlands Airport, and the crew then called London ATC again to request descent. The London controller cleared the aircraft to turn right and descend to FL100, and instructed the crew to call Manchester ATC for onward clearance.

After reducing power on the No 1 engine for the descent, the captain, sensing that the smoke and smell seemed to have cleared, was satisfied the action they had taken in shutting down the No 2 engine was correct, that the emergency was over, and that the short diversion to East Midlands Airport, flying on the No 1 engine only, would pose no problem.

Captain Hunt therefore called the Flight Service Manager (FSM) to the flightdeck to appraise him of the situation.

"Did you get smoke in the cabin?" the captain asked him when he arrived.

"We did, yes," the FSM told him. "We'd just served the passengers their meal when it started."

"Pack everything away and clear the cabin for landing," the captain now told him. "We're going into Castle Donington – be landing there in just a few minutes."

Back in the brightly lit cabin, there were many passengers who did not share the captain's calm. Having heard the noise "like a car backfiring", accompanied by the vibration and "shuddering" of the whole aircraft, having seen the smoke entering the cabin, and smelt "burning" which seemed like "rubber", "oil", or "hot metal", they were understandably perturbed, especially as the aircraft was now descending steeply in the dark and they had no idea of what was happening. Those in the rear section of the cabin who had seen signs of fire coming from the No 1 engine were even more concerned. The abruptness with which the cabin crew had then begun whipping away their meal trays – before some people had even started eating – did nothing to ease their anxiety.

Less than a minute later the FSM returned to the flightdeck to speak

A typical British Midland Airways Boeing 737: G-OBMB [23832] was the airline's second 737-300, its -33A designation identifying it as an Ansett Worldwide order. After a decade of pure-jet experience with DC-9s, BMA opted for later generations of the Boeing 737, with deliveries commencing at the end of 1987. Currently operating a mix of -300s (5), -400s (6, excluding G-OBME), and -500s (14), BMA has all its 737s on long leases. The fleet also includes a dozen DC-9s and a few Fokker 70s and 100s. British Midland's livery, 10 years old in October 1995, features blue upper and grey lower surfaces, with white titles and the fiery orange "BM" logo topped by a diamond in white or silver. (with acknowledgement to Richard Vandervord/ADC)

to the captain again. "Sorry to trouble you," he began diffidently, "but some of the passengers are very panicky."

Captain Hunt immediately responded to the FSM's report by making an announcement to the passengers. There was trouble with the right engine which had produced some smoke in the cabin, he explained over the PA system. But it was now shut down and they could expect to land at East Midlands Airport in about 10 minutes.

Numbers of passengers in the rear cabin who had actually seen the sparks and flames being emitted by the engine on the left hand side were puzzled by the captain's reference to the right engine. But the captain's tone was authoritative and reassuring, and no one felt sufficiently sure of themselves to mention the apparent discrepancy to any of the cabin crew. Unfortunately too, none of the three cabin crew who had also seen the symptoms of fire apparently assimilated the captain's words. By this time also, although some passengers were conscious that the aircraft was still vibrating excessively, the smoke and smell of burning had dissipated.

With the aircraft now only a few nautical miles south of East Midlands Airport, Manchester ATC provided the crew with radar vectors to descend to the north of the airport and to intercept the localiser of the ILS for Runway 27.

Throughout this descent the captain flew the aircraft manually while the first officer handled the numerous radio communications. The workload on the flightdeck remained high as the latter obtained details of the East Midlands weather and attempted to program the Flight Management System (FMS) computer to display the landing pattern at the airport. The weather observations passed to the aircraft were: wind 250°/10 knots; visibility 10km; cloud 7 oktas, base 1,700 feet; temperature 9°C; QNH 1018.

During a break in the numerous radio exchanges as the descent continued, the captain began to verbally review the crew's handling of the emergency. "Now – what indications did we actually get?" he said to the first officer, "... rapid vibrations in the aeroplane ... smoke ..."

At this moment he was interrupted by an ATC transmission passing a new radar heading, a further descent clearance to FL40 (4000 feet), and instructions to change frequency to East Midlands Approach Control. As soon as the first officer established contact on the new frequency, he began reading aloud the One Engine

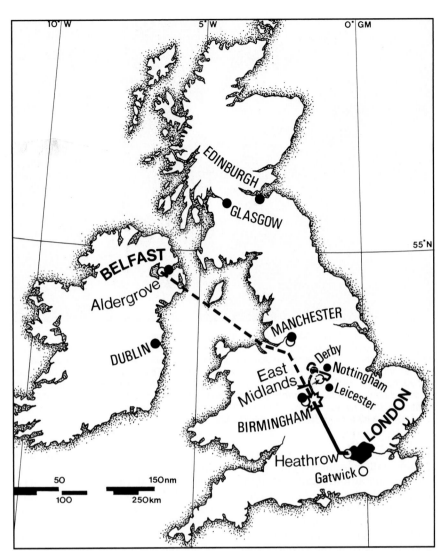

Map of the British Isles showing Flight BD092's route from London-Heathrow to Belfast-Aldergrove, skirting the Manchester Control Area and crossing the Irish Sea on Airway Blue/Bravo 3. British Midland took over the London/Belfast route with Vickers Viscounts on October 31, 1974, initially operating from Gatwick, after British Caledonian withdrew its service. The block time of 90 minutes was reduced to 55 three years later when DC-9s replaced the Viscounts. (Matthew Tesch)

Inoperative Descent and the Approach checklists.

These in turn were interrupted when Approach Control requested the crew to make a test call to the airport fire service, and the Approach checklist was only completed when the aircraft was 15nm from touchdown, descending through 6500 feet. A minute later the captain accepted a new vector of 220 degrees to take the aircraft south of the extended runway centreline and increase its distance from touchdown.

When 13nm from touchdown, it was vectored back towards the runway centreline and the crew increased power on No 1 engine to maintain height at 3000 feet. The aircraft was then cleared down to 2000 feet and the captain began a slow descent, calling successively for increased increments of flap. After intercepting the runway localiser at 2000 feet above ground level (AGL),

the captain requested the undercarriage be lowered and, as they passed the outer marker 4.3nm from touchdown with the runway lights in sight, he called for 15 degrees of flap.

All power lost!

A minute later, when only 2.4nm from touchdown at a height of 900 feet AGL, the No 1 engine abruptly lost all power.

The captain at once instructed the first officer to relight the No 2 engine, and raised the aircraft's nose in an attempt to stretch the glide to reach the runway threshold. Seventeen seconds later the fire warning for the No 1 engine began sounding, followed by the Ground Proximity Warning. Accepting the inevitable, the captain called urgently to the passengers and cabin crew over the PA system: "Prepare for crash landing! Prepare for crash landing!"

Two seconds later, as the airspeed

For the crew of G-OBME, the airline's operational base at East Midlands (Castle Donington) Airport was the obvious place to which to divert when the engine problem developed over the densely urbanised Midlands on January 8, 1989. This earlier view shows the company's engineering and maintenance base on the western side of East Midlands Airport, with four Viscounts, three BAC-111s, an Argosy and a Vanguard on the apron. BMA's ancestry can be traced back to 1938, its direct corporate lineage beginning with the formation of Derby Aviation (later Airways) in 1953. The all-737 holiday charter operator Orion Airways later joined BMA with a major base at East Midlands.

fell below 125 knots, the stick shaker stall warning began operating, and the aircraft sank heavily to the ground in a nose-high attitude 1030m short of the runway threshold.

The initial impact, on the edge of a field immediately short of the M1 motorway skirting the airport's eastern boundary close to the village of Kegworth, was heavy enough to sheer off both main undercarriage legs and the fuselage tail skid. Still travelling at more than 100 knots, the aircraft continued through the motorway's wooden fence, cut a swathe through trees on its sloping eastern embankment, passed over its eastern lanes, demolishing a lamp standard in the centre strip as it did so, and crashed into the motorway's western embankment. This final major impact fractured the fuselage severely in two places, the tail section jack-knifing over the centre section and coming to rest almost upside down.

Airport fire service crews waiting in position by the runway were watching the lights of the aircraft as it approached. Seeing it descend below the motorway embankment, they set off at high speed to the accident site via the runway and the airport's eastern crash gate. Arriving only five minutes later, they immediately extinguished the fire in No 1 engine which had grown in intensity, and laid a blanket of foam as a fire protection against leaking fuel.

They were quickly joined by units from the Leicestershire, Nottinghamshire and Derbyshire fire services. Ambulances from the same counties followed the fire vehicles to the scene and, assisted initially by passing motorists, their crews set about recovering the survivors from the wreckage and moving them to hospital. RAF helicopters were subsequently called in to uplift some of the more seriously injured.

In the darkness and confusion of the wreckage, the task proved to be enormous. With the cabin flooring completely disrupted in the forward section of the cabin, many of the passenger seats had broken free and compressed forward, trapping and squashing their occupants. In other parts of the cabin, passengers were trapped by fallen overhead lockers, and cabin partitions. In many cases, metal cutting equipment had to be used to reach and free the victims. Despite the fact that a total of 74 ambulances attended the scene, assisted by personnel from the Army, the RAF and the Derbyshire Miners' Rescue Team, it was eight hours before the last victim could be extricated.

Thirty nine passengers were found to have been killed in the impact. Sixty seven passengers and seven crew members, including the two pilots, were seriously injured. Only four passengers and one flight attendant escaped with minor injuries. Eight of the seriously injured passengers subsequently died in hospital.

INVESTIGATION

A team of eight experienced investigators from the Air Accidents Investigation Branch of the UK Department of Transport reached the site of the accident not long after midnight, while survivors and the dead were still being recovered from the wreckage. Three of them had just returned from the investigation of the Boeing 747 disaster at Lockerbie in Scotland which had occurred less than three weeks previously.

The investigation established that the approach to East Midlands Airport's Runway 27, the elevation of which is only 280 feet AMSL, lay over level farming country, passing above the village of Kegworth and then the M1 motorway 1500 metres from touchdown. Runway 27 had an available landing distance of 2280

Plan of East Midlands Airport: Popularly referred to as "EMA", it was actually assigned the designation "CDD" (Castle Donington, Derby). Originally an RAF Station and an Operational Conversion Unit for Wellington bomber crews during WW2, it was taken over by a consortium of city and county councils triangulated by Derby, Nottingham and Leicester. With a new runway and purpose-built civil facilities, it was opened on April 2, 1965. Part of BMA's original business, operating from Derby's previous grass airfield at Burnaston, was the transport of Rolls-Royce Avon engines, fresh from the nearby RR works at Derby, to the Caravelle assembly line at Toulouse in France. (Matthew Tesch)

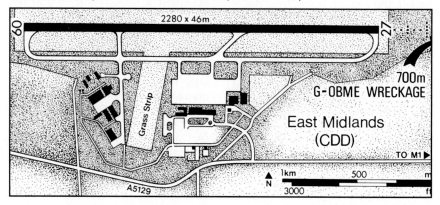

metres and was equipped with high intensity approach lighting extending for 900 metres from the threshold. Precision approach path indicators were installed for a three degree glideslope. All lights were illuminated at the time of the accident.

Impact

The Boeing 737's first ground contact was made by the tail skid and rear fuselage on slightly upsloping ground only 29 metres short of the motorway's eastern embankment boundary fence, with the aircraft in a 13 degree nose up attitude. The aircraft's groundspeed at the time was calculated at between 104 and 111 knots, with a descent rate of between 8.5 and 16 feet per second. Almost simultaneously, the main undercarriage struck the ground less than 15 metres from the motorway fence.

The initial impact was severe enough to tear off the tail skid and the APU door, while drag loads imposed by the soft ground immedi-

(below) Aerial perspective of G-OBME's flightpath, taken from the official investigation report. The plot begins (lower right), with the Boeing 737 climbing northwest through FL280. The subsequent orbit and meandering track reflect the flightdeck workload. The captain had disengaged the autopilot and was hand flying the aircraft, the first officer was occupied for some minutes attempting to reprogram the diversion to East Midlands Airport into the FMS computer, and radio communications were constant as the crew dealt with vectors, procedural calls and handoffs. In addition, the close proximity of the aircraft to East Midlands entailed losing nearly 30,000 feet over a very short time and distance. (UK DoT/AAIB)

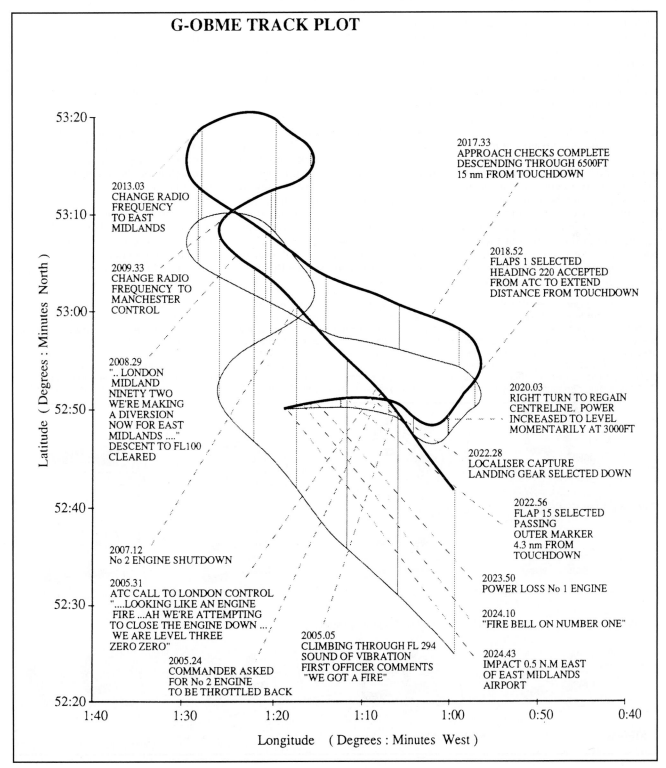

G-OBME TRACK PLOT

2017.33
APPROACH CHECKS COMPLETE
DESCENDING THROUGH 6500FT
15 nm FROM TOUCHDOWN

2013.03
CHANGE RADIO
FREQUENCY
TO EAST
MIDLANDS

2018.52
FLAPS 1 SELECTED
HEADING 220 ACCEPTED
FROM ATC TO EXTEND
DISTANCE FROM TOUCHDOWN

2009.33
CHANGE RADIO
FREQUENCY TO
MANCHESTER
CONTROL

2008.29
".. LONDON
MIDLAND
NINETY TWO
WE'RE MAKING
A DIVERSION
NOW FOR EAST
MIDLANDS ...."
DESCENT TO FL100
CLEARED

2020.03
RIGHT TURN TO REGAIN
CENTRELINE. POWER
INCREASED TO LEVEL
MOMENTARILY AT 3000FT

2022.28
LOCALISER CAPTURE
LANDING GEAR SELECTED DOWN

2022.56
FLAP 15 SELECTED
PASSING
OUTER MARKER
4.3 nm FROM
TOUCHDOWN

2007.12
No 2 ENGINE SHUTDOWN

2005.31
ATC CALL TO LONDON CONTROL
"....LOOKING LIKE AN ENGINE
FIRE ...AH WE'RE ATTEMPTING
TO CLOSE THE ENGINE DOWN ...
WE ARE LEVEL THREE
ZERO ZERO"

2023.50
POWER LOSS No 1 ENGINE

2024.10
"FIRE BELL ON NUMBER ONE"

2005.24
COMMANDER ASKED
FOR No 2 ENGINE
TO BE THROTTLED BACK

2005.05
CLIMBING THROUGH FL 294
SOUND OF VIBRATION
FIRST OFFICER COMMENTS
"WE GOT A FIRE"

2024.43
IMPACT 0.5 N.M EAST
OF EAST MIDLANDS
AIRPORT

Latitude (Degrees : Minutes North)

53:20
53:10
53:00
52:50
52:40
52:30
52:20

1:40   1:30   1:20   1:10   1:00   0:50   0:40

Longitude   (Degrees : Minutes West)

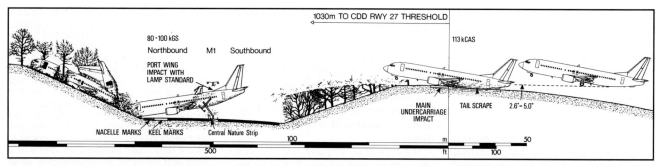

North-facing sectional view of the Boeing 737's impact sequence. The first impact, on rising ground just short of the eastern embankment of the M1 motorway, was relatively gentle and went almost unnoticed by those seated towards the front of the aircraft. But the blunt nose-dive into the lower western embankment slope imposed severe deceleration forces, resulting in the worst head, limb and torso injuries as the cabin floor structure collapsed and passenger seats broke free. (UK DoT/AAIB)

ately failed both main undercarriage legs rearwards, but at this stage the airframe remained otherwise intact. Debris left behind as the aircraft continued through the tops of the trees on the motorway's sloping eastern embankment was almost entirely from the wing leading edges and engine cowlings.

As momentum carried the aircraft above and across the motorway itself, the port wing tip struck a lamp standard in the centre nature strip, fracturing it at its base and removing the outboard two metres of the wing.

Finally impacting with great force against the lower portion of the motorway's western embankment, the entire aircraft structure was violently deflected up the sloping ground. This major impact wrenched off the nose leg, crushed the underside of the nose, and tore out the fuselage belly skin over the entire length of the passenger cabin. With the lower fuselage structure thus disrupted, the forward fuselage broke off from the centre section and, as the wings sliced through trees on the western embankment, deceleration forces jack-knifed the tail section over and to the right of the centre section where it came to rest nearly upside down. The centre section, though extensively damaged by contact with trees, remained intact with the wings still attached. Although inverted, the tail section sustained less damage than the other fuselage sections.

Wreckage

Both engines remained partially attached to their pylons, which in turn were still partially attached to the wings. But both nacelles were severely crushed and much of their forward sections had been torn away. Both engines had sustained extensive impact damage, with their forward sections clogged with earth and tree debris. A more detailed examination of the engines, however, revealed major differences in their internal condition.

The fan blades of the No 1 engine had been severely damaged by hard object ingestion and a large number of blade fragments were found lying forward of the fan disk. Other blade fragments were found along the

Because it was one of the first accidents involving an aircraft fitted with seats meeting the US FAA's new "16g force" requirements, the crash of G-OBME prompted even more industry interest than usual. Unfortunately, as with many survivable crashes, the seat designs held up better than their floor attachments. The fact that much of the cabin floor collapsed when the fuselage fractured in two places rendered the seat integrity almost inconsequential, most catastrophically in the crushed forward section. Moreover, far from providing any clear assessment of seat crashworthiness, the accident drew attention to the structural shortcomings of the cabin's overhead stowage bins, most of which collapsed on top of the already injured passengers. Computer simulations of the crash forces developed in the accident also highlighted the dangers of single lap-strap restraint in forward facing seats. This sequence of drawings takes a half-second "slice" from G-OBME's major impact, to show the likely effects at 50 millisecond intervals. (Matthew Tesch, with acknowledgement to UK DoT/AAIB)

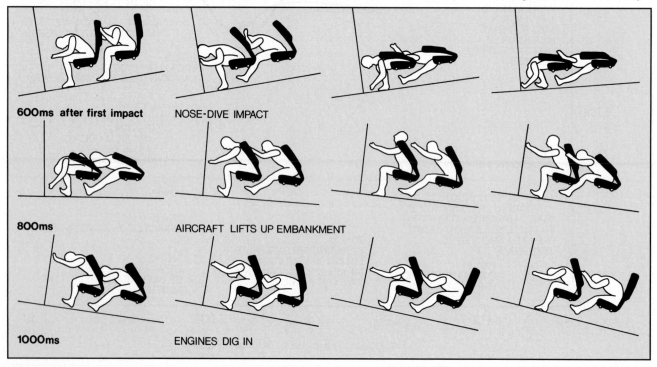

600ms after first impact

NOSE-DIVE IMPACT

800ms

AIRCRAFT LIFTS UP EMBANKMENT

1000ms

ENGINES DIG IN

wreckage trail, and several small pieces were even recovered from a farm piggery under the final flight path some three kilometres short of the crash site. The engine had also suffered severe external fire damage, the fire having emanated from the fuel system in the base of the engine fan case, the unions of which had apparently been loosened by vibration.

By contrast, the No 2 engine exhibited ground impact damage only, with no evidence whatever of fire. There were also clear indications that the engine had not been running when the aircraft struck the ground.

Recorders

Both the Flight Data Recorder (FDR) and the Cockpit Voice Recorder (CVR) were recovered in good condition and together enabled the events leading up to the accident to be reconstructed with a high degree of accuracy.

The first sign of any problem had occurred 13 minutes after takeoff while the aircraft was climbing through FL283. At the time the crew experienced vibration and a smell of burning, the CVR picked up a "rattling" sound and the FDR showed fluctuations in lateral and longitudinal accelerations. The FDR also showed that severe vibration had occurred in the No 1 engine, accompanied by marked fluctuations in fan speed (N_1), a rise in exhaust gas temperature (EGT) and low, fluctuating fuel flow.

When asked by the captain which engine was causing the trouble, the first officer had actually said: "It's the le- ... it's the right one."

"OK – throttle it back," the captain had responded. At this time, all the No 2 (right) engine's indications were steady.

But within two seconds of the closure of the No 2 power lever, the fluctuations in lateral and longitudinal accelerations ceased, the No 1 engine fan speed settled at 3% below its previous stable speed, and its EGT stabilised at 50°C above its pre-

vious level. These engine parameters remained fairly stable for a further minute until the engine's power was reduced for descent, but the indicated vibration remained at maximum and the fuel flow continued to be erratic.

The captain's order to shut down the No 2 engine came 43 seconds after the onset of the vibration, but its execution was delayed when he added: "Seems to be running all right now. Let's just see if it comes in."

After further radio traffic concerning the aircraft's diversion to East Midlands Airport and a flight attendant's instruction to passengers over the cabin address system to fasten their seatbelts, the first officer told the captain he was about to start the "Engine Failure and Shutdown" checklist, adding: "Seems we have stabilised ... we've still got the smoke." The fuel cock for the No 2 engine was closed and the APU started two minutes and seven seconds after the initial onset of the vibration.

View of the wreckage of the Boeing 737, looking west from the southbound lanes of the M1 motorway. Note the missing 2m section of the outboard port wing (left, behind fire tender) and the groundscrape marks from the first impact on the belly of the near-inverted rear fuselage. The compressive crushing of the fuselage during the second impact is evident at both ends of the midships section. The inertia of the nose section carried it further up the embankment as the engines dug into the ground and the tail section broke away.

At 8.12:28pm, almost seven and a half minutes after the onset of the engine trouble, the captain attempted to review their situation during a break in radio traffic. "Now – what indications did we actually get?" he began to the first officer. "Just rapid vibrations in the aeroplane ... smoke ..." He was interrupted by further radio transmissions, and the first officer then began the One Engine Descent and Approach check list which was completed at 8.17:33pm. Shortly afterwards the captain called for one degree flaps.

At 8.20:03pm, after the aircraft had been given its final vector to intercept the runway centreline, power was increased on the No 1 engine to level the aircraft briefly at 3000 feet. As this occurred, maximum vibration was again recorded on the FDR. The aircraft was then cleared down to 2000 feet and the captain called successively for two degrees, then five degrees of flap and, on descending to 2000 feet, for the undercarriage to be extended.

At 8.23:49pm, with 15 degrees of flap now lowered and the aircraft 2.4 nautical miles from touchdown at a height of 900 feet, there was a crackling noise on the CVR, possibly the result of electrical interference as the No 1 engine lost power. Immediately afterwards the first officer made a transmission to East Midlands tower indicating they were having trouble with the second engine as well. The captain told him urgently: "Try lighting the other one up – there's nothing else you can do."

Seventeen seconds after the loss of power, the No 1 engine fire warning bell sounded and the first officer asked if he should shut the engine down. The captain replied in the negative, indicating his intention to try to "stretch the glide". Seven seconds later again the ground proximity warning sounded and continued with increasing frequency as the aircraft sank below the glidepath. Again the captain called desperately: "Try opening the other one up!" but the first officer replied: "She's not going!"

A minute after the loss of power and 10 seconds before impact, the captain called over the cabin public address system: "Prepare for crash landing! Prepare for crash landing!" The stall warning stick shaker then began to operate as the airspeed fell below 125 knots, and sounds of impact began as the CVR ceased recording at 8.24:43pm.

Engine examination

Both engines, complete with their remaining cowlings and pylons, were removed from the wings and taken first to the BMA company base, then airfreighted to the manufacturer's facility at the SNECMA works in France for detailed examination.

All the damage to the No 2 engine was found to be the result of ground impact, with no evidence of any external fire. Apart from this damage, the internal condition of the engine was consistent with that of a fully serviceable low time engine which

So near, yet so far – and rarely was a cliche so apt. This low-level aerial view of the crash site, taken from short final leg to East Midlands' Runway 27, emphasises the pitifully slender margin between life, injury and death that existed for those aboard G-OBME. Had the No 1 engine finally expired but two seconds earlier or later, the aircraft would have touched down on open ground, avoiding the motorway cutting which wrought such havoc. As it was, the M1 remained closed for four days before investigators completed their onsite work and the debris could be cleared. In the foreground is the cordon surrounding the initial impact marks made by the aircraft's tail skid and main undercarriage. (UK DoT/AAIB)

had little or no rotational energy at impact.

The No 1 engine on the other hand, showed evidence of severe damage both internally and externally. All fan blades had suffered considerable hard object damage, only nine of the 38 retaining their full length. Although there was only slight evidence of hard object ingestion within the booster section, all stages of the core compressor exhibited some hard object damage. Throughout the engine, there was also evidence of severe, circumferentially uniform, rubbing of blades on their tip paths and rotating seals.

There was considerable sooting of the engine core, centred around a damaged combustion nozzle attachment. Sooting was also found on the inside of the high pressure compressor case and inside the low pressure shaft. Most of the external fire damage was towards the rear of the fan case. It appeared to have entered the inside through a split in the fan case-to-frame joint caused by crushing. There was no evidence that this fire had been driven by a fierce airstream – in other words it had occurred *after* impact.

The fracture surfaces of all the fan blade failures were examined metallurgically and, with the exception of blade No 17, were found to be overload failures. The failure of the Number 17 blade exhibited several features consistent with fatigue and, after cleaning, it was examined both optically and with an electron microscope. The characteristics of the fracture were those of a high cycle fatigue failure which had evidently originated on the pressure face of the blade, 1.0 to 1.5mm from the leading edge.

Misidentification

At this stage of the investigation, it was obvious that the explanation for the accident was in essence very simple – an engine failed, the crew misidentified which of the engines was at fault, and mistakenly shut down the wrong one – precisely the sort of error that had plagued the propeller driven, piston engined era of aviation from the time that twin-engined aircraft first became capable of flight with one engine inoperative.

When these facts became known throughout the aviation industry worldwide, there was enormous controversy and concern as to how such a basic, long recognised error could have been committed by the highly trained, experienced crew of the latest version of a proven jet design, fitted with the latest in new technology flightdeck instrumentation.

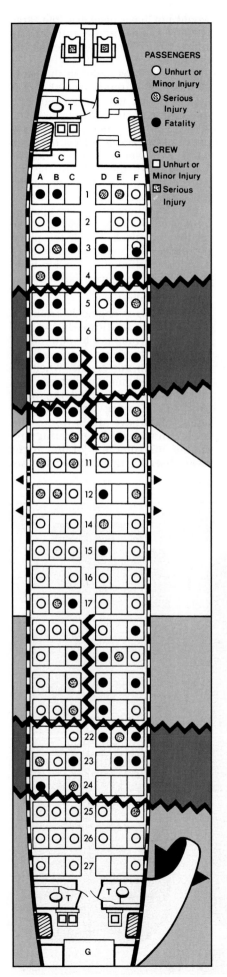

Amid all the speculation as to how such a disastrous mistake could have been made, there were even suggestions that the aircraft's engine instrumentation wiring had somehow been reversed during manufacture.

An extremely detailed investigation was therefore made of all the factors which could possibly have contributed to the misidentification.

Why?

Detailed examination and testing of the aircraft's controls, instrumentation, and electrical systems established that both sets of main engine controls, and the primary and secondary EIS, together with their associated wiring, were all functioning as designed at the time of impact and were correctly displaying input information.

The captain, who had been flying since 1964 and logged over 13,000 hours, had undergone conversion training on Boeing 737-300 aircraft 13 months before the accident. The first officer had done so seven months before the accident. Both had then done a further one day course on the Boeing 737-400 when the type was introduced to the company three months before the accident. This included an introduction to the Boeing 737-400's solid-state EIS. At this time however, no flight simulator equipped with EIS was available to company pilots. At the time of the accident the captain had flown 23 hours on Series 400 aircraft and the first officer 53 hours.

Although the Boeing Company had issued an Operations Manual Bulletin on CFM56-3 engine vibration, recommending a reduction of power when the aircraft's vibration indicators read in excess of four units, this had not been available at the time of the captain's 737 conver-

Interior plan of the aircraft, showing the pattern of fatalities and survivor injuries. All but six of the fatalities occurred at the two fuselage breaks, most of them in the crushed and collapsed forward cabin. Perhaps the most poignant death was that of the young mother in seat 3F, whose body protected her injured infant – a finding which added to calls for greater efforts to improve crash restraint for all passengers. As confirmed by the computer simulations, most survivors suffered pelvic fractures from lap-straps, the deceleration forces bending bodies around these single-point harnesses so that heads, hands, knees and feet impacted the seat or bulkhead in front of them. Significantly, the three cabin crew and 13 passengers seated furthest aft escaped with the least injuries, despite "riding" the rear fuselage through its vertical pivoting and inverted impact. (Matthew Tesch, with acknowledgement to UK DoT/AAIB)

sion training. However, pending an amendment to British Midland Airways' operations manual, the bulletin had subsequently been issued to all 737 pilots employed by the company. It stipulated that an engine shutdown was not required as vibration levels would decrease as the power lever was retarded.

Questioned after the accident, neither pilots could remember seeing indications of high vibration on the EIS. The captain added that he rarely included vibration monitors in his instrument scan because he believed them to be unreliable. The investigation established that, while earlier types of vibration meter fitted to turbojet aircraft had a history of unreliability, later types such as that fitted to the 737-400 were more reliable and displayed only signals related to the rotating assemblies of the engines.

ANALYSIS

When the flightcrew heard the unusual noise, accompanied by vibration, as the aircraft was on climb to cruising level, neither captain nor first officer apparently assimilated any clear indication of malfunction from the engine instruments. Yet there was no reason why these would not have displayed the large variations in engine indications which the FDR revealed occurred at this time.

The noise was heard in the cabin as a series of thuds, and the FDR indicated this was associated with the stalling of the No 1 engine's fan, with attendant surging of the compressor. The accelerations recorded on the FDR were consistent with the shuddering of the walls of the forward galley reported by one of the flight attendants.

The symptoms were accompanied by a smell of fire and visible smoke on the flightdeck, which the pilots obviously interpreted as evidence of a serious malfunction, leading them to act quickly to contain the condition.

Instrument indications

Yet the No 2 engine instruments showed no variations during this time, and it could not be determined why the first officer concluded the fault lay with this engine. When the captain asked him which engine was at fault, he half-formed the word "left" before saying "right". His hesitation might have arisen from genuine difficulty in interpreting the engine instruments, or he might have observed them during the six seconds of relative stability between the second and third engine surges.

The captain told investigators that the instruments gave him no clear indication of where the trouble lay. Having disengaged the autopilot only seconds after the first engine surge however, his attention at this point would have been primarily on the handling of the aircraft and the flight instruments. His knowledge of the aircraft's air conditioning system had led him to believe the fault lay with the No 2 engine – smoke and fumes were coming from the passenger cabin and, as he understood bleed air for the cabin came mostly from the No 2 engine, the trouble lay with that engine. While this reasoning might apply to other types of aircraft the captain had flown, it did not do so in this case. In Boeing 737-400 aircraft, some of the bleed air for the cabin in fact comes from the No 1 engine.

Because both pilots reacted to the emergency before they had any positive evidence as to which engine was abnormal, the investigators concluded that their incorrect diagnosis was attributable to their hasty action and not to any failure of the EIS.

There then occurred an event that led both pilots into the fatal misconception that the action they had taken in haste was correct. As soon as the No 2 power lever was retarded, the symptoms of engine malfunction appeared to cease. Certainly the compressor surging and associated shuddering ceased at this time, though the FDR showed the high vibration level did not. The smell of burning seems not to have intensified and, having failed to see the continuing maximum reading on the vibration indicator or the fluctuating fuel flow for the No 1 engine, both pilots became convinced that closing the No 2 power lever had dealt with the problem.

Unlike the fluctuations that would have appeared on the primary en-

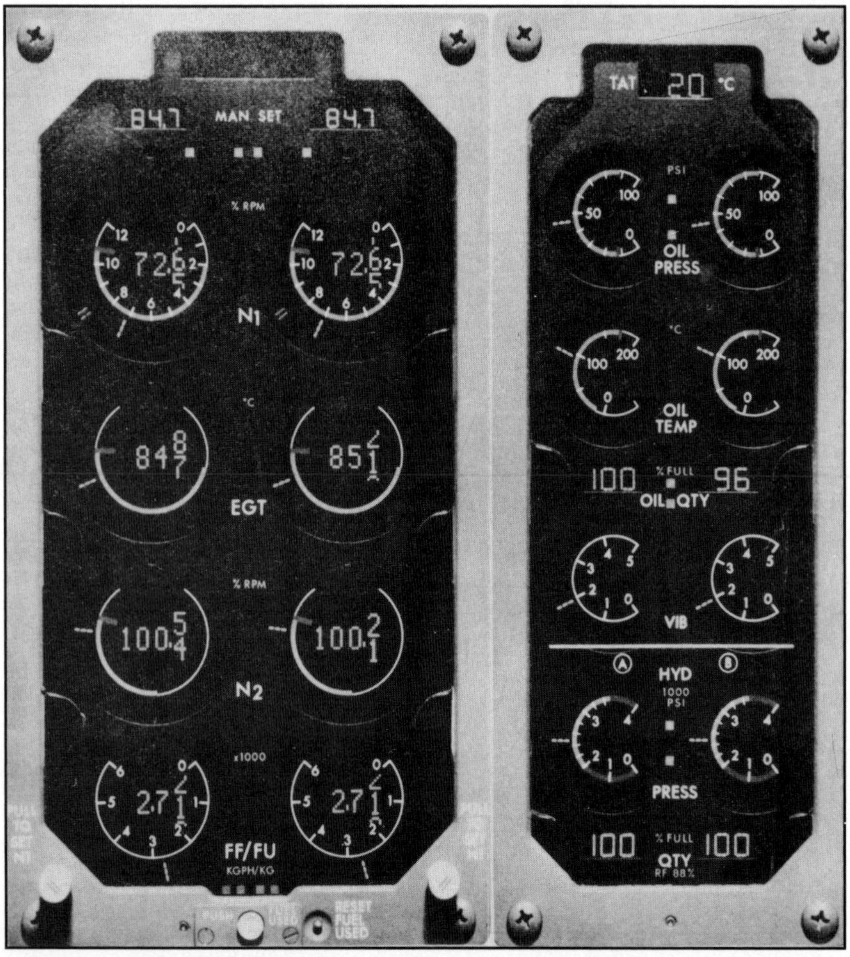

(left) Some idea of the possibility of engine instrument misinterpretation may be gained from a glance at this picture of the "hybrid" instrument layout identical to that on G-OBME's flightdeck. On the left, the primary display indicators are large, well spaced-out, and the red, orange, yellow, green and white colours make for an efficient scan. On the right, however, the secondary display (immediately adjacent, as depicted here) compresses a near-identical amount of information into just over half the area. Not only are the engine vibration "dials" (right, third pair from top) the most simplistic and devoid of colour coding – their electronic three-dash external "pointers" are almost lost against the overall background. (UK DoT/AAIB)

gine instruments, the reading of the No 1 engine vibration indicator rose to maximum when the surging began and remained there for no less than three minutes. Whether or not the crew would have noticed such an abnormal reading on a conventional electromechanical instrument is a matter for conjecture, but undoubtedly it would have been more recognisable.

While the introduction of the EIS represented progress in terms of reliability and maintenance costs, the investigators believed it could be a retrograde step in information presentation. The most obvious difference between conventional electromechanical engine instruments and the EIS is that full-radius mechanical pointers have been replaced by short, light emitting diode pointers moving around the *outside* of their scales. Much less conspicuous than mechanical pointers, they are less able to give the comparative information provided by the strong cue of parallelism.

The vibration indicators' lack of conspicuity appeared to be a particular problem in the Boeing 737-400. Unlike the new technology "glass cockpits" of the Boeing 757 and 767, designed from the beginning with the aircraft themselves, and incorporating engine instrumentation in their CRT-monitored Alert and Status display selections, the Boeing 737-400's EIS presentation had been "evolved" from the older analogue engine instrument arrays fitted to earlier marques of the 737. To keep the EIS panel as much like the earlier electromechanical instrument layout as possible, the two vibration indicators remained as one of four pairs of dials on the secondary engine/hydraulic display, with no exceedence lights or other "attention getters".

The EIS had apparently been introduced without any thorough evaluation of its efficiency in imparting information. The circumstances of the accident emphasised how important it is for such evaluations to take place *before* new developments are introduced to service.

The problem was probably exacerbated in this case by the fact that both pilots were introduced to the EIS before a simulator equipped with this system was available to them. They thus had no opportunity to become familiar within the interpretation of engine problems using the new system. As a result, the first time they saw abnormal engine indications on the EIS was in flight – in an aircraft with a failing engine.

Fire?

Although the crew's initial misidentification of the damaged engine could be regarded as the beginning of the accident sequence, the captain's decision to throttle back the No 2 engine did not in itself lead directly to the accident. It is likely that, had the No 1 engine not ceased

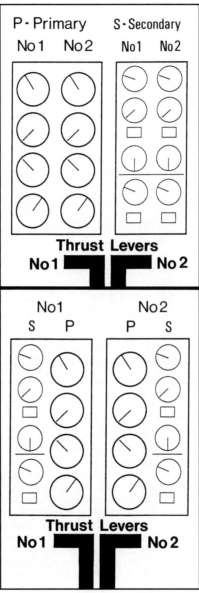

The ergonomic difficulties facing designers of today's flightdeck instrument panels are succinctly summarised in this pair of diagrams from the official investigation report. The top drawing reflects the 737-400's actual layout, the left-right format deferring to a primary-secondary arrangement. The lower drawing shows the option of deferring the "importance hierarchy" to a left-right presentation, keeping all indicators visually and spatially related to their respective power levers. The problem did not arise until sophisticated computerisation eliminated the role of the flight engineer, ushering in the advent of the two-crew flightdeck. Previously, all such "secondary" and systems information was laid out on the flight engineer's panels.

surging (probably as a result of the autothrottle being disconnected) at the same time as the No 2 power lever was closed, the accident would not have happened. Certainly, if the No 2 engine had not been shut down, the accident would not have happened. Some logical explanation had therefore to be sought for the captain's decision to shut it down.

This engine was operating normally but, because its power lever had been closed, the crew could no longer confirm its operation by comparing its indications with those of the No 1 engine. Even so, there was no evidence that the crew consulted the engine instruments or attempted any other analysis before shutting down the No 2 engine.

In the Boeing 737-400's "non-normal" checklists, severe vibration does not necessitate an engine shutdown, provided it is not accompanied by abnormal indications, nor does the presence of fumes or smoke in the cockpit. The crew thus did not comply with published procedures in shutting down the engine. Nor did they follow the more general instructions of the operations manual and their training, requiring them to evaluate all available evidence before taking such action.

However, when the first officer reported the emergency to London ATC, he said: "...at the moment it's looking like an engine fire." It seems likely therefore, that the captain's hasty action was prompted by the belief that the engine was on fire. The operations manual contained no guidance on action to be taken in the event of vibration and smoke or fumes occurring together. Because severe fan shaft vibration usually damages the fan and low pressure compressor abradable seals, and fumes can enter the cabin from these sources as a result, it would have been prudent for the aircraft manufacturer to have included a checklist for such a contingency.

Workload

From the start of the emergency descent, the flightdeck workload remained high. Doubtless this high workload contributed to the crew's failure to notice the abnormal reading on the No 1 engine vibration indicator that was registering for nearly four minutes after the onset of the vibration.

But by the time the captain began reviewing what had happened, some seven minutes after shutting down the No 2 engine, the high reading on the No 1 engine vibration indicator had subsided and there was no other indication of damage to the No 1 engine. And when his review was interrupted by a further radio transmission, he did not resume it, probably because he was confident of the aircraft's safety at this point.

Shortly afterwards, when power was increased on the No 1 engine, it again registered high vibration, which also went unnoticed. At this point in the descent the No 2 engine could still have been restarted but, by the time the No 1 engine lost all power four minutes later, an accident of some sort had become inevitable. Although the first officer attempted to restart the No 2 engine when this occurred, the airspeed was by this time too low for a "windmill" start.

The need to know

It is extremely unfortunate that the observations of the passengers and cabin crew who actually saw evidence of fire in the No 1 engine were not conveyed to the flightcrew after the captain announced on the PA system that he had shut down the "right" engine.

Cabin crew well know that intrusions during busy phases of flight are unwelcome and can be distracting for pilots, especially during an emergency – evident in this case from the fact that the flight service manager made no attempt to enter the flightdeck until called. But the fact remains that, if those who had seen the evidence of distress in the No 1 engine had taken action to tell the pilots, the accident could have been prevented.

The circumstances of the accident were such that the pilots were suddenly confronted with an unseen combination of symptoms beyond their training or experience. Although it could be argued that such a combination of circumstances could hardly have been anticipated, the tragic outcome raised questions concerning the level of technical training available to pilots of modern aircraft. It also illustrated the point that such training should include an appreciation of systems response under abnormal conditions, *particularly those where symptoms have the potential to mislead in the stress of an inflight emergency.*

Lessons for the future

But at least the tragic lesson of East Midlands Airport was not to be lost on the aviation industry.

Precisely five months later, on June 9, 1989, the crew of Boeing 737-400 G-BNNL, operated by the British independent airline Dan-Air,

G-OBME No 17 FAN BLADE

10cm (4 in)

Failure here

Mid-span shroud

OIL TANK   GEARBOX ACCESSORIES

BOEING 737-300/400/500 CFM56

INTAKE 146cm   FAN SECTION   CORE ENGINE   WING

45.7cm

GROUND

The CFM56 engine, jointly produced by SNECMA of France and General Electric in the USA, was a derivative of the latter's well-established CF6 high-bypass turbofan. In its original form, the CFM56 was adopted by the USAF in a fleetwide re-engining program for its K/C-135/137 (B707) tankers and transports. It was then scaled-down specifically for Boeing's 737 family from the -300 series on. Certificated using mathematically-derived – rather than tested – data from background experience, the CFM56-3B/C versions, with higher-rated thrusts for the stretched 737-400, were only just starting to generate in-service occurrence reports when the East Midlands accident occurred. Abrasion of the contact surfaces of the fan blades' mid-span shrouds was found to have induced a pressure fatigue failure of the No 17 blade in G-OBME's No 1 engine. Two similar British incidents five months after the BMA crash showed that the resultant out-of-balance condition of the fan caused frictional contact with the fan casing's abradable lining – leading to heat, smell and smoke, but not necessarily to disaster. (Matthew Tesch, with acknowledgement to Flight International)

also fitted with CFM56-3C engines, suddenly experienced violent vibration and smoke in the cabin while climbing at rated power through FL250 over the English Channel. This time the crew's instrument scan flew immediately to the vibration indicators and No 1 engine was identified as the source of the problem. It was promptly shut down and the flight subsequently made a safe landing on the No 2 engine without further incident. As before, the problem was found to be a fan blade fatigue failure.

Only two days later again, in an extraordinary repetition of circumstances, another British Midland Airways Boeing 737-400, G-OBMG, also operating a London/Belfast service, suffered yet another fan blade fatigue failure while climbing at rated power through FL290, with similar symptoms manifesting themselves. Again the crew knew at once what to look for, correctly identified the ailing engine, shut it down, and landed safely.

Immediately following this third fan blade failure, the engine manufacturer, CFM International, a company owned jointly by SNECMA in France and General Electric in the USA, contacted all operators of the CFM56-3C-1 engine, urging inspections of all fan blades for signs of fatigue cracking and, pending further investigation, strongly recommending engine power be restricted to ratings applicable to the earlier CFM56-3B-2 engine.

Extensive inflight testing by the manufacturer, using a Boeing 707 "flying test bed", subsequently revealed that a previously undetected vibration mode developed in the fan of the CFM56-3C-1 engine while using rated climb power above 10,000 feet. The condition was most severe at altitudes between 25,000 and 30,000 feet and could, in some circumstances, stress individual blades above their design endurance limit.

During further exhaustive testing and research, it was found that the coefficient of friction of the fan's mid-span shroud contact faces affected the vibratory response of the fan, the vibration mode being aggravated as the contact faces become more highly polished with use.

The problem was finally overcome by redesigning the contact angle of the fan's mid-span shrouds, thereby changing the damping characteristics of the outer portion of the fan blades. The engine was then re-certificated at its CFM56-3C-1 design rating.

The tragedy's other lessons for the

future, not only for Boeing 737 and CFM56 operators, but for all involved in the air transport industry, would of necessity take longer in their application.

The crashworthiness of passenger seats, attachments, floor support structure, cabin fittings and individual passenger restraints, shown to be so inadequate in this "survivable" accident, remains a continuing problem.

In the first impact, the Boeing 737's undercarriage broke away without disrupting the integrity of the wings or their fuel tanks and lines – exactly as they were designed to do in a low-speed ground impact, leaving the aircraft structure basically intact and its occupants unharmed.

But in the second, major impact, despite the fact that the aircraft was fitted with newly designed seats which met higher regulatory crash-resistant standards, passengers were killed and seriously injured because the floor collapsed beneath them, and overhead bin assemblies fell bodily from the ceiling on top of them. Moreover, survivors restrained only by their lap-straps suffered pelvic fractures as the high deceleration forces bent their bodies at extreme angles around these single-point harnesses. This flailing also allowed heads, hands, knees and feet to strike the seat or bulkhead in front of them and sustain further injuries.

Learning why a fan blade fails in flight certainly reduces the chances of similar accidents from such causes in the future. But it appears that only a radical change in crashworthiness design thinking can save passengers from death or serious injury in so called "survivable" accidents.

This pair of pictures graphically illustrates the consequences of the CFM56-3's early predilection to fan blade failure. (top) The No 1 fan of Dan-Air's G-BNNL. Culprit blade No 25 at the 4 o'clock position has lost its 10cm tip out from the mid-span shroud, while blades 1 & 37 (12 o'clock) are even more bereft. All other blades have suffered extreme leading edge damage. (middle) This fan from BMA's G-OBMG has had its failed blade removed from the 12 o'clock position, while the remaining blades have escaped with only minor nicks and dents to their tips and leading edges. The final picture (right) uses this nose-on view of Boeing's 737-400 prototype to good effect to show the No 1 engine installation. By side-mounting the engine's oil tank and gearbox accessories, the bottom of the nacelle was flattened to permit adequate ground clearance with the retention of the standard 737-200 main undercarriage. (UK DoT/AAIB)

CHAPTER 13

"Whatever you do, keep us away from the city!"

– DC-10 Captain to Approach Controller

United Airlines McDonnell Douglas DC-10-10 N1819U [46618]
(F/n 3619) – July 19, 1989

Multiple hydraulic primary control systems are designed to ensure "fail-safe" redundancy in today's heavy jet transports. Accepted design philosophy had held that any eventuality grave enough to simultaneously disable them all would in any case result in the loss of the aircraft. But as with JAL's Boeing 747SR in Japan, this concept was shown to be wanting when a manufacturing flaw in an engine fan disk forging, undetected for 17 years, finally flew apart.

Cruising flight

Wednesday, July 19, 1989 was a glorious summer's day over the Mid-West of the United States. Above 4000 feet, scattered cumulus clouds, towering against the clear blue sky, rode majestically southward on the light northerly breeze. By mid afternoon, the temperature on the ground had risen to a warm 80°F (22°C).

For crew and passengers alike aboard United Airlines Flight UA 232 from Denver, Colorado, to Philadelphia, Pennsylvania, via Chicago, Illinois, it seemed a perfect day for flying – the sort of weather that, as one pilot would put it, almost made "it a shame to take the money."

The DC-10-10, cruising serenely 37,000 feet above the ripening grain fields of north-western Iowa which extended to the horizon in every direction, had taken off from Stapleton International Airport, Denver, 2.10pm central daylight time. The eight attentive cabin crew members had served a late lunch to their 285 passengers, four of whom were very small children seated on their parent's laps, and now they were preparing to screen a film.

On the flightdeck too, all was calm, the mature and highly experienced crew conducting the flight with the taken-for-granted professionalism that is intrinsic to the operation of a heavy jet aircraft in a major US airline.

In command was Captain Alfred Haynes, 57, a veteran United Airlines pilot of 33 years' service with the company. Of the 30,000 hours in his log book, more than 7,000 hours was on DC-10s. His first officer was William Records, 48, a former National Airlines and Pan American World Airways senior pilot who had joined United in December 1985. He had accumulated some 20,000 hours and had nearly 700 hours as a first officer on United's DC-10s.

The third member of the crew was Second Officer Dudley Dvorak, 51, the flight engineer. Although he had been with United Airlines for only three years, he had 15,000 hours of flying time and, prior to undergoing transition training on the DC-10 five weeks previously, he had been a flight engineer on Boeing 727s.

Although United Airlines employed many hundreds of aircrew,

the three on the flightdeck knew one another reasonably well. During the last three months they had flown together as a crew on six trips, and before beginning today's flight they all had a spent a whole day off in Denver.

First Officer Records was flying the aircraft on this Denver-Chicago leg. He had the autopilot engaged and, in accordance with the flight planned cruising speed of Mach 0.83, had the autothrottles selected in the speed mode for 270 knots

At 3.15pm, a little more than an hour after departure from Denver, the DC-10 was approaching an airway intersection north of the town of Alta. Here the flight plan required it to make a right turn from the northeasterly heading it had been flying since passing over Omaha, Nebraska, on to the new heading of 095°M which would take it direct to Chicago.

A bang – and a lurch

A minute later, as the DC-10 was swinging through 080°M during the gently-banked, near right-angled turn on autopilot to capture the new

Resplendent in its "Four Star Friend Ship" livery, immediate sistership N1818U [46617] is seen here before delivery to United on April 9, 1973, three days ahead of the doomed N1819U. United has been a significant DC-10 operator, not only in sheer numbers, but also for its role in the success of the DC-10. In the determined trijet sales battles fought by McDonnell Douglas and Lockheed at the end of the 1960s, American launched the DC-10 first, with an order for 25, but TWA and Eastern countered with substantial orders for the L-1011 TriStar. United's subsequent breathtaking order for no less than 60 DC-10s, announced on April 25, 1968, finally ensured the DC-10's future. American and United DC-10s shared a joint delivery ceremony at Long Beach on July 29, 1971, and N1802U [46601] opened United DC-10 services two weeks later on the San Francisco-Washington DC route.

heading, there was a loud report from somewhere towards the tail and the whole aircraft shuddered. Passengers in the cabin, most of them still finishing their lunch, heard the noise as a loud bang and, as the aircraft lurched, flight attendants who were standing or moving about were thrown off balance. "I guess that means we should fasten our seatbelts," Senior Flight Attendant Janice Brown calmly announced to the passengers over the PA system.

On the flightdeck, instrument indications showed that the tail-mounted No 2 engine had failed and was spooling down, and Captain Haynes immediately called for the engine shutdown checklist. In the process of carrying out the shut-down, Second Officer Dvorak was concerned to see from his flight engineer's console that the hydraulic pressure and hydraulic fluid quantity gauges for the aircraft's three hydraulic systems were all falling.

Meanwhile, instead of straightening out on its selected new heading, the DC-10 was continuing to swing to the right. It was also tending to nose down into a descending turn. When adjustments to the autopilot controls produced no effect, First Officer Records disconnected the autopilot and attempted to straighten the aircraft out with the primary controls. Again there was no response, the DC-10 instead continuing its descending turn to the right.

Loss of control

"It's not responding to control!" Records told the captain with alarm.

Captain Haynes at once took the controls for himself and found the aircraft was not responding to any flight control inputs. Clearly, whatever had occurred to disrupt the control system had effectively "frozen" the control surfaces in the position they had taken up during the airway intersection turn on to the new heading. Easing back the No 1 power lever, the captain reduced thrust on this port side engine, and the aircraft began rolling back into a wings-level attitude.

Haynes then called for the emergency air driven generator, which powers the aircraft's No 1 auxiliary hydraulic pump, to be deployed. This was done and the hydraulic pump selected on, but still no hydraulic pressure could be restored.

The time was now 3.20pm. The aircraft, still descending slowly but now rolling from side to side as it pitched gently fore and aft in a slow phugoid motion, was more or less stabilised on a southerly heading. Calling Minneapolis (Air Route Traffic Control) Centre, the crew reported their plight and requested vectors to the nearest airport for an emergency landing. At the same time they initiated a coded Aircraft Communications and Reporting System (ACARS) message to United Airlines' central despatch facility in Chicago, requesting a call on 129.45 mhz.

Forced diversion – to Sioux City

The Minneapolis air traffic controller working the DC-10 at once suggested that it should divert to Des Moines International Airport, about 100nm southeast of the aircraft's position. Two minutes later however, seeing that the barely controllable DC-10 had again swung to the right and was now heading northwest, the controller asked the crew if they would prefer to go to Sioux City which lay in this general direction.

"Affirmative," First Officer Records replied, and the controller then passed them vectors to Sioux Gateway Airport at Sioux City, Iowa.

Sioux Gateway Airport, six nm south of the city on river flats adjoining the east bank of the Missouri River, has an elevation of 1098 feet, and in mid 1989 it had two bitumen-surfaced serviceable runways. Runway 17-35 was 6600 feet (2013m) long with overruns of about 800 feet (244m) at both ends, while Runway 13-31 was 9000 feet (2745m) long with 1000 feet (305m) of overrun at its southeastern end. A third, concrete surfaced runway, 6888 feet (2100m) in length and aligned 04-22, had been closed to traffic sometime previously (see airport diagram).

In the DC-10's passenger cabin, as the flight attendants were hurrying to clear away the lunch trays, Captain Haynes came on the PA system himself, informing the passengers with characteristic understatement

The four stars were a belated 1973 addition to United's livery, but the days of "Mainliners" and "Friend Ships" were numbered. On June 17, 1974 DC-8 N8031U was rolled-out to reveal the "double U, triple stripe" colour scheme (see Chapter 3). DC-10-10 N1804U [46603] "Curtis Barkes" is shown in the now-familiar livery on departure from San Francisco in May 1978. United went on to operate 48 DC-10-10s (registrations N1801U to N1849U, omitting '1840 and '1848), plus six second-hand Series 30s. (with acknowledgement to APS/ Ian Mackintosh)

that they "had lost the No. 2 engine" and that they "might be late arriving in Chicago". He concluded by asking Senior Flight Attendant Janice Brown to report to the flightdeck.

When she did so a few moments later, Haynes told her to secure the cabin and to prepare the passengers for an emergency landing and evacuation. Returning to the cabin, she quietly and separately informed the other seven flight attendants. Determined to keep things "normal" for as long as possible, she did not tell the passengers at this stage because she did not want to alarm them

Meanwhile, the company's despatch facility in Chicago had been unsuccessful at first in establishing two way communication with the crew. But at 3.23pm another ACARS call back to the aircraft resulted in voice contact. Second Officer Dvorak at once asked Despatch to put them through to the company's maintenance headquarters in San Francisco. "Immediately," Dvorak demanded, "It's a MAYDAY!"

A fourth crew member

With no manual backup available, the pilots had no way of moving the ailerons, elevators, rudder, flaps, slats or spoilers. Their only hope of controlling the DC-10 was by manipulating the thrust generated by the two remaining engines. They were also faced with the uncontrolled pitch oscillation of the aircraft. Despite the best efforts of the crew, they found it impossible to re-establish stabilised flight.

By 3.27pm the Chicago despatcher had put the aircraft in touch with San Francisco Maintenance. Second Officer Dvorak then explained at some length that they had lost of all

three hydraulic systems, and asked for whatever advice and assistance they might be able to provide. San Francisco could offer no immediate advice not already available to the crew, but undertook to contact the company's Flight Operations department and call the aircraft back.

One of the cabin crew now came forward to the flightdeck to report that a passenger in the First Class cabin, identifying himself as an off duty company DC-10 captain, had offered to come to the flightdeck if he could be of any assistance. "OK – let him come up," Captain Haynes told her.

Captain Dennis Fitch, 46, was in fact a DC-10 check and training pilot based at the company's flight training centre in Denver, Originally a pilot with the Air National Guard, he had been with United Airlines for 21 years. Nearly 3000 hours of his 23,000 hours' experience had been logged on DC-10s.

As the DC-8 photograph in Chapter 3 shows, positioning the triple cheatline with the middle (red) stripe flanking the window line can cramp airline titles. In the late 1980s, United lowered the cheatline by one stripe-width on all but its Boeing 747s, and increased the size of its titles and symbols, as shown in this recent picture. DC-10 N1819U was wearing this amended livery as it cruised high above Iowa's grainfields on the summer afternoon of July 19, 1989. (with acknowledgement to Airliners magazine/Steven Aaltvick)

"We don't have any controls!" Haynes told Fitch grimly as he entered the flightdeck. "Could you go back and check if you can see any external damage through the cabin windows?"

"What's the hydraulic quantity reading now?" First Officer Records asked the flight engineer when Fitch had left.

"It's zero," Dvorak told him.

Records: "On all of them?"

Dvorak: "That's right."

Captain Haynes: "Quantity is all gone? You got a hold of San Francisco Maintenance?"

Dvorak: "Yes – but he's not telling me anything yet."

Haynes (with concern): "We're not going to make the runway, fellas."

Fitch now returned to the flightdeck from the passenger cabin.

"We have no hydraulic fluid," Captain Haynes told him. "That's part of our main problem."

"OK – both your inboard ailerons are sticking up slightly – but they're not damaged as far as I can tell – and the spoilers are locked down. But there's no movement of the primary flight control surfaces. I don't know ... what would you like me to do?"

Rudimentary control with thrust alone

The captain asked Fitch if he would take over the power levers, which appeared to be their only remaining means of control, while the crew tried to sort out the problem with advice from Flight Operations in San Francisco.

Kneeling on the floor between the two pilot seats so he could manipulate the No 1 lever with his left hand, and the No 3 with his right, Fitch began to experiment with power settings in an attempt to dampen out the gentle low frequency phugoid motion which the aircraft had developed, and to overcome both the rolling of the aircraft from side to side and its continuing tendency to enter a descending turn to the right.

It proved vastly more difficult than he expected. Indeed, it seemed almost impossible to achieve and maintain a stable pitch attitude. As he continued to experiment, he commented to Haynes that the flight attendants were slowly securing the cabin for an emergency landing.

"They'd better hurry," the captain retorted. "I think we're going to have to ditch."

Meanwhile the aircraft, still pitching and rolling to some extent, flew wide clumsy orbits to the right, progressively losing height as it did so.

Changing frequency to Sioux City Approach Control, Haynes reported to the controller that the aircraft had

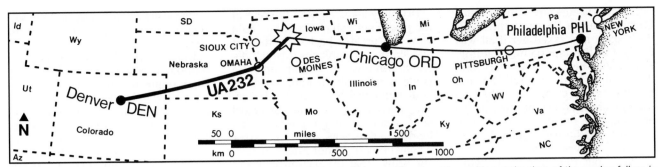

Planned route of United's Flight UA232 from Denver to Philadelphia via Chicago. The aircraft's position at the time of the engine failure is shown. (Matthew Tesch)

no hydraulic fluid and therefore no elevator control and that they might have to make a forced landing. As the captain was speaking, Fitch, increasingly frustrated by the near impossibility of the task set him, and the bare minimum of control available, burst out: "Get this thing down – we're in trouble!"

Fitch's comment convinced Haynes they would have to attempt a landing at Sioux City with a minimum of delay. Telling the first officer to obtain the V speeds for a no-flap, no-slat landing, he called Approach Control again to ask for the ILS frequency of the duty runway, the heading they would need to fly to the runway, and its length. The controller provided

the frequency, reported that Runway 31 was 9000 feet (2745m) long, and gave the DC-10's radar position as 35nm northeast of Sioux City's Gateway Airport. At this point the DC-10 was flying a northerly heading after completing the second of two erratic descending orbits of some five nm radius.

Emergency preparations

Haynes instructed Dvorak to start dumping fuel, using the quick dump system, and the fuel load was jettisoned down to the level of the system's automatic cutoff valves, leaving some 33,500 pounds (15,200kg) in the aircraft's tanks. The captain then asked Fitch if he could manipulate

the power levers to maintain a 10° to 15° turn to the left. "I'll try," Fitch replied, without conviction.

Having consulted the aircraft's flight manual, First Officer Records declared 200 knots to be the "clean manoeuvring airspeed" they would require for a no-flaps, no-slats landing. To the captain he added: "That's 200 and 185 on your bugs, Al."

At 3.40pm, 24 minutes after the onset of the emergency, San Francisco Maintenance called the aircraft back to report that personnel from the company's Operational Engineering department were being contacted to lend assistance and that the crew could expect further advice in about another five minutes.

What the anxious crew of Flight UA232 could not see: this plan view of the DC-10's tail assembly shows the damage inflicted by the fan disk's uncontained failure. With the CF6 engine spinning clockwise at high RPM, the starboard tailplane suffered the worst damage. But the energy of the shattered fragments was also enough to sever the fuselage tailcone from its hinged mounting, and pepper the port tailplane with fragments. (Matthew Tesch, with acknowledgement to NTSB)

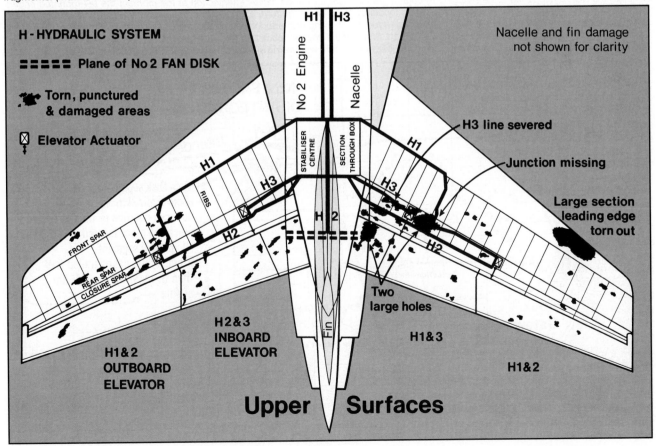

Captain Haynes now called Senior Flight Attendant Brown to the flight-deck again and asked her if all was ready for the emergency landing. Explaining they had only very limited control of the aircraft, he told her they were going to attempt to put the aircraft down on the runway at Sioux City. But it was going to be difficult, and he was doubtful of its outcome. Because it was not possible to damp out the aircraft's phugoid motion, touching down at a pre-determined point and airspeed would be impossible. The final moments of the landing would therefore be a matter of chance. He told her that, when the landing was imminent, the warning, "brace, brace, brace" would be made over the PA system to alert everyone in the cabin.

Sioux City Approach Control now called the aircraft to inform the crew that the airport's emergency vehicles would be standing by the runway when the DC-10 touched down.

Tailplane damage

A few moments later, another member the cabin crew came to the flightdeck and spoke to Second Officer Dvorak. She told the flight engineer she had seen damage on one of the aircraft's tailplanes. Conveying this to Captain Haynes, Dvorak and asked if he should go back and investigate for himself. The captain agreed.

Dvorak walked back to the rear of the passenger cabin where he could view the greater part of both port and starboard tailplanes through the cabin windows on either side. He could see that the leading edges of both tailplanes had sustained damage, particularly on the starboard side, where a major piece of the leading edge was missing. After commenting to Senior Flight Attendant Brown that the passenger briefing would have to be "quick and dirty" (ie a blunt abbreviated briefing in place of the longer, more detailed and more tactfully worded emergency briefing), he returned to the flightdeck and reported what he had seen on the tail. "That's what I thought," Captain Haynes answered.

The crew now set about lowering the undercarriage, using the alternative extension procedure because of the lack of hydraulic pressure. It locked down satisfactorily.

No sooner had they accomplished this when San Francisco Maintenance called again, with the information that, "Engineering is assembling right now and they're listening to us." Replying, Second Officer Dvorak told San Francisco that they were now down to 9000 feet, were intending to attempt a landing at Sioux City, and that they had just completed the alternative undercarriage extension procedure. But the

engineering department had no further useful advice they could offer to the crew.

Unknown to the crew, Flight Operations personnel in San Francisco then requested the Chicago company despatcher working the DC-10 to ask the crew if they would consider a landing attempt at Lincoln, Nebraska, 105nm to the south, instead of Sioux City. Flight Operations were concerned about crosswinds at Sioux City Airport and the crew's need for a longer runway to give the difficult landing the best chance of success. Although the despatcher transmitted this enquiry to the aircraft, she received no reply.

The despatch office in Chicago also received a call from United Airlines staff at Sioux City, reporting that a company DC-10 was obviously in difficulties to the east of the airport. The despatcher immediately telephoned the Sioux Airport tower, requesting that all available emergency, fire, and rescue vehicles be readied for the aircraft's landing.

Triumph of skill and judgement

Approach Control now reported the DC-10's radar position as 21nm northeast of the airport, and requested the crew to widen their turn to the left in order to keep the aircraft away from the city, as well as to position it for a right turn on

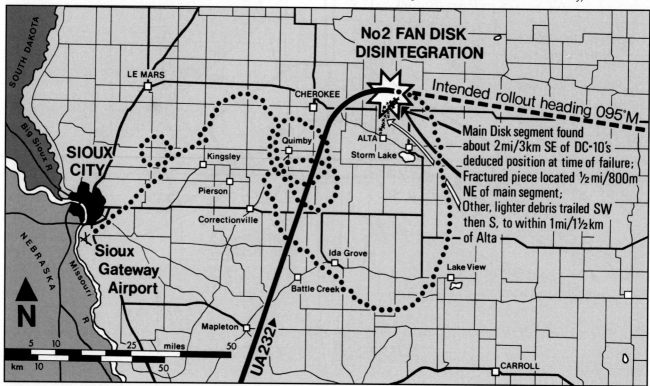

Because the DC-10 happened to be swinging through a gradual right turn at an airway intersection at the moment the tail-mounted engine disintegrated, its "frozen" control surfaces left it with a tendency to continue the turn, as this map of the aircraft's radar-plotted track shows. But the sole left turn which the hard-pressed crew succeeded in achieving was enough to position the DC-10 to the northeast of Sioux City, on a relatively direct heading for the city's Gateway Airport. Much of the engine debris that fell to the ground north of Alta was only discovered during the harvest season some time after the accident. (Matthew Tesch, with acknowledgement to the NTSB & Rand McNally)

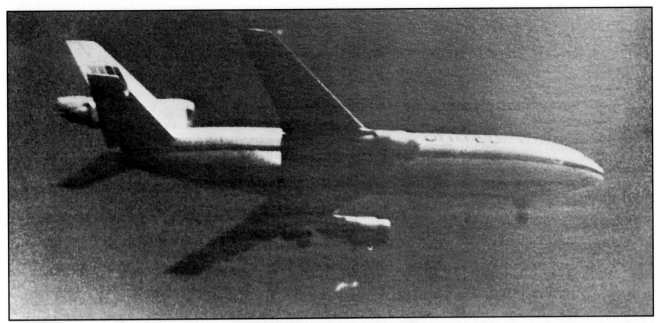

An amateur photographer snapped this picture of the crippled aircraft during its final approach. The hole in the leading edge of the starboard tailplane is visible, as is the fact that the tailcone is missing; the undercarriage has been manually extended, but slats and flaps remain retracted. In their fight to retain control with engine power alone[(1)], the DC-10 crew had small, but crucial advantages over the hapless Japanese Boeing 747 crew in a similar predicament four years before – the undamaged fin gave the aircraft some measure of flight stability, and a "dead-heading" check pilot joined the United crew on the flightdeck. The check pilot's remarkable skills in handling the power levers undoubtedly allowed the operating crew to concentrate even more closely on their critical individual tasks. (NTSB)

to final approach.

"Whatever you do, keep us away from the city," the captain responded ominously.

Instructing the crew to fly a heading of 180°, the controller alerted them to the presence of a 3400 foot radio tower five miles to their right, and asked how steep a turn the aircraft could make.

Captain: "We're trying to make a 30° bank!"

Fitch, frustrated by his struggle to turn the aircraft to the left with the power levers and at the same time maintain a relatively stabilised attitude, called out with exasperation: "I can't handle that steepness of bank ... Can't handle that amount of bank!"

First Officer [recognising the near-impossibility of Fitch's task]: "We're going to have to try it straight ahead, Al!"

Approach: "If you can hold that altitude, your turn on to 180° will put you about 10 miles east of the airport."

Captain: "That's what we're trying to do!"

First Officer: "We'd better try and set up a shallow descent."

Captain: "We want to get as close to the airport as possible. Get on the air and tell them we got about four minutes to go."

First Officer [beginning to transmit]: "Sioux City Approach ..."

Captain [correcting him]: "No ... tell the passengers!"

First Officer Records then made the announcement over the PA system.

In the cabin, as the flight attendants stood at their demonstration positions, Senior Attendant Brown read the Short Emergency Landing Preparation briefing over the PA system. The cabin crew then helped passengers individually, giving brace-for-impact instructions to parents of infants and small children. They also assisted small children in passenger seats by providing pillows as padding to enable the adult lap belts to be tightened around them.

At this stage Captain Fitch abandoned his vain attempts to turn the DC-10 to the left against its continuing tendency to swing to the right, and instead allowed it to enter a turn to the right through almost 360°. Shortly before 3.55pm Captain Haynes was able to report they were now on a heading of 180°.

Approach: "If you can maintain that altitude, your heading will work out fine for about ... seven miles."

But rather than holding its southerly heading, the aircraft continued to swing to the right. By the time Fitch was able to check the swing, the airport lay directly ahead again.

Approach (a minute later): "Roger – the airport is now at your 12 o'clock and 13 miles."

After Captain Haynes had directed the crew to lock their shoulder harnesses and to stow all loose articles out of the way, the pilots sighted the airport in bright sunshine from about nine miles out: "OK – we have the runway in sight," Haynes transmitted. "And thanks for your help."

Approach: "The wind is now 360° at 11 knots – and you're cleared to land on any runway."

In view of the aircraft's position and the near impossibility of turning to the left, Haynes now decided to continue the approach straight ahead to Runway 22, rather than attempt further difficult manoeuvring on to a final approach for Runway 31. "OK," he told the controller, We're pretty well lined up on this one here ... think we will ..."

Approach: "The runway you're lined up on is Runway 22, which is closed. But that'll work, sir – we're getting the [emergency] equipment off the other runway and they'll line up for that one."

Captain: "How long is it?"

Approach: "Runway 22 is 6,600 feet [2013m] long ... but there's an open field at the far end, and the winds should not be a problem."

Still kneeling between the pilots' seats as he worked the Nos 1 and 3 power levers, Captain Fitch knew from his own experience as a training captain with no-flap, no-slat approaches at necessarily high airspeed, that he would have to juggle the power with great care to control the final descent.

Concentrating hard as the aircraft's smooth oscillations in pitch and roll continued, and using the first officer's airspeed indicator in conjunction with his visual judgement, he constantly changed the power settings to maintain a satisfactory descent profile intended to

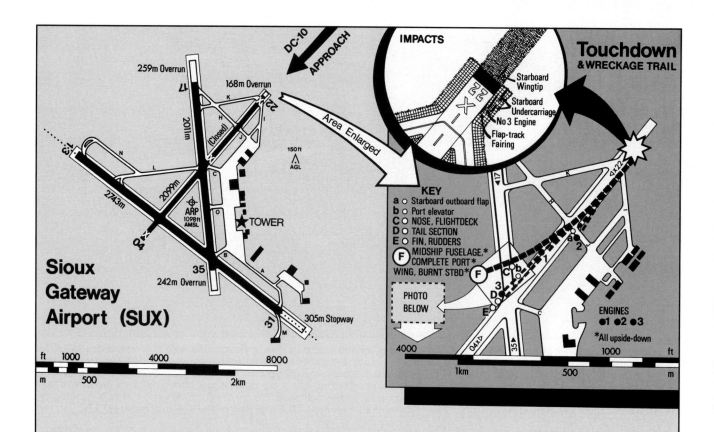

Sioux Gateway Airport (SUX)

DC-10 APPROACH

259m Overrun
168m Overrun
201m
(Closed)
2099m
2743m
ARP
1098ft
AMSL
TOWER
35
242m Overrun
31
305m Stopway
150ft
AGL

ft 1000 4000 8000
m 500 2km

IMPACTS

Touchdown & WRECKAGE TRAIL

Area Enlarged

Starboard Wingtip
Starboard Undercarriage
No 3 Engine
Flap-track Fairing

KEY

a ○ Starboard outboard flap
b ○ Port elevator
C ○ NOSE, FLIGHTDECK
D ○ TAIL SECTION
E ○ FIN, RUDDERS
(F) MIDSHIP FUSELAGE,*
COMPLETE PORT *
WING, BURNT STBD*

PHOTO BELOW

ENGINES
● 1 ● 2 ● 3
*All upside-down

4000
1km 500 m
1000 ft

(above) Diagrams showing layout of Sioux Gateway Airport and the spread of wreckage from the DC-10's spectacular breakup. The aircraft's phugoid oscillations and directional instability could be managed only at the price of a flat approach at high speed – the moment power was reduced for landing, the nose would inevitably drop and the right-turn tendency reassert itself. That the crew managed to nurse the crippled DC-10 for as long and as far as they did – literally to within 100 feet over the runway threshold – was a superb feat of airmanship. Although 111 people died in the valiant landing attempt, no les than 185, including all four crew on the flightdeck, survived. (Matthew Tesch, NTSB & Wide World Photos)

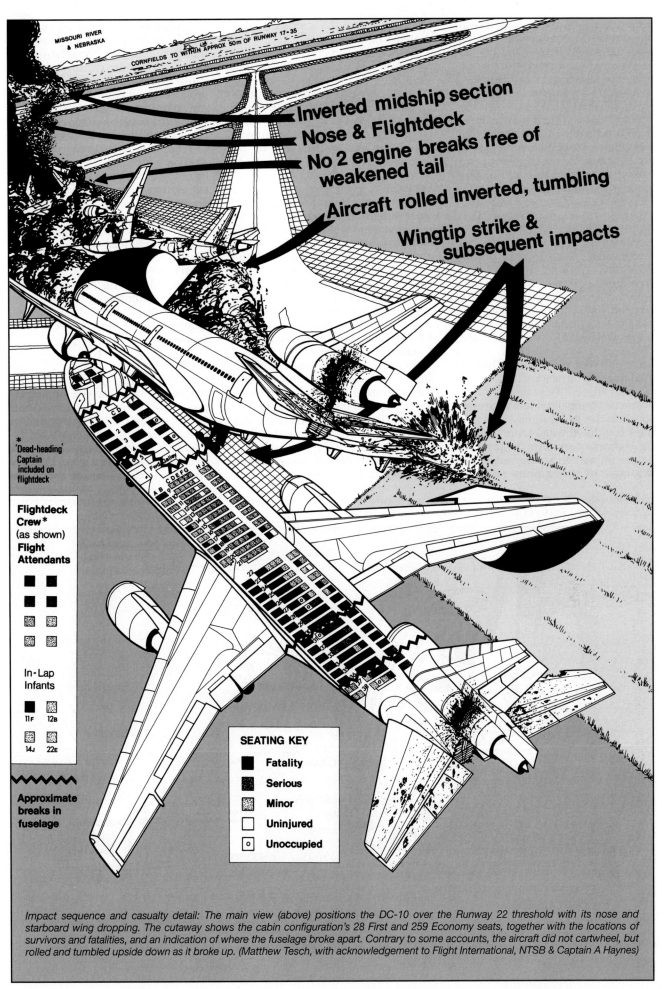

MISSISSOURI RIVER & NEBRASKA

CORNFIELDS TO WITHIN APPROX 50m OF RUNWAY 17-35

Inverted midship section

Nose & Flightdeck

No 2 engine breaks free of weakened tail

Aircraft rolled inverted, tumbling

Wingtip strike & subsequent impacts

* 'Dead-heading' Captain included on flightdeck

Flightdeck Crew*
(as shown)
Flight Attendants

In-Lap Infants

11F   12B

14J   22E

Approximate breaks in fuselage

SEATING KEY

■	Fatality
▨	Serious
▦	Minor
□	Uninjured
⊡	Unoccupied

Impact sequence and casualty detail: The main view (above) positions the DC-10 over the Runway 22 threshold with its nose and starboard wing dropping. The cutaway shows the cabin configuration's 28 First and 259 Economy seats, together with the locations of survivors and fatalities, and an indication of where the fuselage broke apart. Contrary to some accounts, the aircraft did not cartwheel, but rolled and tumbled upside down as it broke up. (Matthew Tesch, with acknowledgement to Flight International, NTSB & Captain A Haynes)

bring them over the runway threshold at a height of about 100 feet. He also succeeded in keeping the aircraft fairly well aligned with the runway. The airspeed was fluctuating around 215 knots and the sink rate was 1,600 fpm.

When about four nautical miles from touchdown at a height of 1000 feet, First Officer Records made an announcement over the PA system, calling for all in the cabin to now assume the brace position "for the roughest landing you've ever made!"

Attempting the impossible

Sixteen seconds later, as the aircraft neared the ground, the Ground Proximity Warning System began sounding. Fourteen seconds later again, the aircraft had almost reached the runway threshold at a height of about 100 feet.

Captain Haynes: "Close the throttles!"

Captain Fitch [urgently]: No – I can't pull 'em off, or we'll lose it! That's what's turning us!"

First Officer: "We're turning!"

The aircraft, its high approach speed unchecked, had now swung to the left of the runway centreline and the high sink rate alarm of the GPWS began sounding. At the same time the nose of the aircraft began to pitch down and the starboard wing dropped rapidly.

First Officer [urgently]: "Left Al! ... Left throttle! ... Left throttle! ... Left throttle!

Despite Fitch's desperate efforts to correct the aircraft's attitude with power, the starboard wingtip struck the ground just short of the runway threshold and to the left of its centreline.

Catastrophe

A moment later the starboard main undercarriage impacted the left hand edge of the runway heavily and was sheared off. Skidding out of control to the right at high speed, the DC-10 rolled, demolishing the outer starboard wing as it tumbled on to its back and ignited into an enormous flash fire. Skidding off the runway upside down, the wreckage slid for more than a kilometre, the massive fuselage breaking apart as it did so.

Breaking off first, the flightdeck slid off the runway to the left and came to rest at the edge of intersecting Runway 17-35. The inverted centre section of the fuselage, the biggest portion of the aircraft still intact, with most of the port wing still attached, also slid off the runway to the left but continued across Runway 17-35 into a field of tall ripening corn where it went on burning, though not fiercely. The relatively intact tail section continued down Runway 22, finally stopping just beyond the intersection of the two runways.

The fuselage sections containing the First Class cabin immediately behind the flightdeck, and the Economy cabin between the trailing edge of the wing and the No 2 engine air intake, were demolished as the aircraft broke up.

Firefighting, ambulance and emergency rescue crews waiting on the airport, together with a medical crew hovering overhead in a helicopter, moved into action at once, all the fire vehicles rushing to the intersection of Runways 22 and 17, the position from which the separated sections of the fuselage were most accessible.

Survivors

As the medical team's helicopter touched down by the side of the runway, those on board, fully expecting that all on the DC-10 had been killed in the spectacular impact, were astounded to see numbers of survivors emerging from the two metre tall grain crop in which the major section of

Main elements of the DC-10's tail-mounted engine are identified in this General Electric CF6-6 cutaway drawing. The fan section lost in flight when its disk fractured is indicated. (Matthew Tesch & NTSB)

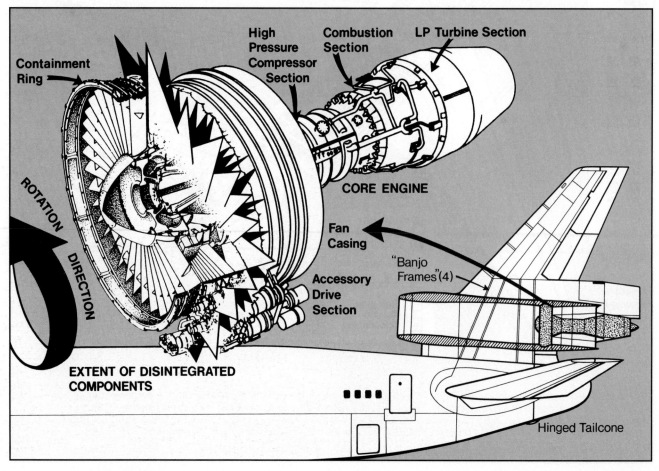

the fuselage had come to rest. Some of them appeared to be almost unscathed.

But the teams' joy was short-lived. As they leapt from the helicopter to render assistance, they caught sight of mutilated bodies littering the runway behind them – victims unlucky enough to have be seated in the sections of fuselage destroyed in the breakup.

Although the flightdeck area was badly damaged when it broke away from the fuselage just aft of the forward cabin doors, its shoulder harnesses and lap belts remained intact and restrained the four crew members. Suffering varying degrees of injury, they were extricated from the wreckage by the rescue teams.

Fighting the fire

Meanwhile, the senior fire officer, after quickly checking the tail section which included the rearmost part of the cabin containing 10 passenger seats and two flight attendant seats, left it to the ambulance crews to attend to the injured and ordered all fire units to move at once to the main section of the aircraft where the fire appeared to be intensifying. As they did so they encountered more survivors from this section of the wreckage walking towards them along Runway 17.

The first fire tender to arrive sprayed a massive blanket of foam over the entire inverted centre section. The fire, burning beneath the starboard wing box area on the exterior of the wreckage, was hard to reach, but fortunately for the time being the 12-knot northerly wind was helping to keep the flames away from the fuselage itself.

This portion of the fuselage contained seats from row 9 to row 30 as well as four flight attendant seats at doors 2 and 3 on each side. The greatest amount of structural deformation and collapse appeared to be in the area of the port wing.

More survivors were clambering from the break at the front of wreckage as the fire tender arrived and were sprayed with foam as they escaped. From them, firemen learnt that others who had already made their escape were somewhere in the surrounding field of corn, which was high enough and dense enough to be totally disorienting to anyone amongst the crop on foot. Other passengers were still in their seats inside the wreckage, hanging upside down by their seatbelts, and it was obvious that the collapsed structure was impeding their escape, particularly towards the rear of the fuselage section.

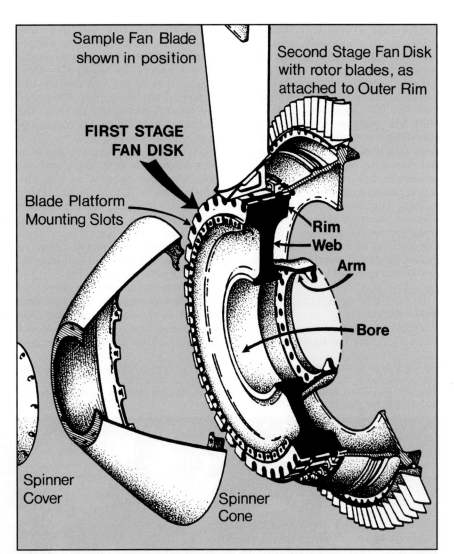

Close-up cutaway view of the CF6 fan assembly, showing relationship of other components to fan disk. For further details of this engine, see Chapter 4 in this volume, and Chapters 13 and 15 in Volume 1. (NTSB)

Three minutes after it had arrived on the scene, the first fire tender had exhausted its onboard water supply but, by this time, a second vehicle was in position and continued the mass application of foam. Firemen also used a hose from this vehicle to attack the wing box area that could not be reached with the foam and to help protect passengers still leaving the front of the wreckage. But a few minutes later, the second tender had also exhausted its water supply.

While this firefighting was in progress a third unit, a water supply tanker, was also brought into position. Hoses were connected to resupply the fire tenders, but a mechanical failure prevented any water being transferred. The tanker was then disconnected and pumping units from the Sioux City fire service were brought in to replace the tanker.

But by this time the unchecked fire had intensified again and had spread from the wing structure into the interior of the fuselage. Another

two hours passed before it could be brought under control. As a result, 35 passengers who had survived the impact, but who were trapped in their seats because of injuries or cabin deformation, died from smoke inhalation.

Casualties

All the flight attendants and passengers were in a brace-for-impact position as the crew attempted to land the aircraft. Four in-lap children were on board, three of them under two years of age, and parents were instructed to place them on the floor and hold them there when the parent assumed the protective brace position.

One woman said her son "flew up in the air" upon impact but she was able to grab and hold him. One child held on the floor sustained minor injuries. Two mothers could not hold on to their children and were unable to find them after the crash. One was rescued by an escaping passenger who heard her cries and re-entered the fuselage to find her. The other child died of smoke inhalation. One three year-old boy who was given pillows to help tighten his seat belt remained restrained throughout the impact sequence and was not injured.

Of the 296 occupants of the aircraft, 110 passengers and one flight attendant lost their lives in the accident. Of the 35 passengers who died as a result of smoke inhalation, 24 had suffered no serious injuries. The other fatalities were the result of multiple injuries sustained in the impact. Of the other 185 occupants, 47 sustained serious injuries, 125 minor injuries, and 13 escaped unhurt. One passenger died a month after the accident as a result of his injuries.

INVESTIGATION

Impact evidence

NTSB investigators who arrived at Sioux City early the following morning established that the final catastrophic moments of the accident sequence had been triggered when the crew's extremely limited control was unable to prevent the DC-10's starboard wing dropping sharply as the aircraft was about to cross the runway threshold at an extremely high approach speed.

As a result the wing tip, the starboard main undercarriage, and the No 3 engine nacelle struck the ground immediately short of the threshold, tumbling the aircraft on to its back. The primary high speed impact and those that followed then broke the aircraft up as it continued down the runway and left the inverted centre section on fire.

The empennage came to rest on its starboard side against the remaining stub of the starboard tailplane near the intersection of Runways 04-22 and 17-35. Most of the No 2 engine

air intake, portion of the aft fuselage, and the stub of the starboard tailplane, were intact. The separated fin and rudder were just west of the empennage.

The port tailplane had separated into three main sections, but the starboard tailplane had broken into a number of pieces which were scattered along both sides of Runway 22. The biggest piece was a three metre outboard section from which most of the leading edge was missing.

No 2 engine damage

Portions of the No 2 engine stage 1 fan blades and stage 2 booster blades were embedded in the sheet metal of the empennage, and two fan-to-shaft flange nuts were found lodged in the air intake acoustic panels. Four punctures in the fin appeared to be fragment damage sustained before impact with the ground.

Even this poor quality picture showing the NTSB's "reconstruction" of the No 2 engine's fan disk cannot disguise the massive fracture which removed a third of its circumference. During the investigation the DC-10's entire tailplane assembly was painstakingly "reconstructed" in a Sioux Gateway hangar, enabling the airborne damage caused by the disintegrating disk to be differentiated from that sustained in the ground impacts. (NTSB)

Examination of the interior of the empennage showed that, except for the breached hydraulic systems, there was no evidence of pre-crash damage to the components of the flight control systems, or the APU.

The No 2 engine came to rest to the left of Runway 22, some 1850 feet (564m) beyond the initial impact point and had been extensively damaged by tumbling after being torn from its empennage mountings. The rear end of the fan forward shaft, with about 20 percent of the shaft cone wall section, remained attached to the engine. Six fragments of the conical section were recovered at the accident site, representing about 75 percent of the fan forward shaft. The entire aft fan case was also recovered at the accident site, as well as about 90 percent of the stage 2 fan.

The lower starboard half of the fan containment ring was found on the right side of Runway 22, in line with the direction that the empennage had skidded after separating from the fuselage.

The No 2 engine fan module could not be found amongst the wreckage on the airport and further examination of the engine and its components confirmed that the fan rotor assembly, as well as part of the fan forward shaft, had separated from the engine in flight.

Air intake and banjo frame damage

Examination of the tail structure revealed that, apart from damage that had obviously been sustained in the ground impacts, the No 4 (rearmost) aluminium banjo frame forging was cracked through at the 3:30 position and a piece was missing from its rear edge between the 2:30 and 4:00 positions. In addition, most of the engine inlet adapter assembly between the No 4 banjo frame and the fan containment ring – the inlet bellmouth, bolted to the front flange of the fan forward casing, and the adapter ring, designed to accommodate movement between engine and airframe – had been torn away.

Other wreckage

Shortly after the accident, farmers living north of the town of Alta reported by telephone that aircraft parts had fallen on to their properties. The following day, NTSB investigators who went to area recovered the DC-10's fuselage tailcone, together with various parts from the No 2 engine, including half the fan containment ring, and numerous smaller pieces.

A few days later, various parts of the No 2 engine adapter assembly were found in the same rural area near Alta. They included two pieces of the adapter ring and bellmouth assemblies, fan blade fragments, a segment of aluminium from one of the four large banjo forgings in the tail mounting, and other smaller components, including two hydraulic accumulators from the engine-driven hydraulic pumps and two pieces of braided hydraulic hose clamped together. The recovered piece of aluminium was found to match part of the section severed from the No 4 banjo frame forging. It also contained titanium alloy smears from the fan section of the engine.

Photographs

A householder who lived on the eastern side of Sioux Gateway Airport had taken a number of photographs of the DC-10 as it was on final approach to its disastrous landing. They showed clearly that the fuselage tail cone and the fan cowling door for the No 2 engine were missing. The remainder of the No 2 engine installation – mounting beam, reversers, and core cowl – appeared to be intact. Damage was also evident on the starboard tailplane. Using the photograph with the sharpest image, details of this damage were incorporated into a three-dimensional scale drawing of the tailplane setting out the extent of the inflight damage.

The aircraft

United Airlines operated a total of 55 DC-10s, 47 of which were DC-10-10s and eight were DC-10-30s. The aircraft involved in the accident, N1819U, powered by General Electric CF6-6D high bypass ratio turbofan engines, had been delivered new to United Airlines in 1971. Up to the time of its departure from Denver on the ill-fated flight, it had flown a total of 43,401 hours in the course of 16,997 cycles.

Its maximum certificated takeoff weight was 430,000lbs (195,220kg) but the gross takeoff weight on departure from Denver was only 369,268 pounds (167,648kg) and its computed centre of gravity well within calculated limits for this weight.

Hydraulic flight controls

The DC-10-10's primary flight controls comprise inboard and outboard ailerons, two-section elevators, and a two-section rudder. Secondary flight controls consist of leading edge slats, spoilers, inboard and outboard flaps, and a dual-rate adjustable tailplane or horizontal stabiliser. Each primary and secondary control surface is powered by two of three independent hydraulic systems.

The three independent, continuously operating hydraulic systems are intended to enable full control of the aircraft in the event of one or two hydraulic systems failing. The integrity of at least one hydraulic system is required for continued flight and landing and there is no provision for manual reversion.

Each hydraulic system derives power from both a primary and a reserve pump driven by a different engine. Either pump can supply full pressure to the system. Backup power is automatically provided by two reversible motor pumps, which transmit power from one system to another without fluid interconnection as long as fluid is available in the unpowered system.

Electrical power can also be used to drive either of two auxiliary pumps provided for the No 3 hydraulic system. Should there be an extreme emergency in which all engine-driven pumps become inoperative, an air-driven generator can be deployed to supply electrical power to one of these auxiliary pumps.

The hydraulic components and lines are physically separated to minimise the aircraft's vulnerability to multiple hydraulic failures in the event of structural damage.

Empennage "reconstruction"

The rear fuselage and all identified pieces of the empennage were moved to a hangar for reconstruction as a mockup, vertically mounted on a wooden trestle and scaffolding, with a wire grid to support the smaller pieces of wreckage. A viewing platform was built around the mockup to enable any part of it to be examined in detail.

The port side tailplane was found to contain numerous holes where engine debris had punctured the skin, but there was no evidence that this damage had severed hydraulic lines or caused any significant leakage of fluid.

On the starboard tailplane however, far more serious inflight damage was found to have been inflicted. In addition to numerous skin punctures similar in character and extent to those on the port side, there were three large holes in the starboard tailplane. One spanwise hole at the outboard leading edge, visible in the photograph taken during the aircraft's approach to the airport, extended back to the front spar. Efforts were made to identify the source of this damage, but although its dimensions were similar to the size of a major piece of the fan disk, no positive match was possible.

The second hole, also visible in the inflight photograph, was forward of the inboard elevator where some components of the flight control hydraulics are located. The exact size and shape of this hole could not be determined because of ground impact damage. The third hole was in the inboard elevator where there were no critical components.

Hydraulic system damage

During the reconstruction of the empennage, it was determined that a section of the starboard tailplane was not amongst the wreckage recovered from the airport, and the photograph taken during the aircraft's approach confirmed that this section was missing before impact. The missing piece contained the No 1 hydraulic system tubing which supplies hydraulic fluid to the starboard inboard and outboard elevator actuators.

Examination of the empennage wreckage revealed that the No. 3 hydraulic system pressure line had been severed in the inboard area of the starboard tailplane. Holes penetrating the upper and lower skins of the tailplane were found in the area of the severed line. The hole sizes and shapes conformed to the dimensions of a fan blade base platform. All three hydraulic system reservoirs were found empty.

No 2 engine fan disk

Three months after the accident, two pieces of the stage 1 fan disk, each with fan blade segments still attached, were found in fields north of Alta. Together, the two pieces made up almost the entire disk, with the exception of one dovetail post.

The different locations in which the two pieces were found suggested that the smaller segment was flung to the north of the 082°M heading the aircraft was flying at the moment of failure, while the remainder of the fan disk assembly was thrown southwards. With the northerly winds prevailing at the time, trajectory calculations predicted that both pieces of the disk assembly would fall to the south of the aircraft's ground track, where they were actually recovered.

Two massive fractures in the disk had resulted in about a third of the rim separating from the remainder of the disk. The circumferential fracture was typical of an overstress failure stemming from a pre-existing fatigue crack in the bore of the disk. The parts were taken to the General Electric factory in Evandale for examination, and the smaller segment later went to the NTSB's Materials Laboratory in Washington for further evaluation.

Some nine months after the accident, a farmer working his fields in the area where the pieces of disk were found, came across the front flange of the No. 2 engine rotor shaft and a major section of the fan booster disk. These parts were also examined at the NTSB's Materials Laboratory.

Fan disk fracture

Examination of the fracture surfaces of the fan disk disclosed that the near-radial, bore-to-rim fracture was the primary fracture. It had

Douglas engineers accepted the penalties of complex installation and access difficulty in their "straight-through" design of the DC-10's No 2 engine mounting. (Hawker Siddeley, Boeing and Lockheed instead faced the tricky aerodynamic challenges of "S-ducts" on their Trident, 727 and TriStar). This picture shows the No 2 engine of a Laker Airways DC-10-10 being lowered from its mounting – with no less than six cowlings, two inboard elevator sections, and the hinged tailcone, cleared away for access.

gradually propagated from a fatigue region on the inside diameter of the bore, the strength of the disk finally being weakened to the extent that the catastrophic separation occurred. Metallurgical examination revealed that the fatigue crack had actually originated in a small cavity on the surface of the disk bore. The cavity had apparently formed within a melt-related hard alpha defect in the titanium alloy of the disk during manufacture.

Fan disk history

General Electric's CF6-6 engine was certified by the FAA on September 16, 1970. Its fan assembly consists of the stage 1 disk with large fan blades and retainers, the stage 2 disk and smaller blades, the spinner cone and cover, and various mounting and balancing hardware.

The stage 1 fan disk weighs 370 pounds (168kg) and is a machined titanium alloy forging about 32 inches (80cm) in diameter. The rim, about five inches thick, contains axial "dovetail" slots to retain the fan blades. The stage 2 fan disk is bolted to the aft face of the rim. The primary loads imposed on the stage 1 disk are those resulting from centrifugal forces.

The manufacturing process of the failed stage 1 fan disk had been completed at the General Electric Aircraft Engines factory at Evandale, Ohio, in December, 1971. The disk was installed in a new engine in the factory's assembly facility, and the engine was shipped to the Douglas Aircraft Company in January, 1972, where it was installed on a new DC-10-10.

The several different engines in which this fan disk was subsequently installed over the following 17 years were routinely overhauled and the fan module dismantled. On six occasions during these years the disk was removed and subjected each time to fluorescent penetrant inspections. At the time of the accident, the disk had accumulated 41,009 hours and 15,503 cycles.

Its last shop visit was in February 1988, 760 flight cycles before the accident, when the engine in which it was installed was removed because of corrosion in the high pressure turbine nozzle guide vanes. At that time, the disk had accumulated 38,839 hours and 14,743 cycles since new. Following this inspection, it was installed in the No. 2 engine on the aircraft involved in the accident.

Simulator study, using thrust for control

A simulator re-enactment of the events leading to the crash was conducted to determine if DC-10 crews could be taught to control the aircraft and land safely without hydraulic power to the flight controls. The DC-10 simulator used was programmed with the aerodynamic characteristics of the accident aircraft and a number of DC-10 rated pilots – line captains, check and training captains and production test pilots – were then asked to fly the accident profile with wing engine thrust as the only means of control.

The use of differential thrust produced a yawing moment and a yaw angle. Because of the aircraft's wing sweep and dihedral, the yaw angle produced a rolling moment and a roll angle. The roll angle produced a turn on to a new heading.

Increasing and decreasing thrust on both engines had a limited effect on the pitch attitude, but the aircraft tended to oscillate about its centre of gravity in the pitch axis. Pilot-induced thrust variations were required to control not only this long period (about 60 seconds) phugoid or pitch oscillation, but also asymmetric rolling moments induced by airframe damage.

The whole exercise proved extremely difficult because of the need to use the No 1 and No 3 power levers asymmetrically to maintain both lateral and direction control, coupled with the simultaneous need to increase and decrease thrust to maintain pitch control. It was not possible to control the pitch oscillations with any degree of precision, and the pilots found that, despite their best efforts, the aircraft would not maintain stabilised flight.

Required manoeuvres could be implemented, via thrust variations on the wing engines, but only after a delay of as much as 20 to 40 seconds. Because of this, any thrust changes required in the course of manoeuvres for a landing had to be anticipated by at least this amount of time. Thus, any required changes within 20 to 40 seconds of touchdown could not be fully accomplished.

Moreover, because airspeed is primarily determined by pitch trim configuration, there was no direct control of airspeed. Consequently, the possibility of landing on a runway at a particular point and airspeed became largely a matter of chance.

ANALYSIS

Crew performance

The loss of all the three hydraulic systems, and consequently of control, combined with airframe vibration and visual assessment of damage to the tailplane, convinced the crew that the structural integrity of the DC-10 was in jeopardy and it was essential to land without delay. The captain's ready acceptance of the check captain to assist on the flightdeck showed the value of flightdeck resource management training.

The simulator re-enactment demonstrated that crews could not be taught to land safely without hydraulic power to the primary flight controls. In general, the simulator exercises showed that speed, touchdown point, direction, attitude, and vertical velocity could all be control-

led separately, but it was virtually impossible to control all parameters simultaneously. The investigators concluded that the damaged aircraft, deprived of all three hydraulic control systems, could not have been successfully landed on a runway. All that the crew managed to achieve was highly commendable and greatly exceeded reasonable expectations.

Overall, the simulator re-enactment showed that such a manoeuvre involved many unknown variables, and the small degree of control available during approach and landing rendered a training exercise virtually impossible.

Even so, the results did provide advice that could be helpful to any crew in a similar situation. McDonnell Douglas made this information available to the industry in

These three production line photographs show the construction of the DC-10 tail assembly and the No 2 engine mounting. (top) Two of the four "banjo frames", comprising the primary nacelle and fin-box structure, before delivery to McDonnell Douglas' Long Beach assembly line. (bottom) This view of the now-recognisable DC-10s on the production line shows the tail installation more clearly. The pylon protruding rearwards from the top of the nacelle supports both the No 2 engine and the upper fin. (McDonnell Douglas)

the form of an "All DC-10 Operators Letter."

Prior to the accident, McDonnell Douglas, the FAA, and United Airlines had considered a total loss of the DC-10's hydraulic flight controls so unlikely that there was no need for a further backup system.

Fan disk failure

Metallurgical examination and evaluation during the investigation established that the fatigue crack which led to the catastrophic failure of the stage 1 fan disk had initiated in a small cavity in the titanium alloy of the disk. The cavity was within a melt-related, nitrogen-stabilised hard alpha inclusion in the material of the disk, formed during the alloy manufacturing process. Hard alpha inclusions, which have a melting point substantially higher than defect-free titanium alloy, result from localised excess amounts of nitrogen or oxygen introduced through atmospheric reaction with titanium in its molten state.

The defect remained undetected through ultrasonic, macroetch, and fluorescent penetrant inspections during the manufacturing process. The macroetching procedure might not have been capable of detecting the flaw because it was performed on the forging rather than on the final machined part. The cavity itself was most likely created within the metallurgical defect in the alloy during the final machining or shot peening process and would have been evident if the part had been macroetched in its final form.

Inspection methods

United Airlines' maintenance records indicated that the stage 1 fan disk, the fan booster disk, the fan shaft, and the No 1 bearing had all been inspected in accordance with the airline's maintenance program and General Electric's CF6-6 shop manual. None of the engines in which the fan disk had been installed had experienced overspeeds or bird strikes. The disk had been through six detailed inspections in its lifetime, all of which appeared to be in accordance with the airline's FAA approved maintenance procedures.

The airline's maintenance program was comprehensive and based on industry standards. The company's inspection requirements for the CF6-6 stage 1 fan disk were consistent with airline practice and complied with Federal regulations. The airline's procedures for selecting and training its inspectors were also consistent with industry practice.

But it was clear that the adequacy

of inspections was dependent upon the performance of individual inspectors – in other words, it was possible for human factors to degrade inspection performance, denying it the detailed attention such a critical process warranted. This same issue was addressed in the wake of the Aloha Airlines Boeing 737 accident near Maui, Hawaii, in April 1988 (see Chapter 11), when the NTSB recommended some formalisation of maintenance inspector training to the FAA.

The investigators believed that manual inspection procedures used in the industry to inspect the vast majority of aircraft structural and engine components were inherently susceptible to human factors that could reduce the probability of detecting a defect. Automated eddy current, ultrasonic, and fluorescent penetrant inspection equipment could be employed by airline maintenance centres using existing technology. The investigators also believed the FAA should initiate a research program to identify other emerging technologies that could simplify or automate inspection processes.

Hydraulic control design

The three hydraulic systems installed in the DC-10 are physically separated to protect the integrity of the systems in a single-event-failure.

The concept of three independent hydraulic systems was by no means unique. Boeing and Airbus had three such systems on some of their most recent aircraft types, while Lockheed and Boeing had four independent systems on their TriStar and 747 widebody aircraft. The investigators saw no inherent advantage in additional independent hydraulic control systems beyond those already existing.

However, in reviewing alternative flight control concepts, the investigators believed that backup systems should be developed for primary hydraulic controls. These would be particularly important for the coming generation of widebody aircraft. Manual reversion systems were likely to be impractical because of the effort required to deflect large, heavily loaded control surfaces. The investigators recommended that the FAA encourage continuing research into backup systems that employ an alternative source of motive power.

The investigators believed that Douglas could have taken additional precautions in the design of the DC-10 if the potential effect of a catastrophic No 2 engine disintegration had been predicted. The fan

containment ring, severed by the fan disk failure, was designed to withstand only one fan blade failure.

It was therefore recommended that the FAA analyse the dispersion pattern, fragment size, and energy level of parts flung from the engine in this accident and include the results in aircraft certification documentation.

The investigators attempted to obtain historical data and recent operating experience on engine rotating part failures and instances of non-containment, but little was available. The investigators believed the FAA should review reporting requirements for manufacturers and operators with a view to establishing a data base of these events. Such a system could monitor rotary part failures in turbine engines, provide a data base for design assessment and comparative safety analysis, and establish a background for a review of certification requirements.

Survival

Well executed cabin preparation improved the prospects of survival for occupants seated in areas of the aircraft where the fuselage remained intact. Passengers were in protective brace positions, seatbelts were tightly fastened, and the cabin was properly secured.

With the exception of two elderly passengers who died of asphyxia from smoke inhalation, all the occupants in seat rows 9 to 21 were able to escape from the wreckage of the fuselage, despite an increasing amount of smoke filling the cabin. Although most passengers were able to do so without assistance, several said they were assisted by others.

The greatest degree of structural collapse was in the area of the cabin near the port wingbox. Consequently, passengers in this section of the fuselage had less space in which to extricate themselves. Thirty three passengers in this section died of smoke inhalation. Of these, 12 had blunt trauma injuries that might have incapacitated them or slowed their escape; but the other 21 had not sustained any serious injuries. Escape for passengers seated on the port side of cabin in rows 22 to 30 was hampered by the fatal combination of fuselage deformation and immediate exposure to smoke. But most passengers in these same rows on the starboard side were able to escape because there was less crushing of the fuselage in that area.

All other fatalities in the accident resulted from blunt force injuries. These passengers were seated in ar-

eas of the cabin where the structural integrity of the aircraft was destroyed.

Emergency management

Overall, the emergency plan previously established by local Sioux City authorities, a recent full-scale disaster drill at the airport, and nearly half an hour's warning of the impending landing attempt, greatly assisted the prompt and efficient response by the emergency teams. But several difficulties affected the ability of the fire service to control the fire in the aircraft's starboard wing root and to rescue survivors promptly.

Both the crop of corn in which the major section of fuselage came to rest, and the wind direction, limited the fire tenders' access to the east side of the inverted cabin wreckage. The height and density of the crop also hampered the firefighters in finding debris and survivors. Some survivors were lying on the ground in need of attention, while others were pushing through the cornstalks, trying to find their way out of the crop and away from the burning wreckage. In view of these difficulties, the investigators believed the FAA should reassess its policy on allowing agricultural crops to be cultivated on airports. The FAA should ensure that nothing be able to interfere with rescue and firefighting activities.

And, as tragically demonstrated by the needless fatalities in the burning cabin, all fire service equipment should be tested at full capacity prior to acceptance and then tested periodically. This practice would provide both training and opportunity to identify equipment deficiencies.

ACTION RESULTING FROM THE ACCIDENT

Fan disk inspections

Even before the pieces of separated disk were recovered from the fields north of Alta, it was thought probable that the fan disk separated as a result of material defects. Six other disks had been produced at the time from the same titanium ingot and because such defects can be shared throughout a particular "heat" process, General Electric began checking with all operators of its CF6-6 engines to identify and remove the other six suspect disks from service.

Because ultrasonic inspections alone were apparently insufficient to ensure the long-term airworthiness of engine fan disks, the investigators issued a Safety Recommendation to the FAA suggesting that, with the assistance of General Electric, an alternative inspection method be developed for the bore of the disks and that this be repeated at specified intervals to ensure any developing cracks were detected.

Hydraulic system enhancement

Two months after the accident, McDonnell Douglas announced design enhancements to the DC-10's hydraulic systems that would preserve a measure of control if a catastrophic inflight failure again dam- aged all three control systems. The enhancements consisted of an electrically operated shutoff valve in the supply line and a check valve in the return line of the No 3 hydraulic system; a sensor switch in the No 3 hydraulic reservoir, and an annunciator light on the flightdeck to alert the crew if the shutoff valve activated.

The shutoff valve, located forward of the tailplane, would close automatically if the sensor switch detected that hydraulic fluid in the No 3 reservoir was dropping below a preset level. If severe damage breached the No 3 hydraulic system anywhere in the aircraft, the shutoff valve would block flow in the No 3 hydraulic lines routed through the tail.

In the event of a DC-10 sustaining damage similar to that near Alta, the system enhancement would provide longitudinal control using stabiliser trim at half rate input, and lateral control with the port inboard aileron and the starboard inboard and outboard ailerons. Slat extension would also be available, but not the flaps. As well, operation of the spoiler panels, brakes, nose wheel steering, un-

dercarriage, and lower rudder would be preserved. The enhancement was mandated by the FAA, effective from July 20, 1990, and was to be incorporated in all DC-10s by July 20, 1991.

McDonnell Douglas subsequently incorporated the enhanced hydraulic system in the MD-11, and all future MD-11 aircraft were to be manufactured with the shutoff valve system installed.

Industry task groups

A Systems Review Task Force was formed after the accident to consider design concepts that would provide a further alternative means of control in the event of the total loss of all normal flight control systems. Boeing, Douglas, Airbus, Lockheed, General Electric, Pratt & Whitney, and Rolls-Royce were

Exterior view of a DC-10, showing relationship between the aircraft's three independent hydraulic systems and the primary and secondary controls they power. Reversible motor-pumps between Engines/Systems 1 & 3 and between 2 & 3, together with non-reversible units between 3 & 2 and between 2 & 1, provided ample back-up in accordance with airworthiness certification requirements in force at the time of the aircraft's design. Both the Boeing 747 and Lockheed TriStar have four independent hydraulic systems, Boeing subsequently becoming convinced that this additional redundancy was justified by the very first accident to a 747. This occurred at San Francisco in 1971, when a Pan Am 747 struck a number of approach lighting stanchions immediately after lifting off. Although three of the aircraft's four hydraulic systems were ruptured, the one intact system enabled the crew to maintain control, dump fuel and return for an emergency landing. In its investigation of the Sioux City accident, the NTSB was much less concerned that the DC-10 had only three hydraulic systems, than with the fact that their critical lines and components all converged into an area vulnerable to damage from an uncontained engine failure. (Matthew Tesch, with acknowledgement to McDonnell Douglas & NTSB)

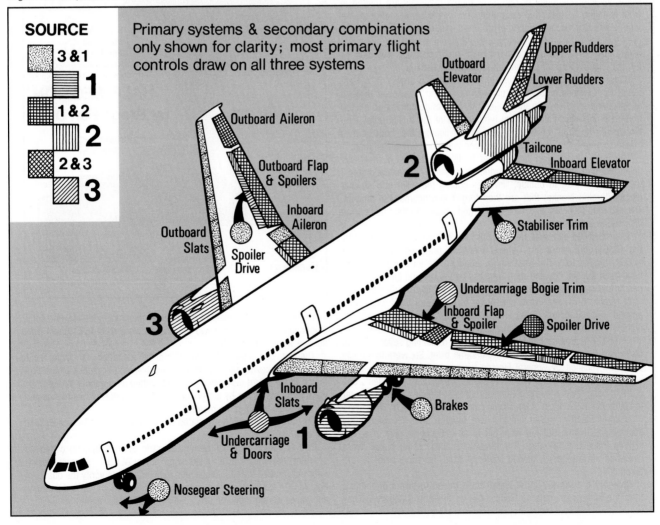

among the airframe and engine manufacturers represented.

An Engine Containment Working Group was also set up. The group would seek to identify which engine parts required reassessment, characterise their damage potential, and examine their design, in-service inspection, and repair. The group would also study improved design concepts.

Inadequate allowance for the effect of secondary damage on flight controls had now resulted in two major airline accidents – the DC-10 and the JAL Boeing 747 in Japan four years before. Other widebody aircraft in the world transport fleet could well benefit from a systems safety review.

Damage tolerance in airline transport engines

As well as the fan disk failure in the DC-10 accident, there were many examples of engine components failing before reaching their life limit. The investigators believed this demonstrated a need to revise certification, design, and maintenance philosophies for turbine engines. For example, certification processes for rotating parts in engines currently assumed that materials used in their manufacture were always defect free.

Because of these concerns, the investigators recommended that the FAA require operators to incorporate a damage tolerance philosophy into the maintenance of all engine components whose fracture or sepa-

ration could pose a threat to aircraft structure or systems.

Footnote:

(1) Directional control of the DC-10 on wing engines alone was shown to be possible in June 1972, when the rear cargo door of an American Airlines DC-10 blew out after departure from Detroit, immobilising the tail-mounted No 2 engine, jamming the rudder controls, and leaving the elevators with very little movement. (See "Air Disaster" Volume 1, Chapter 15). In that instance it was the captain's earlier simulator experiments in controlling the trijet with wing engine thrust alone which stood him in such good stead when the possibility suddenly became a reality.

A METALLURGICAL PAPER TRAIL

Even though it was many weeks before pieces of the failed No 2 engine stage 1 fan disk were found on the plains of northwest Iowa, it was quickly apparent that some kind of structural, metallurgical or fatigue problem had caused the disintegration of the disk. A team of NTSB investigators therefore concentrated on tracking the service, maintenance and manufacturing histories of the disk. Their findings constitute a substantial part of the NTSB's final report on the accident.

"There are three primary steps in the manufacturing of titanium alloy fan disks," explained the NTSB report. In the Materials Processing stage, varying quantities of raw alloy source materials are melted in what is called a "Heat" and each produced Heat is serial-numbered for production records. A number of different methods have been used over the years to produce Heats with minimum anomalies, the most usual after 1972 being a "triple-vacuum-melt" process, specified by General Electric Aircraft Engines after extensive research.

Causes of anomalies resulting in brittleness and cracks in a Heat range from excess amounts of nitrogen or oxygen introduced through atmospheric reaction with the molten titanium, to contaminated source materials. Increasing the furnace temperature of the molten alloy, and increasing the time the Heat spends in the liquid state, both help to minimise anomalies, but do not guarantee their complete dissolution.

The Heat becomes an "Ingot" after its final melt, then is mechanically reformed into a "Billet" for further processing. "The second step," the NTSB went on to outline, "involves cutting the billet into smaller pieces (forging blanks) that are then forged into geometrical shapes. The last step involves machining the forged shape into the finished fan disk shape [see diagram].

The failed fan disk was traced back to a 3175kg ingot produced by the TIMET corporation for General Electric's principal subcontractor ALCOA. Significantly, the Heat which produced the ingot was found to have been the last "double-melt" process before General Electric specified "triple-vacuum-melt" Heats and other quality improvements.

In March 1971, the ingot, now down to a 2816kg billet which had passed ultrasound tests, was shipped to ALCOA, there to be cut into eight 317kg forging blanks, each assigned its own serial number.

The NTSB teams succeeded in locating the remaining seven CF6 fan disks which had been forged from the same billet. Six were in service and were recalled by General Electric for detailed analysis. Two disks were found to have what the NTSB called "rejectable anomalies", one of them being evaluated as containing nitrogen affected defects similar to that found at the origin of the fatigue crack in the accident DC-10's disk.

General Electric moved quickly: two months after the Sioux City accident, a Service Bulletin went out to all CF6 engine operators, assigning inspection priorities. The already recalled "sister disks" were classified as Category I, having been cut from the same billet as the failed disk.

Category II disks (52 in all) were those traced to billets originating from the same raw material "feedstock" as those in Category I. They

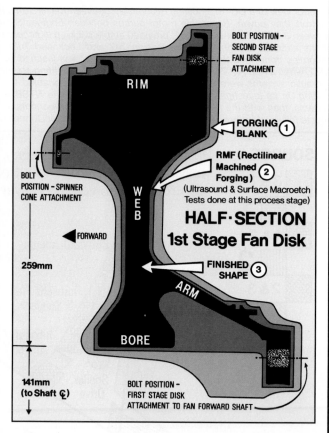

BOLT POSITION – SECOND STAGE FAN DISK ATTACHMENT

RIM

FORGING BLANK ①

RMF (Rectilinear Machined Forging) ②
(Ultrasound & Surface Macroetch Tests done at this process stage)

HALF-SECTION 1st Stage Fan Disk

BOLT POSITION – SPINNER CONE ATTACHMENT

W E B

FORWARD

259mm

FINISHED SHAPE ③

ARM

BORE

141mm (to Shaft ℄)

BOLT POSITION – FIRST STAGE DISK ATTACHMENT TO FAN FORWARD SHAFT

were required to be inspected by either contact or immersion-ultrasonic inspection methods within two months, or were to be withdrawn from service within five months.

The net was cast wider for 213 disks identified as having been manufactured using the superseded "double-melt" process which produced the accident disk. These were classified as Category III disks and were to be inspected by either contact or immersion-ultrasonic inspection methods within three months.

Six days later, the FAA mandated the General Electric Service Bulletin as an Airworthiness Directive.

In July 1990, a further General Electric Service Bulletin called for operator inspections of all disks supplied by ALCOA. "General Electric informally stated that this inspection was initiated to verify the quality of any ALCOA disks that may have been affected by record keeping anomalies during manufacture," declared the NTSB report.

CHAPTER 14

"Reverser's deployed!"

– Boeing 767 First Officer to Captain

Lauda Air Boeing 767-3Z9ER OE-LAV [24628] "Wolfgang Mozart"
– May 26, 1991

Certification procedures for thrust reversers on jet transport aircraft have traditionally included tests, supported by theoretical analysis, to demonstrate that inadvertent inflight deployment was fully controllable. But the catastrophic and mysterious loss of a 767 in darkness over Thailand raised serious questions as to the validity of such certifications.

An independent airline

Among the number of scheduled services to and from the Far East which Lauda Air, the flourishing independent Austrian airline, was operating in 1991 were Flights NG003 and NG004, a Boeing 767 service from Vienna to Hong Kong and return, with an en route call at Bangkok each way.

Founded by world champion racing driver Niki Lauda as a charter operation as recently as 1978, initially with two Fokker F27 Friendships, the company wore down an obstructive Austrian transport bureaucracy to began jet operations with two leased BAC 111s in 1985. At the end of that year Lauda himself, having won his third Formula One world championship, retired from motor racing to apply his energies full time to the development of his air services, and in May 1986 applied to the Austrian Ministry of Transport for licences to operate international scheduled services out of Vienna with Boeing 767s.

Austrian Airlines, the state owned national flag carrier, jealous of its prerogatives and intolerant of competition, vigorously opposed the application. But after 18 months of tireless lobbying and skilful campaigning, backed at all times by popular support from an admiring Austrian public, Lauda Air finally succeeded.

Licences to operate to ports in Australia, New Zealand, Korea, Taiwan, Hong Kong, Thailand, South and Central America – but not to Europe, the United States, China or Japan (the traditional preserve of Austrian Airlines) – were granted in October 1987, making Lauda Air Austria's first and only independent airline flying regular scheduled routes.

With only four Boeing 767-300s for its long distance flights (configured for 246 passengers instead of the usual 290 to provide more leg room in economy class), in addition to several Boeing 737-300s and -400s, Lauda Air's fleet, though modern, was extremely modest for an international airline. But thanks to high standards of cabin service, and great attention to small detail in all aspects of its operations, the company fulfilled the aspirations of its adopted motto, "Service is our success", beyond all expectations. Within two years Lauda Air's international network had been extended to include services to more than 50 countries across the globe – from the Canary Islands to Australasia – resulting in Lauda himself being nominated "Man of the Year" for 1989 by the prestigious Austrian business magazine *Trend*.

Return flight to Vienna

Flight NG004 – the return leg of the regular "one stop" Vienna/Bangkok/Hong Kong service on the night of Sunday May 26, 1991, being flown by Boeing 767 OE-LAV *Wolfgang Mozart* (another of Lauda Air's "quality" touches was to name its aircraft after famous classical composers and movie stars) – promised to be no different in essence to the many similar flights Lauda Air had operated over this route since its inaugural trip three years before in 1988.

Departing from Hong Kong shortly after 9.30pm local time, the flight's relatively short 950nm leg to Bangkok occupied just under two and a half hours and was entirely uneventful in excellent flying conditions. At Bangkok, the aircraft was refuelled and refurbished for the long nonstop leg to Vienna and the 213 Vienna bound passengers booked on the flight were ushered aboard.

The pilot in command for this 11 hour plus marathon was an experienced American airline pilot, Captain Tom Welsh, 48. His first officer, Austrian national Josef Thurner, 41, was also highly experienced. Eight flight attendants were in the cabin to care for the needs of the passengers during the long haul back to Vienna. Of all the crew, Josef Thurner was perhaps the better known, thanks to having been copilot to Niki Lauda himself on a Boeing 737 service to Bangkok which became the subject of a highly affirmative article on the airline and its history in the January 1990 issue of *The Reader's Digest* magazine.

Don Muang departure – and trouble!

The far eastern weather remained benign when, at 10.45pm local time, the Boeing 767 was pushed back from its loading gate at Don Muang Airport's international terminal. With a ground temperature of 26°C, there was the usual high humidity of about 80%. But there was little cloud below the six octas of cirrus at 30,000 feet and, with the moon only two days past full, the night surface visibility was excellent. The only wind was a light southeasterly breeze of about six knots off the South China Sea.

The Don Muang Airport weather office forecast for the air route between Bangkok and Rangoon indicated broken layer tops at FL 300 (30,000 feet), with isolated embedded cumulonimbus clouds reaching as high as FL 400. The QNH altimeter setting was 1007 mb.

The engines were started and the aircraft was cleared to taxi for Runway 21 Left. At 11.02pm it was cleared for takeoff and instructed to contact Bangkok Departures on 119.1 mhz when airborne.

Two minutes later, after a normal takeoff and a right hand turn onto its northwestern departure track, the crew called using the Departures frequency. The aircraft was then identified on radar and cleared to 11,000 feet on climb, tracking direct to the Limla beacon.

At 11.05pm, as the Boeing 767 was climbing through 5000 feet, the crew were instructed to change frequency and call Bangkok Control on 128.1 mhz. Bangkok Control then also radar identified the Boeing 767, clearing it to climb and maintain Flight Level 310 (31,000 feet).

Shortly afterwards, the Lauda Air company base at Bangkok received a routine "after departure" call from First Officer Thurner, passing the aircraft's Estimated Time of Arrival at Vienna as 0308 UTC.

It was to prove the aircraft's final transmission. Only 12 minutes later at 11.17pm, the Bangkok air traffic controller monitoring the Boeing 767's progress was startled to see its target disappear from his radar screen. Radio calls to the aircraft by Bangkok Control, Bangkok Departures, and other aircraft that were airborne in the area at the time, all failed to elicit any response.

Fears for the aircraft's safety were confirmed a little later when the Thai Department of Aviation's Rescue Co-ordination Centre in Bangkok received a radio call from a police outpost advising that people of the mountain village of Phu Toey, in rugged, sparsely settled and heavily forested country some 200km northwest of the city, had reported hearing, and in some cases seeing, a big aircraft explode into flames in the air and fall into the jungle.

But why? The Boeing 767 was less than two years old, and appeared to be in superb operating condition. Whatever had overtaken it, only 15 minutes after a perfectly normal departure from Bangkok's Don Muang Airport, had done so swiftly and apparently without warning of any kind. There had been no radio transmissions from the crew of any impending danger.

An unforeseen encounter with extreme turbulence hardly seemed possible. Although Bangkok's weather radar had earlier shown an area of weak precipitation along the aircraft's intended route, this mild storm area was northwest of the accident site – in other words the aircraft had not yet reached it when the accident occurred. And there had been no pilot reports of any weather activity in the general vicinity of the accident site. Indeed, air traffic controllers saw no weather returns on their radar screens at around the time of the accident.

An act of sabotage was surely the obvious answer. Could it be another Lockerbie disaster?

INVESTIGATION

While notification of the tragedy was transmitted to aviation authorities in Austria (country of registration) and the USA (country of manufacture), Royal Thai Police, Thai Department of Aviation, and military personnel left Bangkok to travel overland to the area in which the wreckage had evidently fallen, ready to begin a ground search early the following morning.

The search parties found that the Boeing 767 had indeed come down in the jungle, about five kilometres northeast of Phu Toey village in the Ban Dan Chang district of Suphan Buri Province.

But rather than locating any main impact crater, the searchers' first evidence that there had been a major air disaster was the finding of the Boeing 767's starboard tailplane, lying in the jungle a short distance to one side of a mountain track. As the search operation continued, other aircraft components and wreckage, some badly burnt by ground fires that had persisted for several hours after impact, others quite untouched by fire, were found scattered apparently at random across the jungle-clad mountain slopes.

While representatives from Lauda Air and the Austrian civil aviation authority flew from Vienna, and investigators from the NTSB, the FAA, and Boeing came from Washington DC and Seattle, the advance parties at the scene tackled the distasteful task of recovering the bodies of the aircraft's 223 occupants. Like the

One of the rare published pictures of the ill-fated OE-LAV, turning in for the apron at Vienna's picturesque Schwechat Airport. Sistership OE-LAU [23765] "Johann Strauss" was the airline's first widebodied type and, consequently, the most photographed of Lauda's aircraft. With the 6.42m (21'1") stretch of the basic 767-200 fuselage, Boeing offered its -300 customers a choice of midship exits to meet regulatory requirements for the additional passenger capacity. Roughly half (including Lauda Air) have opted for an extra pair of full-size doors just forward of the wing leading edge, the others choosing twin overwing window exits instead.

Lauda's "flagship" 767, OE-LAU, is seen "cleaning up" after getting airborne from Las Palmas in June 1988. The patriotic red and white of the airline's livery is offset by the belly colour, best described as "charcoal grey". Difficult to discern, even in good colour reproductions, is the third red pinstripe (in addition to the pair beneath the window line) which, aligned with the wing leading edge, breaks up almost the full length of the belly colour.

wreckage, these too were widely scattered amongst the jungle undergrowth and, before they could all be located and removed, were subjected to hot sunshine and tropical rain showers. The bodies were all taken to the Royal Thai Police's Institute of Forensic Medicine for pathological examination. Only 72 could finally be positively identified, even with the assistance of forensic science experts from Vienna.

Wreckage examination

With the international accident investigation team assembled at the crash site, it was quickly obvious from a preliminary survey that the Boeing 767 had broken up in the air before falling to the ground. Though many of the components were widely scattered amongst the jungle undergrowth, most of the wreckage was eventually found within a one square kilometre area (see diagram showing wreckage distribution), but some lighter sections, including pieces of the rudder, were found up to two kilometres away.

The eyewitness evidence of the local villagers that the aircraft had exploded, or at least caught fire, in the air was confirmed when the investigators examined various pieces of the wreckage. Some sections of the aircraft had clearly been affected by fire in the air, probably as a result of fuel from the disrupted fuel tanks igniting as it was released.

Evidence of inflight fire on the fuselage included airstream soot patterns and the fact that the fuselage section was found in an area where no ground fire had occurred. The separated outboard sections of both wings were also found in areas of no ground fire, yet they had been substantially fire-damaged. On the starboard wing section, the fire had burnt through several fuel tank access panels. Furthermore, one of the sooted fractures on this section was abutted by a "shiny" fracture surface. This indicated that the wing section had separated before being exposed to fire in the air, and was then further fractured by ground impact.

The separated port side midships cabin door was sooted, but was found lying in an area of no ground fire. The door frame itself was untouched by fire or soot, indicating that, as the door fell away during the breakup of the aircraft, it passed through a mass of burning fuel.

Generally, the inflight fire damage appeared to be limited to the outboard sections of the wings and an area of the starboard side of the fuselage above the wings and aft of the main spar. It was possible however, that other inflight fire damage was masked by the ground fires that followed some of the impacts. Much of the fuselage further aft was entirely devoid of signs of fire, indicating that the aircraft was not on fire until it began to break up. The lack of any fire damage to the empennage certainly indicated it had separated from the fuselage before the fire developed. Moreover, the absence of any sign of soot on the cabin outflow valve, or in the cargo compartment smoke detectors, showed that no fire had occurred during pressurised flight.

Similarly, no evidence could be found to support the theory that the disaster was the result of sabotage. No sign of shrapnel or explosive residue could be detected in any portion of the scattered wreckage. As expected, both the aircraft's gross weight and its c of g position were well within prescribed limits, and there was nothing to indicate that any failure of the aircraft's structure or engines could have led to the accident.

Examination of the fan cases of both engines however, revealed evidence of cowl load forces much greater than those that occur during normal operations.

The PW4000 engine installation was designed for the maximum aerodynamic loads on the cowlings that occur during aircraft rotation for takeoff. Fan rubstrips inside the fancase function as airseals for the fan blade tips, and under normal operating conditions a 1.25mm (0.50 inch) deep rub in the strip (considered a minor depth rub), centred at the bottom of the fan case can be expected. The rub results from upward aerodynamic forces acting on the cowling at aircraft rotation, forcing the lowest section of the rubstrip lightly against the tips of the spinning blades.

But the rubstrips found in the wreckage of the two engine cowlings contained rubbing substantially deeper than those typical of normal operations, indicating cowl load forces much greater than expected during takeoff. Furthermore, the forces were essentially *down* from the top of the cowl, suggesting the aircraft experienced a nosedown pitch, accompanied by abnormal rolling and yawing loads.

A startling find

As more and more of the scattered wreckage was progressively identified and physically examined, there was a surprising, totally unexpected finding in the condition of the thrust reverser mechanism on the port engine. The hydraulic actuators for each of the two halves of the thrust reverser sleeve were found in the fully deployed position – showing conclusively that the port engine thrust reverser had deployed, presumably during flight, before the aircraft crashed.

Examination of the thrust reverser system components recovered indicated they were functional at the time of the accident.

Inflight breakup

Detailed examination and analysis of the major items of wreckage showed that the inflight structural failures were the result of violent buffeting, and the application of excessive control forces in combination with abnormally high airspeeds.

Pieces of the rudder and port elevator had separated from buffeting overloads then, as the crew attempted to control the aircraft and recover from its high-speed dive, the starboard tailplane failed in a down-and-aft direction from these manoeuvring overloads. The imbalance resulting from download still present on the port tailplane then introduced a torsional overload to the left, as evidenced by wrinkles in the rear spar of the tailplane centre section.

This resulted in the failure of the fin and port tailplane. The damage indicated that the fin tip failed from bending in both directions before the fin itself, together with the attached upper portion of four fuselage frames, failed to the left.

With the loss of the tailplane, the aircraft pitched down violently, the resulting excessive negative loading causing both wings to fail in a downward direction, rupturing the fuel tanks and releasing many tons of raw fuel into the air which immediately ignited. The wing failure was probably followed by the breakup of the fuselage.

The complete breakup of the aircraft – tail, wing, and fuselage – probably occupied only a few seconds.

Flight recorders

The aircraft's Sundstrand Digital Flight Data Recorder and Fairchild Cockpit Voice Recorder were both located at the wreckage site. Both had been damaged by impact and the DFDR had also been badly affected by prolonged ground fire, probably over a period of several hours.

The recording tape inside the DFDR had melted as a result of this thermal exposure, and it was impossible to extract any data from it. Despite the damage to the CVR however, its tape was relatively intact and it was successfully read out. The readout, beginning 15 minutes before takeoff from Bangkok and ending during the inflight breakup of the aircraft, confirmed the wreckage evidence that the thrust reverser on the port engine had deployed in flight.

The first 20 minutes of the readout, covering the engine start, taxiing to the runway, takeoff, and initial climb, appeared to be perfectly normal and routine, and it was only in the last few minutes of the flight that any problems became apparent.

The following extract from the transcript, covering the final 12 minutes and 21 seconds of the recording, begins at 11.05pm, when ATC transferred the aircraft, now climbing through 5000 feet, from the Bangkok Departures frequency to that of Bangkok Control. Local pm time is shown in hours, minutes and seconds:

11.05:09: F/O: Bangkok [Control], good evening – Lauda Four.
11.05:11: CTR: Lauda Four – Bangkok Control?
11.05:13: F/O: We are out of 4500 [feet] for 11,000, direct to Limla.
11.05:18 CTR: Lauda Four – radar identified, maintain Flight Level 310.
11.05:22: F/O: We are re-cleared to Flight Level 310 and maintaining – Lauda Four.
11.05:40: F/O [to Capt]: Do you want me to delete this speed restriction?
11.05:43: CAPT: Yeah.
11.06:19: CAPT: And the after takeoff check?
11.06:20: F/O: Landing gear's off – flaps up – after takeoff check's complete.
11.06:23: CAPT: OK – and we got altimeters at thirteen.
11.06:52: F/O [on company frequency after calculating aloud in German to himself]: Bangkok ground – Lauda Four?
11.06:57: LAUDA: Lauda Maintenance – Bangkok. Go ahead.
11.06:59: (F/O passes brief details of aircraft's departure from Bangkok, concluding with their ETA for Vienna.)
11.07:14: LAUDA: 0308 – thank you!
11.07:48: CAPT [to F/O – evidently referring to message that has appeared on EICAS screen]: That keeps ... that's come on [again]!
11.08:52: F/O [to Capt]: So we past transition altitude – 1013.
11.08:54: CAPT: OK.
11.10:21: CAPT [to F/O – who has evidently been consulting Boeing 767 Quick Reference Handbook for a minute or so]: What's it say in there about that? Just ah ...
11.10:27: F/O [reading aloud from book]: Additional system failures may cause inflight deployment – expect normal reverse operation after landing.
11.10:35: CAPT: OK – just ... ah let's see ... [evidently takes book from F/O to consult it briefly himself].
11.11:00: CAPT [handing book back to F/O]: OK!
11.11:43: F/O [still concerned about message on EICAS screen]: Shall I ask the ground staff?
11.11:46: CAPT: What's that?

Lauda Air's corporate history is brief, but its equipment history reflects a fascinating evolution. After Formula One World Champion driver Niki Lauda founded Lauda Air in 1978, the company began holiday and motor-racing charters using a pair each of Mysteres and Friendships. But only after tireless campaigning in the face of monopolistic resistance from flag-carrier Austrian Airlines did Lauda Air gain official sanction for its planned scheduled services. During this time the company leased two BAC111-525FTs from Romania's TAROM to build jet experience. OE-ILD [256] is seen here at Vienna.

11.11:47: F/O: Shall I ask the technical men?

11.11:50: CAPT: [uncertainly] Ah ... you can tell 'em about it ... it's just ... Ah no ... it's probably ... ah water or moisture or something, because it's not just on ... it's coming on and off.

11.12:03: F/O: Yeah.

11.12:04: CAPT [considering possible implications of EICAS message]: But ... you know it's a ... it doesn't really ... it's just an advisory thing ...

11.12:19: CAPT [still considering EICAS message]: Could be some moisture in there or something.

11.12:27: F/O: Think you need a little bit of rudder trim to the left, eh?

11.12:30: CAPT: What's that?

11.12:32: F/O: You need a little bit of rudder trim to the left.

11.12:34: CAPT: OK.

11.13:14: (F/O begins adding numbers aloud to himself in German – continues until 11.16:33pm.)

11.17:01: F/O [suddenly]: Reverser's deployed!

11.17:02: (Sound of airframe shuddering.)

11.17:04: (Sound of metallic snap.)

11.17:05: Captain utters involuntary expletive.

11.17:06: (Sound of metallic snap.)

11.17:08: (Sound of four cautionary tones.)

11.17:11: (Sound of siren warning for one second.)

11.17:16: (Siren warning starts again and continues until end of recording.)

11.17:17: CAPT [desperately – simultaneously with further sound of metallic snap]: Here – wait a minute!

11.17:19: (Sound of two metallic snaps.)

11.17:22: Further expletive from captain.

11.17:23: (Sound of wind noise background increases in volume.)

11.17:25: (CVR begins vibrating – continues until end of recording.)

11.17:27: Unintelligible word from captain.

11.17:28: (Multiple bangs of inflight breakup begin and continue until end of recording.)

11.17:30: End of recording.

In addition to transcribing the verbal exchanges recorded by the CVR, the tape was also examined for any significant engine or other background sounds.

Apart from the normal sound "signatures" produced by the engines after the power levers were advanced for takeoff, no other definite engine sounds could be identified during the recording.

Background wind noise, produced by the aircraft's increasing airspeed, could be heard rising in intensity from the time of the thrust reverser

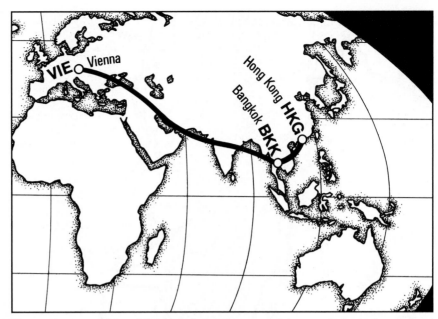

The proliferation of "big twin" designs in recent years and the progressive easing of operational restrictions has meant, among other things, that one-stop services to Europe are no longer the exclusive province of flag carrier Boeing 747s. Bangkok represented not only the "one-stop" on Lauda's scheduled Vienna-Hong Kong return service, but also a means of picking up valuable traffic from a second Southeast Asian hub port. (Matthew Tesch)

deployment until the end of the recording 30 seconds later, but its percentage increase could not be determined. During this time also, a vibration in the recorded sounds could be heard, probably as a result of airframe buffet. But neither the NTSB nor Boeing could obtain any meaningful data from the recorded vibration.

In the final seconds of the recording, several alarms could be heard sounding, but NTSB investigators, working with Boeing engineers, found there was insufficient information to form definite conclusions as to their precise cause.

The situation so far

The physical evidence from the wreckage recovered at the crash site, together with that from the readout of the CVR, showed conclusively that the port engine thrust reverser had deployed in flight, and that the aircraft had broken up in the air.

But how were these two events connected? And what chain of circumstances could have caused an obviously uncommanded deployment of the thrust reverser while the aircraft was climbing normally to cruising level?

In the meantime, as a precautionary measure, the FAA, acting on Boeing's advice, issued an Airworthiness Directive (AD 91-15-09) to all 767 operators on July 3 1991, instructing them to carry out tests, inspections and functional checks of the thrust reverser systems on all

Boeing 767 aircraft powered by PW4000 series engines.

The aircraft

There had been no doubt of the airworthiness of the aircraft before it began its ill-fated flight. The Boeing 767-3Z9ER (ie a 767-300ER built to the specification of Lauda Air); powered by two Pratt & Whitney PW4060 engines, had been delivered new to Lauda Air only 18 months before on October 16, 1989, and up to the time of the accident had flown only 7444 hours in the course of 1135 flight cycles.

The Boeing 767 is an advanced technology aircraft fitted with a so-called "glass cockpit", three pairs of Cathode Ray Tube (CRT) screens replacing most of the former electro-mechanical flight, navigation, and engine instruments. In addition, many of the aircraft's systems are electronically controlled, using integrated computer technology.

The two Engine Indication and Crew Alerting System (EICAS) CRT screens in the centre of the instrument panel have several functions. As well as replacing the "conventional" rows of analogue engine instrument dials with electronically projected images of the engine indications, they are able to display a Warning-Caution-Advisory hierarchy of up to eleven message lines on each screen from multiple "pages" stored in the system's memory. In addition, the EICAS screens display system status information inflight, and maintenance data while the

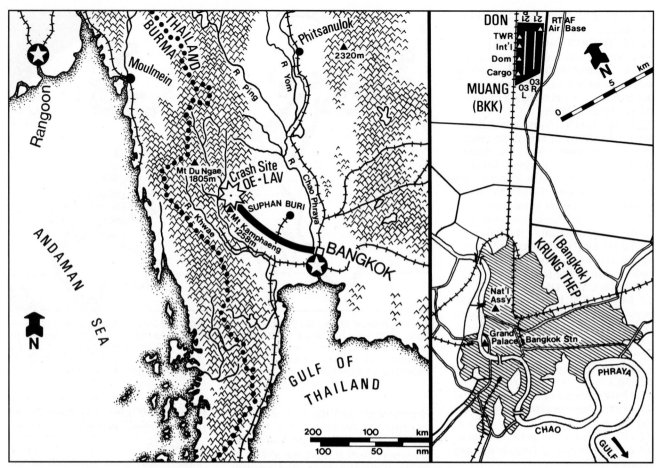

The main map shows the location of the Boeing 767's wreckage, 95nm northwest of Bangkok. The site of the accident was in the densely-jungled mountain chain which, extending south from the Sino-Burmese Shan plateau, forms the spine of the Malay Peninsula. The inset shows Bangkok and its Don Muang Airport. (Matthew Tesch)

aircraft is being serviced on the ground.

With the exception of some recurring maintenance messages concerning the thrust reverser system, generated by the aircraft's electronic Propulsion Interface Monitor Unit (PIMU), there was nothing to suggest that the aircraft was other than fully airworthy. These computer-generated messages had been recurring over a period of 18 months, despite Lauda Air's continuing efforts to correct the problem in accordance with the Boeing Fault Isolation Manual.

The computerised Airplane Communication Addressing and Reporting System (ACARS) fitted to the aircraft, designed to automatically transmit takeoff and cruise reports to ground receiving stations, had successfully transmitted and recorded a normal takeoff report 15 minutes before the accident.

Previous takeoff and cruise reports from the automatic system were also available to the investigators, and a review of this data revealed no anomalies in transmitted aircraft and engine parameters.

Technical logs, component records, and Lauda Air Maintenance Control's troubleshooting file were

reviewed as far back as November 30, 1989, when the aircraft was only six weeks old. Since August 14, 1990, numerous maintenance actions had been logged on the port engine thrust reverser system, nearly always in response to recurring PIMU messages of "EEC CH-B REVERSER RNG FAIL" and "EEC CH A/B REV CR-CHK FAIL." More than 20 of these actions had been logged during the five months preceding the accident.

In addition, the technical log for May 4, 1991, only three weeks before the accident, showed that the outboard auto-restow sensor for the port engine reverser had been found out of tolerance, and was adjusted after a crew reported an amber "REV" signal remaining on the EICAS screen after landing.

Most of the corrective maintenance involved removing and replacing valves or actuators, and making adjustments to the system. Typically, the PIMU message would not then recur for several flights. The most recent maintenance, involving replacing the port engine's thrust reverser locking actuator, had taken place at Vienna only the day before the accident, shortly before the aircraft left for Bangkok and Hong

Kong on the flight from which it would never return.

Throughout this time, Lauda Air maintenance staff had continued to follow all the troubleshooting steps in the Boeing Fault Isolation Manual, but without definitively correcting whatever was prompting the recurring PIMU messages. Despatch of the aircraft with the PIMU messages concerned was permitted under time-limited despatch conditions outlined in the airline's maintenance plan. Lauda maintenance staff were progressively conducting a full inspection of the port thrust reverser wire bundle for damage when the accident occurred.

Thrust reverser system

The thrust reversers on the Boeing 767's PW4000 series engines reverse only the high-volume bypass airflow from the fan, while the primary high-pressure flow from the engine core remains unaffected.

As shown in the diagram in this chapter, when reverse thrust is selected, hydraulic actuators slide ("translate") the two halves of the reverser sleeve on the engine cowling rearward, exposing the forward-angled cascade grid segments. At the same time, powerful hydraulic rams fold blocker doors, mounted within the half sleeves, into the huge volume of bypass air from the engine's fan to redirect its flow through the stationary cascade vanes. Reverse thrust is intended to provide additional retarding force during landings and rejected takeoffs, and is restricted to ground operation only.

The actual thrust reverser mechanism of the PW4000 engine is almost identical with that fitted to the P&W JT9D-7R4D engine, but its control system is entirely different. The JT9D-7R4D's thrust reverser mechanism is operated mechanically through cables from the flightdeck, but that of the PW4000 is electronically controlled through the engine's Full Authority Digital Electronic Control (FADEC) system, the Electronic Engine Control (EEC) using power lever and reverser position inputs to command thrust levels – forward or reverse.

Normal operation of the thrust reverser requires the aircraft to be on the ground to close the air/ground switch on each main undercarriage leg, with the relevant power lever in the idle-stop position. When the reverse thrust lever is lifted, the Hydraulic Isolation Valve (HIV) is opened electrically, admitting hydraulic fluid to the thrust reverser system via the Directional Control Valve (DCV). Further movement of the reverse thrust lever then opens the DCV electrically, sequentially directing fluid to the hydraulic actuator lock and actuators themselves, which move or "translate" the reverser half sleeves on the engine cowling to the deployed position.

When the sleeves unlock to leave their stowed position, in transit to their deployed position, the illuminated abbreviation "REV" appears on the lower EICAS screen in amber light. When both halves of the reverser sleeve reach their fully deployed position, the "REV" display changes to green.

The EEC incorporates thrust limiting logic to obviate inappropriate applications of thrust while the reverser sleeves are in transit, to ensure selected thrust is always in the direction of command. When the power lever position indicates reverse thrust has been commanded, the EEC limits thrust to idle if the sleeves are less than 70% deployed. And when the power lever position indicates forward thrust has been commanded, the EEC assumes the reverser has been commanded to the stowed position and limits thrust to idle while the reverser is more

than 15% deployed. When the reverser is 75% stowed, the thrust-limiting function changes to allow 90% of maximum forward thrust.

Should a disparity develop between a reverser command signal (from reverse thrust lever position or undercarriage air/ground switch) and the hydraulic pressure being supplied to the reverser system via the HIV, the fault is indicated by the illumination of an amber "REV ISLN" warning lamp on the flightdeck's centre pedestal, and by the EICAS message "L [or R] REV ISLN VAL" (Left or Right Reverser Isolation Valve). Inadvertent pressurisation of the reverser system in flight is one such disparity and would certainly trigger these warning signals.

Other evidence

The disposition of the scattered main wreckage, all within one square kilometre, indicated that the aircraft had broken up at relatively low altitude and at a steep angle of descent.

An estimation of this altitude was attempted, using the readout from the CVR. Although the extent to which the airspeed increased between the deployment of the reverser and the end of the recording could not be confirmed, the high speed likely to have been achieved during the descent suggested that the aircraft probably broke up at an altitude below 10,000 feet.

Because fire damage to the DFDR had eliminated a source of information critical to the success of the investigation, the possibility of extracting useful flight data from non-volatile memories in various computerised components of the aircraft's systems was examined.

The best available source of flight conditions during the minutes leading up to the accident appeared to be the EEC non-volatile memory parameters for the port engine. Electronic circuit boards and microchip components from the EEC were therefore analysed on behalf of the investigators by Pratt & Whitney and Hamilton Standard.

The results of the EEC analysis by these companies lacked the time correlation normally provided by the DFDR, but indicated an anomaly had occurred between channels A and B reverser sleeve position signals, resulting in the thrust reverser deploying inflight at an altitude of 24,700 feet, at a speed of Mach 0.78, and with the engine set to climb power. It also showed that engine thrust was automatically reduced to idle at the same time, and that the recorded Mach number increased from 0.78 to

0.99. The fuel cutoff switch was probably also selected to cutoff within 10 seconds of the reverser deployment. Physical examination of the cutoff switch at the wreckage site confirmed it was in the cutoff position at impact. The EEC analysis suggested the aircraft was operating beyond its maximum dive velocity of Mach 0.91 when it broke up.

ANALYSIS

Engineering simulation

Immediately after the accident, a number of airlines operating Boeing 767 aircraft attempted to replay the circumstances of the accident in their flight simulators. But these efforts yielded erroneous results because the simulators, not designed to cover such use, did not contain the performance parameters required to duplicate all the conditions of the flight.

But acting on behalf of the Accident Investigation Commission of Thailand, the NTSB requested Boeing to develop an engineering simulation that would faithfully reproduce the flight conditions that evidently developed when the Lauda Air Boeing 767's port engine thrust reverser inadvertently deployed inflight.

Boeing's difficulty was that, although this had evidently occurred at an airspeed of around Mach 0.78, no high speed flight test or wind tunnel data were available on the effect of reverse thrust at such speeds for any type of aircraft. Furthermore, to be suitable for a valid engineering simulation, inflight reverse thrust data were needed for an aircraft of similar configuration to the Boeing 767. This was essential because the intensity and position of the reverse thrust airflow – the thrust reverser "plume" – directly affects the controllability of the aircraft.

Aircraft such as the 707, 747, DC-8 and DC-10 have actually been subjected to reverse thrust deployment inflight, and all models of the DC-8 (including those retrofitted with high-bypass fan engines) were actually certificated for the use of reverse thrust on the inboard engines during flight. But differences in wing and engine geometry, reverser design, and the number of engines fitted, all affect the way an aircraft will react if a thrust reverser happens to deploy inflight. Available data suggested that the further the engine was positioned from the wing, the less likely its reverse thrust plume was to seriously disrupt the airflow around the wing.

For example, by comparison with

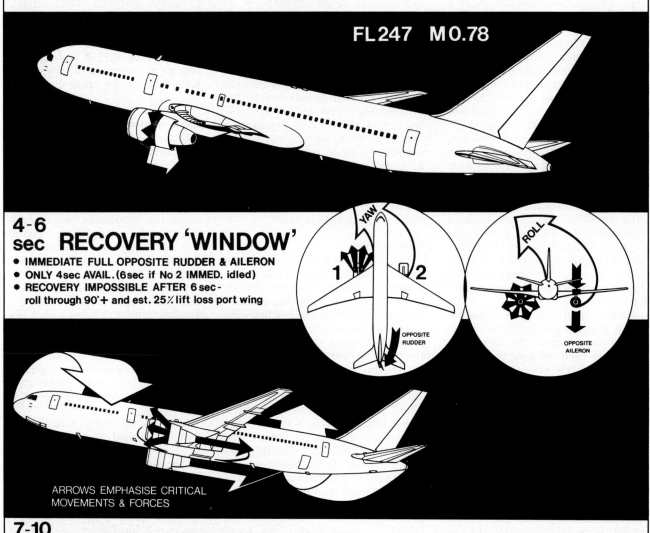

0-3 sec REVERSER DEPLOYMENT

FL 247 M 0.78

4-6 sec RECOVERY 'WINDOW'

- IMMEDIATE FULL OPPOSITE RUDDER & AILERON
- ONLY 4sec AVAIL. (6sec if No 2 IMMED. idled)
- RECOVERY IMPOSSIBLE AFTER 6 sec – roll through 90°+ and est. 25% lift loss port wing

YAW

1 2

OPPOSITE RUDDER

ROLL

OPPOSITE AILERON

ARROWS EMPHASISE CRITICAL MOVEMENTS & FORCES

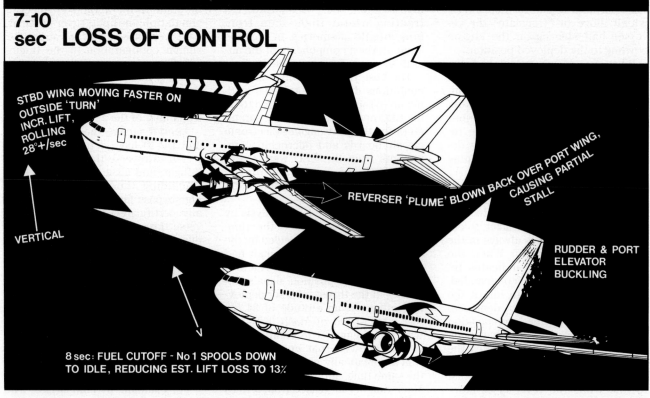

7-10 sec LOSS OF CONTROL

STBD WING MOVING FASTER ON OUTSIDE 'TURN' INCR. LIFT, ROLLING 28°+/sec

VERTICAL

REVERSER 'PLUME' BLOWN BACK OVER PORT WING, CAUSING PARTIAL STALL

RUDDER & PORT ELEVATOR BUCKLING

8 sec: FUEL CUTOFF – No 1 SPOOLS DOWN TO IDLE, REDUCING EST. LIFT LOSS TO 13%

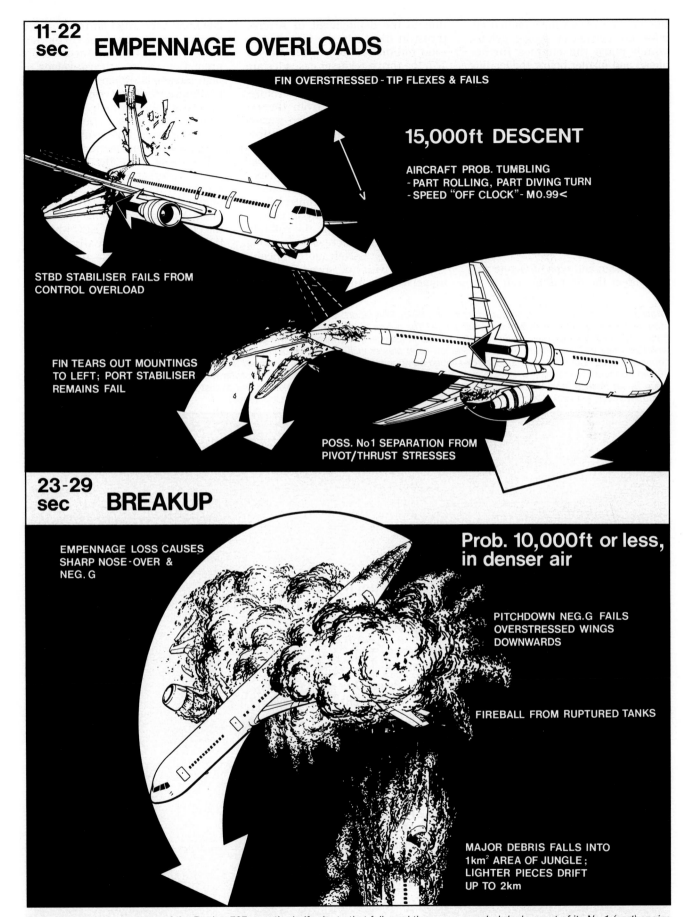

EMPENNAGE OVERLOADS

FIN OVERSTRESSED - TIP FLEXES & FAILS

15,000ft DESCENT

AIRCRAFT PROB. TUMBLING
- PART ROLLING, PART DIVING TURN
- SPEED "OFF CLOCK" - M0.99<

STBD STABILISER FAILS FROM
CONTROL OVERLOAD

FIN TEARS OUT MOUNTINGS
TO LEFT; PORT STABILISER
REMAINS FAIL

POSS. No1 SEPARATION FROM
PIVOT/THRUST STRESSES

23-29 sec BREAKUP

EMPENNAGE LOSS CAUSES
SHARP NOSE-OVER &
NEG. G

Prob. 10,000ft or less, in denser air

PITCHDOWN NEG.G FAILS
OVERSTRESSED WINGS
DOWNWARDS

FIREBALL FROM RUPTURED TANKS

MAJOR DEBRIS FALLS INTO
1km² AREA OF JUNGLE ;
LIGHTER PIECES DRIFT
UP TO 2km

Probable breakup sequence of the Boeing 767 over the half-minute that followed the uncommanded deployment of its No 1 (port) engine thrust reverser. The drawings are based on the investigation's deductions and wreckage interpretation. Despite differences in cause and circumstance, it is interesting to note the similarities to the inflight breakup of the BOAC 707 near Mt Fuji in 1966 (see "Air Disaster" Vol 1, Chapter 5). The 767 accident, in darkness and sparsely-populated mountainous terrain, lacked the concise photographic and eyewitness evidence available in Japan, and its investigation was further hampered by the destruction of the aircraft's DFDR. (Matthew Tesch)

the 767, the 747's wing-mounted engines are carried on longer pylons, which place the engines further ahead and further below the leading edge of the wing. And, in the case of the 707, the reverser mechanism is located in the rear of the engine nacelle, below and behind the wing leading edge, making its reverse thrust plume even less likely to affect wing lift. With aircraft that have three or four engines, each engine produces a smaller percentage of the total thrust, so that if one engine should develop reverse thrust in flight, there will be less thrust/drag asymmetry than on a twin engined-aircraft.

The design and type of engine will also affect the overall aircraft reaction to the deployment of reverse thrust in flight. On the high bypass ratio turbofans fitted to the Boeing 767, the thrust reverser cascades are slightly below and *ahead* of the wing. At high thrust levels therefore, the plume of thrust from the reverser, as well as producing a yawing moment, disrupts the airflow over the wing, resulting in a significant loss of lift on that side. The loss of lift on one wing in turn produces a rolling moment, which must be promptly corrected if control is to be maintained. Any delay in corrective action will result in the roll rate and bank angle increasing, making recovery progressively more difficult.

Starting with low speed 767 wind tunnel data (up to airspeeds of about 200 knots) recorded during Boeing's design and development of the aircraft type in 1979, and theoretically predicting reverse thrust values at high airspeeds, Boeing developed a preliminary inflight reverse thrust simulator model which employed a 10% lift loss factor. Investigators then evaluated the results in Boeing's own 767 engineering simulator.

For these tests, the port engine thrust reverser was configured to provide reverse thrust effect at the beginning of reverse cowl movement, rather than being phased to the cowl position. The EEC was configured to automatically initiate thrust reduction to idle after 10% reverser cowl movement (about two inches or 50mm), and to command

Wreckage distribution chart, reproduced from the official Thai report, showing principal identifiable components of the 767 spread over more than one square kilometre of mountain jungle. The nature of the terrain (elevation 1960 feet) is evident from the meandering access tracks. Although no upper winds were cited in the report (Bangkok's surface wind was a six knot southeasterly), some idea of the fall of the wreckage may be gained from the chart. The left-hand cluster includes the biggest and heaviest pieces of the Boeing's structure, the centre grouping is of still large, but aerofoil-shaped components which could be expected to drift as they fell and, at the top right, some 2000m northeast of the main wreckage area, a field of lighter and smaller debris. Much of the wreckage was burnt beyond investigative value by an intense ground fire which, fed by the jungle foliage, raged unchecked in the almost inaccessible terrain for many hours. (Matthew Tesch, with acknowledgement to the Thai Aircraft Accident Investigation Committee)

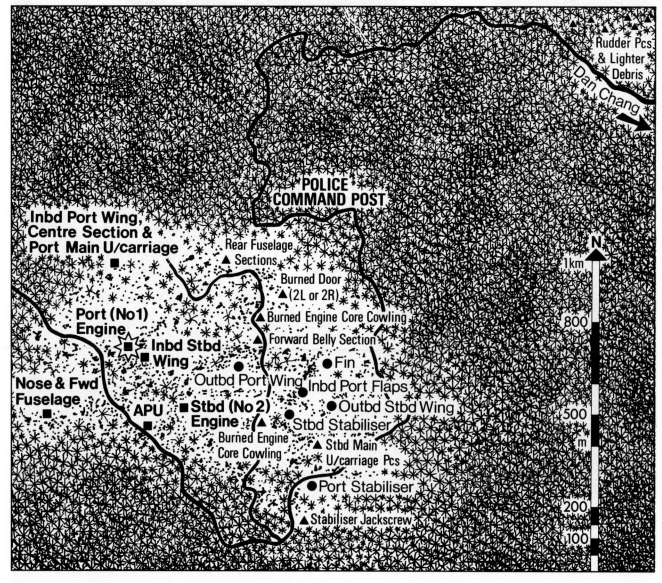

The flightdeck of a Boeing 767 showing its three pairs of "glass cockpit" CRT screens. The two EICAS screens in the centre of the instrument panel not only replace the former twin columns of analogue engine dials with simple electronic counterparts – they also display a Warning-Caution-Advisory hierarchy of up to eleven message lines on each screen from multiple "pages" stored in the system's memory. Apart from these alerts, the EICAS system also displays system status information inflight, and maintenance data on the ground.

idle power at 15% of thrust reverser travel.

The starboard engine was set up to be controlled by the pilot with the power lever. Tests were run with pilot-commanded thrust reduction to idle following reverser deployment on the port engine, then repeated with no thrust reduction on the starboard engine.

The investigators' simulator tests using Boeing's preliminary model proved to be inconsistent with the evidence provided by the CVR, which left little doubt that a trained and highly experienced airline crew very quickly lost control of the aircraft after the port engine reverser deployed. Yet according to the simulator tests, based on the 10% lift loss factor, the crew should have had time to react to the reverser deployment emergency, as well as sufficient control authority, to recover the aircraft to a normal flightpath.

Another simulation model was therefore developed using additional data not previously available. For

this purpose Boeing ran further wind tunnel tests on a scale model aircraft, which included inboard aileron effectiveness, rudder effectiveness, and loss of lift in a flaps-up configuration at different angles of attack and reverse thrust levels. Because scale model high speed testing would have required considerably more time, low speed data obtained from the tests were extrapolated as before.

The wind tunnel test results showed a reverser deployment *lift loss of approximately 25%* with an engine at maximum climb power, reducing over six to eight seconds to approximately 13% as the engine spooled down to idle thrust.

When Boeing's 767 engineering simulator was reprogrammed on the basis of these new tests, the company's Chief 767 Test Pilot found that, if corrective action was delayed more than four to six seconds following deployment of a thrust reverser, he was unable to recover the simulator to normal flight. The varia-

tion in delay was related to the thrust being delivered by the opposite engine.

With the starboard engine remaining at maximum climb power when the port engine thrust reverser was deployed, the Boeing test pilot recovered successfully by applying full opposite control wheel and rudder deflection within four seconds, the EEC automatically reducing the power to idle on the port engine upon movement of the thrust reverser sleeves towards the deployed position. If the starboard engine power lever was reduced to idle at the start of the recovery action, the available response time increased to about six seconds. But if corrective action was delayed more than six seconds after the reverser deployed, recovery became impossible. Loss of lift on the port wing produced a roll rate of about 28 degrees per second within four seconds, resulting in *a left bank in excess of 90 degrees within five seconds*. Immediate, full opposite deflection of both control wheel and rudder pedals was therefore essential to check the rolling moment and prevent the loss of the aircraft.

Using the full authority of the flight controls in this way was not part of normal airline training programs. Furthermore, promptly correcting the roll was not the *only* action necessary for recovery, because the simulator rapidly "accelerated" in the ensuing steep dive.

Examining possible pilot reactions after entering such a dive, the investigators found the load factor reached during recovery from the dive was also critical. With one reverser deployed at Mach numbers above about 0.83, lateral control cannot be maintained at load factors above 2.5g, the effectiveness of flight controls being reduced at high Mach numbers because of aeroelastic effects. This characteristic is common to all jet transport aircraft, not just the 767.

Thrust reverser failure modes

The Boeing 767 thrust reverser system is designed for ground operation only, and incorporates several levels of protection to prevent uncommanded deployment in flight.

Actuation of the reversers on the PW4000 engines fitted to the aircraft involved in the accident required the opening of two hydraulic valves installed in series, and the design of the electromechanical reverser system was intended to prevent the powering of the Hydraulic Isolation Valve (HIV), or movement of the thrust reverse levers, unless the aircraft was firmly on the ground with the engine power levers retarded to their idle position. The investigation disclosed however that, if certain anomalies developed in the actuation of the auto-restow circuitry, they could circumvent the protection afforded by the design.

Electrical failures

The possibility of an electrical failure having resulted in an uncommanded thrust reverser deployment was considered. Testing and analysis of the reverser system design were conducted at Boeing with the participation of the FAA and the NTSB.

To enable the reverser system to deploy, the Hydraulic Isolation Valve must first be opened to provide hydraulic pressure for the system. The HIV could be opened either by a circuit that included the air/ground electrical sensing system, or through the auto-restow circuit. The auto-restow circuit, providing for restowing the reversers after sensing the reverser sleeves out of agreement with the commanded position, powered the HIV to open, regardless of the position of the air/ground switch.

An electrical wiring anomaly in either of these circuits could explain the illumination of the "REV ISLN" indication that attracted the crew's comment a few minutes before the accident. That such an anomaly could occur was supported by the known occurrence of wiring anomalies on other 767 aircraft.

If a second electrical failure, such as a short circuit to the DCV solenoid, subsequently developed then, with hydraulic pressure already available to the system, the DCV could allow the reverser sleeves to deploy. The analysis of the reverser system design showed that certain "hot short" conditions could potentially command the DCV to move to the deployed position, in conjunction with an auto-restow command, for a maximum of one second.

However, the extent to which the findings of this analysis could be applied to determining the cause of the accident was limited. The extensive destruction of the Lauda Air Boeing negated the investigators' efforts to identify any electrical system malfunction. No wiring or electrical system malfunction could be identified as the cause of the uncommanded thrust reverser deployment.

Hydraulic system failures

Tests carried out on Boeing's 767 hydraulic test rig showed that contamination of the solenoid-operated DCV pilot valve could lead to an increase in pressure on the deploy side of the valve. Contamination of the DCV solenoid valve was a latent condition that might not be detected until it affected reverser operation. In this condition, any hydraulic pressure to the DCV resulting from an auto-restow signal opening the HIV could cause an uncommanded deployment of the reverser.

When this discovery was made on August 15, 1991, Boeing immediately notified the FAA, which dispatched a further Airworthiness Directive (AD T91-17-51) to operators, instructing them to *deactivate* the thrust reversers on all PW4000-powered 767 aircraft until further notice.

The precautionary inspections and checks required by the FAA's AD 91-15-09 on July 3 had already revealed that, on some 40% of the reversers checked, the auto-restow position sensors were out of adjustment. Such incorrectly rigged auto-restow sensors could generate an auto-restow signal.

Boeing also carried out tests on other potential hydraulic system failures – blockage of return system flow, vibration, and intermittent cycling of the DCV and HIV, and the effects of internal leakage in the reverse sleeve actuators. The tests disclosed that uncommanded deployment of the reverser was possible with blockage of the solenoid valve return passage within the DCV, or total blockage of the return line common to the reverser sleeves. Uncommanded deployment of one reverser sleeve was shown to be possible when the HIV was energised if the piston seal and cap was missing from an actuator piston head. The testing suggested that this detail might have been overlooked in the original failure mode analysis of the reverser.

Thrust reverser maintenance

It was evident that Lauda maintenance personnel had followed procedures in the Boeing Fault Isolation Manual to resolve the recurring REV RNG FAIL and REV CR-CHK FAIL messages from the port engine PIMU, but without success. After trying the entire procedure several times, Lauda personnel resorted to changing the DCV, HIV and PIMU, but they did not seek assistance from Boeing or Boeing's Vienna-based field service representative. Boeing believed these removals and changes were not related to the PIMU fault messages, and therefore ineffective in resolving the cause of the messages.

Lauda maintenance records also showed that the port engine's thrust reverser actuators had been replaced and re-rigged during this time. No further procedures or other guidance were available in the Boeing manual, and Lauda personnel made the decision to physically inspect the entire thrust reverser wiring harness. However, much of this was unnecessary because RNG FAIL PIMU messages are independent of the operation and indication circuits of the thrust reverser.

Even so, no specific maintenance action could be identified as contributing to the uncommanded thrust reverser actuation that caused the accident.

The DCV for the port engine, a key component in the thrust reverser system, was not recovered until nine months after the accident, when it was returned to the Thai Department of Aviation in exchange for a reward. *Its condition indicated it had been dismantled and reassembled during this time*, but careful examination indicated no anomalies that would have adversely affected the operation of the thrust reverser system.

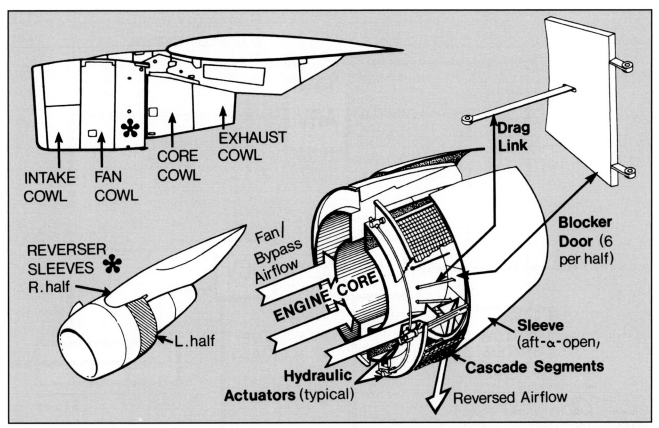

Boeing 767 thrust reverser: although these drawings actually depict a Pratt & Whitney JT9D-7R4E engine on a Boeing 767, any differences between this and the same manufacturer's PW4000 may be disregarded for the purpose of understanding the reverser's mechanical operation and key components. When reverse thrust is selected, hydraulic actuators slide the reverser sleeves on the engine cowling rearward, exposing the forward-angled cascade grid segments. At the same time, powerful hydraulic rams fold blocker doors into the huge volume of bypass air from the engine's fan, forcing this air outwards and forwards through the cascades. The engine does not actually "reverse" of course, and the combusted, high pressure air exhausting from the engine core itself – only a small proportion of the total through-flow in a high bypass engine – remains unaffected. (Matthew Tesch, with acknowledgement to United Technologies – Pratt & Whitney)

The Boeing Despatch Deviation Guide allows despatch of aircraft for up to 500 hours with an EEC maintenance message annunciated. If the message is cleared following a corrective action and does not recur on the next flight, a new 500 hour interval begins. Lauda Air was not therefore remiss in continuing to despatch the aircraft and troubleshoot the problem between flights.

Uncommanded deployment

A review of the thrust reverser system design showed that, when the auto-restow function is required, system pressure to close the reversers is applied during the restow and for five seconds after restow is sensed. The REV ISLN warning lamp illuminates during this period except for the first two seconds. The associated EICAS message appears two seconds after the REV ISLN lamp illuminates.

Interpretation of the crew's comments, "Coming on and off" indicates that they may have been observing cycling of the auto-restow system. The specific interval of illumination of the lamp could not be determined. Nor could it be deter-

mined if the REV ISLN light was accompanied by an EICAS message.

Ten minutes 27 seconds after takeoff, the first officer told the captain there was need for "a little bit of rudder trim to the left." About four and a half minutes separated the REV ISLN indication from the trim discussion, and it seemed probable that the trim requirement was a normal event, not related to the approaching reverser emergency.

Fifteen minutes and one second into the flight the first officer was heard to exclaim: "Reverser's deployed!" accompanied by sounds of airframe shuddering, continuing sounds of metallic snaps and then the captain calling out: "Here, wait a minute!"

The recording ended 29 seconds later with multiple bangs thought to be the aircraft breaking up. But no assessment of the crew's attempts to control the aircraft was possible because of the destruction of the DFDR data. The CVR transcript indicated that the inflight breakup did not occur immediately after the deployment of the thrust reverser, but rather during the subsequent high-speed descent which, as indicated

by EEC recorded data, was in excess of the maximum dive velocity of Mach 0.91.

High structural loadings undoubtedly resulted as the crew attempted to check this descent. The inflight breakup – and the fire that followed as the aircraft's tanks released their heavy load of fuel – then occurred as large control inputs, applied at speeds beyond the aircraft's operating envelope, imposed structural loads in excess of the ultimate strength of the aircraft's structure.

Lack of visual reference could possibly have contributed to the crew's inability to immediately correct the rapid rate of roll that would have developed with the deployment of the reverser, by applying full opposite aileron and rudder. Although there was a near-full moon, the aircraft's climb profile had not yet surmounted the six octas of cirrus cloud at 30,000 feet, and the horizon might have been but dimly visible.

Thrust reverser certification

US Federal Aviation Regulations (FARs) under which Boeing received certification for the 767's propulsion systems stipulated that:

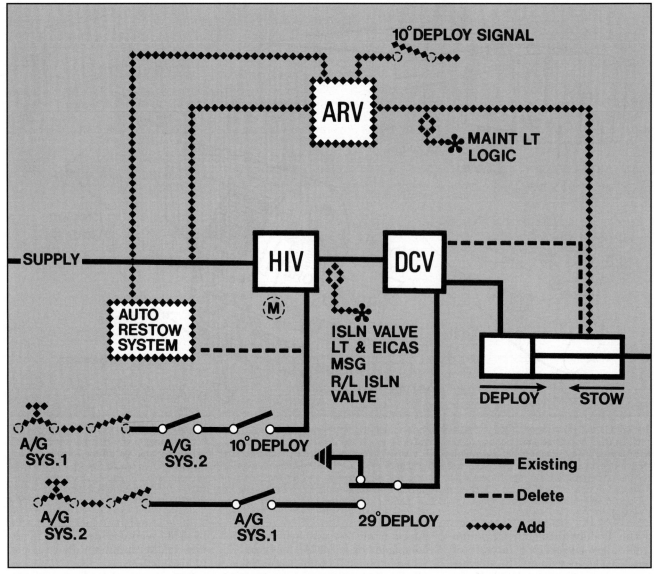

ARV

HIV

DCV

10° DEPLOY SIGNAL

MAINT LT LOGIC

SUPPLY

(M)

AUTO RESTOW SYSTEM

ISLN VALVE LT & EICAS MSG R/L ISLN VALVE

DEPLOY   STOW

A/G SYS.1

A/G SYS.2

10° DEPLOY

A/G SYS.2

A/G SYS.1

29° DEPLOY

Existing
Delete
Add

Schematic diagram of electrics and sensors of a PW4000-powered Boeing 767's thrust reverser system. The core element of the design, the Hydraulic Isolation Valve (HIV), was intended as the "fail-safe" inflight lock of the reverser, regardless of system failures – human, electric, hydraulic or mechanical. But because the actuating Directional Control Valve (DCV) was "downstream" of the HIV in the circuit logic, any failure affecting the DCV itself was outside the protection afforded by the HIV. Changes recommended as a result of the Thai investigation are indicated – not only additional Auto-Restow Valve (ARV) circuitry, but also reinforcement of the Air/Ground (A/G) sensors, ensuring neither partial nor full reverser deployment until both main undercarriage bogies are firmly in contact with the ground.

• Engine reversing systems intended for ground operation only be designed so that during any reversal in flight the engine will produce no more than flight idle thrust.

In addition, it must be shown by analysis or test that:
• The reverser can be restored to the forward thrust position, or the aircraft be capable of continued safe flight and landing under any possible position of the thrust reverser; and
• Each reversing system has the means to prevent the engine from producing more than idle forward thrust when the reversing system malfunctions, except that it may produce any greater forward thrust that is shown to allow directional control to be maintained, by aerodynamic means alone, in the most critical

reversing condition expected in operation.

This requirement for idle thrust following unwanted reverser deployment, both on the ground and inflight, with continued safe flight and landing, dated back to special conditions issued for the Boeing 747-100 in the mid-1960s, and for the DC-10 and TriStar in the early 1970s. The FAA's policy was to require a continued safe flight and landing demonstration of an actual inflight reversal, supported by a controllability analysis covering other portions of the flight envelope.

Such flight demonstrations were usually conducted at relatively low airspeeds, with the engine at idle when the reverser was deployed. It was generally believed that, because

slowing the aircraft during approach and landing reduced control surface authority, a critical condition was thereby created.

Approaches and landings were therefore required to be demonstrated at such presumably critical speeds, and procedures developed accordingly. It was also generally believed that higher speed conditions would involve higher control surface authority and, because engine thrust would be reduced to idle, an aircraft's controllability at these higher speeds could be validly analysed. This belief was borne out at the time by several unwanted thrust reverser deployments on Boeing 747s at moderate and high speeds with no reported controllability problems.

The original engine installation on

the 767 was the P&W JT9D-7R4. In-flight thrust reverser controllability tests involved deployment with the engine at idle power, at an airspeed of approximately 200 knots.

This was followed by a general assessment of overall controllability during cruise, an approach, and a full stop landing. Boeing demonstrated control of the aircraft in cruising flight at 10,000 feet and 220 knots, after which the engine remained in idle reverse thrust for the approach and landing. Controllability in other portions of the flight envelope was substantiated by an analysis prepared by Boeing and accepted by the FAA.

The tests and analysis performed on this version of the aircraft were later applied to engine installations such as the PW4000, based upon the similarities in thrust reverser mechanical design, and engine characteristics. But the circumstance of this accident, in particular the aerodynamic effects of the reverser plume on the wing, called into question the adequacy and interpretation of these FAA requirements.

First, the port engine thrust reverser was not restored to the forward thrust position before impact and the wreckage evidence was inconclusive as to whether it could have been re-stowed. Second, the aerodynamic effects of the thrust reverser plume on wing lift, as demonstrated by simulation, showed that earlier assumptions regarding high speed flight and its beneficial effect on control effectiveness did not take into account the effects of reduced lift resulting from this factor. The consideration actually given to high-speed inflight thrust reverser deployment during design and certification was not verified by flight or wind tunnel testing and appeared to be inadequate.

Much information had yet to be gathered on reverser-wing relationships in high speed flight, but experience with other large transport aircraft suggested that not all are affected to the same degree as the 767. Future controllability assessments should therefore include validation of all relevant assumptions made in the area of controllability. This was particularly important for the coming new generation of large twin-engined aircraft with wing-mounted high-bypass engines such as the Airbus A330 and the Boeing 777.

Although the investigation was finally unable to identify any specific component malfunction that caused the Boeing 767's uncommanded reverse thrust actuation on the port engine, it resulted in an FAA determination that electrical and hydraulic system failures could certainly have been responsible.

Design changes resulting from the accident

Following the testing and engineering re-evaluations accomplished as a result of this accident, Boeing proposed design changes to the thrust reverser system to preclude its recurrence.

The changes were mandated by FAA Airworthiness Directives for all PW4000-powered Boeing 767s.

Boeing 767s in service were subsequently modified in accordance with a Boeing Service Bulletin by Boeing engineering teams. The fleet modification was completed by February 1992. Design reviews and changes were also undertaken for other transport aircraft.

The 767 design changes included:
• Replacing the solenoid operated HIV with a motor-operated HIV;
• Adding a dedicated stow valve;
• Adding new electric wiring from the electronics bay and flightdeck to the engine strut. Critical wire isolation and protective shielding would now be required;
• Adding a new reverser test/reverser system maintenance indication panel to the flightdeck;
• Replacing existing reverser stow proximity targets with improved permeability material to reduce nuisance indications;
• Adding a thrust reverser deploy pressure switch.

The original design of the 767's PW4000 thrust reverser system required multiple failures before it could deploy inflight, and the design changes addressed each of the possible failure modes identified by the investigation. The design changes were expected to effectively prevent further uncommanded inflight deployment – even in the event of further multiple failures.

ABOUT THE AUTHOR ...

Bob Fripp

Macarthur ("Mac") Job's advice on aviation safety has been read for many years by thousands of Australian pilots.

A former Senior Inspector with the Air Safety Investigation Branch of the then Australian Department of Civil Aviation, he presided over the heyday of its acclaimed pilot safety education magazine *Aviation Safety Digest* from 1964 to 1978, editing (and for the most part writing) every issue throughout this time. As Editor of the *Digest* he sought to establish a rapport with his readership by talking to them as fellow pilots in their own language — letting the accidents the *Digest* reviewed in detail tell their own story, rather than merely lecturing. That he succeeded admirably was borne out – not only by the fact that the *Digest* was avidly read by well over 30,000 pilots, aircraft owners and operators and other key people in the aviation industry – but also by that, under his editorship, the *Digest* received the prestigious US Flight Safety Foundation's *Publication of the Year* award.

In a unique position to study the way accident investigation has continually contributed to safer flying operations, Macarthur Job came to see that the high standards to which today's airways systems, both in Australia and the world at large, have developed over the years since airline flying began after World War 1, came about only as a result of successive major accidents that progressively revealed weaknesses in ground support facilities, in airline operational standards, and in crew training.

Far from being an armchair theorist, Macarthur Job is himself an experienced pilot, earning his living in earlier years as a Flying Doctor pilot in outback Australia, and later as a charter and aerial work operator. A full time aviation writer specialising in air safety since leaving the Department in 1978, he has variously been Editor of several well known aviation publications and today contributes regularly to monthly *Australian Aviation* magazine on air safety topics.

Married with five adult children, he still holds a commercial pilot's licence. His particular delight today is flying vintage aeroplanes – aircraft from that fleeting moment in aviation history when, as author and pilot Nevil Shute once put it, "messing about with aeroplanes" was "sheer enjoyment a man can never forget".